MOURNING ART & JEWELRY

Maureen DeLorme

4880 Lower Valley Road, Atglen, PA 19310 USA

Library of Congress Cataloging-in-Publication Data

DeLorme, Maureen.
Mourning art & jewelry / by Maureen DeLorme.
    p. cm.
ISBN 0-7643-1964-7
1. Mourning jewelry--United States. 2. Bereavement in art. 3. Mourning customs--History. I. Title:
Mourning art and jewelry. II. Title.
NK7312 .D45 2004
739.27--dc22
2003027126

Designed by Bonnie M. Hensley
Cover design by Bruce Waters
Type set in Bodoni Bd BTSouvenir Lt BT

ISBN: 0-7643-1964-7
Printed in China
1 2 3 4

Published by Schiffer Publishing Ltd.
4880 Lower Valley Road
Atglen, PA 19310
Phone: (610) 593-1777; Fax: (610) 593-2002
E-mail: Info@schifferbooks.com

For the largest selection of fine reference books on this and related subjects, please visit our web site at
www.schifferbooks.com
We are always looking for people to write books on new and related subjects. If you have an idea for a
book please contact us at the above address.

This book may be purchased from the publisher.
Include $3.95 for shipping.
Please try your bookstore first.
You may write for a free catalog.

In Europe, Schiffer books are distributed by
Bushwood Books
6 Marksbury Ave.
Kew Gardens
Surrey TW9 4JF England
Phone: 44 (0) 20 8392-8585; Fax: 44 (0) 20 8392-9876
E-mail: info@bushwoodbooks.co.uk
Free postage in the U.K., Europe; air mail at cost.

Contents

Acknowledgments

Assembling a book displaying some of the finest memorial art in private collections under one volume would not have been possible without the generous support of contributors. The privilege of being able to photograph these exceptional collections is equal only to the joy in becoming acquainted with their owners, each of whom has generously, and often sacrificially, made this book possible.

My greatest indebtedness goes to Darlene Bolyard, of Things Gone By, who has been my friend and source for outstanding mourning jewelry and memorial items for many years. Her recommendation of me to Schiffer Publishing was the catalyst in enabling me to put my long-held dream of writing a book on this subject into fruition. The many outstanding pieces from her business and personal collections comprise large portions of the sections on mourning jewelry, hair art memorials, and rare objects of remembrance in this book.

I am also deeply indebted to other contributors as well, who have each made a significant contribution to the completion of this book. To all of them I extend a heartfelt expression of appreciation:

Sandra Hall, of Antiques & Goodies, donated her wonderful *In Memoriam* plate of Queen Victoria for this book, a perfect accompaniment to the section on Queen Victoria.

Sandra Johnson kindly sent slides of her rare antique hair art memorials from the Napoleonic Wars, which are truly outstanding.

Jim Mathews generously contributed the memorial of little "Dorothy's" shoes, the poignant cabinet photographs of the black child and her "empty shoes," and the rare Mexican postmortem images from his extensive archival collection of historically significant photographic memorials.

Ann McIntyre very graciously sent her rare, one-of-a-kind hair loving cap, as well as her fabulous 19th century hair albums and embroidered memorials. These unusual items filled a much-needed place in this volume.

Judy Jay, of Time Dances By, generously contributed some of her fabulous collection of mourning jewelry and the rare posthumous painting on ivory of the dead bride. Her pieces added immensely to this book.

Charlotte Sayers, of London, England, graciously went the extra mile in acquiring photographs of her rare pieces of 17th century Stuart mourning rings and gold slides, some of the finest late medieval pieces outside of British museums held in private hands.

Dr. Anita Schorsch, of the Museum of Mourning Art in Drexel, Pennsylvania, provided some wonderful examples of items from the Museum's rare collection of historically significant early American mourning funeralia, for which I am very grateful. I truly appreciate the time Anita took in providing the slides of the rare American mourning embroideries in silk, memorial watercolors, and creamware memorial pitcher included here.

Charles Swedlund generously contributed slides of the beautiful framed hair memorials, mourning jewelry, postmortem images, and other outstanding items such as the rare cremation urn and shell obelisk from his extensive collection of memorial art, one of the finest of its kind in the United States.

Laura Swenson sacrificially sent pieces of her wonderful mourning jewelry collection (some of it in memory of her parents), to be photographed for this book. Her generosity and enthusiasm for this endeavor has been much appreciated and a pleasure.

Patricia Comstock Wilczak kindly sent slides of some of her outstanding collection of funeralia and mourning clothing. Her collection includes unusual examples rarely seen, for which I am very grateful to be able to show a small portion.

Photographic historian and postmortem image collector Ben Zigler contributed some wonderful postmortem images for this book. The extra efforts he expended in providing the best quality presentation of some of his exceptional collection is truly appreciated and I could not have completed the chapter without him.

A number of friends have also personally contributed to this book through their own collections and areas of knowledge and expertise:

The many hours spent with our friends Lyn Iversen and Chris Lamoreaux at their beautiful home photographing their Victorian memorials were both invaluable in terms of their collections as well as an enjoyable time spent in their company. The same is also true of our friends Jerry Lesandro and Larry Martin, who opened up their gorgeous Victorian home to our camera and allowed us to photograph their wonderful memorials and coffin plate collection. The hours spent with them preparing for this book were made all the more pleasurable by their friendship and laughter.

My friend Holly Majka has been a wealth of information on mourning customs and clothing, particularly as pertaining to the Civil War era. Her own excellent volume, *Life in the Midst of Death*, has been a valuable resource to me in preparing for this book.

Our friends Del and Linda McCuen provided a beautiful Campbell memorial lithograph from their wonderful collection of Victoriana.

David and Judith Peebles donated their wonderful collection of mourning sheet music, and have shared many hours talking about, and helping me prepare for this book. I am also indebted to Judith for her extensive knowledge of 19th century writer Fannie Fern, and as a kindred spirit with me in her love of history, she fills an especially significant part of my life.

Randy and Kellen Perlman contributed some of their wonderful collection of immigrant memorial art and antique reliquaries from their unique shop, OBJX. Their enthusiastic support and friendship have enriched my life and the creation of this book.

My friend Dale Suess, of Oakland, California, has always freely offered his extensive knowledge of the history of the funeral industry, Victorian mourning customs, and cemetery art and symbolism over the course of many years, which has not only been invaluable to me, but which I consider of great importance in the development of my interest in this field.

I am also indebted to Adelina Cramer and her daughter Cassandra, who beautifully modeled for some of the mourning clothing shown in this book.

And to my editors, Donna Baker and Douglas Congdon-Martin, whose assistance and advice were invaluable in preparing this book for publication.

Lastly, as always, my family has been my greatest support. To my father, who, even in his advanced years, continually encouraged me in my book endeavor; and to my son John, whose own interests lie far afield of memorial art, but who has supported me nonetheless, I thank you and love you immensely. And, to my sister Cynthia, who lived this dream with me for many years, believing in it for me before I did myself, to her I owe an especial appreciation and love.

Finally, to my husband, Richard, who spent many hours taking hundreds of photographs, patiently listening to my thoughts and ideas, and text readings ad infinitum, words cannot express my love, and a very grateful "Thank You" from the bottom of my heart.

Preface

As a collector of memorial art, I have often been confronted with the same dilemma faced by many collectors of this genre, that of whether or not to admit of my interest in (and not infrequent obsession with) this field of antiques. We collectors of memorial art are sometimes reluctant to share our interest in social settings, unsure as we are of what the response will be from those listening! Facial expressions exhibiting a mixture of fascination, amazement, and occasionally mild disdain invariably find us explaining our interest in mourning art in the most favorable terms possible. And, in the antiques market, we are sometimes referred to as "morbidity collectors," a euphemism which tends to reflect the prevailing public view of death as a subject matter. Our current cultural perceptions of death and grief expression are fraught with such reticence and fear that societal taboos stigmatize them as matters for open discussion, much in the way sexual topics were to Victorian sensibilities.

In spite of this, however, interest in memorial art has been rising considerably over the last thirty years, testifying to its growing respectability among dealers and collectors. No longer simply the subject of scholarly study in university settings and museum archives, memorial art is being enjoyed for its artistic and sentimental qualities as well as its historical value in private collections. Prime examples of mourning jewelry and memorial art are increasing in value exponentially, often commanding high prices, further validating the significance of memorial art in the European and American antiques marketplace.

Today, the earliest medieval examples of death art, or *ars moriendi*, are almost exclusively found in European church archives and museums, but outstanding examples of 18th and 19th century mourning art are readily available to private collectors of art and social history, both in the United States and in Europe. My own interest in this field, combined with my acquaintance with others fascinated about this genre, has inspired me to write a book on the subject of memorial art for collectors, dealers, and historians alike.

As a collector of modest means, I have aimed at presenting a wide variety of price ranges for those interested in purchasing memorial art, whether it be a single moderately-priced item, or museum-quality, one-of-a-kind pieces of mourning art or jewelry. The values given in this book provide only a general price range, however, and are not intended to set prices or to reflect a universal standard of pricing in this field. Prices for individual pieces can vary according to the marketplace, whether American or European venues for example, or even from the East Coast to the West Coast. Furthermore, values can deviate in venues such as Internet auctions versus auction houses versus specialized dealers. True appraisals also depend on condition, rarity, artistic beauty, and historical merit, as well as intangible or subjective characteristics such as emotional content and aesthetic qualities, which can often be "in the eye of the beholder."

It is my hope that this book will introduce the reader to the varieties of memorial art and their historic significance, as well as to the exceptional efforts expended by the living for the sake of beauty in what was basically a remembrance of a *death*. Additionally, it is hoped that the wide variety of memorial art exhibited here will reveal something of the emotional and spiritual connection we share as mortal human beings facing this most universally mysterious aspect to human existence: that of the end of life.

This book is intended to be much more than an apologetic for this field of collecting, however; rather it is intended as a historical narration as well as an antiques guidebook. Thus, I have detailed some anecdotes from sources containing memoirs and accounts to illustrate the human component in the creation of mourning tokens and keepsakes. For it is in the personal records of the events that punctuated the lives of Europeans and Americans that we are introduced, in a sense, to the original "owners" of our memorials, enabling us to become intimately connected to them through the objects we both have loved. Today, aspects of Victorian mourning rituals and practices are within the distant memories and recollections of older Europeans and Americans, and many people possess a postmortem photograph or two, or images of relatives in mourning attire, in their family photograph albums. It cannot be overstated that history is not truly "animated" until we understand something of the lives of ordinary people, including their practices and perspectives when facing death.

Those of us passionate about this genre know that a spiritual element of the *soul-life* exists in a piece of mourning jewelry, a commemorative painting, or the postmortem photograph, an essence rarely found in other areas of collecting. Mourning art has *passion,* and an attachment with the past similar to that felt by genealogists studying their family history. The ubiquitous Victorian expression, "those who have gone before," has literal significance to collectors of mourning art in a way completely foreign in other objects of inanimate function and history. For many of us, when we finger the beautiful mourning locket with its poignant curl of hair, we are curious to *know* the person who wore it – and the person who died. We long for some link or union with the faces that stare back at us from 19th century photographs or posthumous paintings. These faces are both *them* and *us.* Additionally, collecting memorial art is a form of stewardship, a gift held in trust to cherish and care for the memorial object as though it were our own, for in more than a monetary sense – it is. For us, both the mourner and the mourned are "gone but not forgotten."

Today, grief expression is private and restricted: shortened memorial services replace lengthy funerals; cremation replaces burial; roadside floral arrangements replace those exhibited on the homes of mourning families; flat gravestones replace fabulous cemetery monuments; and visible artistic remembrances are seen only in commemorating public tragedies, not in the passing of ordinary individuals. While postmortem photographs are still being taken today, they are done secretively, and will probably never reach the zenith of artistic symbolism nor open acceptance seen in the Victorian era. Similarly, although locks of hair from deceased family members are still kept as keepsakes, they are put away from public view, and few are fashioned into mourning jewelry. No one creates memorials for the living room, and death masks are made only in the forensics lab. It is sad, really. In our rush to move faster, stay younger, live longer, and push death out of our collective conscious, we have abandoned that aspect

to life that Victorians knew was most important: the continuity of love in human relationships which exists even after death.

"Family love is this dynastic awareness of time, this shared belonging to a chain of generations…We collaborate together to root each other in a dimension of time longer than our own lives."[1]

Victorians recognized that a death bears fruit as well as bitterness: it raises the human consciousness by the longing to *know,* to *believe,* to *trust,* and to *hope* in something eternal. Loss was mitigated by adornment; grief was encapsulated in the hand. Truly then Death *had* lost its sting: it was not only swallowed up in victory, it was swallowed up in beauty.

Introduction

"For a moment of night we have a glimpse of ourselves and of our world islanded in its stream of stars – pilgrims of mortality, voyaging between horizons across the eternal seas of space and time."[2]

Throughout history, archeologists and historians have evaluated cultures and civilizations on their philosophies regarding death and the manners in which they memorialize their dead. The noted French historian Michel Vovelle observed regarding death, "In the human adventure it stands as an ideal and es-sential constant. It is a constant which is quite relative, moreover, since people's relationships with death have changed, as have the ways in which it strikes them."[3]

Traditionally, mourning rites have helped individuals and their societies cope with the intrusion of death in sev-eral ways, namely: (1) they resolve the necessity of the disposal of the body; (2) they provide for the preparation of the soul of the deceased to the "other side"; (3) they satisfy, through ceremony, the fact of separation; (4) they bring together the community for security and support; and lastly, (5) they provide a framework for mourners in which to emotionally cope, until the intensity of grief has passed.

While all cultures throughout world history have had their own religious and artistic interpretations of the end of life, this book will focus primarily on European-American memorial art and mourning jewelry, which has been part of social and religious life for centuries. From the fabulous sepulchres of medieval Europe to simple Puritan tombstones, from the primitive burial mound with wooden cross to the ornate Victorian mausoleums, death has been quite visible in Western culture. Death art is not limited to the cemetery, however. Medieval posthumous paintings of royalty, members of the aristocracy, and those in Church hierarchy, were numerous, along with mourning jewelry, death masks, and other visual expressions of mortality. In contrast to today, where we tend to keep funerals and memorial services to a speedy minimum, and our grief private, memorial art from the Middle Ages through the Victorian era clearly shows that death rites and grief expression were much longer, more ritualized, very public, and highly artistic. Death had a *face* in *ars moriendi* throughout the Middle Ages and well into the Victorian era.

Throughout the Middle Ages, mourning art was primarily directed under the auspices of the Roman Catholic Church, which was concerned with keeping its rites and doctrines everpresent in the minds of the faithful as well as the irreligious. Sentimental grief expression was virtually non-existent in the earliest examples of commemorative art, and instead memorials were intended to promote the concepts of heaven for the faithful and hell for sinners. The focus in early mourning art was on portraying death in frightening visual concepts representative of the judgment of an angry God. Grotesque symbols of the prevailing death philosophy of *memento mori*, or "Remember that thou must die," permeated virtually all death art, from sepulchre design, death masks and wax effigies, to posthumous portraiture.

For centuries, these design concepts in memorial art remained unchanged, until the influences of the 18th century Enlightenment and Romantic movements softened and sentimentalized death perspectives and visual representation. Skulls and crossbones, hourglasses, and cadavers, all ubiquitous in medieval memorial art, all but disappeared under the elevated views of the Enlightenment's "Age of Reason" and the sentimentalized ideals of Romanticism. Contemporaneously, a newly prosperous and burgeoning middle class arose during the Industrial Revolution in both 18th century Europe and America, resulting in the movement of memorial art into virtually every middle class home. Along with the birth of the undertaking industry and merchants dealing in mourning clothing, fabrics, and other trappings, an increase in stylized grief ritual arose as a commercial influence in mourning practices. It is during this post-Industrial Revolution era that we see memorial art steadily rising in popularity, reaching its zenith in Civil War America, and in Queen Victoria's England.

At the same time, however, both countries experienced the added burdens of war deaths in addition to low life span averages and high childhood mortality, death statistics which had remained unchanged for centuries. Although French society struggled to cope with the same upheavals of war deaths and social changes which occurred in England and America during the 18th and 19th centuries, France remained orthodox in Catholic religious belief, and by extension, death philosophy and ritual expression.

Nevertheless, under the influences of the Enlightenment, classical designs of Etruscan urns, Egyptian shrouds, obelisks, and weeping Grecian mourners, appear in 18th century memorial art, mourning jewelry, and tombstone architecture of Britain, Europe, and America. France and other Catholic countries were as equally influenced by the sentimentality of the Romantic Movement as were England and America, and thus, memorials and mourning jewelry exhibit the same iconography of the idealized *"good death"* as seen in the exemplars of Victorian Protestantism. Thus, the veneration of hair in mourning jewelry and other artistic mediums, death masks, posthumous memorial paintings, postmortem photography, etc., are as commonly seen in French mourning culture as in English and American venues.

It is during the 18th and 19th centuries that some of the most beautiful and numerous examples of mourning art were created; it is these that are the most readily available to the collector, and which are described in this book. Although Queen Victoria did not begin her reign until 1837, her influence was so pervasive that her name has been given to describe the entire 19th century in which she reigned. Thus, I have used the word "Victorian" or "Victorian era" to describe the influences prevalent during the 19th century as usually defined by that terminology, even where French memorial art and mourning jewelry is included. The same applies to other "Anglo" terms used for the various eras described, such as "Stuart era" to refer to the 17th century, "Georgian era" to apply to the 18th century, etc.

Memorial art and mourning artifacts reflect not just an outdated cultural phenomenon of the past, they also represent an emotional "bridge" from present-day collectors to the men, women, and children who did not keep silent about their grief as we do today, but shared it publicly for all to see. Death was not abstract in the sensibilities of those living in prior centuries; it had a corporeal *face* and an audible *voice*. In the following chapters we will take a more intimate look at what our predecessors said, what they wore, and what they created while coping with dying, death and grief.

Historical Background
Memento Mori

Death in the Middle Ages

Everyman. I know thee not. What messenger art thou?
Death. I am Death that no man dreadeth, for every man I rest, and no man spareth; for it is God's commandment that all to me should be obedient.
Everyman. O Death, thou comest when I had thee least in mind!
Death. I give thee no respite. Come hence, and not tarry.

—*Everyman*, c. 1500

In medieval Europe, people interpreted their position in the world in terms of a divinely ordered universe with the Catholic Church as God's representative emissary to mankind. Society was viewed as having been organized by God for the good of humanity, and the established order was in the form of a hierarchy with God enthroned at the summit, kings below Him, and in descending order, the princes of the Church, the nobility and aristocracy, the merchant classes and yeoman, and at the bottom, the peasants. One accepted one's lot in life without question, as being divinely ordained by God, and all issues of life, from birth to death, were governed by the religious tenets of the Church, which defined and shaped philosophies surrounding these events. Memorial art, known as *ars moriendi*, was also interpreted under the auspices of Church doctrines which governed dying rites, funeral and burial practices, and artistic representations of death. Grief expression was generally subdued, if not nonexistent, with little sentimentality. Death was pictorially graphic and macabre in form, intended to impress upon the faithful the importance of adhering to Catholic doctrinal rites surrounding dying and death and the future state of the soul. Thus, skulls and crossbones, skeletons, and cadavers figured prominently in memorial art of the Middle Ages, and artistic portrayals of death and grief conveyed the prevailing *memento mori* or "Remember that thou must die" philosophy.

In contrast to today, where we tend to divide human existence into two distinct spheres of birth and death, medieval funeral ritual and death philosophy interpreted individuals as having, in essence, two compositions: the *natural* body, and the *social* body. This was to maintain a sense of social cohesion and prevent the dissolution of the community by the death of any one individual. The memorial image of the *natural* body did not affect the Church philosophy of the continuity of the soul, nor the society in which the deceased dwelt. This is exemplified by the royal proclamation "The King is dead; long live the King," whereby the *natural* body of the King was deceased; but the *social* body represented by his royal position survived and continued.[4] Commemorative art fulfilled this societal need by representing the idea that although the deceased was dead, he or she still "lived" in the consciousness of the community by the visual remembrances of paintings, sepulchral design, mourning jewelry, etc. Members of royalty and aristocracy were preserved in leather and wood effigies or wax death masks, in addition to posthumous paintings. Every effort was made to create an effigy as lifelike as possible to "deny" the decay of the *natural* body, and so maintain the influence of the individual in the *social* body.

The Elizabethan artist, John Colt, was commissioned to create an "image rep[re]senting his Late Maiestie" [sic], at the funeral of Elizabeth I in April, 1603. Henry VIII's effigy was also "made veray like unto the Kings Ma[hes]tis person" [sic], and the 1612 effigy of his son, Henry, the Prince of Wales, actually had movable limbs to simulate "life."[5] These practices were not unlike those that existed in ancient Egypt and Rome, which in fact, influenced death imagery in Western Europe during the Middle Ages. Herodotus, the 5th century B.C. Greek historian, relates the Egyptian practice of carrying a wooden image of a corpse at the banquets of the wealthy, and a similar custom existed in Imperial Rome, where miniature bronze skeletons were given away at funerals. And even as early as the first century of the Christian era, Roman wine cups used at funerals of the wealthy depicted skeletons and rose wreaths around the perimeter, not unlike European *memento mori* representations of the Middle Ages.

Commemorative art during the Middle Ages was aimed at being instructional to the living rather than as simply a memorial to the life lived by the deceased. The medieval art form known as *transi*, which depicted the body covered with worms, snakes, and toads (representative of the corruption and decay of the natural body), was intended to horrify and repulse. An engraving in 1480 depicted Death as a figure covered with toads and snakes in the *transi* style, summoning a well-dressed youth and attempting to warn him of the nearness of death.

With the stress placed on the living to be ever aware of the fragility of life, memorial art frequently portrayed death as a cadaver walking about touching his bony hand on the shoulders of royalty and peasant alike. Design elements throughout the Middle Ages (and well into the Victorian era), reflected philosophical and religious beliefs much as metaphors did for poetry and literature during these, and later, centuries. Medieval poetry gave anthropomorphic characteristics to death as *memento mori*, just as was done visually in commemorative art. The 13th century legend of three living kings addressing three dead men no doubt contributed to the popularity of the "Dance of Death" theatrical presentations (called "morality plays") of two centuries later. And a 16th century English ballad entitled "Death and The Lady" portrayed Death as an actor speaking directly to an aristocratic woman, and by extension to the society in which she lived:

"My name is Death, cannot you see?
Lords, dukes, and ladies bow down to me.
And you are one of those branches three,
And you fair maid, and you fair maid,
And you fair maid must come with me."

Eighteenth century woodcut print from 16th century French play, *La Grande Danse Macabre*, showing Death taking aristocratic ladies away by force.

Medieval artists such as Albrecht Durer, the 16th century German painter and engraver, gave anthropomorphic qualities to Death as a figure riding upon a horse holding a scythe, perhaps representing the biblical plagues of pestilence literally fulfilled in the Black Death decades of the 14th century. Even marriage portraits of the Middle Ages contained *memento mori* symbolism, to convey the states of life and death as two halves of the whole, in contrast to our views today which tend to separate life and death in opposition. Frequently, the betrothed are shown placing their hands on a skull rather than on a Bible, their vows symbolic of the transience of life within the context of marriage. One 16th century Dutch painting even included the moralizing words "The Word of God hath knit us twain and death shall us divide again," with a graphic depiction of the husband's future state as an emaciated corpse underneath the marital portraits of man and wife. The macabre dominance of the cadaver in the painting is also combined with the sobering words, "We Behold Our End." The contrast between artistic interpretations of marital love between the Middle Ages and the Enlightenment of the 18th century and the Romanticism of the Victorian era could not be more antipodal.

Even after the Protestant Reformation, emphasis was still placed on spiritual preparedness by the faithful, and death imagery and emblems of mortality continued to permeate all aspects of daily living, both in the private and public spheres. With elimination of the religious doctrine of purgatory under Protestantism, however, the possibility of masses and prayers being offered for the salvation of sinners after death was no longer a part of Reformed Church ritual. Protestant doctrines stressed immediate judgment upon death, and thus, macabre and morbid symbolism in memorial art continued the *memento mori* death philosophy common in the pre-Reformation era.

The widespread popularity of the 16th century French "Dance of Death" plays, one of which was illustrated by Hans Holbein the Younger in a series of woodcuts, was intended to prepare the sinner for the Judgment by the daily reminder of the expectation of death. Portraits by Holbein also frequently portrayed Death as a skeleton with a scythe hovering in the background over the shoulder of the [living] sitter. In the woodcuts shown here from *La Grande Danse Macabre,* we see Death depicted as a cadaver walking about in the halls of Kings, as well as the huts of peasants, summoning each to death and judgment. Note the grotesque representation of Death, even to the point of the incised abdomen with entrails exposed. This portrayal not only depicts death as the dreadful consequence of sin, it also alludes to early attempts at autopsies to understand disease and death processes. This play was one of the so-called *mystery* plays, which were theatrical productions held under the sponsorship of the Church to convey the *memento mori* death philosophy, primarily to the illiterate. These *mystery* plays were not the "mysteries" with which we are familiar today, but were in fact moralistic and religious works, the precursors of Shakespearean-era secular dramas and comedies.

Memento mori symbolism appeared in all forms of jewelry, especially memorial rings, and even devotional objects such as rosaries with beads in the form of Death's heads (skulls and crossbones) conveyed the prevailing societal views of the end of life. Pieces of mourning jewelry with macabre symbolism were intended to serve as virtual talismans against dying unrepentant, and English literature frequently referred to Death's heads in memorial jewelry. Shakespeare describes the concepts of *memento mori* in several of his plays, such as *Henry IV, Part Two,* in which the character Falstaff declares "Do not speak like a death's head; do not bid me remember mine end." In *The Merchant of Venice,* the character of Portia humorously declares, "I had rather be married to a Death's head with a bone in his mouth than to either of these!"

Additionally, Death's heads are often seen portrayed in combination with infants in *ars moriendi.* Sixteenth century art in European museums occasionally depicted women breastfeeding infants with Death's heads and hourglasses (sometimes "winged") painted into the scene, often with skulls placed on nearby tables. This allusion to birth and death within the same artistic context was meant to illustrate the well-known medieval expression of, "The first cry of the newly born child is its first step towards the grave." The juxtaposition of death symbolism with new life was also represented in children's utensils, where silver infant feeding spoons were sometimes cast with death's heads; in one rare medieval British example, a spoon with a skull was also engraved with the words, "Live to Die" along the shank!

German *memento mori* medals struck in the 1600s showed the portrait of a young woman with the Latin inscription *QVAE SIM POST TERGA VIDEBIS,* or "Who I am you will see on the reverse." Upon turning the medal over, a skeleton was shown contemplating an hourglass. Other 17th century European memorial medals depicted a lovely woman and the inscription "I am Beautiful" on one side, and her as a cadaver or skeleton on the obverse, with the inscription, "I was Beautiful." The intended message was clear: Death ultimately conquers beauty and vanity. Other *memento mori* symbols of the Middle Ages are the phoenix in a burning nest, symbolic of the resurrection; a serpent with its tail in its mouth, symbolic of eternity (later becoming an emblem of eternal love in the Victorian era); and butterflies, symbolic of the immortal soul and a favorite death concept of Plato.

Memorial rings of King Charles I, beheaded in 1649 during England's Civil War, show the King wearing an earthly crown. They are inscribed "VANITAS" on one side, with a Death's head wearing a celestial crown and inscribed "GLORIA" on the reverse. How prophetic this ring proved to be is shown by the fact that Charles I, so hated during his reign for vanity, became in death a sympathetic figure, during the unrest and violence of the Cromwellian period. In the Restoration of the monarchy of his son, Charles II, the beheaded monarch achieved the "GLORIA" denied him in earthly recognition, albeit posthumously. *"These matters be kings' games, as it were stage plays, and for the more part played upon scaffolds."*[6]

Upon the death of Charles II in 1685, a medal was struck depicting Time seated next to a tomb, with one foot on a skull, holding a scythe and hourglass in one hand, and extending a laurel wreath with the other. The inscription

13

reads *"TO THE COLD TOMB ALL HEADS MUST COME,"* a reference to a 16th century poem which declares, "Your heads must come to the cold tomb; Only the actions of the just smell sweet, and blossom in their dust." Death is seen as the great leveler of mankind, where both King and pauper end in the grave.

Death's head memorial rings were sometimes surrounded with projections to serve as rosaries, and Martin Luther, the father of the Protestant Reformation, wore a gold finger ring with a small Death's head in enamel, inscribed with the words *"MORI SAEPE COGITA"* ("Think often of death"). Such Death's head rings were also popular with English Puritans. In some rings, the Death's head formed the entire bezel, in others, an intaglio (incised in recess) design was cut, and still others were in cameo form. An extraordinary 17th century English ring, now in a British museum, is formed of two skeletons holding a tiny sarcophagus with a lid, which, when opened, shows a smaller skeleton in the interior. And another English gold pendant of the same era is shaped in the form of a skull, which opens to show a figure of a reclining skeleton, his neck resting on an hourglass – a somewhat humorous depiction of death in an otherwise macabre context.

Eighteenth century woodcut print from 16th century French play, *La Grande Danse Macabre*, showing Death coming for the King and Pope.

Eighteenth century woodcut print from 16th century French play, *La Grande Danse Macabre*, showing Death taking a peasant woman and snatching a baby from its cradle. The deaths of children were such a common event in the Middle Ages that over half of all poor children born ultimately died before the age of five. Parents unable or unwilling to care for children often placed their unwanted offspring outside their cottages or hovels to either die from exposure or be taken in by others.

Some memorial rings enclosed an actual piece of bone, probably a saint's relic, encased in the bezel; in still others, locks of hair were preserved. In contrast to *memento mori,* these souvenirs became *memento illius,* a reminder not of the nearness of death, but an admonition to pray for the dead. Reliquaries of saints' bones were venerated as virtual relics of God, imbued with healing and spiritual powers, and were more widely cherished as memorial keepsakes in European Catholic countries. Saints' relics were usually enclosed in beautiful tiny frames adorned with materials such as silk, glass beading, sequins, gold leaf, and precious metals, and their veneration was a precursor to the keeping of other personal objects of remembrance, such as hair and teeth of the deceased in later centuries. These souvenirs substituted for the absence of the *corruptible* body as *incorruptible* fragments.

Popular inscriptions on 16th and 17th century memorial rings are "Live to die, Dye to live"; "Breath paine, Death gaine"; "As I am, you must be"; "Prepared be to follow me"; "Heaven is my happiness"; and "Fallen to Rise," in addition to the ubiquitous "memento mori" and "respice finem."

The common symbol of a skull and crossbones arose out of designs created in charnel houses and church ossuaries of the Middle Ages. For centuries, the

Nineteenth century French reliquary with bone relic of St. Benedict (Joseph Labre, 1748-1783), the patron saint of the poor, an *Agnes Dei,* set into a black enamel metal frame. 2.75" x 3". *Courtesy of OBJX.* $350.

wealthy and those affiliated with the Church were buried under the floors and inside the walls within cathedrals, preferably in the nave and as close as possible to the altar. It was felt that by being buried within a cathedral, one's salvation was assured, and the soul that much closer to heaven. Medieval churches throughout Europe show outstanding sepulchres with effigies of royalty and other notables, along with burial plaques on floors and walls denoting the resting places of the aristocracy. Tombs were located within the church in order of desirability, with eastern facing sepulchres the most sought after, and those along the north walls the least coveted. The wealthy insured the location of their burial by generous contributions to the Church either in life, or by bequest after death.

The burial of the poor, however, was an entirely different matter throughout the early Middle Ages. Like the potter's fields of later centuries, bodies were buried *en masse* in central pits inside charnel houses, which were large outdoor enclosures adjacent to the north side of parish churches with open galleries around the perimeter. When the bodies had been reduced to a skeletal state in the pits, the bones were then disinterred and heaped in piles inside these perimeter galleries, or ossuaries. Family members often visited the charnel ossuary, creating elaborate designs with the bones, which became known in France as *presentoirs.* It is in these displays that the skull and crossbones, originally a design element in the *presentoir,* evolved to become a universal icon for death.

Handmade 19th century French reliquary of silk brocade and velvet, decorated with sequins, enclosing a bone fragment of St. Amand, 6th century French missionary. 1.25" in diameter. *Author's collection.* $150.

In the post-Reformation era, memorial art also began to portray the concepts of the "*good*" death versus that of the "*bad*." The innocent death of a child, the heroic soldier martyr dying for country, the quiet death of the elderly, the peaceful death of the "good wife," contrasted vividly with the death of the wicked. Stoneware memorials of the 17th century often portrayed the deaths of wealthy children in the beautifying artistic poses more typical of the 18th century, post-Enlightenment era. These artistic representations of "good" deaths were beautifully executed with peaceful deathbed features, or animated facial expressions as heaven approached.

The "bad" death was also portrayed in memorial art of the late Middle Ages. Deaths at sea, by accident, or in battle where the body was never recovered, were especially feared, as no obsequies and assurances of salvation of the soul were possible after the Reformation's elimination of masses for the dead out of purgatory. This concept of the "bad" death continued into the Victorian era, where the absence of previously expressed religious beliefs by the deceased also made the determination of salvation uncertain. Throughout Western history, suicides were thought the epitome of the "bad" death, and this philosophy existed well into the Victorian era, with the attendant stigmatization in terms of burial rites and absence of traditional comforts to family members.

The deaths of the "wicked" were also intended to be profoundly frightening to all members of society. Paintings of the Middle Ages frequently depicted the fate of sinners cast into hell, or the souls of the wicked at judgment. In a 16th century painting by William Blake, entitled, "The Death of the Strong, Wicked Man," the soul of a dying man is seen struggling against his future judgment before God, extending his hands out to resist being wrenched from his writhing physical body. This genre of painting was another form of *memento mori* intended to impress upon the faithful and agnostic alike the fear of falling unrepentant into the hands of God without the Catholic rites of absolution performed prior to death.

Representations of dying, death, the corpse, and memorialization remained static for centuries until the 18th century, when profound changes occurred which forever altered the fundamental concepts of death and mourning in Western culture. In the next two chapters we will look at how death philosophy and visual representations of the end of life were radically altered by new philosophical ideas emerging from the birth of humanism of the Enlightenment. These revolutionary ideologies accompanied an evangelical religious fervor occurring coincident with the Industrial Revolution, and conflicts within the British Empire, the French Revolution, and the rise of colonial America.

Ossuary in late medieval church in the Czech Republic, typical of such decorative bone depositories throughout Europe in the Middle Ages.

La Mort De Toi

Death of "The Other" in the Age of Enlightenment

By the 18th century, four societal changes occurred in Western culture that permanently refashioned death perspectives and memorial art. The first of these changes involved new secular ideals being discussed in French drawing rooms and written about in French literature, arising from a philosophical movement which ultimately became known as The Enlightenment. Spurred by anti-royalist and anti-clerical intellectuals and writers, such as Francois Voltaire, Jean-Jacques Rouseau, and Baron de la Montesquieu, new ideals of political and religious freedoms, social reforms, and the elimination of class-structure and cultural chauvinism began to influence French thought. These ideals brought about both the best and the worst in human behavior in the decades following the inception of this movement, in the upheavals of the French Revolution. Enlightenment principles spread beyond French borders and influenced Western political and religious philosophies, ultimately laying the foundation of political thought behind American constitutional government. After centuries of images of the "Sinner's Death" in frightening contexts, this new secular philosophy also changed the visual interpretation, definition, and portrayal of dying and death. The Catholic Church had been facing spiritual upheaval under the Protestant Reformation, and, even though Protestants still believed in the concept of hell, *memento mori* death imagery was being challenged by new ideologies emerging

"It is often said that something may survive of a person after his death, if that person was an artist and put a little of himself into his work. It is perhaps in the same way that a sort of cutting taken from one person and grafted on to the heart of another continues to carry on its existence even when the person from whom it had been detached has perished."

—Marcel Proust, 1871-1922,
Remembrance of Things Past

among these secular philosophers and scientists about mankind's God-given ability to reason. Rather than suffering and death as a judgment of God against sin, under the new humanistic philosophies, mankind was elevated to a higher plane where God is seen as watching over His children while they discover His miraculous ways through science and logic.[7]

Between the medieval God of judgment and the subsequent "personal God" of the Victorian evangelical movement, an ambiguous and opaque De-

ism became the faith of the Enlightenment, which tended to obscure death into abstract philosophical concepts. This is the first extensive attempt among members of the clergy and intellectuals to understand the three great issues mystifying mankind – to wit, life, death, and immortality – in contexts apart from parochial Church definitions. Thus, with the gradual elimination of Church-governed portrayals of the end of life, the new humanism interpreted death in ways no longer inspiring horror and fear. For the first time in Western culture, one's lot in life was not preordained by God; rather any individual could rise above his circumstances, no matter how lowly, to achieve greater social status, wealth, and prestige. Human progress now held the keys to human betterment, and the resultant consequence was a more prosperous standard of living and a longer life. This new "Age of Reason" brought with it principles of equality, self-rule, and self-improvement through the belief in universal education and the pursuit of knowledge, which greatly influenced America's founding fathers, these views being seen in the very wording of the Declaration of Independence and the Constitution.

A revival of interest in classical mourning motifs and design arose out of the new humanism, and provided a middle ground between the orthodox Catholic religious views, which tended to discourage empirical thought, and the Enlightenment principles of reason. This rise in Neoclassicism resulted in softer representations of death imagery, so that the terrors of the deathbed and the uncertainty of salvation were now replaced with a more serene and sentimental *expectation* of paradise. Instead of cadaverous skeletons grabbing the unaware to death and judgment, angels now escorted the deceased to his or her heavenly home.

Coincident with The Enlightenment of the 18th century was a collateral philosophy known as the Romantic Movement. Romantics, mostly members of the art and literary worlds, interpreted death in two contexts: in one view, death allowed for the ultimate communion of man with nature, as mankind itself returned to the dust. In the other view, death was seen as the catalyst for the elevation of emotional sensitivities in art and literature, particularly poetry. Edward Young's classic *Night Thoughts on Life, Death, and Immortality,* published in 1742, and Thomas Gray's 1750 *Elegy in a Country Churchyard* helped awaken and advance the new exalted sensations surrounding death. Now, new expressions of emotionalism influenced family relationships in the home and at the deathbed. In contrast to the Middle Ages, where little, if any, grief expression was portrayed and death was viewed as the consequence of sin and the judgment of God, society now began to view death and loss in highly sentimentalized imagery. And, where death had once been artistically portrayed through Church influences as an *individual* experience, or *La Mort de Soi,* ("mine own death"), by the Age of Enlightenment, the new romantic perspectives altered it conceptually into that of "The Death of the Other," or *La Mort de Toi."*

This new romanticism is seen in 18th century American, English, and European memorial designs of Grecian-style mourners weeping over tombs, burning hearts above monuments (symbolic of marital love and passion), and beautiful, classical-style urns surrounded by flowers and angelic beings. The introduction of the *"romantic death,"* that is, the concept of immortal love existing after death, also now appears in literature. In the 1774 German ballad, *Leonora,* Wilhelm, the lover of Leonora, is killed in battle, and she is overcome with obsessive grief. Unable to continue among the living, Leonora is carried away by the dead Wilhelm to the underworld, in a portrayal suggestive of the union of sexual love with death, lurid imagery sometimes alluded to in Victorian literature and art of the Romantic poets, writers, and artists of a century later (see photos on next page).

Language itself changed as perspectives about death and grief were softened. Letters of the 18th century describe the deathbed scene in wording diametrically opposed to the frightening references of the Middle Ages. Those present at the deaths of family members describe the passing of loved ones in a new vocabulary, and verbiage such as "lovely in death" or "beautiful in her last repose" make their first appearances in death narratives. Typical is the following description of the passing of "Olga," a young woman from a prominent 18th century French family:

> *"The most consoling transformation had taken place. All traces of the malady had disappeared. The room had become a chapel in which our angel lay sleeping, surrounded by flowers, dressed in white, and once again beautiful, more beautiful than I had ever seen her in life."*

The happy reunion of family members in paradise became the overriding focus of death perspectives and commemorative art after the Enlightenment and Romantic Movements. Death is no longer *death* in the same sense that it had been throughout the Middle Ages; it is now obscured in the beautified portrayals of the deathbed scene both in art and literature. For the first time in Western culture, Death had now become an *aesthetic.*

Coincident to these new philosophies, 18th century European and American societies also experienced burgeoning prosperity as a result of the numerous inventions and expanding commerce of the Industrial Revolution. A growing middle class, well able to afford the niceties of a burial plot, tombstone monument, and all the trappings of mourning formerly only available to the wealthy, magnified the commerce for mourning goods.

Although Catholicism continued to govern death ritual in France and other predominantly Catholic European countries, the evangelical religious revivals of the Great Awakening, which occurred in late 18th century England, influenced perspectives about death and the "After Life" throughout England and America. Beginning in the 1750s, England had begun a love affair with children and the domestic home life, to be followed with an outpouring of sentimental art of angelic babies and novels extolling the virtues of happy families. Under the new evangelicalism, the severance of death in the family was resolved by the concept of the "heavenly reunion" where the deceased in bliss looked down upon those still living and watched over them, until all were eventually reunited. Literature and art abounded with themes of this "domesticated heaven," which was viewed as simply a "mirror" of that which existed in the romanticized family sphere in the home. In this new "Cult of Memory," the soul is now seen being carried heavenward by angelic beings, with the heavenly gates opening to welcome the deceased to his or her new home. Gone are the cadavers, the skulls, and the Grim Reaper carrying the dead to judgment. The "Death's Head" of the Middle Ages is replaced by the winged cherub, the beautiful mausoleum now contains the beloved bones, the rural cemetery supercedes the charnel house, and more democratic views and practices govern the end of life. As macabre skeletal iconography faded in memorial and religious art, the skull and crossbones symbol was relegated to those contexts more representative of mass slaughter, such as war and pestilence.

Nevertheless, in spite of the intellectual idealism of the Enlightenment principles, the softened death perspectives of Romanticism, and the beautified, even *feminized* "domesticated heaven" of the Great Awakening, the 18th century was a time of catastrophic change and upheaval for England, France, and America. Not everyone died peacefully in bed surrounded by family members. Political tumult and convulsions influenced memorial art as kings fell, soldiers were killed in battle, revolutionaries altered governments and governmental powers, and citizens died in mob anarchy or at the guillotine. As with other wars and upheavals in years past and those to come, memorials reflected the lives lost.

England struggled financially and militarily to hold onto America and her other colonial interests, fighting against revolutionary Americans in essentially three major conflicts: the French and Indian Wars, the War of Independence, and later, the War of 1812, ultimately losing the American colonies. And, as always, there were the continual conflicts with France. English military heroes such as Lord Horatio Nelson and the Duke of Wellington were immortalized in memorial art and mourning jewelry, and their battles and victories commemorated ubiquitously throughout Britain.

French intellectuals, initially moved by the noble Enlightenment principles of *liberte, equalite, fraternite*, and desiring a more democratic form of government based on the principles of American constitutional ideals, ultimately abolished the French monarchy in one of the bloodiest eras of French history. Economic deprivations and sufferings along with undercurrents of political intrigues at the court of Louis XVI and Marie Antoinette, ultimately led to the terrible atrocities of the French Revolution and the execution of the King and Queen. As the Revolution gained its ghastly momentum, hundreds of thousands of French citizens were executed on the merest of suspicions of royalist sympathy. According to one survivor's recollections:

> *"In that time of horrible memory every French person was either an accomplice or a victim."*[8]

For the American colonists, who barely thought of themselves as "Americans" at all, it was a hopeful time, but life was fraught with as much danger as it had always been in the countries they'd left behind in Europe. Death still omnipresently reigned as the *King of Terrors*.

Lithograph from 18th century German poem *Leonora*, showing her lover Wilhelm attempting to flee with her from the dead of the underworld, the heaving breaths of Wilhelm's steed turning white in the frosty air of Hades.

Leonora is overcome and dies of grief, and is carried to the underworld by the dead Wilhelm in the 18th century German poem, *Leonora*.

The Finger of the Lord Hath Done It

Death in Colonial America

"Dec. 25, 1696 – T'was wholly dry, and I went at noon to see what order things were set; and there I was entertained with a view of, and converse with, the Coffins of my dear Father Hull, Mother Hull, Cousin Quinsey, and my Six Children…T'was an awful yet pleasing Treat."
—From the diary of eminent American colonial Judge, Samuel Sewell

Early colonial settlement in America was comprised of small communities, and the loss of any individual member was a severance within the social fabric of the village. Community life consisted of home and family, workplace, church, and local government, so that the private and public spheres of community life overlapped and combined with one another. Grief was shared with neighbors, and virtually all participated in the "death watch" at the bedside of the dying, then preparation for burial, the funeral, and the "wake." Martha Ballard's 18th century diary of her life as a midwife in colonial Maine relates numerous deaths amongst her neighbors. One such entry on August 20, 1787, is typical:

"Clear. Mr Hinkly brot me to Mr Westons. I heard there that Mrs. Clatons Child departed this life yesterday & that she was thot Expireing. I went back with Mr Hinkly as far as there. Shee departed this Life about 1 pm. I asisted to Lay her out. Her infant Laid in her arms. [sic]"[9]

Life spans in colonial America had little improved from the statistical average of twenty-five years throughout the Middle Ages. Additionally, one of every six women died in childbirth, so that many colonial marriages averaged only seven years, with the husband remarrying once or twice more before his own death. Deaths in childbirth were so common that many women approached marriage with a great deal of trepidation, even considering postponing marriage to their late twenties because of wholly realistic fears of death in birthing if still in their teens. The 18th century maxim of "Those who marry late, protect their fate; those who early wed, make a widower's bed" exemplified the very real threat to women's lives by early marriage and pregnancies.

Epidemics of smallpox, typhoid, dysentery, and other diseases virtually decimated colonists, and because Puritans believed that God created disease as a punishment for sin, it was also a *sin* to interfere by the use of medicine or palliative treatment. Some colonial documents added the notation, "The finger of the Lord hath done it" to obituary lists as the cause of death.

Early attempts at smallpox inoculation were often thwarted by these same Puritan beliefs. Childhood deaths from scarlet fever, diphtheria, whooping cough, and flu took the lives of hundreds of thousands of children from the colonial era through the first three-quarters of the 19th century. Epitaphs in colonial graveyards such as the following tell the typical melancholy story of childhood deaths:

> Youth behold and shed a tear,
> Fourteen children slumber here.
> See their image how they shine
> Like flowers of a fruitful vine.[10]

The prevailing medical treatments of bleeding, blistering, cupping, and purgatives to induce vomiting and diarrhea often directly led to premature deaths, such as that of George Washington in 1799, whose death was precipitated by the overuse of bleeding.

As colonists moved into new territories inhabited by Native Americans, the inevitable conflicts of ambushes, killings, and massacres on both sides took the lives of many early Americans, deaths which were exacerbated by the battles of the French & Indian Wars and the American War of Independence. So routine was early death, that one Kentucky woman wrote, "the most comely sight she beheld" during the wars [French & Indian] "was seeing a young man dying

in his bed a natural death." The scene was so rare that "she and the rest of the women sat up all night, gazing upon him as an object of beauty."[11]

Mourning customs and burial practices attempted to repair the separations caused by death, and to restore community cohesion and security. Family members stayed with the body as "watchers of the dead," until the time of burial when the family invited attendees to the funeral by sending pairs of gloves or funeral rings as announcements. Burial followed in small, crowded churchyards, with monuments carved with the similar *memento mori* symbols popular in the Middle Ages. In partnership with their English brethren, Puritan colonies held fast to the Death's heads, skulls and crossbones of the pre-Enlightenment eras, as can still be seen today in tombstone iconography in New England graveyards.

But with the growth of the new nation and under the philosophies of the Enlightenment and Romanticism, softened memorial art began to supercede Puritan death symbolism, beginning in New England, spreading to the mid-Atlantic states, and into the South with the expansion of pioneer settlement. The popularity of commemorative art in 18th century England, to include such famous military heroes as Lord Nelson, spread quickly to America, where samplers mourning the loss of George Washington took hold in the American psyche. Mourning Revolutionary War heroes was an act of patriotism, and love for one's country analogous to the love for God. Additionally, commemorative art included classically-dressed figures symbolic of the Roman ideals of justice, virtue, wisdom, liberty, nobility, sacrifice and courage, so much a part of Enlightenment thought. These allegorized figures are usually seen standing next to the tomb or monument, sometimes in conjunction with a portrait or bust of Washington or other colonial notables.

Initially beginning with 18th century military and presidential heroes, American memorial art later included Lincoln, Garfield, Grant, McKinley, etc. in the Victorian era. Pottery, ceramics, jewelry, handkerchiefs, and other memorial tokens extolling the virtues of 18th century American heroes expanded rapidly to include "generic" remembrances com-

patible to everyone's family member. The commerce created by the romanticism of grief resulted in large productions of mourning memorabilia, textiles, ceramics, and prints available to the American middle class market from England.

Mourning pictures on silk grew in popularity in the decades following the death of George Washington. Originally copying English designs, Americans soon created their own death iconography. Academies and boarding schools emerged for the education and social enhancement of young girls. In these "dame schools," female students were taught the skills of needlework by embroidering mourning samplers, sometimes in combination with watercolors on silk, commemorating the deaths of family members. Painted and embroidered mourning samplers with obituary information recorded on Grecian-style tombstone plinths or steles were the most frequently executed. Background garden-style surroundings included symbols from Greek funerary customs along with Christian iconography associated with death, such as urns, tombs, churches, weeping willows, symbolic trees and floral vegetation, and mourners, first dressed in white clothing in the 18th century, later in black dress during the Victorian era. Britannia, weeping over the tomb in Grecian-style clothing, is seen as a common memorial figure in English mourning art, and in America, the design was altered to a more "generic" Grecian figure distraught with grief by a tomb, urn, or other monument.

A new "language" of mourning saw its visual representation in a variety of symbols, easily understood to virtually everyone. In addition to weeping willows, other floral vegetation achieved new symbolism for the mourner: evergreens symbolized the eternal life of believers; thistles, symbolic of Christ's Crown of Thorns, represented the pain inherent in living in a sinful world; the dove came to symbolize the Holy Ghost, etc. The following poems on 18th century mourning samplers embroidered by young girls are typical of the melancholic language embodying Puritan-influenced colonial pessimism and fatalism:

> "I have seen the bright azure of morn,
> With darkness and clouds shadowed
> o'er.

I have found that rose is a thorn,
Which will wound when its bloom is no
more.
Our pleasures are born but to die,
They are linked to our hearts but to
sever,
And like stars shooting down a dark sky,
Shine loveliest when fading forever."

And,

"When I am dead, laid in grave,
And all my bones are rotten,
By this may I remembered be
When I should be forgotten."

Excavations in Pompeii and Herculaneum in the 1740s exposed Europeans and Americans to classical design concepts, which in turn, greatly influenced memorial art. The Neoclassical Etruscan urn was extensively used as a mourning symbol because of its association with antiquity and the burial of the ashes of the dead in ancient civilizations. The love of classical design also overflowed into scenery of the 18th century, where picturesque pastoral landscapes on a grandiose scale, with marble temples, lakes, and pools reflective of this new love of classicism influenced early concepts in American rural cemeteries and parklands. These design elements and symbols became integral elements of memorial art and jewelry in the 18th and 19th centuries.

Historian Anita Schorsch, in her classic exhibition book, *Mourning Becomes America*, states that the floral and garden themes seen in early American memorials reminded families of the original Garden of Eden, the Garden of Gethsemene, and the heavenly realms described by poets and artists of both the 18th and 19th centuries. Thomas Gray's *Elegy in a Country Churchyard* called up visions of peaceful burial settings for the deceased and the mourner, overflowing with trees, flowers, and birds, for quiet melancholy contemplation. The idealized garden also symbolized the growing awareness of pollution in the increasingly industrialized cities in both America and Europe, and a desire to dwell in bucolic natural scenes was simultaneously emerging in the new rural garden cemetery movement in America.

Trees figured prominently in early American memorials, as reminders of the Tree of Life and the "tree" upon which Christ was crucified. Depending upon the growth habit and shape of the tree, various aspects of life, death, and grief could be artistically portrayed. The weeping willow was both a memorial symbol because of its melancholy drooping aspects, but it was also popularly used in cemeteries because of its tendency to soak up vast amounts of water, thus keeping the graveyard drier. Dignity and strength are seen in the bushy foliage of the oak and elm, and the motif of an oak tree cut down or fallen is seen as symbolic of a life cut short. Some memorials depict a dead branch or tree to symbolize death, the former life of the deceased once one of vigor and strength, now reduced to being withered and dead. Evergreens also represented the Resurrection and eternal life, and the upward ("towards heaven") growth of cypress, yew, and cedar trees depicted the hope of immortality of the Christian faithful. Imaginary garden themes in 18th century memorial art often included streams of water as well, which not only represented the River of Life in the "new heavens and new earth" to be created by God at the end of time, but also symbolized the cleansing of sin in water baptism.

Numerical symbolism is sometimes seen in memorial samplers, and design elements were often grouped together for additional interpretive meaning. Memorial art using three main artistic elements represented the Trinity; the number four indicated the material world; and the war between the spirit and the flesh was represented by groups of three and four together in the same composition. Triangular design of the entire scene was a theologically-based artistic arrangement dating back to the Middle Ages and based on the concept of the triune Godhead.[12]

The grieving mourner was a central figure to the memorial scene. Originally depicted in religious art as the Mourning Madonna, a veil over her head symbolic of the renunciation of the flesh and the corporeal world, the weeping figure became the very personification of grief with her bowed head symbolic of Christian resignation. Usually dressed in white, graceful raiment, the mourning figure grieving over the tomb was a leitmotif

quite similar to the then-contemporary Empire clothing fashions of the day, in which ladies wore white, gauzy muslin in both social and mourning settings.

The classic mourning figure is also seen in pottery and ceramics, most notably those by Josiah Wedgwood in 1770, but other pottery manufacturers such as Leeds in England also commemorated her in earthenware plaques, vases, patch boxes, tea pots, etc., referring to her as Grief personified, or Andromache, the mourning wife of slain Hector in Greek mythology.

Many 18th century memorial samplers also depicted architectural elements such as Grecian-design mausoleums, Puritan churches, or Federal-style period homes, usually in the background surrounding the melancholy mourner and tomb. Occasionally, when the family home is depicted in embroideries or watercolors, all the window shutters are shown closed except those of the "death room," symbolically left open to allow the soul of the departed to make its ascension towards heaven. Irish (and other immigrant) folklore frequently advised the keeping open of a window in the death room for this purpose.

After the burial, wakes held in the colonial-era home, or the "House of Mourning," often included memorial tokens of remembrance such as black or white gloves and scarves, black-bordered handkerchiefs, and rings. These memorial jewels were often gold, inscribed with the name and date of death, enameled in black, white, or black and white together, and incorporating the skull, coffin, and other *memento mori* symbols, in combination with urns and willows, along with the hair of the deceased. The quality of the ring depended largely upon the wealth of the deceased, and these memorial rings passed from one generation to the next.

Once the deceased was buried and "waked," the community largely returned to the business of living. A century later, the American colonies were a new "country" upon the world's stage, and a young woman would ascend the English throne to influence an entire century with her royal charisma and her grief.

Beautiful in the Last Repose

Death in the Victorian Age

Death is a dialogue between
The spirit and the dust.
"Dissolve," says Death. The Spirit, "Sir,
I have another trust."

Death doubts it, argues from the ground.
The Spirit turns away,
Just laying off, for evidence,
An overcoat of clay.
                    —Emily Dickinson, 1830-1886

The Victorian era saw memorial art reach a zenith in beauty and popularity unmatched before or since. No other era in Western culture has ever exhibited to such an extent the artistic emphasis on death and loss as a visible part of the consciousness of an entire population. Life spans were still quite short in the first three-quarters of the 19th century, with the average age of early Victorians at death being forty to forty-five. In industrialized cities such as Manchester, England, the life spans were considerably lower due to the foulness of the rapidly expanding city, and inhabitants often did not live past the age of seventeen. Additionally, traumatic upheavals such as war added to the already

high mortality from disease. American soldiers died in the Mexican War, Spanish-American War, and the horrific battles of the Civil War during the 19th century. England lost untold numbers of men in the Crimean War, the Indian Mutiny, the Napoleonic Wars, and the Boer War, among others. And France, after already enduring the horrors of the French Revolution of the 18th century and a second revolution of 1848, suffered still more catastrophic losses in the Franco-Prussian War, the fratricides of the Paris Commune of 1871, as well as the numerous battles of the Napoleonic Wars.

Thus, the pressures of continually facing death as an intrusion into every-

day family life made the need to keep both the *presence* of the "Lost Beloved" near while simultaneously bidding farewell, a Victorian preoccupation. Victorians met this need by creating an extensive mourning culture employing elaborate mourning dress, jewelry, and funeral trappings; memorial portraits (both drawn and painted); postmortem photographs; sculptures, busts, and death masks; and a myriad of commemorative artifacts. The elaborate funeral processions, the fabulous monuments and mausoleums, and the pervasiveness of memorial art were so much a part of Victorian life that historians have often described this era as having been "obsessed" with death. Additionally, romanticism so permeated Victorian sensibilities, that the *Beautiful Death* philosophy evidenced a virtual eagerness about the end of life and the promise of bliss awaiting on the other side, as attested to by numerous letters and memoirs in England, France, and America. In contrast to today, where we tend to keep grief privately endured, the hearts of Victorians were laid bare for all to see.

Victorians not only beautified death itself, but also the act of dying and the deathbed scene. As noted by author Pat Jalland in *Death in The Victorian Family*, there were four primary consolations that gave comfort to Victorians: religious belief, time, private and social memory, and the sympathy of family and friends.[13] The Victorian definition of the "good" death encompassed an ideal in which the dying person was cared for in the home, had sufficient time to take care of spiritual matters, and was also able to make farewells or exhortations to family members. At the time of passing, families hoped some evidence of the after life would be seen in special "visitations," called "hoverings," as the deceased moved from the earthly realm into that of the heavenly, what today are sometimes referred to as "near-death experiences." Memoirs of family deaths from this era described deathbed scenes in flowery prose, and many were later published as "consolation literature," desirable today to collectors and historians.

The earliest treatise on the subject of dying the "good death" was published in 1651 by Bishop Jeremy Taylor. Called *The Rule and Exercises of Holy Dying*, this form of consolation literature was reprinted for centuries, and was so ubiquitous in Victorian homes that the 19th century English novelist George Eliot referred to this staple volume in her novel, *Adam Bede*. Numerous other religious memoirs were published in Victorian England and America, such as *Death-Bed Thoughts*, published in 1838 in England, and *The Gates Ajar* published in 1869 in America. Parental memoirs of children's deaths were published as comforts to grieving parents, as seen in *Agnes and The Key to Her Little Coffin* (1857), *The Empty Crib* (1873), and *Our Children in Heaven* (1870). Secular examples of romanticized deathbed scenes were also popular among writers of non-religious works,

such as the death of Little Nell in Charles Dickens' *The Old Curiousity Shop.*

In the Victorian era, there was also a desire to develop the deathbed scene into almost melodramatic theatre, with the dying and his or her family members virtual "actors" playing specific "roles." The dying were encouraged to relate beatific visions of the "heavenly realms" as a sign of salvation and as an assurance of ultimate reunion, as well as a "message to the living" left behind. The dying were also encouraged to give an example of a "triumphant" death to edify living family members, often problematic in an era of few effective palliative remedies. Consolation literature of the mid to late 1800s abounds with references to the utterances of the dying while delirious, and fanciful imagery of the "Other Side" gave comfort to those witnessing the passing. This was the Victorian ideal of the "good" death, which contrasted sharply with the medieval definition of the same.

Deaths from consumption (or tuberculosis as it is known today) were especially romanticized in the Victorian era. Because the disease usually struck young adults, the lingering dying process and pale pallor of the sick appealed to Victorian tastes of the romanticized death as set forth in the sampler shown later in this chapter. In this c. 1840s memorial, an embroidery on punched paper, the maker eulogizes the consumptive death of her brother in the classic description of the symptoms of "fading away," as seen in the language of the poem:

As spring came and the trees were all blooming,
Death our dear brother was calling.
Pale and wan he grew and weakly,
Bearing all his pains so meekly.
That to us he grew still dearer,
As the trial hour grew nearer.
But he left us sad and lonely,
Watching by his semblance only.
Yet he spake of realms more fair,
We hope ere long to meet him there.

Here in one archetype, we have all the classic elements of the Victorian idealized deathbed scene embodied in *The Beautiful Death*: the long, lingering dying process allowing for spiritual preparation; the pale skin color as epitomized Victorian definitions of beauty; the pres-

ence of the family for emotional farewells; the courage and fortitude under suffering; the visions of heavenly realms viewed in euphoria; and the hope of eventual family reunion.

Artists such as Dante Gabriel Rossetti, W. Holman Hunt, John Millais, and other Pre-Rafaelites frequently portrayed the deathbed scene of consumptives in romantic ideals of young innocent women fading away. And Edgar Allen Poe, upon hearing of the death of a young woman to consumption, exclaimed, "I would wish all I love to perish of that disease. How glorious! To depart in the heyday of the young life, the heart full of passion, the imagination all fire."

The family life of the Brontes, the famous 19th century English family of writers of *Jane Eyre*, *Wuthering Heights*, and *The Tenant of Wildfell Hall*, was one of a series of early deaths, mostly from consumption. When Mrs. Bronte died of ovarian cancer at thirty-eight, she left behind her six young children, two of whom also died shortly thereafter of consumption. Of the well-known sisters Charlotte, Emily, and Anne Bronte, only Charlotte lived into adulthood, as all eventually succumbed to the ravages of consumption. Their beloved only brother, Branwell, also died an early consumptive death precipitated by dissipation and alcoholism, leaving their father Patrick Bronte to outlive his entire family. The family's personal experiences with consumptive deaths are seen in their writings, both in poetry and literature. In *Jane Eyre*, Charlotte described a deathbed conversation between the dying Helen Burns and Jane, in what must have been a familiar remembrance from her own experiences at the deathbeds of her siblings. The death of Edgar Linton in Emily Bronte's *Wuthering Heights* mirrors the same romanticized dying scene, where Edgar blissfully gazes at his daughter, his eyes "fixed on her features that seemed dilating with ecstasy." As he kisses his daughter Catherine, he murmurs, "I am going to her [his first wife Catherine]; and you darling child, shall come to us!" This description of the unnaturally bright and glistening eyes was a common feature of the consumptive termi-

24

nal state, as Charlotte so poignantly described in a letter dated June 13, 1849:

"It is over. Branwell – Emily – Anne are gone like dreams – gone as Maria and Elizabeth [her two baby sisters] went twenty years ago. One by one I have watched them fall asleep on my arm – and closed their glazed eyes…"

An 1850s handwritten account of a dying teenager named "Charlie," by his aunt who witnessed his passing, is typical of the almost lachrymose language used by Victorians in describing deathbed scenes. As Charlie passed, his aunt recounted how death "snatched him from the warm embrace of beloved ones and consigned him to the dreary grave," but that he [had been taken] "from a world of temptation and sin unto God." She added that although Charlie had been relinquished with "streaming eyes and bereaved heart," it was "well to murmur not, selfish one as thou too, if faithful, shall reach the joys of heaven." The letter is a mixture of encouragement to piety and the realities of dying when the family members were "in an agony of suspense, hoping and fearing to hear the results." After a long nighttime deathbed vigil, "in the morning all was over." Charlie's father was no longer able to control his feelings, and "then came the bitterness of grief when he could not be comforted." The family and friends all came to the house to sit and watch at night with the "sweet sleeper," while they awaited the burial. Charlie's aunt then went on to describe the "lovely broken band of brothers and sisters so deep in sorrow" as they carried Charlie's coffin to the cemetery, where she herself took one final look, then the "the coffin was closed and Charlie gone from our sight forever."

Deathbed accounts in letters and diaries of women who died in childbirth were also quite numerous in the 19th century, as pregnancies and birthing were inherently risky in an era with little understanding of obstetrical care. Women frequently died of sepsis, convulsions, and hemorrhaging in childbirth, as well as catastrophic injuries from the overzealous administration of toxic therapies and interventionist procedures. Eliza Clitherall recorded the death of her daughter in childbirth, relating, "On the 30th my blessed Gena was confin'd of a little boy; on the 2nd of Dec'r her chastin'd spirit took its flight. Another sad call to our family to 'Prepare,' [as] this is the third member of our family who has in the past few months died in childbirth." [14]

As recounted by author Sally G. McMillan, Ann Eliza Jewell and her husband left their home in Missouri and made a trip to a healing spring in Georgia in hopes of alleviating their symptoms from severe summer diarrhea. On their trip back to Missouri, Ann went into labor, giving birth to a premature child. Her husband, despite his own poor health, was forced to leave her and return home to attend to domestic matters. As Ann continued to decline from childbirth, she determined to return to him "if it was but to take one look farewell and then die." Barely able to move, she managed to get on board a boat for St. Louis, but was moved to a private home on shore as she began to further deteriorate. Her sister, Julia, rushed to her bedside in time to see her kiss her newborn babe farewell and expire. Her husband never saw his wife again, for he had died on his journey to retrieve her. [15]

In those situations where the dying lapsed into unconsciousness, or death occurred suddenly where no dying declarations or visions of the "other world" could be uttered, Victorians were robbed of those consolations so dear to their idealized interpretation of the "good death." In these so-called "bad" deaths, which occurred more frequently than not (especially with illnesses such as cholera and typhoid where fevers and delirium prevented coherent dialogue between the dying and those at the bedside), there was no possibility of assurances of future family reunions in blissful paradise.

Willie Lincoln, son of Abraham and Mary Lincoln, died unconscious from typhoid fever and internal hemorrhaging in February 1862. Mary, distraught with grief after losing her second son to illness, sought comfort in a popular consolation book of the period, *East Lynne*, by Ellen Price Wood. In this novel, the long-suffering child, a boy the same age as 11-year-old Willie, proclaimed as he died, "Jesus is coming for me; I see heaven, a beautiful city, precious stones, pearly gates, beautiful fruits and flowers." But, such vocal assurances were denied to Mary Lincoln, and to many family members at bedside vigils. [16]

Grief, while permitted to be openly expressed through mourning ritual, was also to be controlled so that excessive grief would not display even the slightest evidence of unbelief in Christian assurances of resurrection and future family reunion. Mourning was to be a mixture of restrained emotion and pious resignation to God's will. Any violation of these standards was abhorrent to Victorian religious sensibilities.

Spiritualism also made its entrance into the Victorian psyche, by offering the living a "revelation" of the after life experienced by their deceased loved ones. Queen Victoria, Empress Eugenie (wife of Napoleon III), and Mary Todd Lincoln attended séances held by prominent spiritualists, and all believed their dead husbands (and in Mary's case, her dead children as well), appeared as ghostly incorporeal beings to bring comfort and assurance of guidance. It was believed that Queen Victoria's groundskeeper John Brown was quite knowledgeable in contacting the dead, and Empress Eugenie sought the services of Madame Blavatsky, the infamous conjurer and spiritualist of Europe.

Out on the isles of Guernsey off the coast of Britain, French political dissidents living in exile under the symbolic leadership of famed French writer Victor Hugo engaged in spiritualism as a humorous pastime. They professed to have contacted the spirits of Hugo's dead daughter, as well as those of Moliere, Shakespeare, Dante, Racine, Jesus, Plato, and even the dove of Noah's Ark and Balaam's ass!

New York and Boston became centers for the spiritualist movement in the 1850s and 1860s, and séances were held in many middle and upper class homes. In Boston alone, a city of 177,000 people, there were an estimated 40,000 spiritualists and four spiritualist newspapers, and Boston became the home of a number of "spirit" photographers who advertised their abilities to show "proofs of the After-Life." In 1885, author Elizabeth Stuart Phelps collected and published what she described as messages dictated to her from the spirits of the dead. *Songs of the Silent World* was as much of a commercial success for Miss

Phelps as were her earlier books, *Gates Ajar* and *Between the Gates*, both published just after the Civil War.

For Americans living in towns and cities, adherence to mourning customs provided some comfort in the form of ritual, just as they did in English and European households. Windows and mirrors were covered and draped with crape, in the belief that this would prevent the death of anyone who might see his reflection in the glass and thus be doomed to die by the spirit of the deceased. This belief goes back to the Greek myth of Narcissus, where the fear of viewing one's reflection in a pool of water would tempt the water spirits to steal the soul. The practice of turning mirrors to the wall was a part of mourning ritual in Christian, Jewish, and African-American households. In some superstitious homes, clocks were stopped until after the funeral, and when re-started, were set two minutes ahead so that the "Hour of Death" would never again occur in the home.

The houses of mourners would also be suitably dressed to give evidence to the community of recent bereavement. Crape bunting decorated the outside of the homes, and ribbon and crape wreaths hung on the front doors as a signal to the community of the family's loss, in black for an adult death, and white for a child's. Mutes, uttering not a word, would be posted outside the homes, staring at passersby with appropriately lugubrious facial expressions. Funeral feasts with special mourning tea-sets were employed in the wakes following the funeral, where tables of foodstuffs such as oyster pudding, sandwiches, shrimp gelee, fruit salad with sour cream, and cakes provided a repast for the mourners. Among the Pennsylvania Germans, large "dead-cakes" made of flour, sugar, butter, pearl ash salt, and caraway seed were made for visitations, then kept as a memento of the person who died. And in Dutch funeral feasts a raisin "funeral pie," known as *leicht boi* in Pennsylvania and New England, was commonly served. So ubiquitous was this pie at funerals, that the expression "There'll be raisin pie yet," would be related amongst family members when all hope was lost, and death imminent.[17]

Ponderous funeral rituals of upper class Victorians were status symbols, and bordered on the ostentatious as the century progressed. Death for some upperclass Victorians held a certain prestige. Numerous "Feathermen," carrying trays or "feather boards," walked in the funeral procession alongside the carriage horses, which were festooned with dyed black harnessing, silk rosettes, and ostrich plumage. The funeral procession of former president and Civil War hero

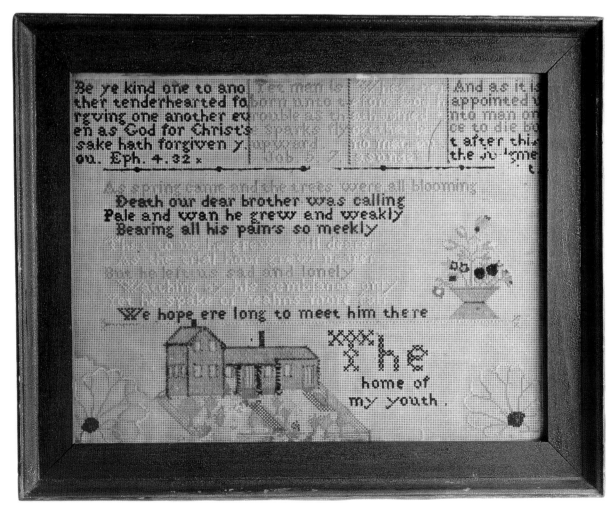

Berlin wool-work embroidery, c. 1840s, memorializing the death of the maker's brother, in the elegiac poetry representative of the idealized deathbed scene popular in the 19th century. 18" x 12". *Author's collection.* $250.

Ulysses S. Grant, in 1885, is one such example of an unbelievably elaborate Victorian funeral. The purple and gold draped catafalque transporting Grant's magnificent casket was eighteen feet long as well as high, drawn on a caisson by twenty-four pairs of matched black horses, each caparisoned in somber mourning, and each attended by mutes in mourning attire walking alongside. Fifty thousand mourners walked behind the caisson in the procession, thirty thousand of which were Civil War veterans. The procession was witnessed by several million people along the route, and was so long that from the first appearance of the funeral train coming into a town, it was three and a half hours before the caisson carrying Grant's body arrived.

In England, the death of the Prince Consort to typhoid fever, in December 1861, plunged Queen Victoria into life-long mourning, and further popularized the wearing of mourning clothing and jewelry among British subjects. All wore mourning attire at Court for many years after Albert's death, with the Queen herself in seclusion, refusing even to be present to open Parliament. During the Queen's mourning, England itself mourned for its own husbands, sons, brothers, and fathers lost in the Crimean and Napoleonic Wars, the Indian Mutiny, etc., just as American families mourned their losses in the Civil War and other conflicts of the 19th century.

In addition to deaths from statistical averages universally typical for this century, France endured war deaths just as in England and America. As previously stated, the Napoleonic Wars of 1800-15 and the Franco-Prussian War of 1870-71 added numerous losses and grief for French family members already trying to recover from deaths incurred during the French Revolution, Paris Commune, etc. The customs of mourning clothing, jewelry, and framed memorials continued in France just as they had in England and America. Cemeteries such as Pere La Chaise reflected the High Victorian sentimentalities surrounding death and grief just as was seen in 19th century Protestant cemeteries in England and America.

For prosperous Victorians, the accoutrements of mourning fashion were readily available through mourning warehouses in England, France, and America. For many, however, the need to memorialize grief and loss was adjusted and altered to fit their circumstances, which were often enormously burdensome. Where few visible tokens of remembrance were able to be kept or created, Victorians made concessions to vicissitudes, and their letters, diaries, and memoirs often substitute as the only *memento mori* possible. In the following chapters, we will step into their lives through their personal accounts and their faces.

When my mother died I was very young,
And my father sold me while yet my tongue
Could scarcely cry 'Weep! Weep! Weep! Weep!
So your chimneys I sweep, and in soot I sleep."
[William Blake, 1757-1827, from *The Chimney Sweeper*]

Sisters In Mourning

Mary Todd Lincoln and Queen Victoria

"What is to be, is to be, and nothing we can say, or do, or be, can divert an inexorable fate, but in spite of knowing this, one feels better even after losing, if one has had a brave, whole-hearted fight to get the better of destiny."

—Mary Todd Lincoln, in a letter to a friend upon the death of three-year-old son, Eddie Lincoln

Mary Todd Lincoln and Queen Victoria could not be more dissimilar in familial background, personality and temperament, and perspectives about children and religion, yet they shared one common unifying experience: that of lifelong grief over a beloved husband cut down in the prime of life. Mary was emotionally high-strung, outspoken, loved and spoiled by her husband, and prone to histrionics and melodramatic fits of temper. When she married Abraham Lincoln in November of 1842, she ecstatically anticipated all the fulfillment of married life outlined for her in the Victorian view of the happy domestic sphere: a devoted husband, a beautiful home, a growing brood of healthy and prosperous children. Literature of the day exhorted women to be,

> *"Best pleased to be admired at home,*
> *And hear reflected from her husband's praise,*
> *That her house was ordered well.*
> *Her children taught the way of life."*

And, certainly, Mary Todd Lincoln did her best to fulfill these expectations. However, while she outwardly expressed agreement with these Victorian views of women as exemplars of Christian virtue, she often tended not to observe these roles for herself, but desired instead to be in the limelight of White House parties, beautifully dressed as befitted, in her view, the wife of a President. Strongly opinionated, she frequently intruded into the "male" world of politics as a way of augmenting her husband's advancement through personal contacts and by paying visits on those she felt would aid in Lincoln's political career. Her actions brought her a great deal of condemnation, and many of Lincoln's cabinet officers disliked her.

After President Lincoln was assassinated, Mary did not "go gently into that good-night," as befitted the proper Victorian widow, but continually besieged the Senate and the House for a widow's pension, a provision not part of the Federal budget at that time. Sadly, her reputation for emotional outbursts combined with her growing mental instability were quickly destroying the last vestiges of sympathy for her as the widow of the martyred President.

Mary often expressed the wish to "forget myself," as she faced tragic events so frequently she believed her life marked by the cruelty of fate or the capriciousness of Providence. As a child, she lost her mother, the death foreshadowing others in Mary's life. Born into a wealthy Lexington, Kentucky family, Mary saw her family divided by the Civil War, more than half of them fighting for the Confederacy (including all three of Mary's half-brothers), while other family members remained loyal to the Union cause. The Todd family would lose some of its sons in the war, further reminding Mary of past deaths endured and presaging deaths yet to come. They were, in fact, "shadows before nightfall."[18]

Death also intruded more intimately in striking the happy home that Mary worked so hard to create for her own sense of security. The first to die was three-year-old Eddie Lincoln, who took sick in December, 1849, with what was initially thought to be diphtheria, but by mid-January, 1850, the dreaded diagnosis of consumption was finally acknowledged. After fifty-two days of the typical consumptive symptoms of racking coughs, gasps for air, anorexia, and exhaustion, Eddie died. Mary was prostrate with grief, and Lincoln repeatedly attempted to exhort her by saying, "Eat, Mary, for we must live."[19]

There was a lull of several years before the next blow was struck. During the depressing second year of the Civil War, the First Lady decided to hold a party in the White House to cheer her husband, and to brighten the dreary scene of the winter's gloomy weather and course of the War. Much preparation went into the February 1862 affair, and everyone in Washington was in attendance. It should have been a relief from the worries of the progress of the War, but upstairs, Mary and the President were consumed with their own anxieties: eleven-year-old Willie Lincoln was sick with a fever. Two weeks later, Willie was dead, probably of typhoid fever from the Potomac River, long the primary source of water for the White House, but now contaminated from the 140,000 military troops with open latrines surrounding the Capitol. Mary's grief so engulfed her that Lincoln led her to a window one day and pointed to the Washington Lunatic Asylum in the distance. "Mother," he said, "Do you see that large white building on the hill yonder? Try to control your grief or it will drive you mad and we may have to send you there."

Willie had been weakened by an earlier bout of scarlet fever, and his death was long and difficult. As he lapsed into unconsciousness, Mary was robbed of the consolations of deathbed assurances through "last words" so precious to Victorians, a comfort that was to be denied her in all three of her children's deaths, and that of her husband as well. This no doubt contributed to Mary's unorthodox obsession with spiritualism and divergence from conventional Christian views and behavior in mourning.

Mary had finally come out of the three-year grief from Willie's death when the severest stroke of her life occurred. On April 6, 1865, General Robert E. Lee surrendered the Army of Northern Virginia to the United States Army of the Potomac, ending the bloodiest conflict in American history. Eight days later, on Good Friday, April 14, Mary and the President decided to go to the theatre to see *Our American Cousin,* for the first relaxing time together they had had since the War began. An hour and a half into the play, Mary slipped her hand into that of her husband's, whispered intimately into his ear, and a shot rang out. In the ensuing chaos, Mary's cry was heard above all else, "Oh, my God, and have I given my husband to die?"[20]

Again, Mary was robbed of the deathbed consolations and loving farewells. She later said to a friend, "In my hours of deep affliction, I often think it would have been some solace to me and perhaps have lessened the grief, which is now breaking my heart – if my idolized had passed away, after an illness, and I had been permitted to watch over him and tend him to the last." Like her sister in mourning, Queen Victoria, Mary went into seclusion and experienced grief so intense that she was bedridden with overwhelming despair. Her African-American secretary Lizzie Keckley described Mary's paroxysms of grief as, "the wails of a broken heart, the unearthly shrieks, the terrible convulsions."[21]

A *carte de visite* photograph taken in 1867 of Mary Todd Lincoln in mourning dress shows that her outfit was intended to reflect "first stage" attire, but her veil was embellished with floral decorations typical of Mary's love of dress

trims, an addition which would have been considered quite *taboo* according to etiquette requirements of that era. She was never able to fully come to terms with her overwhelming grief, nor reach the expected Christian "resignation and acceptance" required of women in the 19th century. She was superstitious her entire life, seeing ominous "strokes" to follow her in every fortuitous event. In one of the many ironies of her life, Mary purchased $1,000 worth of deep mourning attire immediately after Lincoln had related to her one of his many prophetic dreams of his own death while napping on Election Day in 1860. Mary's later obsession with spiritualism was heavily influenced by the superstitions and premonitions both she and Lincoln experienced throughout their marriage, but particularly during the Civil War years. Her resistance to social constraints, and poignant attempts to still maintain a sense of her former (antebellum) self, is seen here in her tragic addition of feminine floral trims. Mary was struggling to maintain her mental stability when this photograph was taken.

Six years after the death of her "idolized" husband, Mary lost the remaining son to whom she was close: eighteen-year-old Thomas, or "Tad" Lincoln. After criss-crossing the Atlantic desperately looking for a home for herself and her son, virtually a woman without a country, Tad caught cold from the chilly winds off the coast of England. The cold lingered, and then worsened, until the dreaded diagnosis was finally made: Tad was dying of consumption. After weeks of suffering Tad died, leaving Mary once again feeling overwhelming abandonment and grief, declaring, "Ill luck presided at my birth and has been a faithful attendant ever since." She did not travel to Springfield, Illinois, where at this point, almost all her family were buried, but lived the rest of her life in aimless wanderings between America and Europe, accompanied only by relentless grief and her several suitcases full of old clothing and memories. Her one remaining son, Robert, with whom she was never close, had her committed to an asylum for a time, an act for which she never forgave him. On the anniversary of Tad's death, July 15, 1882, Mary collapsed in her bedroom, lapsing into a coma, and died in the early morning hours of July 16,

1882. The recognition denied her in life, she finally received in death in the form of a lavish funeral, whereupon she was then finally reunited with her beloved husband and sons in the burial vault in Oak Ridge Cemetery in Illinois.

Carte de visite memorial for Abraham Lincoln, "The Martyr President," c. 1865, *Author's collection.* $75-100.

Carte de visite of Mary Todd Lincoln in mourning dress, taken in 1867. *Author's collection.* $175.

Queen Victoria

"Princess Alice whispered to me, 'This is the death rattle' and went for her mother. Then in that darkened room they knelt; the Queen and her elder children…watching in agonised silence, the passing of that lofty and noble soul. Gentler than an infant slumber it was at last. The poor Queen exclaimed, 'Oh yes, this is death.'"[22]
—Sir Charles Phipps, at the deathbed of the Prince Consort

Mary Todd Lincoln's sister in mourning, Queen Victoria, was not spared her own "shadows before nightfall," the greatest of these being the death of her beloved Albert, the Prince Consort, in December 1861. The Queen had already endured the death of her mother, the Duchess of Kent, a few months prior in April 1861, but she had been relatively unacquainted with death. After her mother died, she noted in her diary, "I had never been near a coffin before…The dreaded terrible calamity has befallen us, which seems like an awful dream…Oh, God! How awful! How mysterious! The constant crying was a comfort and relief…but Oh! The agony of it!"

Six months earlier, in October of 1860, the Prince Consort had taken a spill from a carriage while he and the Queen were vacationing in Coburg, Germany, the country of his birth. Although the accident was not particularly severe, the Prince was quite shaken, his brother Ernest noting that the Prince seemed despondent and unwell for days afterward. Albert had suffered from ill health and a delicate nature his entire life, and the accident was a debilitating precursor to the illness that eventually overtook him the following year. Over the next two months, the Prince's condition worsened, as he suffered with violent headaches, chills, and attacks of illness, which he kept secret from the Queen. He confided to Victoria, the Princess Royal, "My attack was the real English cholera," but in fact, the Prince was succumbing to typhoid fever, contracted from the polluted drains of Windsor Castle.

After pushing himself beyond his endurance in matters related to the Queen and to English affairs of state, Albert had little emotional and physical reserves to cope with the profligacy of the Prince of Wales, the future Edward VII, who was spending considerable time in the theatres and disreputable districts of London. Prince Albert's efforts to redeem his son from the potential ridicule and legal consequences of his liaison with an actress left him completely undone emotionally and physically. He lost the will to live, declaring to the Queen at one point, "I do not cling to life…I am sure if I had a severe illness I should give up at once, I should not struggle for life. I have no tenacity of life." Over the coming weeks, chills and insomnia further debilitated Albert, who persisted in handling affairs for the Queen, along with attempting to guide the Prince of Wales' behavior along more appropriate paths. By early December, Prince Albert was becoming increasingly bedridden but restless and continuing to suffer from insomnia, inability to eat, and rapid, labored breathing. On the morning of December 14, 1861, with the Queen, various physicians, and their children beside his bed, the Prince began to decline, breathing rapidly.

At the end, the Queen recalled in her diary, "I took his dear left hand which was already cold, tho' the breathing was quite gentle and I knelt down by him…Two or three long but perfectly gentle breaths were drawn, the hand clasping mine, and…*all, all,* was over…I stood up, kissed his dear heavenly forehead & called out in a bitter and agonising cry "Oh! My dear Darling!" [sic], and then dropped on my knees in mute, distracted despair, unable to utter a word or shed a tear!"[23]

The abject grief of the Queen caused her to be dubbed the "Widow of Windsor," and the yards of crape formed so much a part of her mourning dress that she became something of a "Crape Deity" according to author John Morley, in *Death, Heaven and the Victorians.* The Queen herself described her grief in an 1862 letter to Earl Canning:

"To the Queen it is like death in life! Her misery, her utter despair, she cannot describe! Her only support, the only ray of comfort she gets for a moment, is in the firm conviction and certainty of his nearness, his undying love, and of their eternal reunion! Only she prays always, and pines for the latter with an anxiety she cannot describe."[24]

The Queen commissioned many memorial pieces of Albert, including photographs of her and her children in mourning, sculpted busts of Albert, mourning handkerchiefs embroidered with tears, memorial portraits of the Consort, and ceramic memorial plates and objects. A postmortem photograph of Albert hung over the Queen's bed, and she slept with his nightshirt. His clothing and shaving items were laid out each morning and evening as though he were still alive to use them. The Queen had been widowed at forty-two years of age, a year younger than her sister in mourning, Mary Todd Lincoln, and the love of both women for their husbands was legendary.

The Queen had depended on the Prince Consort for virtually every detail of her life, from the clothing she wore to his advice on English affairs and European crises. She was overwhelmed with grief, and became a recluse, unable to perform public duties, and barely capable of seeing to private ones. She wrote in a letter that she could look forward to "nothing but a pleasureless and dreary life," a despair echoed in writings by her sister in mourning, Mary Todd Lincoln. She was finally persuaded to open Parliament in 1866, under considerable pressure, but it was an ordeal for her and she was still reclusive from grief in the 1870s. Rumors began to surface that the Queen was possibly insane from grief, and emotionally incapable of performing her duties – the similarities of accusations to those regarding Mary Lincoln unmistakable. In due course, however, Queen Victoria came out of seclusion to resume her role as sovereign, one she had never totally abandoned when out of the public eye, but she continued to wear mourning for the remainder of her life.

Unlike Mary Lincoln, Queen Victoria did not lose any of her nine children in childhood, but three preceded her in death in adulthood: Alice, in 1878, at the age of thirty-five, probably from diphtheria; Leopold, in 1884, at the age of thirty-one, from hemophilia; and Alfred, in 1900, at the age of fifty-six, of cancer of the throat.

Queen Victoria died at Osborne in January 1901, at the age of eighty-one, supported on her deathbed by her grandson, Willy, the Kaiser of Germany, son of Princess Victoria. After a period of declining health in mind and body, the Queen had rallied to show patriotic spirit at the beginning of the Boer War in 1899, and stayed the course virtually to the end of her life, only discontinuing her lifelong diary four months before her death. Her long reign had seemed a rock of stability in a rapidly changing world, the monarchy bridging the gap between the insular world of early Victorian life, and a world of bewildering transformation and increasing upheaval. When she died, the novelist Henry James described her passing succinctly: "We all feel a bit motherless today: mysterious little Victoria is dead and fat vulgar Edward is king."[25]

Memorial card for H.R.H. Prince Albert, the Prince Consort of Queen Victoria, with beautiful die-cut iconography of willows, cherubs, drapes, and weeping mourners. 3" x 4.5". *Author's collection.* $100+.

"Her—over all whose realms to their last isle, the shadow of Her loss draws like eclipse, darkening the world." Beautiful Queen Victoria "In Memoriam" ceramic plate with inscription, "She wrought her people lasting good," c. 1901. 8" in diameter. *Courtesy of Antiques & Goodies.* $275.

Buried at The Side of the Road

Death in Westering America

"We halted a day to bury her and the infant that had lived but an hour, in this weird, lonely spot on God's footstool away apparently from everywhere and everybody. The immense, lonesome plain; the great fathomless ocean – how insignificant seems the human body when consigned to their cold embrace!"[26]
—From the diary of pioneer Catherine Haun, on the trail to California in 1849

On February 2, 1848, in a treaty between the United States and Mexico ending the war between the two countries, a huge expanse of land from Texas to Oregon was ceded to America, expanding the nation from the Atlantic to the Pacific. Between 1840 and 1870, hundreds of thousands of men, women, and children rode and walked over 2,400 miles to the western states, in literal fulfillment of Manifest Destiny. They came from all walks of life, from all over the world. Some were escaping poverty and the crowded cities of Europe, some were fleeing slavery, and still others simply wanted to better themselves. For all, the desire to own a piece of land was something sacred, and the siren call was irresistible.

The landscape was formidable. When pioneers looked out on the fathomless prairies, the seemingly insuperable mountains, the enormous expanses of desert, the huge and sometimes frightening rivers, they were facing a landscape unlike anything they had seen in the East or in their native lands. As writer Ian Frazier has so eloquently pointed out, it was in the West that Americans ultimately shaped their own identity from their European roots; it was the watershed where they declared, "This is the place where we became a *people*, unlike the people we were in Europe."

As men and woman moved west, however, they struggled to maintain familial relationships even as the hardships of the trail threatened to cast family members to the four winds. The physical separation of leaving family and friends "back home" was compounded by the permanent dissevering of loved ones to death on the trails west. With the lack of accessibility to mourning accessories and clothing, to say nothing of primitive and hurried roadside burials, adherence to appropriate mourning requirements was all but impossible for pioneers. Many diaries recount numerous deaths on the journey, and the attempts by families to appropriately bury their dead loved ones under appalling circumstances.

Westward trails to California and Oregon were littered with thousands of makeshift graves, attesting to the tribulations endured. Diseases such as cholera ravaged wagon trains, as watering holes became contaminated by waste from people and animals. Pioneer women died in childbirth at alarming rates, often surpassing the statistical levels in the East, where one in eight women died in childbed. Historians have estimated that three-quarters of pioneering women in the 19th century were in some stage of pregnancy, became pregnant on the trail, or were nursing newborn infants. Considering that most pioneers walked the majority of the distance from starting points in the east to their destinations, one can only imagine the sufferings endured.

Children died by the thousands, either from disease or accident, just as adults did. Pioneer diaries recorded children falling out of wagons and under the feet of oxen, or wandering off, never to be seen again. They drank bottles of laudanum and died. They accidentally shot themselves or were shot by other children. They drowned in rivers. They broke limbs which, when poorly set, resulted in their deaths, or they sustained minor cuts and scrapes which later became infected, leading to deaths from septicemia.

For many pioneers, the painful loss of loved ones was magnified by the necessity of burial in hurriedly-dug graves, never to be revisited. Lodisa Frizell, a pioneer mother on her way to California, noted in her journal:

"The heart has a thousand misgivings and the mind is tortured with anxiety, and often as I passed the fresh made graves, I have glanced at the side boards of the wagon, not knowing how soon it might serve as a coffin for some one of us."[27]

This was all too true for Lydia Allen Rudd, who lost her daughter Margaret on the trail west. Composing a poem, she sent it, along with locks of the child's hair, to family and friends back home. In the last stanza of her poem, she expressed a common feeling for 19th century parents:

Shall we not all meet there to love,
With love that has no trembling fears?
In that dear home far far above
This dark and dreary land of tears?[28]

In contrast to today, where we keep children away from the dying, pioneer children were not spared the realities of death and decay on the trail west.

32

Twelve-year-old Ada Millington described the death of her little brother, George, on the trail to California in 1860. Her parents' pathetic attempts to keep George's body with them for as long as possible caused Ada to note in her diary,

"We couldn't bear the thought of leaving his little body among the sands of this wilderness surrounded by Indians and wolves. We used spirits of camphor very freely on George's clothes and think we will try to take his body on at least another day."[29]

Husbands died fording rivers, or of serious accidents and disease. Some were simply worn out to death from exhaustion, just as women were. Others brawled with fellow pioneers and were shot. Statistically few of all pioneer deaths were actually due to Indian raids or massacres, the major fear of most westering Americans.

The Henry Sager family suffered more than their share of trials on their way to Oregon. En route, and in the middle of the desert, Mrs. Sager gave birth to her seventh child, and endured considerable discomfort as a rainstorm flooded the wagon, washing over her and her newborn infant. At one point, the wagon team bolted on an embankment and overturned, severely injuring Mrs. Sager, already exhausted from childbed. A few days later, her nine-year-old daughter Catherine jumped out of the wagon, catching her skirt on the wheel axle, which then threw her under the feet of the oxen crushing one of her legs. Day after day brought new troubles. At another point along the trail, Henry Sager, while trying desperately to turn a herd of stampeding buffalo away from his wagon and family, was himself critically injured and ultimately died. A pioneer diary written by a witness to the event recounted his last moments:

"It soon became apparent to all that he must die. He himself was fully aware that he was passing away and he could not be reconciled to the thought of leaving his large and helpless family. His wife was feeble in health, the children small, and one likely to be a cripple for a long time."[30]

After her husband's death, Mrs. Sager courageously attempted to continue on to Oregon, but was soon debilitated by "camp fever" after her difficult childbirth and injuries sustained in the accidents. She became delirious, and despite the care of other pioneer women, died and was buried at the side of the road. In less than a month, the seven Sager children were orphaned, the oldest being fourteen years of age, and the youngest only a few months.

After being taken in by other pioneering families, the Sager children eventually arrived at the Marcus and Narcissa Whitman mission in southeastern Oregon, where they were adopted by the Whitmans. Nevertheless, trouble continued to plague their lives. Three years after they arrived at the mission, Cayuse Indians attacked, killing both the Whitmans and twelve others, among them two brothers of little Catherine Sager.[31]

Another pioneer family suffered similar tragedies. William Smith, his wife, and children left Missouri by wagon train in 1846, headed for "the grate North West to Parts unknown." Sickness and accidents took their toll, delaying the wagon party for six weeks while they waited for the sick to either recover or die. After too long a delay, William finally decided to push on, but just as that decision was made, he suffered a heart attack and died. He left his wife with the care of nine children, one of whom was dying, another crippled, and the youngest, a toddler. Ellen Smith "put her sadle [sic] on the White ox an Put the three little boys" on board, packed the bedding around them, and attempted to walk with the older children, pushing the oxen along heading west. It was too late to turn back. The hardships were too much for sixteen-year-old daughter Louisa, who was already ill with fever. As she lay dying, Louisa requested that her mother dig "a Grave six feet deep for she did not want the wolves to dig her up and eat her."

Pioneer wife Elizabeth Smith Geer, who lost her husband on the trail to Oregon in the 1850s, wrote of her overwhelming feelings regarding the experience in a letter sent back home to friends and family:

"Today we buried my earthly companion. Now I know what none but widows know; that is, how comfortless is that of a widow's life, especially when left in a strange land, without money or friends, and the care of seven children...I have not told you half we suffered. I am not adequate to the task."[32]

With the completion of the transcontinental railroad on May 10, 1869, pioneering by wagon and on foot diminished in the following decades, along with the attendant deaths and diseases. Congress officially closed the "wilderness frontier" in 1890, which belatedly reflected what had been long-established fact: that Americans had already settled most of the country. In a timeline that Thomas Jefferson predicted would take a thousand years to accomplish, Americans had overspread the continent in less than fifty.

"All America lies at the end of the wilderness road, and our past is not a dead past, but still lives within us. Our forefathers had civilization inside themselves, the wild outside. We live in the civilization they created, but within us the wilderness still lingers. What they dreamed, we live, but what they lived, we dream."

Johnny Has Gone For a Soldier

Death in Civil War America

"There are nights here with the moonlight cold and ghastly, and the whippoorwills, and the screech owls alone disturbing the silence when I could tear my hair and cry aloud for all that is past and gone."

—From the diary of Mary Chestnut, Southern wife and memoirist, on the loss of her home, family members, and friends during the Civil War

The American Civil War, or the War of Northern Aggression, as Southerners termed it, was probably the last great "romantic" war for Americans. It has been described by some historians as the "Great American *Iliad*," for it was the longest war fought anywhere in the Western world between the surrender of Napoleon I in 1815 and World War I. Families, both North and South, saw the war as having a divine purpose, and the cause to which they resolutely held their loyalty, necessitating a noble sacrifice. Loyalty to "country," vis a vis, one's state, was akin to allegiance to one's blood. For Southerners, it was the maintaining of a way of life without governmental interference, or as one Rebel soldier put it when asked by a Yankee why he was fighting so tenaciously, " 'Cause ya'll down heah." For Northerners, it was

a war not only for the abolition of slavery but to maintain the American vision begun only eighty-five years earlier, that of one country united on the principles of life, liberty, and the pursuit of happiness. For them, it was inconceivable that there could ever be a Constitutional concept of "*e pluribus duo*" for America.

When "Johnny had gone for a soldier," he joined over three million Americans who fought against each other, resulting in 1,095,000 casualties and over 632,000 deaths, almost equaling all the deaths in all the wars fought by Americans up to the present day – combined. At Antietam, the single bloodiest day in American history, there were over 23,000 casualties; Confederate losses alone being twice as much as all American deaths on D-Day during World War

II. Casualties on both sides worsened with each battle: over 50,000 at Gettysburg; over 96,000 during the fighting from the Wilderness to Petersburg in 1864; and on and on. At Cold Harbor, the one assault that General Ulysses S. Grant regretted ordering his entire life, Union troops pinned strips of paper to their coats to aid in identifying their bodies, such was the expectation of dying. One soldier prophetically noted his own death in his diary, "June 3rd. Cold Harbor. I was killed." He was among 7,000 other soldiers killed or wounded in less than an hour of fighting.

At the time the Civil War began, the country was essentially in a state of uneven coexistence due to the predominantly agrarian lifestyle of most Americans and the oxymoronic demands placed on that lifestyle by the need for cheap human labor through slavery in order to fulfill the vision of taming the continental wilderness through settlement.[33]

Peaceful coexistence between immoral and inequitable societies was, of course, impossible and in complete antithesis to the Enlightenment principles of American constitutional foundation. Thus, the prophecy of abolitionist John Brown in 1860, that the sin of slavery would not be expunged from the land without the shedding of blood, was apocalyptically fulfilled in the violent battles on American farmlands between April 12, 1861, and April 9, 1865.

Of the 31 million people living in America at the time of the Civil War, over half were under the age of twenty-one, and with virtually every able-bodied man and boy involved in the War, there were few families that were not personally impacted by grief and loss. Among the youngest Civil War soldiers was nine-year-old Edward Black, who joined the 21st Indiana as a musician, and little Johnny Clem, the ten-year-old "Drummer Boy of Shiloh." And many soldiers, such as Union Brigadier General Galusha Pennypacker, were still not old enough to vote by the end of the war.

One of the oldest enlisted men was Curtis King, who joined the 37th Iowa at the age of eighty; other elderly men refused to stay home as well, fighting alongside sons, grandsons, and great-grandsons on both sides. At least 450 women are known to have disguised themselves and fought in the War for either patriotic motives or to be with a husband. Most soldiers were native-born whites, but approximately 500,000 immigrants were brought into the war voluntarily or out of necessity for employment once in their new country. Three brigades of Cherokees, Choctaws, Chickasaw, and Seminoles fought for the Confederacy, while one brigade of Creeks enlisted in the Union forces.[34] And, after Abraham Lincoln delivered the Emancipation Proclamation on January 1, 1863, approximately 186,000 African-Americans fought for their freedom on the Union side.

Civil War drummer boy, typical of many little boys in armies and navies on both sides during the War Between the States.

36

When a Confederate force bombed Fort Sumter, South Carolina, on April 14, 1861, ushering in the four-year-long War Between the States, virtually every American household prepared itself for the possibility of memorializing fathers, brothers, husbands, and sons. Civilians on both sides, but particularly in the South, were personally impacted by horrific battles in their pastures and front yards. When a shell came crashing through the window of his house during the First Battle of Bull Run on July 26, 1861, at the *start* of the Civil War, farmer Wilmer McLean had had enough. He decided to move his family to a quieter part of the country, to a peaceful little village called Appomattox Court House. In one of the many ironies of the Civil War, it was there, four years later, that fate again intervened. The *final* battle of the War was fought in Wilmer McLean's front yard, and it was in his front parlor that the war ended. On April 9, 1865, Confederate General Robert E. Lee signed the terms of surrender to Union General Ulysses S. Grant, seated on Wilmer McLean's parlor furniture. Thus, the war began and ended on Wilmer McLean's property, and one can only marvel at the thoughts that must have gone through his mind as he mused on this odd bit of kismet.

The battles were horrific, great "crimson gashes" as one historian described them. Early in the war at the battle of Shiloh, so many Union and Confederate forces fell that it was possible to walk across the entire length of the battlefield on top of bodies without ever stepping foot on the ground. The loss of life at Shiloh alone surpassed that at Napoleon's Waterloo, yet there would be twenty more battles like Shiloh ahead in the remaining years of the conflict.

Throughout the War, the fighting brought out the best and worst qualities among men who still thought of themselves as Americans, who spoke the same language, had attended the same schools, had come from the same towns, and had the same cultural (and sometimes familial) backgrounds as those fighting against them. Acts of heroism and valor were done by both Union and Confederate soldiers, and often when not engaged in battle, opposing sides traded cigarettes or food items, sang songs, and chatted with each other across battle lines, out of sight of offic-

ers. As the war progressed, however, and battlefield deaths increased, the desire for revenge took hold in many a soldier's heart, as evidenced by one Yankee's letter written following the Battle of Gaines' Mill, June 27, 1862:

"My two tent mates were wounded, and after that I acted like a madman. I snatched a gun from the hands of a man who was shot through the head, as he staggered and fell. At other times I would have been horror-struck, and could not have moved, but then I jumped over dead men with as little feeling as I would over a log. The feeling that was uppermost in my mind was a desire to kill as many as I could. The loss of comrades maddened me."[35]

Despite battlefield losses, however, twice as many soldiers died of disease and infection than were killed in fighting. Hospital conditions were appalling before volunteer nurses working under the severest of conditions brought some semblance of hygiene and comfort to wounded and dying soldiers. Still, battlefield casualties were horrendous, making caregiving almost impossible at

times. When Clara Barton, the famous Civil War nurse, attempted to comfort and treat soldiers after Antietam, she wrote that it was necessary for her to frequently wring out her skirts so that she could walk among the ailing and wounded soldiers without the weight and impediment of her blood-soaked hems.

Like many women both North and South, Mary Chestnut, wife of Jefferson Davis' aide-de-camp, kept a detailed diary of the War, and the friends and family members who were lost. In 1863, after the battle of Sharpsburg, she wrote the following entry typical of the devastating impact the deaths of husbands, fathers, brothers, and sons had on civilian women on both sides:

"My friend Colonel Means, killed on the battlefield, his only son wounded and a prisoner. His wife had not recovered from the death of her other child, Emma, who had died of consumption early in the war. She was lying on a bed when they told her of her husband's death. She did not utter one word. She remained quiet so long, someone removed the light shawl she had drawn over her head. She was dead."[36]

*"Fold it up carefully, lay it aside;
Tenderly touch it, look on it with pride;
For dear to our hearts must it be evermore,
The jacket of gray our loved soldier-boy wore."*
[From *The Jacket of Gray* by Caroline Augusta Ball, 1865]

Civil War artifacts, including tintype of Union officer with wife and child; ambrotype of Confederate soldier from South Carolina; autographed *carte de visite* of Varina Davis, wife of Jefferson Davis, President of the Confederate States of America and memorial *carte de visite* for Confederate dead; Grand Army of the Republic Reunion ribbon dated 1886; GAR veteran's mourning medal; Union issue soldier's Bible; hand-forged bullet mold and powder measure; gaming pieces including chess piece carved from .58 caliber bullet, and brass case with carved bone dice; soldier's religious medal and wedding band dug at battlefield; Civil War-era bleeder used in treating illness. *Author's collection.* $25-350.

Helen A. Kimbell wrote a letter to the chaplain of the U. S. General Hospital at Hampton, Fort Monroe, on August 9, 1863, inquiring as to the status of her husband, a Union soldier. The letter is a poignant reminder of the anxiety and torment suffered by wives and family members on both sides of the Civil War, when uncertainty of the status of their male relatives was not only emotionally traumatic but could be financially catastrophic as well. The date of Helen's letter is approximately one month after the battle of Gettysburg, and it is possible that her husband was mortally wounded in the conflict, and had deteriorated to such an extent that he had sent his final communication to his wife through the chaplain. In euphemistic language typical of the Victorian era, she states:

"Dear Friend,

Now, therefore I write to you hoping you will be kind enough to inform me of his situation whether living or if he has been called to join the past accumulated throng of martyred ones on the other side of the river. I need not tell you that we are feeling very much afflicted and I might say his father, mother, and myself, as he is their only child, the hope and strength of their old age. I cannot endure the thought that he will not get well. If he dies will you tell me as nearly as you can his messages to his home and friends. Also if we can have his remains brought home for burial. This is a very painful theme if my husband is getting better; do not pain him by his seeing this. I am only waiting to hear from him again; to come to him I shall even if I hear again that he is alive. Please write me again and oblige a mourning Friend.

Respectfully yours, Helen A. Kimbell"

Judging by the content of her reply, it is unlikely that Helen's husband survived. Her request to know any "messages" he might have uttered to his "home and friends" was intended to mean dying utterances, which would have assured his family members of future heavenly reunion, a comfort treasured by Christian families on both sides of the War. The ability to return remains to family plots back home was also brand new with the advent of embalming in 1863 by Civil War field surgeons and doctors.

Helen's belief in her husband's martyrdom was a view shared by families on both sides of the War, and the euphemism of the state of death being likened to crossing over to the "other side of the river" is echoed in Confederate General Stonewall Jackson's immortal dying words, "Let us cross over the river and rest under the shade of the trees."

Large c. 1865 Civil War shadowbox memorial using the hair of various family members surrounding a *carte de visite* photograph of a Union officer who died or was killed in battle. This hair wreath is composed of hair of various lengths and colors, from children's curls to elderly gray, and the lengths of hair were wound around thin wire, then fashioned into floral designs. The creator further embellished the wreath with tiny glass beads and yarn "flowers." 20" x 24". *Author's collection.* $350-400.

For families, North and South, the struggle to maintain some semblance of continuity in the midst of chaos was all but impossible, especially for women in the South. In the early months of the War, the bodies of soldiers received all the proper Victorian rituals for burial and mourning. After the First Battle of Bull Run on July 26, 1861, the Confederate slain were escorted through Charleston, South Carolina, by Confederate troops, and business was suspended while the bodies lay in state. More than a thousand soldiers accompanied the dead soldiers from the church services to their burials in Magnolia Cemetery. A year later, burials were more haphazard, with one Confederate woman noting that at Richmond Cemetery, "six or seven coffins dropped into one yawning pit, and hurriedly covered in, all that a grateful country could render in return for precious lives." By the war's end, battlefield dead were simply thrown in ditches, or as one Mississippi woman remembered it, "in bunches, just like dead chickens."[37]

President Abraham Lincoln spoke of "the mystic chords of memory" that wove Americans to each other and to their ancestors. Thus, mourning art, dress, and jewelry reached its zenith in the public expression of those "chords of memory" in Civil War America, just as Prince Albert's death was the English catalyst for mourning customs and art in Britain. Even though the wearing of mourning clothing and jewelry was well entrenched by the mid-1800s in both countries, its popularity soared, propelled by these two pivotal events. Prior to leaving for their military units, many male family members left locks of their hair with their mothers, wives or sweethearts, to be made into mourning jewelry in the event of their deaths. Both Union and Confederate soldiers sat for photographs before battlefield engagements, so as to leave a living photographic record in the event they did not return alive.

For Northern women, the ability to mourn was eased somewhat by access to mourning warehouses and goods. For Southern women experiencing the shortages caused by Northern blockades, however, acquiring appropriate mourning clothing and accessories became increasingly difficult as the War dragged on. For families on both sides, mourning itself sometimes became a "luxury" in which few could indulge, as many women were forced to assume the role of breadwinner, or otherwise take over duties formerly those of their husbands. Survival for Southern women to feed themselves and their children became a priority, and many women, both North and South, volunteered as nurses in field hospitals to escape from grief or to give a sense of purpose to overwhelming despair.

As the war progressed, depression over the continual war losses altered the perception of death in the minds of those at home. "People do not mourn their dead as they used to," Kate Stone observed in April, 1864, "Everyone seems to live only in the present – just from day to day – otherwise I fancy many would go crazy."[38] Not only did families suffer grief and depression, but a general numbness set in. Diaries and letters describe the "hardening" that came upon survivors after hearing of war deaths; perhaps the deadness was a coping mechanism against the incomprehensible losses and pain. After Kate Foster heard of her brother's death, she noted that "My heart became flint. I am almost afriad [sic] to love too dearly anyone now."[39]

Former slaves burying Union dead after battle.

"No more shall the war-cry sever,
Or the winding rivers be red;
They banish our anger forever
When they laurel the graves of our dead!
Under the sod and the dew,
Waiting the Judgment Day:
Love and tears for the Blue,
Tears and love for the Gray."
—Francis Miles Finch, *The Blue and The Gray,* 1867

As with the deaths of children, Civil War era Americans struggled to accept with passivity and resignation the Christian doctrinal requirements of submission to God's will. Susan Caldwell complained bitterly of her inability to "gain power over my own rebellious heart," and Sarah Estes confessed in 1862 that "sometimes in my wickedness, I feel as if God had forsaken us." After being left widowed and homeless, another Southern wife, Cornelia McDonald, described "dreadful hours of unbelief and hopelessness." Responses ran the gamut from quiet Christian acceptance to outright rejection of God, and many struggled to reconcile the realities of their experiences with the plethora of Christian narratives encouraging sufferers that redemption and consolation was available to them in the midst of their trials.

Civil War-era punched paper embroidery, possibly memorializing more than one death. Its material content is quite unusual. Rather than using threads or wool to create the lettering, beadwork was employed for the words, "In Memory of the Departed," along with tiny white stars as embellishment. The rare aspect of this memorial is the use by the maker of mourning crape as a wreath material, occupying the central portion of the piece. Much superstition attended the retaining of crape in the household after the required period of mourning was over, so the use of this fabric as a material in the creation of the memorial is quite rare, even while it seems somehow fitting. 12" x 10". *Author's collection.* $450.

Men were not the only ones to suffer deaths during the War Between the States; women too lost their lives for a variety of reasons, often exacerbated by the hardships war imposed on already-stressed single-parent households. The tragedy of orphaned children of the Civil War was vividly brought home upon the discovery of an ambrotype of three children found clutched in the hands of a dead soldier on the battlefield of Gettysburg. Sgt. Humiston of the 154th New York Volunteers was killed in the terrible fighting of the 3-day battle of July 3-5, 1863. When the Union burial detail came upon the officer's body several days later, they found that he had been looking upon his children while in his last moments on earth. The pathos of this scene was so representative of the problem of children orphaned by Civil War soldiers' deaths, that the ambrotype of little Frank, Frederick, and Alice was reproduced in 1864 in *carte de visite* photographic format to raise money for the support of orphans.

Toward the end of the war, families on both sides began to lose the fervor of patriotic zeal for their cause. Women especially began to write tearful letters to their husbands, sons, brothers, and fathers, pleading for them to come home. An extraordinary example of the change of heart for the War is seen in the evolution of a Southern children's speller. In 1864, Marinda Branson Moore published the *Dixie Speller*, and in its series of readers, primers, and spellers, one lesson contained a political pacifism not seen in Moore's earlier patriotic Confederate school volumes.

"This sad war is a bad thing.
My pa-pa went, and died in the army.
My big brother went too and got shot.
A bomb shell took off his head.
My aunt had three sons, and all have died in the army. Now she and the girls have to work for bread.
I will work for my ma and my sisters.
I hope we will have peace by the time [I] am old enough to go to war.
If I were a man, and had to make laws, I would not have any war, if I could help it.
If little boys fight old folks whip them for it; but when men fight, they say, "how brave!"[40]

In spite of the tearing of the fabric of the Victorian home throughout the Civil War years, women continued to create memorials for loved ones whenever possible. In fact, the Victorian "Cult of Memory" reached its pinnacle of expression in the mid-1860s, primarily because the home remained the center of what has been called "the cult of true womanhood," the place where the realm of domesticity was separated from the outside, masculine world of men. As the social expectations of women and men were viewed as being in opposition, the absence of men in the household did not prevent women from continuing the roles already well established. It was assumed their "feminine nature" predisposed them to the domestic skills expected of them as cultural norms in the 19th century, and so middle class women participated in the Victorian "domestic theatre" of mourning ritual and the creation of memorial art.

Women were, for the most part, unwilling participants in the Civil War drama, and while patriotism initially influenced many women to encourage their men to fight for Northern and Southern causes, as the War progressed, suffering, hardship, and grief considerably lessened their zeal. For the fighting men, both North and South, however, their philosophy was entirely different: they knew that they were part of a "grand adventure," one which they would never forget, and which for many was the defining moment of their lives. As one soldier declared, "Ours is a generation touched by fire."[41]

FRANK, FREDERICK & ALICE.

Carte de visite of little Frank, Frederick, and Alice, the "Orphans of the Battlefield," children of Sgt. Humiston who was killed at the Battle of Gettysburg, July, 1863. *Author's collection.* $150.

That Little Company of Angels

Deaths of Children in the Nineteenth Century

I wonder, Oh! I wonder where,
The little faces go;
That come and smile and stay awhile,
Then pass like flakes of snow.
  —Epitaph on English child's grave in India during colonial period

Children's deaths were particularly agonizing for Victorians, just as they are today. Historians have estimated childhood deaths at between one-fifth and one-third of all children under the age of ten during the 18th and 19th centuries, with regional epidemics experiencing childhood death rates as high as fifty percent. Today, *every* effort is made to ensure successful childhood through safeguards at home, school, and in the community. For Victorians, however, the loss of a child was an *expected* experience, so much so that many parents did not name their children until they had reached their first year of life. Literature and sermons of the era cautioned parents against becoming too attached to their children because of the expectation of early childhood death. Letty Lewis, of South Carolina, attempted to control her maternal feelings towards her daughter, declaring, "I have often felt superstitious about indulging such an extent of feeling toward the little angel as I do."[42] And Dr. Samuel Brown (step-uncle of Mary Todd Lincoln) attempted to guard himself against just such a commitment of love towards his infant daughter, stating that he, "scarcely had the fortitude to indulge my parental affection for my poor dear little Nancy," who shortly thereafter died, along with her mother.

Even after a child's first-year milestone was reached, letters and memoirs were replete with parental reservations and fears that their children would not survive infancy, much less reach adulthood. In industrialized cities such as Manchester, England, the infant death rate for impoverished mothers was forty to fifty percent but even among the wealthy, disease took an enormous toll. As seen in the memorial card pictured, disease struck the Broadhurst family in February, 1865, carrying off the father Samuel, and his three young sons in the space of fifteen days.

The Broadhurst family was, unfortunately, not unique in losing so many children. Inscribed on an 1864 tombstone for a father named Joseph Barras of Brampton-on-Swale, Yorkshire, are all his deceased children, listed as follows:

Joseph May 23rd 1843, aged 8 years.
Eleonor July 20, 1843, aged 2 years.
William April 20, 1845, aged 12 years.
George Dec. 13, 1848, aged 12 years.
Eleonor July 11th, 1852, aged 5 years.
Ann Oct. 15, 1855, aged 1 year.
Timothy Jan. 1, 1859, aged 16 years.
Robert Feb. 15, 1867, aged 17 years.
Marmaduke Proctor Sept. 26, 1868, aged 16 years.

It was no wonder that Victorians viewed children as "temporary travelers in a world of sorrow."[43] Parents were comforted, however, by the plethora of consolation literature dealing with childhood death in this era. As the loss of children was so universal, this subject was addressed frequently from every pulpit, and in various forms of literature, whether secular or religious. Children taken as "jewels" for the "Crown of Christ," or "flowers" for God's "heavenly garden" were popular Christian concepts to assuage grief. In *Agnes and The Key Of Her Little Coffin*, the author and father of little Agnes described the "privilege in being selected by Christ to contribute an infant soul to his mediatorial crown." He compared it to the pleasure a "peasant" receives when a "nobleman or his lady stops at his gate and asks for a slip from some beautiful plant" in the peasant's garden. And in *The Empty Crib: A Memorial of Little Georgie*, by Rev. Theo. L. Cuyler, pub-

lished in 1868, the concept of God as a gardener plucking children for His heavenly garden is again set forth in an inscription on the dedicatory page, as:

"Who plucked that Flower? Cried the gardener, as he walked through the garden. His fellow-servant answered, "The Master!", and the gardener held his peace."

For many, these conventional explanations for childhood death cauterized the pain. Yet, diaries and memoirs show that parents did not always find these explanations adequate to assuage the gaping holes in their hearts. Grieving (then as now), was individualized: some moved easily from initial grief into Job-like resignation; others never reached acceptance. Yet, no consolation literature of the 19th century addressed the latter condition, as any departure from the accepted doctrines of Christian submission to God's will was viewed as rebellion. Victorians were encouraged to

be "satisfied with all He gives and contented with all He takes away," as advised by the 1858 consolation book, *Our Little Ones in Heaven*. Christian parents frequently walked a tightrope between the freedom to mourn openly and yet not grieve too excessively, as this could be interpreted as anger against God. The discouragement of excessive grief even came in the form of poetic admonitions from the dying child, or from the grave in the form of an epitaph directed to the parents. The following poem entitled "The Dying Child" from *Our Little Ones in Heaven* virtually chastises the mother for clutching her child too firmly to "this world":

"Why does thou clasp me as if I were going?
Why dost thou press thy cheek thus unto mine?
Thy cheek is hot, and still thy tears are flowing;
I will, dear mother, will be always thine!
Do not sigh thus, – it marreth my reposing;
And if thou weep, then I must weep with thee!
Oh, I am tired, – my weary eyes are closing;
Look, mother, look! The angel kisseth me!"

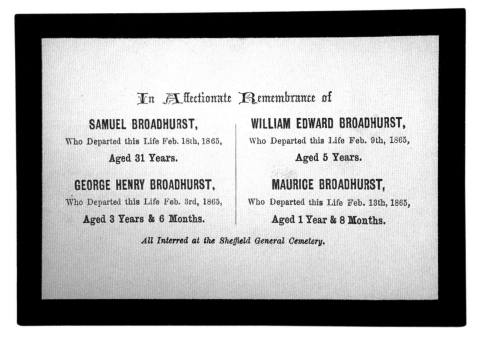

Extraordinary memorial card listing the deaths of a father and three of his children in the space of fifteen days in February, 1865, probably from a catastrophic disease such as typhoid or cholera. 4" x 5". *Author's Collection.* $50.

A beautiful Scottish sampler embroidered in wool on canvas by the mother of three children who had died is sewn in surprisingly colorful threads with charming lambs belying the stark message in the obituaries of the infants. No doubt the anguished mother poured out her grief in the stitches, as she recorded,

"Eliza Naylor Who Departed This Life February 6 1852 Aged 1 Year And Also William Naylor Who Departed This Life October 17 1857 Aged 5 Months And Also Martha Naylor Who Departed This Life June 7 1866 Aged 2 years."

An added poem below the obituaries speaks volumes:

"What Peaceful Hours I Once Enjoyed How Sweet Their Memory Still But They Have Left An Aching Void The World Can Never Fill They Sleep In Jesus And Are Blessed."

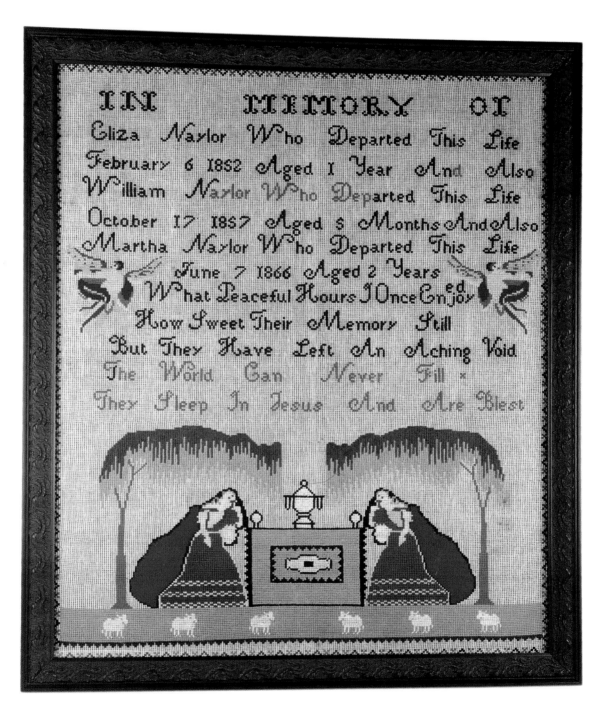

Beautiful large memorial sampler embroidered in wool on canvas, mourning the loss of three very young children who died between the years 1857 and 1866. The pain of the mother's grief is graphically lamented in her poem below the obituary information, and the touching row of lambs at the bottom adds to the poignancy of their deaths. 28" x 30". *Author's collection.* $500.

Consumption (or tuberculosis), was the most lethal disease in the mid-19th century, carrying off more young victims than all diseases combined, including cholera. The symptoms of "wasting away" combined with unnaturally sparkling eyes and frequent episodic mania caused the English writer Charles Dickens to describe consumption as "a disease in which death and life are so strangely blended that death takes the hue of life and life the gaunt and grisly form of death; a disease which medicine never cured, wealth never warded off, or poverty could cause exemption from." But other ubiquitous diseases of childhood, often taken for granted today as non-fatal, such as measles, chicken pox, etc., took the lives of thousands of children. Influenza was often fatal as well, as parents had no understanding of how this disease (or any other) spread or how to treat it. The prevailing medical recommendations advised parents to withhold fluids during fevers, which sometimes lead to the deaths of children from dehydration, rather than from the illness itself, as seen in the postmortem daguerreotype of a young child that is illustrated here. Dehydration was also a potentially fatal consequence of severe parasitical infestation and malaria brought about by the "mushetoes" that plagued Southern regions of the United States.

The medicines given to children were frequently so toxic that they precipitated death, but to parents watching beloved children tormented by raging fevers, or in delirium from pain and breathlessness, any treatment, no matter how potentially lethal, was preferable to the agonizing and helpless waiting at the bedside. Doctors generally administered medications or treatments directly when called to the home, or wealthy families went to local apothecaries to purchase the required "drugs." Apothecaries frequently displayed thick syrups in decanters of red, blue, and green with cut glass stoppers in their windows to entice passersby.[44] Consumers could also purchase pills of various colors, or black, brown, or white powders scraped from large cones and put into small twisted pieces of paper, all of which promised cures but rarely delivered. Most popular among treatments for adults and children alike was calomel, a universal panacea for everything from stomachache to gout. Used as a purgative to induce vomiting, it was so toxic it is a wonder that more children did not succumb to its poisonous chemical toxicity, as it was in fact, pure mercury sulphide. Frequently added to calomel was "oxymel of squills," a popular syrup concocted of vinegar, honey, and ground-up bulbs of the scilla plant. Another favorite remedy was "mellipidus," a preparation made of ground up wood lice. Some physicians tried spirits of turpentine, muriatic and nitro-muriatic acid, iron, quinine, sarsaparilla, prepared chalk, acetate of lead, and sulphate of morphia as remedies.

Children often endured bleeding, blistering, and cupping to induce diarrhea, sweats, and the "expression of poisons" to the surface of the skin. Cupping was a practice whereby glass "cups" were heated and placed on the skin of the back to form a suction, often actually creating blood loss through capillary breakage on the surface of the skin. Other methods of treatment included the forcible pumping of various mixtures into the mouths of young patients of such ingredients as coal gas, iodine, creosote, and carbolic acid. And, some physicians even lanced children's jugular veins to abort convulsions. One can only imagine the terrible suffering endured by children in prior centuries by these horrific medical procedures and medications, which of course, frequently hastened children's deaths.

Death also came suddenly, whether from catastrophic accident or disease, as so poignantly summed up by an American mother named Abigail Malick, when she stated,

"The minute I heard the news I burst in a flood of tears and grief. So the world goes: one minute in good health and the next in eternity."[45]

The diary of 19th century frontier mother, Agnes Reid, described her anguish at the loss of her twin daughters:

"We named them Finetta and Heneaga for my two best friends and they lie buried on the bench that rises north of the house. Their little coffins had to be made of what material we could find. During the life of the babies, I slept with both of them and with little Charlie, and Francis in a trundle bed by the side of me. Then when I could see the first one failing I was reconciled that she must go but I was sure we would raise the other, and even after she died, the children and I consoled each other that the cradle was not empty. But when the second one had to, all that I had borne during the months seemed to curse me. When I looked at her little dead face I wanted to scream and run away from it all."[46]

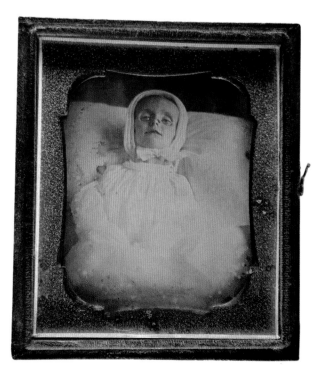

Sixth plate daguerreotype of dehydrated child, whose jaw and hands have been tied up preparatory to placement in the coffin. *Author's collection.* $450-500.

In keeping with the overwhelming desire to look upon the body of a loved one after death, the popularity of post-mortem photographs of children during the 19th century stands out as a unique form of *ars moriendi*, and great effort was expended to position the child to appear asleep and in the *"Beautiful Death"* pose so popular in this era. When one realizes that often these postmortem photographs were the only tangible and visible remembrances Victorian parents had of their children, their significance as a memorial keepsake cannot be underestimated. Fixation with the child's body consumed many Victorian parents, who often desired to hold, kiss, as well as look upon their dead children. Louisa Park, a 19th century mother grieving over her infant son, resisted the urge to visit the vault containing her little boy's body, believing that it would promote "excessive" or "hysterical" grief. She later regretted her decision, exclaiming,

"Oh what would I not have given to have kissed once more his cold cheek before it moulders to dust. What satisfaction it would be to me – how much pleasure I should take if I could, every day, enter his gloomy mansion and there indulge in meditation and give vent to the feelings of my heart."

Between 1850-60, John Callcort Horsley lost four sons and a daughter to scarlet fever, a major killer at the time of infants and young children. In a letter to his wife, he recorded his anguish at the loss but confidence in a future family reunion, and enclosed to her, "a little memorial of the day for you, a locket in which you can place dearest Hugh's hair." The keeping of precious locks of children's hair was ubiquitous in the 18th and 19th centuries, and poignant examples can be seen in the section on Mourning Jewelry.

Scarlet fever also took five of the seven children of Archibald and Catherine Tait, all in the space of three weeks in March and April, 1856. Both Archibald and Catherine kept daily records of their struggles to keep their five little girls alive, aged 1-1/2 to nine years. Catherine cut off and burned each little girl's long red hair in a vain attempt to stop the contagion, but ultimately, their "little company of angels left us one by one for their home in heaven."

Archibald recorded his attempts to muffle the sounds of the hammers used to make the little coffins, and to keep the church bells from tolling, so that the still living children would be unaware of the deaths of their siblings.

Their memoirs of the tragedy were later published as a form of consolation literature aimed at comforting other bereaved parents. One such father later wrote Archibald (who by then had become the Archbishop of Canterbury under Queen Victoria), of the comfort provided him by the Tait memoirs. He had lost all nine of his children along with his wife in the space of one year.

Diaries, letters, and memoirs of the 18th and 19th centuries abound with detailed accounts of children's illnesses, dying, and death; like all death accounts, they often resonate with the abiding internal struggle between the quotidian and the eternal. The prevailing views of the "domesticated heaven," in which death was believed to be simply a temporary separation, comforted many Victorian parents, as in the case of pioneer mother Sarah Hale, who noted the passing of another child as,

"Another little girl has been given and taken, and now there are seven here, and four awaiting us on the other side."[47]

Many times, Victorians consoled themselves that the deaths of their children were, in fact, a "blessing," as their deaths took them away from this world of "sin and woe." This was the assurance which brought comfort to W. H. DeCourcey Wright of Baltimore after the loss of his young son in 1845. He poured out his resignation in his diary:

"Yet a few years, and his devoted Father, Mother and Sisters will repose beside him in the Grave and their spirits, I trust in the Almighty ruling all things, be reunited with his and those of my other dear lost babies, in the place of happiness, where the tortures of this life will be all forgotten. It is true my dear boy was taken at a period of life, while yet unacquainted with any of its pains and disappointments, and everything was happiness before him; but a few years more would have removed the illusions of youth and exhibited to him the unworthiness of existence."

Although the prevailing Christian views of death, with its promises of bliss in the afterlife, consoled many parents on the loss of their children, not everyone serenely faced their losses with Christian acceptance. Some struggled with the same anger and loss of faith common to parents today. One such English mother, married to a minister, alternated between expressions of Christian hope and frenzied utterances of anguish and rage in her journal entries, as she grieved over the loss of her second child:

"Here I set with empty hands. I have had the little coffin in my arms, but my baby's face could not be seen, so rudely had death marred it. Empty hands, empty hands, a worn-out exhausted body, and unutterable longings to flee from a world that has had for me so many sharp experiences. God help me, my baby, my baby! God help me, my little lost Eddy!"[48]

In another tragic 19th century family, Caroline Mordecai Plunkett, of North Carolina, lost two children in the space of three days, and eight months later her husband died. Her third child, born three months after her husband's death, lived for only nine months. This last death proved to be more than Caroline could bear; she spent her last days in a mental institution.[49]

Published in an 1800s Baltimore newspaper, a mother's weeping poem spoke for parents everywhere in the 19th century, when simply viewing the lock of a child's hair could completely undo parental self-control.

*Hide them, O hide them all away—
His cap, his little frock,
And take from out my aching sight
Yon curling, golden lock;
Ah, once it waved upon his brow! –
Ye torture me anew –
Leave not so dear a token here –
Ye know not what ye do!*

Interestingly enough, however, the deaths of their adult children were far more devastating to Victorian parents than those of their infants and toddlers. Parents expected to lose their young children, and while it was painful to be parted from them, their deaths were not considered as severe an anguish due to

46

the short period of time in which they enjoyed the presence of their babies. Adult children, on the other hand, were part of their parents' lives for far longer periods of time, and thus the parents had a greater emotional investment in them. Parents felt relieved to have brought their children through the "terrors" of childhood illnesses, and to have raised them to adulthood. Their hopes and dreams were invested in them and the assurances of comfort in their old age. Thus, when bereft of their adult children, parents were often destitute emotionally as well as financially. In the c. 1840s book, *A Gift for Mourners*, the writer, a minister, noted regarding the death of an adult son that,

"had he died in infancy, before affection was riveted, or expectation raised, the affliction had been less pungent. But death seized him in his flower and prime – at the very age which rendered him capable of realizing to a fond mother the hopes of many years, and of rewarding her for a thousand cares and labors."

Victorian children themselves knew intimately of the fragility of life, as they routinely witnessed the deaths of grandparents, parents, and siblings in the home. Being present at deathbeds no doubt prepared them for their own deaths. In a 19th century account of the death of one young boy, his family testified that some weeks before he died, the child had "seen an angel" who had spoken to him, saying "When it is the Master's time I will come for you." Later on, while playing with friends, he ceased talking and looking towards an open window, exclaimed, "My angel has come," whereupon he sank on his pillow and died.

Children were also "prepared" for the imminence of death through Sunday School lessons such as *A Child's Memorial: Containing An Account of the Early Piety and Happy Death of Miss Dinah Doudney of Portsea*, in which a graphic account of little Dinah's death is combined with admonitions to Christian virtue and pious behavior on the part of the book's readers. This account also included the true story of "Miss Sarah Barrow," who was burned to death on April 4, 1805, further extolling the value of a Christian death to childish readers. Not every Victorian parent felt inclined

that such morbidly explicit reading material be shared with their children, however enough of this material has survived to indicate that instruction on approaching death was a major part of religious education for children.

Furthermore, it was not uncommon for children to carry the corpse of a friend or sibling to the grave, and awareness of their own mortality is shown in the following Victorian children's skipping games:

Grandmother, Grandmother,
Tell me the truth.
How many years am I
Going to live?
One, two, three, four…?

And,

Mother, Mother, I feel sick,
Send for the doctor, quick, quick, quick.
Doctor, doctor, shall I die?
Yes, my dear, and so shall I.
How many carriages shall I have?
One, two, three, four…

Some children's prayers and poems on death are familiar to us even today, such as the somewhat innocuous (but nevertheless moralistic) prayer of the 1781 *New England Primer*:

Now I lay me down to sleep;
I pray the Lord my soul to keep.
If I should die before I wake,
I pray the Lord my soul to take.

And what child has not grown up playing "Ring Around A-Rosy" never knowing that its words have their roots in the plagues of pox of the Middle Ages:

Ring around a-rosy,
A pocket full of posy,
Ashes, Ashes…
We all fall down.

The symptoms of rose-colored rings around the sores, followed by victims collapsing (or "falling down") in death, necessitated the holding of "posies" of flowers to the nose to mask the smell of the many corpses left decaying in the streets throughout the towns of Europe. And, in a vain effort to prevent contagion, the clothing and bedding of the dead would be burned in thousands of piles, which left the polluting "Ashes, Ashes" floating in the air overhead.

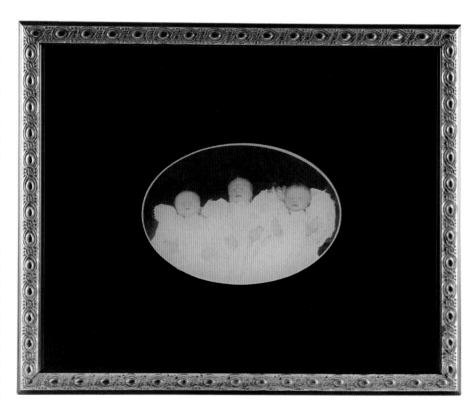

Postmortem cabinet card of triplets, "Julie, June, and Gene," who were born and died on the same day, March 23, 1901. 10" x 8". *Author's collection.* $250.

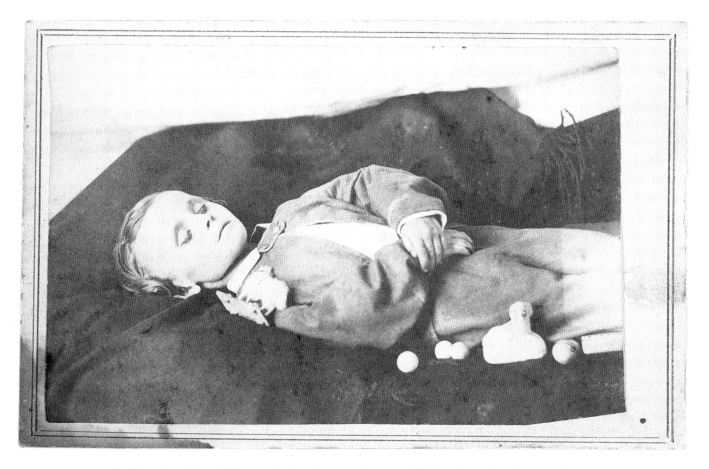

In this heartbreaking c. 1870s *carte de visite* of a young boy, some of his favorite toys have been placed around him, along with two symbolic figural items: a chalkware or porcelain reclining lamb, and a cotton lamb on wheels, a traditional German Christmas toy. The placement of two lambs in this scene can only be deliberate, and its symbolism representative of the Biblical reference to Christ carrying the lambs (or children) in His arms. *Collection of Ben Zigler.* $450.

An early American child's nursery rhyme book entitled *The Doleful Death of Cock Robin*, which included fourteen original woodcuts, is shown on the following pages. This handmade rag paper book was hand sewn and printed in 1809 in Hallowell, Maine, and is a rare example of how death was visually portrayed to very young children. *The Doleful Death of Cock Robin* nursery rhyme is believed to date from the 14th and 15th centuries in England, and its earliest known printing was in 1744. Although some of the more ghastly realities of death and burial are mitigated by the charming substitution of birds, insects, and animals as participants in the funeral of Robin, nevertheless, the story involves a murder in addition to a funeral.

The poem opens with its title question, "Who Killed Cock Robin?", after which the sparrow admits to the deed "with my bow and arrow." The second verse, which asks "Who saw him die?", is answered by the fly, who replies, "I saw him die with my little eye." In the third stanza, "Who catch'd his blood?", the Fish steps forward and answers, "I, said the Fish, with my little dish," and such are the macabre details of the nefarious act. The scene then shifts to a typical Victorian funeral, with birds, insects, and animals assuming the various roles: a fat wood beetle makes Robin's shroud with his thread and needle; an owl digs Robin's grave; a bird carries him to the gravesite; a rook assumes the role of parson; a linnet holds the light for the

nighttime burial; a lark acts as clerk to record the event; doves act as mourners; two birds hold the pall over the coffin of Cock Robin; and so on. At the end of the story, the tolling of the bell announcing Robin's death is rung by a bull in the church tower, at which point,

> *"All the birds in the air*
> *Fell to sighing and sobbing,*
> *When they heard the bell toll*
> *For poor Cock Robin."*

Learning very early that "tomorrow" was not promised, 19th century children had an understanding of death processes beyond their years. An 1858 poem, excerpted in the popular 19th century consolation book, *Little Ones in*

Heaven, was written by a female poetess, but expressed in the voice of a child.
In it, a daughter asks her mother:

> *"Mother, how still the baby lies!*
> *I cannot hear his breath;*
> *I cannot see his laughing eyes –*
> *They tell me this is death.*
>
> *My little work I thought to bring*
> *And sat down by his bed,*
> *And pleasantly I tried to sing –*
> *They hushed me – he is dead."*

The mother then explains to her
daughter about the butterfly forming
from the dead chrysalis, and that God
would do the same for her brother. At
this explanation, the daughter then joyfully anticipates the transfiguration of her
brother from "this broken cell" to live
with "heavenly things."

A late 19th century young children's
reader, *The Birds' Xmas Carol*, tells the
story of the "Bird" family and their adop-
tion on Christmas Eve of a little girl they
named "Carol." Carol lives with the
Birds for ten years, but on Christmas Eve
of her eleventh year, the heart of the
"little snow bird" quietly ceases to beat,
and she flies to her "home nest." At the
end of the book, the Birds remember
Carol in "every chime of Christmas bells
that peal glad tidings and in every Christmas anthem sung by childish voices."

Such macabre and sobering themes
for children's literature and religious instruction would be unthinkable today.
Yet, *The Death of Cock Robin* as well as
other stories and poetry on dying and
death aimed at children are a window
into the teaching of religious education
in English and American households in
the 17th through the 19th centuries.

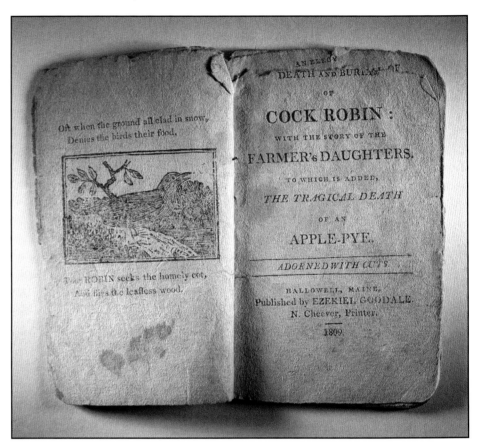

Various woodcuts from a rare 1809 handsewn rag paper book from Hallowell, Maine, of *The Doleful Death of Cock Robin*. Each of the woodcuts depicts an animal participant in the funeral of Robin after his murder by the sparrow. The tale is quite macabre by contemporary standards of children's stories. *Author's collection.* 3" x 4". $125.

(6)
Who saw him die?
I, said the Fly,
With my little eye,
And I saw him die.

This is the Fly,
With his little eye.

(7)
Who catch'd his blood?
I, said the Fish,
With my little dish,
And I catch'd his blood.

This is the Fish
That held the dish.

A 4

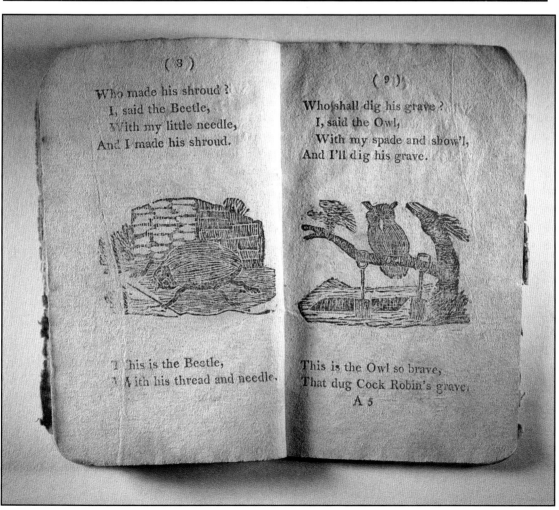

(8)
Who made his shroud?
I, said the Beetle,
With my little needle,
And I made his shroud.

This is the Beetle,
With his thread and needle.

(9)
Who shall dig his grave?
I, said the Owl,
With my spade and show'l,
And I'll dig his grave.

This is the Owl so brave,
That dug Cock Robin's grave.

A 5

Summary

In conclusion, death iconography was visible and universal for centuries in Western culture. In medieval *ars moriendi,* it was most often given human-like features: a body, frequently skeletal or cadaverous, and a countenance. Perhaps anthropomorphizing death made it somewhat *identifiable*, and while still terrifying, it could be perceived as *definable* (and, it was vainly hoped, therefore controllable), simply for no other reason than because it *was* so visibly familiar. Conversely and somewhat surprisingly, death was also imbued in both art and literature with the qualities of omniscience, omnipotence, and omnipresence, characteristics *only* attributable to God. In both contexts, it was given *animation,* an anomalous quality of intrinsic "aliveness" as though death itself had the ability to spiritually create and hold its own life. This seeming contradiction does not appear to have occurred to medieval artists and clergy, or if it did, fear of diversion into heresy kept most conforming to the accepted doctrines of *memento mori* in death iconography without too much philosophical examination. The emphasis was on instructing the living to remember their own imminent death, however that death was artistically portrayed in art and ritual.

In the post-Enlightenment years, the "King of Terrors" of the Middle Ages was diluted and softened into the "Angel of Death," and became less visible, less terrifying, and no longer imbued with God-like attributes. When death became invisible, it melded into the beauty of the 18th century Aesthetic Movement, and *memento mori* became the romanticized deathbed scene of the Victorian era. Lord Byron, the archetypal Romantic poet, described death as "an everlasting mist," its opacity obscuring understanding, but not its visibility – a metaphor that perhaps best explains our current perspectives about death on those rare occasions when we think about it in philosophically or poetically visual terms. It is possible that in venturing to *share* existence with death, those living in prior centuries attempted to *contain* its power and omnipresence through dress, ritual, and art. If it could be drawn or painted, contained within the camera lens, framed on the wall, or held in the palm of the hand, it could be *encapsulated*. Perhaps then, the mist would clear *ever* so slightly.

Today, death has no objectified symbolism universally recognized, and death as a subject matter is almost totally absent from most public and religious contexts and conversations outside of the funeral service, which is – even in that environment – sanitized. Where death was once *everywhere* the "King of Terrors" to whom all bowed down and paid homage, today we simply ignore him as thoroughly as yesterday's news.

Yet as we have seen, there was a time when death iconography saturated European and American life as part of religious orthodoxy and as visual comfort to the grieving. In Section II, we will look at the various forms of 18th and 19th century memorial art and the visible expressions of grief during the two centuries when *ars moriendi* reached its zenith in romantic beauty and popularity.

Section II

Memorial Art and Artifacts

Mourning Clothing and Ritual

Mourning clothing does not appear in European and British historical references before the 14th century. In England during the Middle Ages, only the nobility was entitled to the elaborate visual rites surrounding their funerals. The first appearance of the color black in relation to death was its introduction by St. Benedict in the 6th century, wherein he admonished his monks to wear black to symbolize "the spiritual darkness of the soul unillumined [sic] by the sun of righteousness."[1] Superstition also held that wearing black would trick the devil who, it was believed, could not see the color. By the 11th century, black capes with cowls were commonly worn for outdoor funeral processions, and by the 14th century, black was entrenched as a mourning color for grief, although reds, browns, and grays were still occasionally employed.

In the 15th century, during one of his many bloody campaigns to conquer France, Henry V of England became ill, probably from dysentery, finally succumbing to the disease on September 1, 1422. Little remained of his emaciated body, but his corpse was nevertheless embalmed with aromatic herbs, wrapped in waxed linen, lead and silken cloth, and transported in a coffin, borne on a black-draped bier. Mourners accompanied the bier as it was led on a long funeral procession through France and across the sea back to England.[2] At the funeral of the Earl of Northumberland in 1489, over 2,200 yards of black fabric equipped the

mourners, and those attending the 1547 funeral of Henry II of France were clothed in mourning habits, the lists of which ran to fifty pages.[3]

Mourning ritual and artistic representations of death were governed by the College of Heralds, who in essence, legislated the length and style of mourning clothing worn by mourners and the elaborately embroidered funeral palls draping the coffins of the aristocracy. Heralds regulated the symbolic designs of the coats of arms, armorial displays, and heraldry symbolic of fraternal orders and craftsmen's guilds. By the 17th century, the heralds were slowly being replaced by tradesmen undertakers, who were involved in making and supplying funeral trappings. A 17th century undertaker, Richard Chandler, describing himself as an "Armes-Painter," advertised to furnish "funeralls with 'Coffin burying suit, pall hangings, Silver'd Sconces and Candlesticks, Cloakes, Hatbands, Scarves, Favors, Funerall Escocheons, Coaches, Herse Wax Lights flambeaux links, Torches, Tickets etc and performed after ye same manner as by ye Undertakers at London at Reasonable Rates [sic].'" The transition of tradesmen undertakers replacing the College of Heralds in funeral rites and ritual occurred coincident with the newly emerging merchant class in the 17th and 18th centuries. Soon, the English middle class could fulfill their desire for all the trappings of funeral display formerly only within the provenance of the aristocracy. During the 18th century, white became the color of

mourning, albeit temporarily in western culture, as it was again replaced by black in the 19th century.

By the Victorian era, in both England and America, mourning expression was highly ritualized and codified, so much so that this era has been described by historians as the period of the "Cult of Memory." Women were viewed as "true vessels of grief," and entire books were written on the subject of appropriate clothing and jewelry to be worn for the various stages of mourning.

Most of us are familiar with Scarlett O'Hara dancing in her "widow's weeds" in Margaret Mitchell's classic book, *Gone With The Wind*, but few people realize the extent and detail of the complicated etiquette of mourning dress and behavior. Widows were required to mourn for a husband from 2-1/2 to 3 years, with "first stage" or "deep" mourning evidenced by the wearing of "unrelieved" black clothing, yards of attached crape, and head veil. The mourning dress was made from a variety of so-called "mourning fabrics," such as bombazine, a dull, matte black fabric of silk and wool, created to give the impression of somber woe. Mourning clothing was described by the 19th century phrase, "*a chrysalis of gloom*," so heavy was the portrayal of grief through the multiple layers composed of yards of lusterless fabric enveloping the widow. According to some advice manuals, the only permissible mourning jewelry for "first stage" or "deep" mourning was made of jet, French jet, gutta percha, or onyx. If her social position permitted, a woman in mourning was to stay at home, and not receive visitors, nor pay calls upon friends or acquaintances for the first six months (one year in the case of widows). If, on the other hand, her economic situation required that she go out in public, then she was to wear the mourning veil properly draped over her head and face. The following photographs show women in the first stage of "deep" mourning attire.

Carte de visite of Civil War widow in long veil. Period inscription on the reverse says "Your friend in distress, Sue." *Author's collection.* $75.

Tintype of woman in first-stage mourning attire showing slightly more elaborate trims in hat than seen in Civil War era, c. 1870s. *Author's collection.* $50.

Circa 1860s *carte de visite* of woman in first-stage mourning dress with bands of crape at her hem and sleeves. *Author's collection.* $25.

Crape, the fabric of mourning, was a material of crimped silk, infamous for its dull finish and unstable black dye. Yards of it were fastened about the mourning dress, with wealthier widows able to express their deepest sorrow by the more extensive use of the highest quality crape. Originally produced in the late 17th century by Huguenot weavers, crape was an English staple fabric for mourning among the aristocracy and those at Court. However, such significant quantities were produced by the 19th century after the Industrial Revolution, that the middle class was soon able to afford mourning crape for clothing, along with all the other funereal trappings which had been customarily available only among the wealthy. By the mid-1800s, so much crape was sold in England after the Queen went into mourning, that Courtauld's, originally a small English manufacturer of silk goods, made a fortune in crape, monopolizing the English market and exporting to Europe and America.

Once the first year of mourning was completed, a widow could change her costume into "second stage" attire. Here the wearer was still dressed in "unrelieved" black, but the yards of crape could be removed and substituted with simple trims of crape at cuffs, necklines, and hems. Also, the veil could be removed from around the face and less restrictive mourning jewelry added. Additionally (and especially in the case of mothers mourning the deaths of children), a white collar was acceptable trim on an otherwise unembellished black mourning dress. Queen Victoria was unique in wearing a white "Marie Stuart" bonnet and veil (fashioned after the one worn by Mary Stuart, Queen of Scots, to her execution in 1567).

For "light" or "half" mourning, during the last six months of the second year and into the third year, a woman could exchange her "widow's weeds" for clothing of less somber tones, indicative of her less restrictive social position. Fabrics of gray, mauve and purple, variously referred to as violet, pansy, heliotrope, and scabious, were popular for "light" mourning clothing, and the trims of crape were gone entirely. At this time, the widow could resume her social activities, but not too quickly, nor behave "inappropriately" gleeful among friends, lest her neighbors and friends view her

grief as superficial or insincere. A mourning widow was even encouraged *not* to return to social gatherings the day immediately following the three-year anniversary, as that would also appear overly "anxious" or "anticipatory," but to wait a few days longer.

So pervasively visible were Victorian women in mourning dress, that iconoclastic 19th century English and American novelists poked considerable humor at the customs. English writer Anthony Trollope described one widow as being,

"almost gorgeous in her weeds. I believe she had not sinned in her dress against any of those canons which the semi-ecclesiastical authorities on widowhood have laid down for outward garments fitted for gentlemen's relicts. The materials were those which are devoted to the deepest conjugal grief [sic]."[4]

And, in *Dombey and Son*, Charles Dickens described the mourning gown worn by the widow Mrs. Pipchin as,

"black bombazeen, of such a lustreless, deep, dead, sombre shade, that gas itself couldn't light her up after dark, and her presence was a quencher to any number of candles."

Mark Twain, like his English counterparts, Charles Dickens and Anthony Trollope, also parodied the extremes of elaborate ritual and mourning art in both *Tom Sawyer* and *Huckleberry Finn*. Twain describes fifteen-year-old "Miss Grangerford" spending all her days writing elegiac poetry and creating memorial art in *Huckleberry Finn*. A mourning scene painted by Miss Grangerford is of a "woman leaning pensive on a tombstone on her right elbow, under a weeping willow, and her other hand holding a white handkerchief." Inscribed beneath the mourning scene are the words, "Shall I never see thee more Alas," a typical inscription actually seen in memorial art of both the 18th and 19th centuries. This scene was a popular genre one, in the form of paintings, embroideries, sketches, etc., created by women all over England and America, and universally hung in family parlors. Twain goes on to describe Miss Grangerford's death in a rather humorously mocking manner:

"Everybody was sorry she died, because she had laid out a lot more of these pictures to do, and a body could see by what she had done what they had lost. But I reckoned that with her disposition, she was having a better time in the graveyard."

These novelists would have enjoyed considerable mirth had they lived a century earlier when fashions for aristocratic French ladies at the court of Louis XVI dictated powdered coiffures as high as three feet (known as *poufs*), beribboned and bedecked with tiny funeral urns for widows! In spite of these humorous attacks on mourning dress and customs, however, Victorians took them quite seriously, and for some women, especially those of low income, the obsession with adherence to appropriate etiquette sometimes necessitated spending the equivalent of a year's income for one mourning outfit. The 1890 *Gentlewomen's Book of Dress*, described the lengths to which mourning dress requirements were to be met,

"If she lifts her skirts from the mud, she must show by her frilled black silk petticoat and plain black stockings her grief has penetrated to her innermost sanctuaries."

The mourning widow was so restricted in her dress and social activities, that her widowhood was viewed as almost akin to a form of *suttee*, that Indian practice of wives throwing themselves on their husband's funeral pyres! Nevertheless, 19th century mourning etiquette writer, Mrs. John Sherwood, in her book *Manners and Social Usages*, written in 1884, provided the alternative, and most common, perspective on the wearing of mourning clothing. She stated that wearing black was a mark of respect for the deceased, and furthermore, "A mourning dress does protect a woman while in deepest grief against the untimely gayety of a passing stranger. It is a wall, a cell of refuge." The truth of this statement is evident to anyone today who has borne a devastating personal loss and been forced to prematurely face public view while stifling grief.

Relationships other than widowhood had their own requirements for mourning, which generally followed the following codes:

For mourning the death of a parent – one year.

For mourning the death of a child – one year.

For mourning the death of a sibling – six months to one year.

For mourning other relatives, including those of their spouse – six months.

Mourning requirements were so rigid that some authorities advised a woman to wear half-mourning for three months following the death of her husband's first wife's parents! And deaths other than those in the family necessitated proper mourning observances as well. In England, when an important national figure died, a General Mourning Order was declared requiring the public to observe the principles of mourning dress just as was being done by those at Court. These strictures even applied to foreign dignitaries, as in the case of the death of Czar Nicholas I in 1855, when Queen Victoria ordered that General Mourning be observed in his memory – an irony not lost on the English military considering the Czar's death occurred during the Crimean War in which the nation was fighting against Russia at the time.

Men had their own mourning clothing and jewelry, depending upon their wealth and status. However, the prerequisites for mourning were considerably less restrictive for men, who were only required to mourn a wife's passing for a period of six months. For most, the mourning clothing was usually the man's "best black suit." Some wealthy widowers, however, wore black silk or beaver top hats fitted with "weepers," which were long crape fabric "streamers" intended to dab male tears at funerals. Men's mourning jewelry was usually in the form of stick pins, studs, cufflinks, or watch chains and fobs of black jet, French jet, gutta percha, or vulcanite. Some hair-work watch chains incorporated cords of woven or plaited hair of a deceased wife or child, often with attached fobs containing hair or shaped in memorial symbolism such as urns, etc. Other mourning accoutrements were scarves, black-bordered handkerchiefs, chest banners in black or white crape, and canes, sometimes containing hairwork of the deceased in the handle. As an aside, handkerchiefs date back to the

reign of King Richard II of England (reigned 1377-99), who is credited with being the first to invent their use. Known to have been fastidiously clean in an age when cleanliness was not a priority even amongst royalty, it was observed by his contemporaries at Court that he had made "little pieces [of cloth] for the lord King to wipe and clean his nose."[5] During periods of mourning in these early centuries, these *hand-kerchiefs* were made of black cloth.

Man's late 19th century mourning coat with dull cloth-covered buttons and braid trim. Tailored by Heath Bros., Utica, NY. *Collection of Patricia Comstock Wilczak.* $250.

Man's late 19th century mourning beaver top hat with mourning band. The width of the band denoted the relationship of the wearer to the deceased; the wider the band, the closer the affiliation. *Collection of Patricia Comstock Wilczak.* $200.

Various examples of 19th century mourning handkerchiefs, the earliest example being the white lawn with black border. Here again, the border width would vary according to the relationship to the deceased and the period of mourning. *Collection of Jerry Lesandro and Larry Martin.* $25-50 each.

Even Victorian children observed the etiquette of mourning by wearing black clothing with crape when in mourning for a parent or sibling, and infants were often dressed in white clothing trimmed with black ribbon, or soutache braid. The c. 1860s era infant boy's mourning dress trimmed with black soutache braid is an excellent example of clothing worn by a child of a mid-19th century middle class family, and a similar mourning dress being worn by a little boy is seen in the accompanying 1860s photograph. Late 19th century mourning clothing for children, however, tended to be black and of the same fabrics as worn by their parents, often trimmed with crape. Note the c. 1890s black toddler's silk mourning dress with bonnet (seen here), c. 1860s child's black straw bonnet with silk trim and ties, and c. 1870s infant's bonnet with crape trim (seen on the next page). A young daughter's silk mourning parasol, which would complete her outfit just like her mother's, and a rare mourning skirt lifter, a miniature of what her mother would have used for ease in entering and exiting coaches, are also seen in the accompanying photographs on the next page. Such items would have been used by a child of wealthy or upper-class parents.

Among wealthy and aristocratic families, the nursery would also be in mourning, even including the children's crib sheets, which were occasionally embroidered with black thread to commemorate a death. Such was the case in 1860, when Queen Victoria reproved her daughter, Vicky, the Crown Princess of Prussia, for not putting her five-month-old baby in mourning upon the death of her husband's grandmother. "I think it quite wrong that the nursery are not in mourning," chastised the Queen to her daughter. Queen Victoria put her own youngest child, daughter Beatrice, aged three, in mourning for the husband of her half-sister, proclaiming in a letter, "Darling Beatrice looks lovely in her black silk and crape dress."[6]

Young child's black silk mourning dress, late 19th century, with black silk bonnet. *Author's collection.* $150.

Carte de visite of child in mourning dress with black soutache braid, c. 1860s. *Author's collection.* $40.

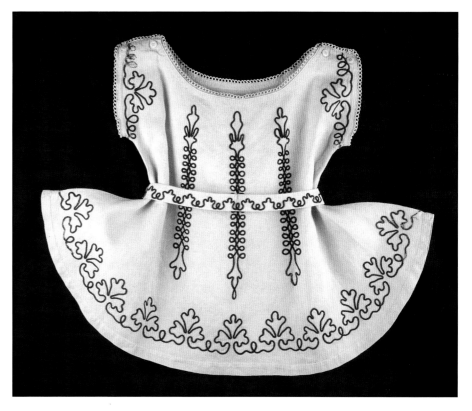

Toddler child's c. 1850-60s mourning dress, white cotton with black soutache braid. This style of dress with black soutache braid was typical for very young children and infants in the mid-19th century. *Author's collection.* $125.

Rare child's black straw mourning bonnet with silk ties, c. 1860s. *Collection of Patricia Comstock Wilczak.* $100-125.

Rare c. 1870s infant's silk and crape mourning bonnet. Even babies were dressed in mourning attire with crape in the second half of the 19th century, but items with crape are difficult to find in this condition. *Author's collection.* $175.

Child's straw mourning bonnet, with the unusual addition of hand-woven black horsehair as trim around the brim. Horsehair was customary as a stiffening material for structural design and strength in bonnets of the 19th century, but in this rare child's mourning hat, the horsehair was used as a decorative embellishment. *Author's collection.* $250.

Close-up of bonnet at right, showing finely woven horsehair lace, which is in two layers overlapping one another, each approximately 2" in width.

Rare mid 19th century child's mourning umbrella, identical to what her mother would have used for visiting. *Collection of Patricia Comstock Wilczak.* $75-100.

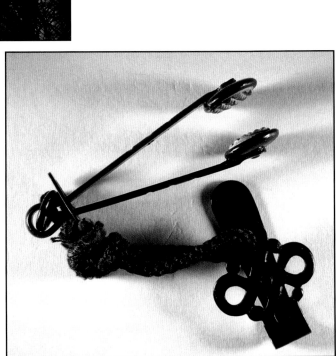

Little girl's c. 1860s mourning skirt lifter, a smaller version to one her mother would use for ease in entering and exiting coaches and lifting skirts from the mud. *Author's collection.* $100-125.

Children in mourning for a sibling or parent are sometimes seen in period photographs, especially in the *carte de visite* format typical of the Civil War era. Shown here are two such children in mourning; one little girl is in mourning dress standing by a table on which her father's Civil War uniform and hat is placed, indicating his passing. She has her hand placed on the table near the uniform, and is wearing his pocket watch around her neck. The *carte de visite* of the older girl shows her also dressed in mourning (note her black fingerless mitts), and standing next to an "empty" chair, a popular prop for photographers to indicate a vacancy in the family.

The often oppressive requirements for mourning, especially when applied to children, were frequently the subject of criticism. Fannie Fern, the 19th century newspaper columnist, vehemently objected to children being "swathed in sackcloth," adding, "Is it Christian or even humane, so to surround them with gloom that 'death shall be a never-ceasing nightmare?'" Ms. Fern advised parents to do "away with this bugaboo nightmare [of] heathenish insignia," reminding them that children will soon enough enter the "portal through which they are certainly destined to pass" without "prematurely draping [them] with the blackness of darkness."

Carte de visite of little girl in mourning dress standing next to a table spread with her father's Civil War uniform and hat. She is also wearing his pocket watch around her neck. *Author's collection.* $75.

Carte de visite of young girl in mourning dress with black fingerless gloves, c. 1860s. *Author's collection.* $40.

As an aside, in the case of infants who died, they were most often laid out and buried in their christening dresses, and older children were customarily buried in their best outfits. The same is true of young, unmarried women, and if no such apparel was available, burial attire made to appear similar to christening dresses could be purchased at most mourning warehouses with which to dress the female child or teenager for viewing and subsequent burial. Teenage boys were buried in their best suit of clothes. The following photograph shows a silk burial dress open in the back for ease in dressing the child, along with a pair of youth-sized silk burial slippers.

Before the emergence of English warehouses of mourning goods, eight days were allowed to the family to have clothing and accessories made and worn. This period of time not only permitted the family the time necessary to obtain a seamstress or purchase the requisite goods, but also put in place a reverse *taboo*, that of a cautionary prohibition against observing mourning too quickly following the death of a family member and thereby implying a vulgar anticipation of the event!

Circa 1900s child's silk burial dress, made to appear like a christening dress, but open in back for ease in dressing inside the casket. *Author's collection.* $100.

Back of child's silk burial dress showing open lacing.

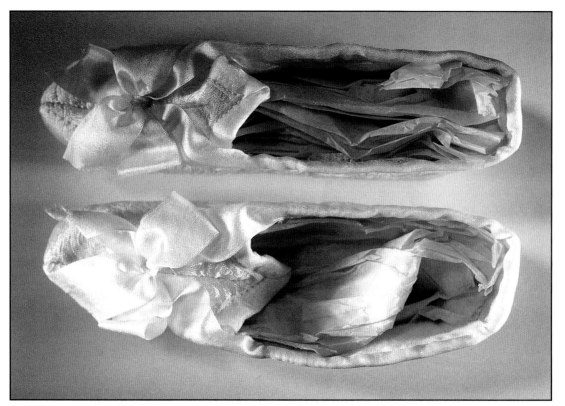

Early 20th century child's silk burial slippers in original box (not shown). Finding burial garments and slippers, especially in original boxes can be difficult, and collectors of funeralia place a high value on such items. *Collection of Jerry Lesandro and Larry Martin.* $125.

The commerce in supplying family members with appropriate clothing, fabrics, and accessories was enormously profitable to European and British establishments specializing in this market. In Paris, the *Grand Maison de Noir* was the grandest of the French mourning emporiums, and English warehouses capitalized on the desire to emulate French customs by calling their establishments *Maisons de Deuil*. These warehouses provided all the accoutrements necessary for a socially proper funeral and necessary clothing. Courtauld's and Jay's of London are the most well-known of these mourning warehouses, but dry goods merchants in America also sought to emulate English and French businesses by importing their mourning wares from these suppliers. In fact, Courtauld's had sales representatives working in America and other European countries to meet the demands for mourning merchandise. The family mourning store of S. S. Williams in Boston, Massachusetts, announced that their "stock embraces all the different grades of the best English and French manufacturers" of mourning wear. Rushton's of London, advertised themselves as manufacturers of hair jewelry, naming royal and aristocratic patrons. And, Priestly's, another mourning supplier, advertised that their patron, the widowed Empress Victoria of Germany, daughter of the Queen, bought her gowns, Marie Stuart caps, and veils of crape from them, in an effort to appeal to American purchasers.[7]

Today, finding good quality examples of mourning clothing, especially those trimmed with crape, can be difficult. Crape was expensive for the average family, and quite perishable, quickly turning brown from sunlight and stains. Most Victorian women threw out their crape after the required period of mourning was over, as prevailing superstition held that the keeping of crape in the home was tantamount to inviting death to touch another family member. Wealthier women could purchase new mourning attire for each death and generally threw out "last year's" mourning dress, while those less financially well off made accommodation to economy by simply purchasing new crape to trim an older outfit.

For collectors, there is a great deal of confusion over what constitutes a true piece of mourning clothing from what was simply a lady's black dress. The wearing of black clothing was commonplace for older women in the 19th century who were not necessarily in mourning for a loved one. This was especially true in Europe, as older widows routinely wore black clothing the rest of their lives, as is still done today in some countries.

Furthermore, for Americans, acquiring the requisite mourning fabrics such as bombazine and crape was sometimes impossible for those women living in frontier areas, as America was still primarily an agrarian country for much of the early 19th century. Added to this obstacle was the fact that many Victorian women were unable to afford expensive crape or bombazine, and thus, poorer women, like their rural counterparts, "made do" with homemade mourning clothing made out of whatever black fabric was at hand. The problem becomes even more apparent when one compares advertisements in ladies periodicals such as *Godey's Lady's Book* which shows examples of *ideal* mourning dress, as advocated by warehouses such as Courtauld's and Jay's, with actual clothing worn by average women in mourning as seen in 19th century photographs. In lieu of the preferable fabrics of bombazine, Henrietta cloth, crepe anglais, and parametta, fabrics such as silk, muslin, polished cotton, and other lower grades of black cloth generally considered unsuitable are clearly shown in the mourning attire worn by women seated for the photographer.

In addition, mourning etiquette books also held to strict standards in mourning jewelry, some advising women that jet was the *only* permissible gemstone for "deep" mourning, others declaring that even jet was not allowed in the first year. Yet, here again, period photographs of Victorian women show them wearing later period mourning jewelry while in obvious "first stage" mourning attire.

Therefore, in spite of the rigidity of mourning etiquette, women (and men) frequently made accommodations to necessity, station in life, and personal desire. Without the addition of crape, which distinguishes a true mourning dress from a regular black garment, determining authentic mourning clothing can be problematic. However, there are some clues which may help the collector in his or her investigation. Mourning dresses of the 1850-70 period are distinguished by their "plain-ness," with no trims and fastened with either hooks and eyes or unembellished, non-shiny buttons. Fabrics tended to be dull, although some mourning clothing was made of silk, alpaca, or Henrietta cloth, which may have a slight sheen. The dress, however, would have had crape added to it during "deep" mourning. A woman could purchase any number of yards of crape and, through the use of mourning pins, fasten the crape embellishment around the bodice and skirt for "first stage" mourning, reducing it in the second year, and removing it altogether in the third.

On the next page we see three examples of 19th century mourning clothing: the first, a late 1850s silk mourning dress worn by a teenaged girl or young woman. It has several period repairs of the same fabric, indicating that the original wearer was probably not wealthy enough to acquire more than one mourning dress. By altering the dress from first-stage or "deep" mourning by substituting the original crape for the velvet bands at the hem and buttons the young woman was able to "make do" with one dress over a number of years. The second example is a c. 1890s first or second-stage mourning dress with bustle. This dress of Henrietta cloth is still quite plain in a decade when trims, ruching, and laces were elaborate, even for mourning attire. Shown in the third example is a simple cotton mourning maternity "at home" dress, c. 1890s, which fastens under the bustline with an adjustable fabric tie.

60

Circa 1890s mourning dress of Henrietta cloth, probably for "first stage" mourning. *Modeled by Cassandra Cramer. Author's collection.* $300.

Side view of 1890s mourning dress showing bustle. *Modeled by Cassandra Cramer.*

Circa 1850s young woman's silk mourning dress with velvet bands and buttons. This dress was probably originally trimmed with crape, then after the first year was over, the crape was removed and the velvet trim and buttons added to "make do." *Author's collection.* $250-300.

Rare mourning "at home" maternity dress, c. 1890s. *Modeled by Cassandra Cramer. Dress courtesy of Ferndale Museum, Ferndale, California.* $250.

By the late Victorian period, mourning clothing in advertisements from *Godey's* show considerably more decorative trim with less crape embellishment, and a consciousness of fashion styles even for "first stage" mourning. Thus, determining true mourning clothing of the late 19th century is difficult for this reason, unless crape trim is evident. Shown here is a c. 1890 advertisement from Peter Robinson's Mourning Warehouse, of London, England. Typical of mourning warehouses of the Victorian era, Robinson's offered to provide everything the mourner needed to properly adhere to etiquette requirements, "no matter the distance."

Robinson's also offered to provide "inexpensive mourning as well as the richest qualities" of goods, adding that *"plushes, silks, velvets"* for *"evening and dinner dresses"* of *"superior and superb variety"* [emphasis added] were available to mourners of every class and economic status. Yet the August 1891 issue of *Ladies Home Journal* advised women that,

*"Widow's [sic], which is the deepest of all mourning, consists of a plain gown of Henrietta cloth or bombazine, with crape upon it or not….A tiny Marie Stuart cap, made of footing and net, is pinned on the head….the real widow's veil should reach to the edge of the skirt, back and front. This is worn so that the whole figure is shrouded for three months; after that it is thrown back, and at the end of another three months, a single veil, reaching to the waist, is worn. This may be worn for six months, and then be laid aside. My dear woman, feathers are not mourning…Lace is not mourning, and except the ribbon to tie your bonnet, ribbon as a decoration is certainly not permissible when mourn-*ing *is worn. All these things are allowable with black, which is assumed for from one to three months, but their use when one is wearing crape is in extremely bad taste."*

In the example shown in the advertisement, we see a late Victorian "deep" mourning dress with hat and veil, composed of a great deal of crape, yet stylishly designed and embellished with ribbon-work in spite of the admonitions mentioned above. Robinson's Mourning Warehouse even advertised in bold type that it provided "Fashions for the Season"! This statement would have been unthinkable a few decades earlier, and represented a new compromise in mourning dress to the dictates of fashion typical in the late-Victorian period, when cultural attitudes surrounding dying and death were undergoing change and increasing aversion.

"Fashions for the Season," Robinson's Mourning Warehouse advertisement, late 1890s, showing the evolution of mourning dress into less austere, more elaborate costuming towards the end of the century.

In the following examples, we will look at other items which made up a mourning outfit for the average middle and upper middle class woman. A Civil War era mourning reticule, entirely hand-crocheted, with hand-faceted jet beading, is shown next. It is beautifully made, with the beading graduated as the bag increases in size.

Another outstanding c. 1850s mourning purse is constructed of finely crocheted beadwork, probably made in memory of a deceased husband. A great deal of memorial symbolism is contained in the mourning scene: two burning hearts, symbolic of marital love sit atop a tombstone monument; an arrow, symbolic of mortality, pierces them, while a dog, symbolic of loyalty, looks on. Overhead, a bird, symbolizing the human soul, places a wreath over the monument. On each side of the tombstone, are funeral trees: cypress trees, symbolic of immortality and heaven because of their upward, vertical growth habit, and cedar, which reminds the owner to "Think of Me."

Memorial ribbons worn to funerals by participants, or given away as memorial remembrances, are available today to collectors of 19th century funeralia and memorial art. Some, like the pallbearers' ribbons shown here, were simply black and white silk or satin emblems pinned to the lapels of mourning coats as part of men's mourning attire. In the case of a funeral for a young unmarried woman or a child, the ribbon would be white, rather than black. Other funeral ribbons were worn by members of fraternal associations such as I.O.O.F. or Modern Woodsmen of America, who often paid for the funerals of deceased members whose families could not afford the burial costs. Shown is an example of such a memorial ribbon for the Rebekah Lodge of the Oddfellows, or I.O.O.F. The c. 1860-80s black Stevensgraph mourning ribbon is an item which would have been given away to attendees at a funeral as a memorial remembrance of the deceased, or, as in this case, a religious admonition or encouragement.

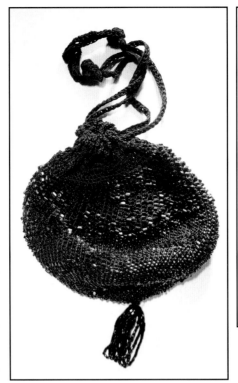

Civil War-era mourning reticule with graduated hand-carved jet beading. 7" long. *Author's collection.* $125.

Early 19th century mourning purse, entirely done in beadwork with mourning symbolism in memory of a husband. 6" long. *Author's collection.* $450.

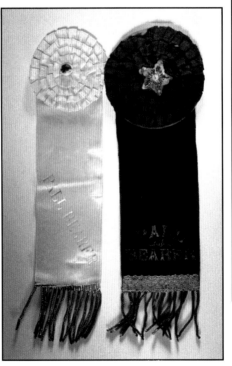

Nineteenth century pallbearer's ribbons, black for an adult funeral, white for a child's or that of a young unmarried woman. *Collection of Jerry Lesandro and Larry Martin.* $75 each.

Commemorative ribbons, such as this one for the Rebekah Lodge of the I.O.O.F., were frequently worn at fraternal funerals. Most fraternal organizations paid for funerals of destitute or impoverished members. Celluloid and silk with metallic fringe. 7" long. *Author's collection.* $50.

Stevensgraph mourning ribbon given out as a remembrance at a funeral. Mourning ribbons such as this are popular with funeralia collectors and this ribbon is of interest to Stevensgraph collectors as well. 5.5" long. *Author's collection.* $75.

Other items available to collectors today are 19th century pallbearers' gloves and casket palls. In the following photographs are some fine examples of other items accompanying a mourning outfit, although finding these pieces in good condition (or even in their original box such as the pallbearer's gloves shown here) can be quite difficult. As noted before, in the case of a funeral for a young child or unmarried woman, pallbearers would have worn white gloves, along with white crape banners across the front of their mourning suits, white weepers on their hats, etc. The rare bonnet with artificial cherries and floral trims reflects the growing acceptance of "fashionable" mourning dress in the era of the "Gilded Age" towards the end of the 19th century.

Pallbearer's gloves in original box, white for the funeral of a child or that of a young, unmarried woman, and black for an adult funeral. *Collection of Jerry Lesandro and Larry Martin.* $150-200.

A late 19th century mourning slat muslin bonnet. Large-size bonnets such as these in various calicos and muslins were primarily worn as outdoor clothing, for both functional and "fancy" wear. Some were worn only as Sunday "fancy bonnets," while others were used to shield the wearer from the intense sunlight in the western territorial areas of the United States. Early mid-century style bonnets were stiffened with several layers of fabric, primarily of crinoline, then stitched in quilted lines for shaping. A cape-like portion covering the back and sides of the neck, called a *bavolet* or *curtain*, added further protection from sunlight, and horizontal lines stitched as casings allowed for the insertion of thin slats of hickory or cardboard for stiffening. Black mourning bonnets in wool crepe or brilliantine, sateen or silk taffeta enabled the wearer to observe mourning etiquette, but were not worn with attached mourning crape. *Collection of Judith Peebles.* $75-90.

Rare c. 1880s crape mourning bonnet with artificial cherries and leaves as trims. This hat reflects the growing acceptance of fashionable trims as part of the mourning dress towards the end of the 19th century in the emerging "Gilded Age," an unthinkable inclusion during the previous decades of the Civil War years. *Collection of Patricia Comstock Wilczak.* $250.

As mourning etiquette authorized that every accessory be appropriately black, even utilitarian objects such as this Civil War era fan would reflect the necessary mourning requirements, yet would provide modesty, privacy, and comfort. *Author's collection.* $75.

Small boxes of "Mourning Pins," c. 1860-80s. These necessary little accessories allowed the mourner to pin the yards of crape fabric to clothing, secure mourning veils to headpieces, and pin undergarments without the "shame" of using shiny, and definitely inappropriate, milliner's pins. Crape and other mourning fabrics were extremely fragile, prone to tearing and fraying, and these little pins helped to hold delicate fabrics in place until the required period of mourning was completed. *Author's collection.* $10-15 each.

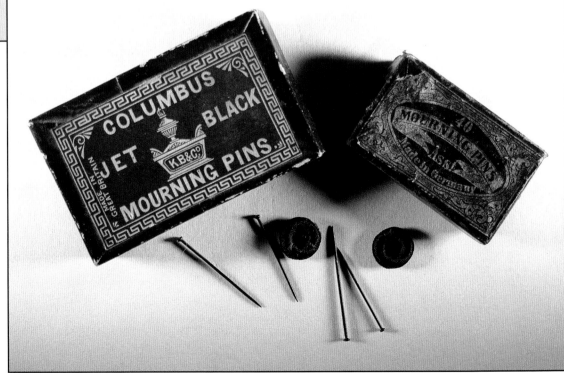

Mourning Jewelry

As described in the Historical Background, mourning jewelry has long been popular in Western culture as tokens of religious admonition and memorials of remembrance. The power of jewelry to mark the significant passages of human life from birth to death has remained relatively unaltered over the centuries. A single brooch followed the life of Empress Alexandra, granddaughter of Queen Victoria, from her first meeting at the age of twelve with her future husband, Czar Nicholas II of Russia, to her execution in a cellar in Ekaterinberg, Siberia, thirty-four years later, during the 1917 Russian Revolution. In 1884, the sixteen-year-old heir to the Russian throne met his future bride-to-be, and gave her a diamond brooch as a gift. In childish embarrassment, however, she nervously thrust the pin back into his hand, accidentally stabbing him in the process. For Nicholas, it was love at first sight, and ten years later when they ultimately became engaged, he once again proffered the diamond brooch. This time, Alexandra joyfully accepted the gift, wearing it on the anniversary of their engagement every year thereafter for twenty-four years. When the bodies of the assassinated Romanov family (Czar Nicholas, Empress Alexandra, and their five children), were finally retrieved in 1991, entangled in the bones of the Empress' body were remnants of the diamond brooch. She had taken it with her into exile and worn it when she was executed.

Dating back to the Middle Ages, mourning jewelry afforded a personal token of reflection and remembrance in the form of rings, pendants, brooches, and watch fobs. Provisions in wills of the Middle Ages instructed that mourning rings be made and given in the form of bequests, and it is known that King Richard II (reigning 1377-99) left one gold ring to each of the five bishops and four noblemen he chose as executors.[8] In addition, a fascinating early piece of mourning jewelry is seen in a c. 1530 portrait of Margaret, the daughter of the Duke of Clarence, who was executed by his brother King Edward IV for treason in 1478. Rather than the customary execution of hanging, drawing, and quartering for convicted traitors, the King permitted Clarence to choose his own method of dying, whereupon the Duke chose to be drowned in a cask of wine. His daughter Margaret wore a miniature wine-cask on a bracelet in his memory, which can be seen in the portrait![9]

Another early example of *memento mori* jewelry is a pendant ornament originally found at Tor Abbey in England, which has been dated to approximately 1546. The gold pendant contains a skeleton inside a coffin, the lid of which is inscribed "Through the resurrection of Christe we be all sanctified." William Shakespeare's will bequeathed memorial rings to friends as well as to three of his actors, and well-known are the 123 mourning rings given to friends of Samuel Pepys, the 17th century English diarist, after his death. Mourning jewelry, originally designed with the ubiquitous *memento mori* individual reminder, changed in the 17th century to *memento illius,* or the commemorative remembrance of "another."

In America, the earliest piece of mourning jewelry made by an American-born and trained jeweler is a gold mourning ring made in Boston in 1693 by Jeremiah Dummer. This piece is now in the Winterthur Museum. Mourning rings are the earliest pieces found in American jewelry, and were primarily the property of wealthy colonists, frequently being the only piece of jewelry owned (even surpassing wedding rings). Just as in England, mourning rings were distributed in 17th century New England funerals, and the early Boston colonist, Judge Samuel Sewall, owned fifty-seven such commemorative rings given to him at funerals.

In the following sections, we will take a closer look at the periods of mourning jewelry defined as the Stuart, Georgian, and Victorian eras. However, as hair appears in many memorial pieces from all three of these periods, and as hairwork is among the most popular form of mourning jewelry for collectors today, it is worth taking a moment here to give some background history and information about hair as a commemorative relic in Western culture.

Many civilizations throughout history have believed that hair holds a sacred quality and retains something of the "essence" or "soul" of the person. Because hair is virtually imperishable, it was often symbolic of immortality, and keeping a lock of hair tantamount to preserving a portion of the beloved deceased. In ancient Rome and Greece, it was common practice to hang a lock of hair over the doors of households in mourning, and even during the time of Christ, contracts were frequently sealed by "swearing on the hair." To secure the terms of an agreement, the beards of men and the hair of women were sometimes used as collateral for their honor. In ancient Hebrew mourning rituals, the tearing out of one's hair was done as an expression of intense grief (Ezra 9:3) and even to this day, strands of hair are often plucked from heads or beards in Jewish mourning custom.

Hair began to emerge as a material in mourning jewelry as early as 14th century Europe, and was often included in *memento mori* jewelry of the 14th through the 16th centuries along with teeth and bone fragments, as seen in saints' relics. By 1600, hair bracelets became popular as a mourning accessory, and the 17th century English poet and clergyman, John Donne, refers to a memorial hair token in his poem, *The Relic*, wherein he describes a "bracelet of bright hair about the bone," of his own skeletal remains.

When my grave is broke up again
Some second guest to entertain,
(For graves have learned that woman-head,
To be to more than one a bed,)
And he, that digs it, spies
A bracelet of bright hair about the bone,
Will he not let us alone,
And think that there a loving couple lies,
Who thought that this device might be some way
To make their souls, at the last busy day,
Meet at this grave, and make a little stay?

It is in the Georgian and Victorian eras that we see the most unparalleled examples of hair-work in mourning jewelry, in which the hair remembrance assumed qualities not unlike virtual shrines to the deceased. To better appreciate the skillful workmanship of hair-work artisans, we will now take a look at the various methods of hair-work, called "devices," which were employed. In the case of Georgian mourning jewelry, background shapes of porcelain or ivory, primarily ovoid, octagonal, rectangular, or navette in form, were painted with water-colored hues of pale pink and blue,

upon which hair devices were applied to create the scene.

Various basic methods for creating the hair-work mourning scene were employed; sometimes the hair was finely chopped and combined with gum arabic or an adhesive known as "musilix," which was made from vegetable and seaweed gums, then painted onto the watercolored background. In another method, the hair was pounded in a mortar and pestle to the consistency of powder and added to distilled water, which held the macerated hair in suspension. The "dissolved" hair was then mixed with sepia pigment and used as a painting medium for the fine details of scenes as well as lettering for sentimental expressions or epitaphs on tombs. In a third method (called *cut work*), strands of hair were spread over glue-covered paper and allowed to dry, whereupon the hair-covered paper was cut into various shapes and arranged into the mourning scene. All of these methods are collectively referred to as *palette-worked* hair, as they were most often created on an artist's palette.

Generally speaking, palette-worked hair of both the chopped and "dissolved" methods are the earliest in design, dating from approximately 1760 to 1825; cut-work methods follow, from 1825 to 1835; and a transitional period, employing both dissolved and cut-work methods (sometimes in the same piece), occurred between 1835-1850. After 1850, the *loupe work* method of hair feathers and curls, called "Prince of Wales" plumes, dominates the hair-work design in mourning jewelry and memorial art. This method of hair-work was created by using a curling iron or metal rod. When the lock of hair had been curled around the iron two to three times, the iron was then placed over a candle flame to heat the hair and thus set the curl.

American artist Francis Rabineau advertised in 1791 that he "paints in Miniature, Crayon and Hair Work, with natural or dissolved hair: mourning pieces for Bracelets, Brest-pins, or Rings, figurative to the wish and desire of the ladies and gentlemen. [sic]" However, not all hair-work was professionally executed, and by the 18th century, academies and schools for young girls taught the skills of mourning art, including the working of hair, in New England and the

American South, as well as schools in Britain.

In a letter to a friend, a woman wrote of her love of a memorial ring containing the hair of her dead sister-in-law, Dorothea:

"Dear Laura has given us each a ring of our Do's hair with a small pearl in the middle. I am so fond of it. We chose a ring – and I am glad for 3 reasons. First because always wearing it helps me to think of her; 2nd because a ring seems to be a bond of love; 3rd it being round, a circle reminds one how one's love and communion with her may and will last for ever if we don't lose it by our own fault. Then the Pearl 'Purity' pleases me so much."[10] [sic]

Hair-work was also created to memorialize patriotic events as well as famous figures. When Lord Nelson was victorious over the French at the Battle of the Nile, his mistress, Lady Hamilton, commissioned a medallion to be struck memorializing the victory. The medal enclosed Nelson's palette-worked hair over opaline glass, and included nautical motifs such as an anchor and trident.[11] Nelson himself kept a lock of hair from a young soldier he had mentored, and who had become very dear to him. The young man was later mortally wounded during one of the many sea battles between the French and English, causing Nelson to exclaim in a letter that the lock of "dear Parker's hair, which I value more than if he had left me a bulse of diamonds," to be his only consolation.[12] At the Battle of Trafalgar, when Nelson himself was mortally wounded, he declared to his close friend Captain Thomas Hardy, his immortal dying words, "I am a dead man, Hardy. I am going fast. It will all be over with me soon. Pray let my dear Lady Hamilton have my hair and all the other things belonging to me."[13] And, when Grace Darling, daughter of the lighthouse keeper at Berwick Bay, England, rescued shipwrecked passengers from a steamboat in 1838, her daring swim to save the drowning victims so touched English hearts, that she was besieged with requests for locks of her hair. Poor Grace complied with the requests until her hair was "embarrassingly short"![14]

Political allegiances were represented in mourning jewelry as symbolically potent emblems of loyalties during revolutions and civil wars in both England and France. A memorial ring worn by a visiting English lord to the French Court brought a prescient shudder of trepidation to Queen Marie Antoinette as the terrible days of the French Revolution began in 1789. The mourning ring contained the hair of the English regicide Oliver Cromwell, who was responsible for the death of Charles I in 1649, and no doubt this English lord was visibly, (and not so subtly) expressing his revolutionary sympathies. One can understand the fears of Louis XVI and Marie Antoinette when even the ancient stones of the Bastille, torn down on July 14, 1789, by a mob of revolutionaries, became memorial gemstones set into brooches and worn as emblems of liberty by the "radical chic" at the French court!

Most eighteenth century mourning jewelry, however, did not have political or patriotic symbolism, but simply commemorated the loss of a loved one. Typically, Georgian mourning scenes were delicate and pale-hued, executed in sepia with dissolved hair on watercolored backgrounds painted onto ivory. Some pieces simply consisted of hairwork designs on ivory, while others incorporated additional tiny slivers of ivory, seed pearls, gold wire, or mother of pearl into the scene of weeping willows, mourners standing by urns, epitaphs, angels, etc., as will be seen by the examples in this volume.

By the Victorian period, mourning jewelry employing hair plumes, or "Prince of Wales" curls, palette-work, or cut-work, and hair plaiting became fashionable, as it was more compatible with the larger-sized brooches and pendants worn with heavy mourning attire. Hair weaving and plaiting involved other forms of design arrangement, and by mid-century, instructions were published and sold along with kits, to enable individuals to create their own hair weaving for placement in purchased mourning jewelry frames from their local jeweler. In America, a man named Mark Campbell published a book with directions for plaiting hair, showing diagrams for various designs of both sentimental and mourning motifs. Plaiting hair became a parlor pastime for many women,

and while *Godey's Lady's Book* reminded ladies that only jet jewelry was suitable for "first stage" or deep mourning, hair jewelry was frequently worn for all the stages of mourning, as a cherished memento of the beloved deceased.

If one so chose, the hair of the deceased could be left with a jeweler to be woven by an assistant, usually a female employee, and placed into a purchased brooch or pendant frame. In 1855, *Godey's Lady's Book* offered to accommodate any woman wishing to have a piece of hair jewelry, by ornamenting the hair into mourning pieces at various prices. *Godey's* extolled the virtues of hair-work by stating:

> "Hair is at once the most delicate and lasting of our materials and survives us like love. It is so light, so gentle, so escaping from the idea of death, that with a lock of hair belonging to a child or friend we may almost look up to heaven and compare notes with angelic nature, may almost say, 'I have a piece of thee here, not unworthy of thy being now'."

Woven hair-work for watch-chains, necklaces, and bracelets was created on a round table, approximately 33" high, which allowed a woman to be seated in a chair and to weave the hair on the table frame placed in front of her. Before weaving, the hair was prepared by boiling in soda water for fifteen minutes, then dried, and separated into strands of twenty to thirty hairs of various lengths. Bracelets required lengths of hair approximately 20-24", and as most women wore their hair long throughout their lives, acquiring hair of sufficient length was not difficult. Almost all hair-work was woven around molds, and fancy designs such as snakes, spiral earrings, and intricate forms in bracelets and necklaces required wooden forms to be carved by

local woodworkers. Simple cords sufficed to form the mold over which watch-chains and necklaces were formed.

Table-worked hair was fashioned upon a padded form on the circular table top, to which pins were placed around at specific distances from one another to create the design in the piece, similar to methods employed in creating bobbin lace. In the center of the table was a hole where the woven hair would be formed underneath. Lengths of sectioned hair were attached to the pins around the circumference, and the hair sections attached with lead weights or bobbins to maintain proper tension. The hair was then woven, in a hand-over-hand method, forming the finished weave inside the central hole. After the design was completed, the finished bracelet, watch chain, or necklace was boiled in soda water again and allowed to dry; any molds in the design were then removed. This method of hair-work was a fashionable parlor diversion and Victorian women could learn the table-work techniques from magazine instructions such as *Godey's*, who published directions in 1850.

In early 19th century Sweden, during the long winters when farming was at a standstill, many small farming families supplemented their income by plaiting hair. Swedish hair-worked jewelry is distinguished by the use of wooden ball "molds," around which the hair was formed, with the balls becoming a part of the jewelry design in hair brooches, necklaces, earrings, and pendants. These wooden ball forms are seen in mourning as well as sentimental hair-work pieces, and distinguish Scandinavian hair-work from other European or American makers. Now we will examine more closely some outstanding pieces of mourning jewelry from the periods just described.

Exceptional English 18K gold mourning ring with *memento mori* skeleton inside bezel "coffin." *Collection of Charlotte Sayers.* $5,000+.

Stuart Mourning Jewelry

The Stuart period generally covers the reigns of James I and II, Charles I and II, the English Civil Wars and the Restoration of the Monarchy, through the reign of William and Mary, to Queen Anne, or from 1603-1714. England during the 1600s was a time of tremendous upheaval, the denouement of which were the English Civil Wars, the abolition of the monarchy, and the execution of King Charles I. The Civil Wars divided men so deeply that a dispassionate interpretation of King Charles' reign and person is difficult to find in historic archival accounts. To his adversaries he was a man of bloodshed; to his supporters a pacific and spotless martyr.[15] The execution of Charles I in 1649 led to a rapid growth in the popularity of mourning jewelry, which originally was worn (often secretively) as a sign of loyalty to the dead King. Locks of Charles' hair were much treasured, and often combined with miniature portraits of the King inside the bezel along with the initials "CR." Other memorial jewelry such as pendants, lockets, and slides (strung on silk ribbon to wear around the neck), with the macabre symbols of *memento mori*, continued throughout the Stuart period. Mourning rings distributed according to wills during the 17th century were generally designed as thin gold bands with black enameling, white enameled skeletons, skulls and crossbones, hour-glasses, or picks and shovels, the emblems of mortality and the grave. Any inscription would be inside the shank, usually of a name and date of death. Some rings had a coffin-shaped crystal bezel in which an enameled skeleton was laid out; other bezels were in the shape of skulls. In the case of slides, ciphers (or initials) of gold wire were often included on top of plaited or curled locks of hair. In others, a crystal bezel (often faceted) displayed an enameled skeleton or skull and crossed bones on one side, with hair on the reverse. These styles of *memento mori* jewelry remained popular until the end of the reign of Queen Anne (1714), and as jewelry from this early period is rare, pieces tend to be expensive.

In the first example (shown on previous page), a beautiful Stuart mourning band conveys the typical *memento mori* skeleton laid out for "burial" inside a crystal bezel "coffin." The band is also enameled in black on 18K gold with floral motifs, (possibly early heraldic designs as well).

The two photographs here depict the classic *memento mori* of the skull and crossbones of the ossuary. The entire band of this 18K ring has *bas relief* crossed bones enameled in white against a black enameled ground, with a skull as the "gemstone." In the second photo, we see the inside obituary inscription of "Hannah Crowe dyed 1677."

Fabulous *memento mori* skull and crossbones ring in memory of "Hannah Crowe dyed 1677," English, 18K. *Collection of Charlotte Sayers.* $7,500+.

Interior view of skull and crossbones ring showing inscription.

Two exceptional 18/15K slides with plaited and curled hair are seen below. Slides were worn with silk "ribbands" around the neck during the Stuart period; later during the Victorian era, slides appear again as fixtures on ladies watchchains to enable them to be adjustable to various lengths. In these examples, the classic skeleton motifs are represented, but here they hold a pick in one hand and an hourglass in the other, one item representing the implement of the grave and the other symbolic of the brevity of life. While these skeletons today seem somewhat humorous, almost reminding us of Halloween, to the wearer in the Middle Ages these symbols were a serious reminder that one must be ever cognizant of the fragility of life. In a time when the Church in Rome exercised sovereign authority over Kings and countries, the importance of adherence to church rites and doctrines was the governing influence over how death was to be visually represented. The skeletons rest on top of the hair of the deceased; in the larger slide, the reddish blonde hair is plaited, in the smaller slide, the hair is a simple curl, perhaps that of a child.

In the second photograph we see the inscriptions on the reverse of these slides, the larger one engraved, "Margaret Hart, Ob. 1 Oct 1685," and the smaller one inscribed, "B.A. May 24, 1689."

Rare Stuart era slides with hair and skeletons, English, 18K gold. *Collection of Charlotte Sayers.* $3,500 each.

Georgian Mourning Jewelry

The Georgian era covers the period 1714-1837, and although many people view the Victorian "era" as 1800 to 1900, in fact, Queen Victoria did not ascend the throne until 1837. During the Georgian period, rococo styles from France began to influence English and American clothing and jewelry design. Neo-classicism reigned supreme as a result of more enlightened philosophical ideas, the exposure of Europeans to the artistic influences of the Middle East, and the ancient civilizations of Greece and Rome being discovered through excavations. Egyptophilia became all the rage as the art and culture of the Pharaohs of Egypt was brought to France (and ultimately Britain) through reports of Napoleon's invasions and the Battle of the Nile. The high-waisted clothing worn by men and the unconstructed, gauzy and light-weight (almost transparent) pastel-hued muslins and silks favored by women in French drawing-rooms and salons became the overriding fashion as a result of the Neo-classicism of Roman and Grecian design elements.

Even mourning clothing was in keeping with the light-colored clothing styles, as paintings and embroideries of the 18th century suggest that female mourners frequently wore white filmy mourning dress, rather than the heavy black clothing seen a century later in the Victorian era. Consequently, mourning jewelry reflected the delicate designs and hues of the current fashions, as seen in the Georgian examples in this section. Crystal bezels containing portraits and/or hair-work now included sentimental messages in the designs around the shank as well, along with enameling in black for mourning deceased adults, and white for mourning children. Bezels became larger, and were ovoid, marquise, oblong, navette, or octagonal in shape. Romanticized mourning scenes such as weeping Grecian-style figures draped over tombs, along with obelisks (reflective of Egyptian influences), urns, weeping willows, and plinths were combined with sentimental expressions of loss or Biblical assurances of future reunion.

Sepia, a brown paint used as a medium for detailed sentimental and mourning scenes and often containing the macerated hair of the deceased, was a popular painting method used in the stylized designs of Neo-classical romanticism. Generally, mourning scenes stereotypically encompassed three or four basic motifs: the grieving mourner, the tomb (usually an obelisk) or an urn, the plinth, and the weeping willow. Expressions such as "Gone to Bliss"; "Fallen to rise again"; "Not lost but gone before"; "Heaven has in store what thou hast lost"; and obituary information were painted in sepia on tombstone plinths. The "winged cherub," or "putti," now replaced the skull and crossbones.

Gemstones such as garnets, amethyst, rubies, and paste stones could be added as embellishments, primarily in second and third stage mourning for wealthier women, although diamonds and pearls were customarily worn as mourning gemstones for those at Court throughout the entire mourning period. The semi-precious stones for later periods of mourning were similar to the *bijoux de fantaisie* (colored gemstones) already worn by aristocratic women and those at the Court of Louis XVI and Marie Antoinette. Glass stones called "paste" were also extensively used in Georgian England and in France in lieu of diamonds, but not necessarily viewed as cheap imitations. Paste stones were leaded glass cut and faceted like diamonds, then set in silver findings against a backing of bright metal, called "foil," to give the stone diamond-like sparkle. They were most popular during the 18th century, and the invention of paste for jewelry is attributed to Georges Frederic Strass (1702-1773), who was born in Strasbourg but worked in Paris as a jeweler. His paste stones were admired for their own merits and qualities; not simply viewed as inferior substitutes for diamonds. Thus, in an era when diamond jewelry was at a height in popularity, there was no shame in wearing paste jewelry, alone or in combination with valuable gemstones, ivory, and other materials.

Rings during this period were much larger than the thin, narrow bands of the previous century of the Stuart era; most popular were the large oval or navette-shaped rings with mourning scenes of figures standing by a tomb with an urn or an obelisk. One historically interesting ring, now in the Victoria and Albert Museum, concerns the death of the Princess Amelia, who was the youngest and favorite daughter of George III and who died on November 2, 1810. The ring, consisting of the letter "A" with a crown in black enamel and bordered by a white enamel inscription "Remember Me," contains a lock of Amelia's hair. As she lay dying, she slipped the ring on her father's finger, murmuring the words "Remember me" – the moment was so shattering for the King, it was said to have contributed to his madness.[16]

Brooches exhibited these same mourning scenes as well, and jewelry often included hair-work using the macerated or "dissolved" hair methods of palette-work in the elements of the scene. Seed pearls and gold wire were added as embellishments on urns and obelisks, and obituary information was written on the plinths in sepia. Backgrounds were usually ivory or ivory substitutes, which were most often water-colored with the motifs of the obelisk or urn and plinth either applied onto the background for three-dimensional effect, or painted onto the ground in sepia along with the mourning figure, trees, and foliage. The naturalistic flora of the background in mourning jewelry of this period is reminiscent of an imaginary "Garden of Eden" in the soft fluid lines of the trees, shrubbery, drooping branches of the willows, etc., and even in the very pale hues of the sepia and dissolved hair-work itself. Where streams or rivers are included, these are subtly suggestive of the bucolic scenery of paintings by the American Hudson River Valley artists of the early 1800s.

Another style of mourning ring became popular in the late Georgian period, however, which contrasts with the softened Neo-classic styles of Georgian period mourning jewelry. This style of mourning ring was more European in appeal, and typically consisted of a wide gold band, enameled around in black or white, usually with the standard "In Memory Of" in Roman capital letters. Frequently, obituary information was inscribed inside the shank as well. The outstanding memorial ring for Napoleon Bonaparte I, shown later in this section (see page 86) is an example of this design style.

In the photograph below, we see a fabulous rose gold English brooch of a grieving mother at her child's tomb, executed in sepia, watercolor, and dissolved hair on ivory, and also incorporating seed pearls, mother of pearl, and gold wire embellishments to enhance the scene. While the mother grieves in hopelessness, her head resting on her hand and dabbing her eyes with a handkerchief, an angel takes her child's "soul effigy" to heaven. This concept of the "soul effigy" was more comforting to the bereaved after a death than the macabre "death's head" imagery of the Middle Ages. This romanticized view evolved as a result of the Enlightenment philosophies and evangelical religious beliefs of the Great Awakenings, which brought more solace in the concepts of a loving God calling people to "come home" as opposed to the God of judgment. In most of these representations, however, the mourners seem unmindful to the event of their loved one being escorted to the heavenly realms, and rather than watching the ascension, are always depicted as overcome with grief at the tomb, oblivious to the angelic resurrection going on around them. The elaborate plinth on the tombstone is decorated with graduated seed pearls and the sepia inscription says "Gone to Bliss," a ubiquitous expression seen on cemetery monuments for both the 18th and 19th centuries. The reverse of this brooch has plaited brown, blonde, and gray hair under a crystal bezel, no doubt that of the parents and the child braided together.

Graphite and pen and ink drawings for designs used in hair-work memorials and mourning jewelry. These sample patterns would be used by workers in hair-work jewelry and memorials as design layouts. *Courtesy of Things Gone By.* $50-75 each.

Beautiful English rose gold brooch of mother grieving at her child's tomb, oblivious to the ascension of her child heavenward by angelic escort. Watercolor on ivory, with sepia, gold wire, seed pearls, and dissolved hair embellishments. Reverse of this outstanding brooch has plaited brown, gray, and blonde hair, no doubt that of the child and her parents woven together. 1.5" x 1.25". *Courtesy of Things Gone By.* $1,750.

72

The spectacular 18K gold French mourning pendant shown here is almost beyond description in the quality of its workmanship, detailing, beauty, symbolism, and hair-work. This pendant has it all in terms of desirability to the advanced collector. The mourning scene depicts a mother grieving at the obelisk tomb of her daughter, whose epitaph gives her date of death as "OB. 29 Feb^y, AE 26," and her initials as "JK 1792." The obelisk itself is comprised of mother-of-pearl, tiny seed pearls, gold and copper wire, enameling in three-dimensional relief against the sepia and water-colored background of weeping willows, cypress, and oak trees all executed on ivory. Note the infinitesimally small urn positioned on the obelisk. A piece of the tomb is broken and lies cast to the ground below, itself comprised of the macerated hair of the deceased child. The moment of resurrection is captured, as out of the tomb flies an angel holding a palm branch (symbolic of victory over death), and the deceased child, enrobed in her burial shroud, is carried heavenward with the celestial messenger. As is typical of such scenes, the mother grieves at the tomb, but appears oblivious to the ascension; however, a snake in the oak to the left observes the miraculous event. The reverse of this outstanding pendant has palette-worked light brown hair overlaid with cipher initials in graduated seed pearls.

Another spectacular tribute, this time to a husband, is shown in the next 18K gold French pendant, probably originally from an aristocratic family. It is followed by additional fine examples of rings, brooches, and pendants and other jewelry from this period.

Spectacular French 18K gold pendant of mother grieving at the tomb of her daughter, while angel escorts daughter heavenward from the broken obelisk tomb; watercolor on ivory, with sepia, dissolved hair, gold wire, seed pearls, dated 1792. 3" x 2". *Courtesy of Things Gone By.* $3,700.

Reverse of French 18K gold pendant above, showing palette-worked hair overlaid with cipher initials in graduated diminutive seed pearls. *Courtesy of Things Gone By.*

A spectacular tribute to a husband is shown in this 18K gold French pendant, c. 1780s-1790s. On this side, his hair, executed in the cut work method of palette-work and overlaid on ivory, frames an interior banner carved from ivory and inscribed with the heartbreaking sentiment, "In Heaven and in My Heart." The banner is set against brilliant blue glass, usually seen in pieces with aristocratic French family origins. *Courtesy of Things Gone By.* $3,500-4,500.

Reverse of French pendant at left, showing an allegorical scene, executed in sepia and dissolved hair on ivory, of a tomb with a silhouette of the deceased husband under the shade of a willow in the cemetery ground of a local parish church somewhere in the countryside of France. The exceptional workmanship of this rare piece along with its poignant sentiment adds to its desirability and value. *Courtesy of Things Gone By.*

This exceptional 1793 Georgian ring is executed in sepia and watercolor on ivory, along with dissolved hair-work. The ring is inscribed "Sara Braikenridge 1793" on the reverse and the initials "S.B." appear on the front plinth; above the mourner at the tomb is a "bow" of hair. The groundwork at the base of the tomb is also done in Sara's hair, which has been finely chopped and placed into the scene in the palette-worked method. *Courtesy of Judy Jay's Time Dances By.* $1,895.

A beautiful pendant in sepia and dissolved hair executed on ivory, inscribed, "In silent sorrow o'er thy tomb I'll mourn," is full of the pathos and romanticism seen in 18th century mourning jewelry under the typical sentimentalities of the Romantic Movement. In this example, the mourner sits in pensive contemplation rather than praying or openly grieving, and fine detailing is seen in the background trees, foliage, and stream, or "River of Life," barely visible to the right. Note the dark melancholy atmosphere of the scene. This rose gold pendant has a velvet backing and the name "E. Fiott" written on the reverse. 1.25". *Courtesy of Things Gone By.* $1,595.

A rare anachronistic memorial piece is seen in this outstanding ivory and pearl 18K gold memorial ring, which contains some of the *memento mori* symbols more typical of the Stuart period; the "Angel of Death" with his scythe and hourglass are all symbols from *ars moriendi* of the Middle Ages. Here, the "Angel of Death" or Grim Reaper as he is more commonly known today, places a wreath of flowers over an obelisk tomb, an unusual act in itself for a figure whose role has always been that of a dreaded harbinger foreshadowing death, not as a sympathetic mourner. The ring is inscribed "Henriette Louise Gebid 12ᵗʰ Apr: 1761, Gestid 5ᵗʰ Junij 1793," and this ring is probably Alsatian in origin, due to the dual French and German inscription. *Courtesy of Judy Jay's Time Dances By.* $2,000.

An unusual brooch showing a grieving father praying at the tomb of his child. This rare and beautifully detailed English 9K gold brooch, is inscribed "T. W. Hooker Obt 16 June 1786 at 5 years." The fact that a woman is not depicted in the scene possibly indicates that she too has passed, as it is rare to have a father depicted as the mourner. The obelisk is unusually ornate with enamel-work, seed pearls, and gold wire, and the ground around it is done in dissolved hair, while the background trees and figure of the father are executed in sepia on ivory. The vitreous blue enameling set with seed pearls around the perimeter is indicative that this was a mourning piece belonging to a member of the aristocracy. *Courtesy of Things Gone By.* $2,800.

An 18th century rose gold English memorial ring with garlanded urn and weeping willow representative of a popular design style of mourning ring during this era. The motifs and inscription were done in dissolved hair and sepia on ivory, and the ground underneath the monument executed in chopped, or "macerated" hair of the deceased. The plinth inscription reads, "Heaven Has in Store What Thou Hast Lost," and on the reverse, "John Hanbury died 9th Feb 1792 Aged 58." *Courtesy of Things Gone By.* $1,895.

A memorial piece, probably from an aristocratic family (as evidenced by the vitreous blue enameling), is seen here. This lovely 18th century rose gold piece also has diamond chips spaced at the navette points and sides, along with two colors of plaited hair, light and dark brown, underneath the crystal bezel. The reverse has more hair laid out underneath an additional bezel. 1.25" x .75." *Courtesy of Things Gone By.* $1,500.

This exceptional Georgian rose gold brooch with multiple mediums and inscriptions on ivory is truly a work of art. Elaborate designs on the plinth with the tiniest of seed pearls set off the monument as a work in miniature, topped with a pearl "urn," itself garlanded with gold wire and topped with an even tinier seed pearl. The plinth is inscribed, "There's Rest in Heaven" in sepia, and a mourner, willow, foliage and ground are all executed in chopped and dissolved hair-work, as well as in sepia on ivory. Around this central scene are the words, "In Death Lamented, in Life Beloved" also in sepia, and surrounding this is plaited light brown hair. The reverse is inscribed, "W. E. Catherine Gaunt born 23 Nov 1770 Died 6 Jan'y 1791 Aged 20." 1.5" x 1". *Courtesy of Things Gone By.* $2,500.

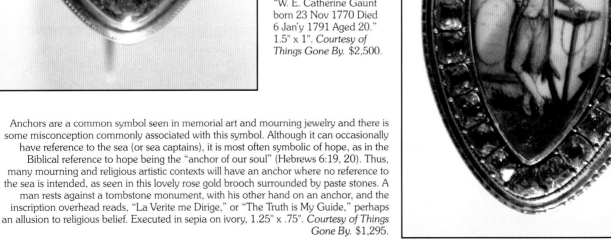

Anchors are a common symbol seen in memorial art and mourning jewelry and there is some misconception commonly associated with this symbol. Although it can occasionally have reference to the sea (or sea captains), it is most often symbolic of hope, as in the Biblical reference to hope being the "anchor of our soul" (Hebrews 6:19, 20). Thus, many mourning and religious artistic contexts will have an anchor where no reference to the sea is intended, as seen in this lovely rose gold brooch surrounded by paste stones. A man rests against a tombstone monument, with his other hand on an anchor, and the inscription overhead reads, "La Verite me Dirige," or "The Truth is My Guide," perhaps an allusion to religious belief. Executed in sepia on ivory, 1.25" x .75". *Courtesy of Things Gone By.* $1,295.

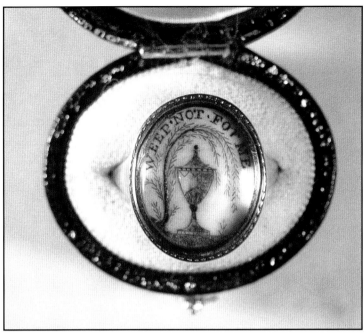

"A tender mother and sincere friend." The wonderful inscription on this beautiful 18K gold ring was the perfect sentiment for the present owner, who purchased it in memory of her mother, Marlene M. Weber Bingman. The c. 1790 ring has a beautiful dissolved hair-work weeping willow over an elaborately detailed urn with seed pearl, gold wire, and tiny diamonds on ivory. *Collection of Laura Bingman Swenson.* $1,395.

This beautiful 1780 ring, inscribed "Weep Not For Me," contains a minutely detailed hair-work weeping willow and urn on ivory with the inscription executed in sepia. Purchased in memory of the present owner's father, Thomas F. Bingman. *Collection of Laura Bingman Swenson.* $1,100.

Lovely sepia brooch with female mourner leaning on an anchor, executed in sepia on ivory with a gold beadwork edge. This French piece is inscribed on the reverse, "Quand vou verrez cici souvenez vous de moi," or "Have this to remember me by," along with the cipher initials "WSP." Here the dead "speaks" to the living through the inscription, rather than the reverse. 1.25" x .75". *Courtesy of Things Gone By.* $1,295.

Lovely 15K gold and black enamel brooch with plaited brown hair under crystal bezel, c. 1800. 1" x .5". *Collection of Laura Bingman Swenson.* $1,000.

An extremely rare French 18K gold brooch with scene of a church and graveyard. The detailing is breathtakingly beautiful and is executed in sepia on ivory with dissolved blonde hair-work in the grounds of the cemetery, weeping willows, and the tiny crosses and monuments, one of which is no doubt the burial site of the deceased being mourned. The church, also undoubtedly real, probably no longer exists, its name and location being unknown. 1.5" x 1.25". *Courtesy of Things Gone By.* $1,595.

A lovely 9K English ring in memory of a one-year-old child, the daughter of wealthy parents, has the typical symbols of urn, plinth, and willow trees, done in sepia work and dissolved hair on ivory, with mother-of-pearl, gold wire, and seed pearls for additional adornment. On the reverse under a bezel is the plaited hair of the child, along with an inscription, "Eliza Rutt Born 5 April 1787 Died 17 April 1788." *Courtesy of Things Gone By.* $1,595.

Outstanding English pendant showing a mourning scene executed on ivory with intricate detailing memorializing two deaths done in elaborate hair-work on both sides and set in 18K gold. A weeping willow overhangs a tombstone with the initials and date of death on the plinth as, "G.E.B. 17 Oct 1756"; another death is recorded inside the serpent with its tail in its mouth (symbolic of eternity), by the initials "MVK" and "Obit 12 Nov 1811." Additional elements in the scene are a butterfly (symbolic of the human soul) flying in the sky overhead, a ship sailing towards the horizon in the background (also symbolic of the soul at death), and the skull and crossbones at the base of the tombstone, an anachronistic motif in this otherwise serenely melancholic theme. The hair-work, in cut-work and dissolved hair methods, was done on translucent opaline glass, along with watercolors to enhance the tableau. 2" x 1.5". *Courtesy of Things Gone By.* $2,195.

Reverse of English 18K gold pendant, showing palette-worked hair plume, wheat stalk, and Forget-Me-Not flowers. *Courtesy of Things Gone by.*

An exquisite Swiss 18K gold brooch with lovely water-colored cemetery scene and dissolved blonde hair on ivory under crystal bezel. This exceptionally beautiful brooch depicts a tombstone set into a garden cemetery with another monument close by. Foliage and trees form a backdrop, and a pathway meanders in front of the tombstone, which is illuminated by a heavenly light from the glowing sky above. Beautifully executed chase work make this c. 1810-30 brooch an excellent example of Swiss mourning jewelry. *Courtesy of Things Gone By.* $895.

An extraordinary rose gold brooch, c. 1780-1800, full of the symbolism so popular in the Regency through the Victorian eras. The scene employs an unusual material in the figure of the shepherdess and the lamb. Papier mâché or ceramic paste was formed in molds for both figures, which were then placed against the ivory ground three-dimensionally; the arm of the shepherdess and two of the legs of the lamb stand out in relief from the background. In symbolic tribute, the female shepherdess, holding a gold wire crook, bestows a wreath made of infinitesimally small snippets of hair on the head of the lamb, a popular symbol for centuries in Western culture to represent children. Overhanging both figures is a delicate tree composed of elaborately chopped and macerated hair-work, that of the young Sarah Wood, whose inscription on the reverse identifies her as having died Nov. 26, 1791, at twenty years of age. The ground and foliage are also done in Sarah's hair. *Courtesy of Things Gone By.* $2,295.

Outstanding 9K gold English memorial ring for three children, executed in sepia and watercolor on ivory. A mourner in classical dress, holding a rose garland, leans over an urn and plinth with an epitaph of "Rest in Peace"; behind the curtain another urn on a pedestal is visible against the water-colored sunset. Inscribed around the bezel in black enameling is "Ben & John Stephenson Lost 22 Dec 1779"; inscribed around the shank in black enamel are the words, "Benj Aged 22; John 20 years." Underneath the bezel is inscribed, "Nancy Stephenson Ob 5 June 1780 Ae 21." The intentional use of the word "lost" as opposed to the usual "obit" or "died" probably indicates that the two sons were lost in a tragic accident, possibly going down in a ship at sea. *Author's collection.* $2,700.

A lovely ivory pendant surrounded with paste stones commemorating the death of a person of Danish ancestry, born in Denmark in 1730 and died in 1782. The entire scene of garlanded urn, willow, and dead branch (symbolic of a life cut short) is executed in chopped hair of the deceased, and the obituary on the plinth is in sepia. The paste stones are cut glass backed with foil, a popular stone in jewelry of both sentiment and mourning, often selected even when gemstones would have been affordable for the wearer. *Author's collection.* $1,295.

Reverse of the memorial pendant of mother and children, showing elaborately braided hair combined with palette-worked hair in the center overlaid with gold cipher of entwined initials. *Courtesy of Things Gone By.*

An extraordinary story of sadness is evident in this large oval pendant of watercolor, sepia, and dissolved hair-work on ivory. The painted mourning scene depicts a widowed mother with her four children given up to hopelessness underneath a weeping willow. As she grieves, holding an infant on her lap, one of her children attempts to comfort her by handing her a handkerchief, while two older daughters console one another. A dog quietly naps at her feet, symbolic of fidelity and the constancy of love, the qualities of her husband, and in the background the family home is painted allegorically, the scene of domestic bliss, perhaps gone forever. Her grief is so overwhelming that this wife and mother is oblivious to the most extraordinary moment, however – that of her husband's soul being taken heavenward by an angel in the clouds overhead; neither she nor her children see his ascension. 3.25" x 2.25". *Courtesy of Things Gone By.* $2,500.

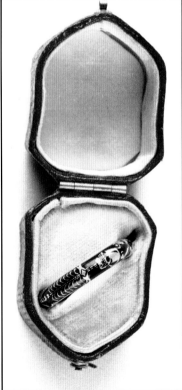

Another anachronistic memorial ring, with outstanding skull and crossbones, hourglass, scythe and shovel, typical of Stuart era *memento mori* iconography and jewelry design motifs. This English 18K gold ring is inscribed "Ellen Savage Ob 16 Oct 1745 at 83," and the detail of the "emblems of the mortality" is truly exceptional, beyond what can be adequately shown here. *Courtesy of Things Gone By.* $8,700.

An emotionally affecting pendant done in sepia with dissolved hair and watercolor on ivory. The scene depicts a widow with her four children at the tomb of her husband; two of the older children are consoling one another, while the two toddlers, as with most young children, are somewhat oblivious to the loss. The plinth is inscribed with the obituary information, "AB 2 July 1804 Aged 42" in sepia. The reverse of the pendant has the plaited hair of the mother and the children combined together as a tribute. *Courtesy of Things Gone By.* $2,100.

79

Strikingly beautiful English 9K gold memorial ring of weeping willow executed in dissolved hair on ivory, with sepia inscription, "In Memory of The Best of Friends." Inscribed underneath bezel, "Hen. Hall, Esq. Ob 23 Aug 1782 Ae 42." *Courtesy of Things Gone By.* $1,975.

An 18th century sepia and dissolved hair-work tribute executed on ivory set in an 18K gold ring in memory of "Suzannah Ward Ob 1 Oct 1779 at 47"; the inscription is in black enamel around the shank. *Courtesy of Things Gone By.* $1,695.

A poignant tribute to a husband is seen in this outstanding 18K gold Georgian brooch, which shows exceptional workmanship in an obelisk outlined with tiny seed pearls and enameling along with sepia painting on ivory in the background cypress trees. The back of the brooch is engraved, "In memory of Patrick Berkley, Ob 2 June 1782 Ae 47 The Best of Husbands." *Courtesy of Things Gone By.* $1,975.

*"Sure, to the mansions of the blest
When infant innocence ascends,
Some angel, brighter than the rest,
The spotless spirit's flight attends."*
[John Quincy Adams]

This outstanding French 18K gold mourning ring, depicting an angel taking a child to heaven, conveys all the pathos inherent in the loss of a child. The detail and watercolor on ivory are still vivid after 200+ years, a tribute to the expert craftsman of this piece. Although the assurance of heavenly security for the child is promised in the personal escort by the angel, the wrenching grief of the event is seen in the dark, roiling clouds in the background. *Courtesy of Things Gone By.* $2,100.

Beautiful Georgian sepia, watercolor, and dissolved hair-work on ivory memorial ring set in 9K gold in its original box; inscribed "T. Foreman died 25 July 1785 Aged 44 years." Scene of mourner grieving at monument and urn with plinth inscribed "Not Lost But Gone Before," with oak and cypress trees in the background; an angel carrying a banner "To Bliss" overhead symbolically informs the mourner of the soul's destination. *Courtesy of Things Gone By.* $2,100.

A touching 18K gold English ring in memory of a little boy, his plaited blonde hair set inside a crystal bezel. Inscribed inside the shank is, "Little ladds Ob 10 Nov 1706." In contrast to the usual practice of the name of the deceased being inscribed, this ring instead gives the deeply personal endearment, "Little ladds," or "Little lad's," there being no standard for spelling and punctuation in the 18th century. *Author's collection.* $1,295.

A beautiful 18K gold ring with sepia-painted urn and willow on ivory, and a black enamel band inscribed "Mrs. C. H. Temayne Ob 19 Aug 1781 Ae 25." This fine quality ring is unusual in its use of the marital status of "Mrs." noted on the ring, as almost all mourning jewelry simply lists the woman's name, with no status given. *Courtesy of Things Gone By.* $1,395.

An 18K gold Georgian sepia and watercolor on ivory ring with a mourner weeping over a obelisk, executed in enameling with chopped and dissolved hair of the deceased filling the "ground" underneath the tomb. The obituary inscription, "Gone Hence But Not Forgot" is written in sepia, as is some of the background foliage. The upper portion of the obelisk is in black enameling with an urn inside on a white oval. Gold painted embellishments highlight the decorations on the monument. The oak tree in the background in sepia symbolizes strength and endurance, and the inscription on the reverse, "Mary Brown Died 26 Jan'y 1793, Aged 68," is an obvious testament to her endurance in an era when longevity, especially for women, was a rarity. *Courtesy of Things Gone By.* $1,695.

A richly symbolic 18K gold brooch with vitreous blue enameling and seed pearls is shown here, with lovely design elements of marital love, intimacy, and fidelity executed in sepia and dissolved hair-work on ivory. This piece probably has its origins in an aristocratic family, as blue enameling is often seen in jewelry for those closely connected to the Crown. The mourner at the tomb is not grieving over it as is usually seen in mourning pieces, but instead is encouraging the dog (symbolic of loyalty) to jump into her lap. She holds a mirror in her hand and stares reflectively into the glass, the symbolism here denoting the fleeting transience of beauty and impermanence of life. This allusion to evanescent beauty hearkens back to the Middle Ages and the *memento mori* tokens depicting the fresh face of youth on one side and the skull on the reverse. Her dress, typical of Neoclassical influences widely popular in the 18th century, subtly suggests sexual love in an otherwise somber context, an unusual element in a memorial piece. Two lovebirds kiss above the monument, another allusion to marital intimacy. The reverse of this wonderful piece has plaited hair of the mourned deceased under a crystal bezel overlaid with cipher initials. *Courtesy of Things Gone By.* $1,895.

A large swivel brooch with cut-work hair flowers and initials in sepia on one side, and a mourning scene done in sepia and chopped hair on the reverse. In this lovely early 1800s brooch, two deaths are commemorated. On one side, a mourner is lying grief-stricken over the tomb, which is inscribed with the initials "MH" on the plinth. A willow overhangs the mourner and the tomb, while a boat on the sea in the background symbolizes the soul sailing towards heaven. The scene is done in chopped and dissolved hair methods of palette-work. On the reverse, elaborate cut-work flowers, done in another method of hair-work, surround another set of initials, "GH". 2.5" x 2.25". *Courtesy of Things Gone By.* $1,975.

A rare brass and black enamel man's mourning ring, c. 1790-1810, with the ubiquitous expression *memento mori*, the admonition for the living throughout centuries in Western Europe. Brass as a material for mourning jewelry is unusual, but the quality and beauty of this ring belies the typical assumptions about this seemingly "base" material. *Courtesy of Things Gone By.* $395.

Reverse of English swivel brooch showing spectacular palette-worked hair flowers around initials of second death being memorialized. *Courtesy of Things Gone By.*

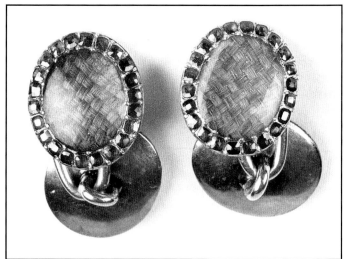

A rare Georgian 18K gold brooch in memory of a beloved pet, a dog, or perhaps a cat. Mourning jewelry for a pet is very unusual and difficult to find, especially in this almost mint condition. It is probable that the hair of the animal was used to create the memorial just as was done with human hair in mourning jewelry for family members. 2" x 1.25". *Courtesy of Things Gone By.* $795.

Lovely pair of English 9K gold men's cufflinks with woven blonde hair and tiny rubies. .50" x .50". *Courtesy of Things Gone By.* $1,395.

A matched pair of exceptional 18th century sepia, watercolor, and hair-work clasps with pearl bracelets are shown here, with each clasp depicting a different mourning scene painted on ivory. In one clasp, the mourning woman (represented as a shepherdess with two sheep, a popular theme in 18th century pastoral paintings) is seen searching for her beloved and is shown writing his name. In the other clasp, she is placing a funeral wreath on a tree in his memory. *Courtesy of Judy Jay's Time Dances By.* $2,500 each.

Full length of one of the matched pair of French sepia and watercolor clasps and pearl bracelets. *Courtesy of Judy Jay's Time Dances By.*

Mourning jewelry occasionally contains obscure symbolism, dissimilar from the usual *memento mori* motifs of urn, plinth, obelisk and grieving mourners. Where obvious memorial design is absent or the meaning is unclear, one must look for symbolic or hidden definition, as in the lovely scene of a mother teaching her son pictured on the French rose gold brooch surrounded by pearls seen here. No doubt this piece represents a real event in the lives of this mother and son, that of teaching her son from the Bible or a religious book. As it is likely that the boy later died (his plaited hair is on the reverse of this piece under a bezel), we can assume this scene of mother and child represented happier times, before death severed their relationship. The dress and setting of this boy and his mother suggest an aristocratic family life. This exceptional piece was executed in painted sepia and dissolved hair on ivory.

Most mourning jewelry is simply inscribed with obituary information, or the ubiquitous sentiments of the day, such as "Not Lost But Gone Before." Some pieces however, have symbols, elements, and inscriptions known only to the wearers. A mysterious hair-work and sepia memorial clasp, c. 1780, is one such example. The scene is beautifully executed on ivory set into rose gold, and surrounded by seed pearls, symbolic of tears. Some elements of the scene are easily recognizable, such as the burning hearts over the tomb, representative of the passion of marital love, and the crown overhead as the promised "Crown of Life" given to all those who "die in Christ." Cypress trees in the background add gloom to the mourning scene while pointing upward in heavenly hope. Two jarring elements intrude into the scene, however: the snake winding around the tomb and threatening to strike at the hearts, and the obscure inscription, "In Spite of Envy." The presence of the snake is interesting, with its symbolism as the progenitor of original sin and "The Tempter" of Eve. The "sin" of envy within the context of marriage carries with it the possible implication of infidelity, which if true, reveals a possible meaning behind the inexplicable inscription.

Lovely brooch of a mother teaching her son, executed in sepia on ivory, surrounded by pearls. 1.5" x 1". *Courtesy of Things Gone By.* $1,200.

Outstanding and mysterious English 18K gold mourning bracelet clasp with unusual themes of serpent entwining the monument with burning hearts and the sepia inscription "In Spite of Envy." Executed in watercolor and sepia on ivory. *Courtesy of Things Gone By.* $1,295.

Another spectacular pendant full of hidden meaning is shown here. This French 18K rose gold pendant is so intricately detailed, it takes some time to study and interpret the scene being represented here. Like the warm affection being displayed between mother and son reading together in the brooch shown earlier, here we see another joyful event, that of a woman's children dancing around a fountain. This was probably not a fanciful depiction, but portrayed a *real* garden fountain, around which the wearer's five children routinely played. However, the scene is not a happy one. All the children but one are dressed in pale-hued clothing; all but one face the viewer. Only the little boy dressed in brown clothing has his back turned and his dark clothing indicates that he is the deceased child being mourned here. Looking on is a large oak tree with a severed limb (symbolic of mortality), which itself forms an "*eye*" as it watches the children play; a bird, symbolic of the soul, perches in one of the branches above. In the background, pale cypress trees, melancholy allusions of despair, remind the viewer that this is not as joyful a scene as might first appear, but that a death is, in fact, being represented. The entire scene has been executed in watercolor and sepia on ivory, with the three-dimensional fountain comprised of a sliver of ivory painted and embellished with gold leaf, gold wire, and almost microscopic-sized seed pearls. The bowl of the fountain is mother-of-pearl with tiny seed pearls, and the little boy's macerated light brown hair forms the ground around the fountain where the children play.

The reverse of this rare pendant is vivid blue vitreous enameling surrounding an interior oval of ivory on which is placed a double curl of the little boy's hair, tied with gold wire, and decorated with a large pearl surrounded by tiny seed pearls. The skill and quality of workmanship of this pendant make it one of the finest examples of Georgian mourning jewelry.

Et in Arcadia Ego. "Even in Arcadia death is lurking." The 17th century French painter Nicolas Poussin portrayed shepherds in a lovely forest glade contemplating a tomb with this sobering inscription. In this spectacular pendant, death subtly hovers in the background of an idyllic scene of happy children playing around a garden fountain, one of which (the little boy in brown suit) is the child being mourned. This rare and outstanding French 18K gold and ivory memorial pendant is full of memorial symbolism, and is executed in watercolor, sepia, and dissolved hair on ivory, with mother-of-pearl and gold wire embellishments. Note the three-dimensional bird in the oak branches above and the melancholy cypress trees in the distance. 3" x 2". *Courtesy of Things Gone By.* $3,800.

Reverse of 18K gold French pendant, showing beautiful flawless enameling, with "loupes" of the little boy's hair and tiny seed pearls. *Courtesy of Things Gone By.*

An extremely rare commemorative piece is seen in the photographs here. This poignant 1821 swivel ring memorializes a political, as well as a royal death, that of Queen Caroline of Brunswick, wife of George IV. The inscription in black enamel reads, "In Memory of Caroline of Brunswick, The Injured Queen of England" on one side, while a lock of the Queen's hair is enclosed on the reverse. This outstanding ring is exceptionally crafted and has black enameling along the shank and around the enclosure for the hair. At the edges of the reversible plaque enclosure are the birth and death dates of Caroline, engraved as "born 17 May 1768," and "died 7 Aug 1821."

Princess Caroline of Brunswick was the wife of the Prince of Wales under George III (later George IV). The marriage, like many royal unions, was a necessity for future succession, as his father, George III, suffered from periods of mental irrationality and instability. Ultimately, the Prince of Wales was made Regent for his father, driven from the bed of his mistress, Mrs. Fitzherbert, and forced to propose to his cousin, Caroline of Brunswick. But the marriage was a disaster. It was barely consummated on the wedding night, due to Caroline's "personal nastiness," as the Prince of Wales referred to her lack of hygiene, whereupon he quickly returned to Mrs. Fitzherbert. Caroline left England and stayed with various friends on the Continent, eventually living with a handsome Italian for an extended stay in Italy.

Upon the Prince becoming King George IV in 1820, Caroline returned to England to assume her rightful place as Queen, to the indignant outrage of her husband. During his regency, and later as King, George had had Caroline investigated and tried for adultery (it had been rumored that she had given birth to an illegitimate child), and attempted to have the marriage annulled. As the King was not a well-liked figure with the English people, all his actions only served to further her popularity and role as the "injured Queen," a position that Caroline considerably enjoyed! When she returned to England, she was received with much enthusiasm, but her attempts to enter Westminster Abbey for her husband's (and her own) coronation were ultimately unsuccessful and she died the following month.

In spite of the marital tumult, a child was conceived on the wedding night of Prince George and Caroline of Brunswick, that of Princess Charlotte, who was born January 7, 1796. Sadly, Charlotte later died in childbirth soon after her marriage to Leopold of Saxe-Coburg, in November, 1817, giving birth to a stillborn infant. (See the section on Ceramics and Pottery for photographs of a memorial sauce boat for Princess Charlotte).

Rare Georgian swivel ring memorializing the death of Queen Caroline of Brunswick, the "Injured Queen of England" and wife of George IV. The craftsmanship in this 18K gold and black enamel ring is exceptionally fine, with ornate chase-work on the sides of the swivel and Caroline's looped hair on the reverse. *Courtesy of Things Gone By.* $7,500-10,000.

Another view of the swivel ring, showing curl of Queen Caroline's hair. *Courtesy of Things Gone By.*

Few other figures in French history evoke such controversy as Napoleon Bonaparte, in a country rich with brilliant and colorful individuals, particularly those arising during two very tumultuous centuries. Like a phoenix rising from the ashes of the French Revolution, Napoleon I, born not in France, but in Corsica, rose to power with a ruthless immediacy evidenced in his style as a military leader. Napoleon so dominated his times that much of European history of the early 1800s is simply referred to as the Napoleonic Era, as all the borders of the countries he invaded were permanently altered in less than a decade. To those who admired him, Napoleon brought unification and solidarity as well as administrative and legal reforms to France at a time when she was still reeling from the upheavals and chaos of the Revolution. To the British, Russians, and other European powers, Napoleon was a despotic threat to an already unstable Continent, and the avaricious "Eagle" was setting his sights for England and other choice conquests. Bonaparte's famous defeat at Waterloo by a combined force of Russians, Germans, English and other allies in 1815 signaled his end. When his empire collapsed, he was exiled to the island of Elba off Corsica, the country of his birth. Although he later escaped and attempted to reestablish his power back in France, this too failed, and he was exiled again, this time to St. Helena, where he died in 1821.

Nevertheless, there were many in France who were loyal to Bonaparte and his vision of a French empire, if not to be ruled by him as Emperor, then through his son by Marie Louise, Napoleon II, known as "l'aiglon," or "the Eaglet." Napoleon II never ruled, however, but was kept a prisoner in Austria after his father's exile, where he died of consumption in 1832 at the age of twenty-one. In the photograph above, we see a rare, perhaps one-of-a-kind 1821 memorial ring for Bonaparte, inscribed, "*a la memorie cherie de Napoleon Bonaparte,*" or "to the beloved memory of Napoleon Bonaparte," inside the shank. On the outside black enamel band are the words, "*on a ecrast l'aigle mais un jour l'aiglon le venoera,*" which translated means, "we have lost our eagle, but one day the eaglet will revenge." The irony of these words in light of the son's imprisonment at the time, make this ring all the more poignant for the French Bonapartist who wore it. The ring has an English hallmark, as many of Napoleon's supporters fled to England after his exile and memorial jewelry made there after his death could be commissioned and worn.

"What is the future? What is the past? What are we? What magical fluid surrounds us and hides from us those things we most need to know? We are born, we live, we die in the midst of the marvelous." [Napoleon Bonaparte, in a letter to Josephine]

Rare French memorial ring commemorating the death of Napoleon Bonaparte I, Emperor of France. English hallmarks of 18K gold, black enamel with interior inscription, "a la memorie cherie de Napoleon Bonaparte," or "to the beloved memory of Napoleon Bonaparte." In black enamel on outside, inscription reads "on a ecrast l'aigle mais un jour l'aiglon le venoera," or "we have lost our eagle, but one day the eaglet will revenge." *Courtesy of Things Gone By.* $4,500.

A small hair-work on ivory brooch with cipher, commemorating the death of a mother. This English 9K gold brooch is inscribed "In memy of deced mother Jane Wife of Heny Mathews Ob 17 March 1811 at 40" [sic]. On the reverse, an additional inscription reads, "Presented by my Luvng Parents as a Tribute of Regard." *Courtesy of Things Gone By.* $575.

*"Could we but climb where Moses stood,
And view the landscape o'er,
Not Jordan's stream, nor Death's cold flood,
Should fright us from the shore."*
[Isaac Watts, 1674-1748, from *A Prospect of Heaven*]

A beautiful German or Austrian pendant, possibly memorializing the sentiments expressed in the famed hymn writer Isaac Watts' poem. This 14K gold double-sided piece has an unusual depiction of Moses viewing the "Promised Land," executed in sepia against a dissolved hair background on one side, with a tomb and willow done in the same process on the reverse. The portrayal of Moses in a memorial context is rare, especially in view of the fact that Moses was denied entrance into the "Promised Land" by God for his angry breaking of the tablets upon which the Ten Commandments were inscribed. Moses was only permitted to *view* the "Promised Land" from afar, as the "Children of Israel" entered it. Perhaps the intent of the wearer was to represent the spiritual view of heaven seen from afar by faith, but only entered into upon death, as was the case with Moses. c. 1790-1810. 1.25" in diameter. *Courtesy of Things Gone By.* $995.

Reverse of pendant, showing weeping willow executed in dissolved hairwork and inscription in sepia on the tomb, "Unverg Mich," which means "Remember me," or "Don't forget me." *Courtesy of Things Gone By.*

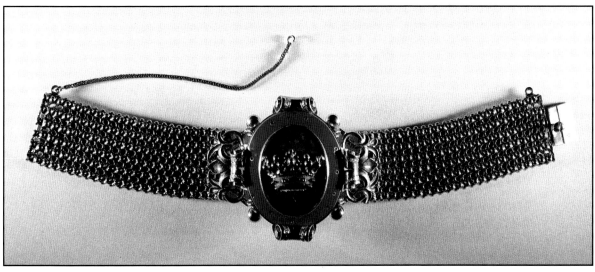

An ornate 18K gold bracelet with links of gold beadwork and a beautiful blue enameled central crown overlaying woven hair under a crystal bezel. This exceptional bracelet shows its true ancestry as having belonged to a member of the aristocracy by its craftsmanship and design as well as by the extensive blue enamelwork. *Courtesy of Things Gone By.* $2,500.

All the grief of a widow is visibly summed up in one plaintive question: "What Will You Do?" on this memorial pendant. The rhetorical question goes to the heart of the matter, addressing the isolation, financial insecurity, and fears of widowhood, often very real for women in previous centuries, where property was held exclusively by men and passed to male children, often leaving widows financially bereft. This enamel pendant is in the shape of a watch, a common symbol for death dating back to the Middle Ages, and the central initials of "FW" under a crystal bezel are no doubt those of her husband. The reverse has a deeply convex bezel over the obituary information, "BORN 12 June 1784 DIED 17 July 1830." 2" x 1.25". *Courtesy of Things Gone By.* $950.

"In Memory of a Beloved Child" – the words speak volumes. This beautiful 18K gold English memorial ring is inscribed with the immortal words around the shank in black enamel, a crystal bezel enclosing a tiny plait of red hair. Inside the shank is inscribed, "Thos. Cooper Hawkins Ob 3 Jan 1825 At 3 Yrs." The ring is enclosed in its original red leather box. *Courtesy of Things Gone By.* $975.

An outstanding Georgian memorial ring, with a rose-cut crystal bezel enclosing a skull, surrounded by cut garnets. The band has decorative scrollwork in black enamel set into 18K gold, which reads, "R. Andrews Ob 28 Dec 1764 Ae 83." This anachronistic ring contains the *memento mori* motifs more typical of the Stuart era of the 1600s, and somewhat out of fashion by its 1783 date when Enlightenment philosophies had softened death iconography. *Collection of Charlotte Sayers.* $2,895.

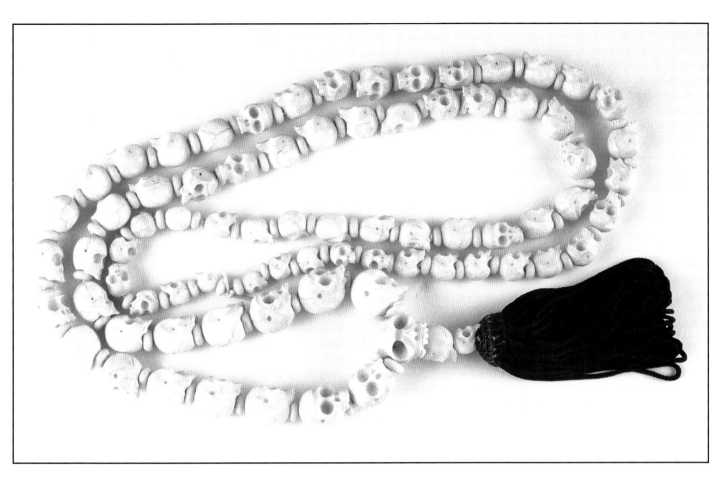

An extraordinary ivory or bone skull necklace, c. 1810, with all the design elements of the medieval ossuary in its graduated skulls, each carved accurately down to the cranium plates. The skulls are strung on silk cord, separated by tiny bone or ivory beads, and finished with a black silk cord fringe. Although its purpose is unclear, it appears to be monastic or clerical in origin rather than a item for personal adornment. 20" long. *Courtesy of Things Gone By.* $850.

Mourning jewelry in silver is somewhat rare; most pieces were made of various grades of gold from 9K to 18K, as well as in gold-filled, plated, and rolled gold. The brooch shown here is even more unusual in that it is a sepia executed work on ivory of an urn with the initials "R.B." and the date, "21-10-22," or October 21, 1822. The frame is in a process of silver called "niello," which is a technique of design work in which an artist carved a design into the piece of sterling, then carefully filled in the cut portions with black metal, in a type of metallic marquetry. Niello was an ancient technique revived in the 19th century by a German jeweler working in Paris, and the effects created by this method are quite striking. 1.25" x 1". *Courtesy of Things Gone By.* $295.

Victorian Mourning Jewelry

When Victoria Alexandrina became Queen in 1837, her ascension to the throne coincided with a transition into an era of more outward displays of despondency. Changes in fashion from the high-waisted gauzy muslin clothing of the French Regency period evolved into the corseted and heavier clothing of the 19th century. The heavy black lusterless "chrysalis of gloom" fabrics came into vogue for Victorians, along with mourning jewelry of larger designs to accommodate the alterations.

When Queen Victoria lost her beloved Albert, she wore only jet jewelry for the first few years of her bereavement, which reflected the deepest grief appropriate to her yards of crape mourning attire. Her choice of jet was also a gesture of support for the English Whitby jet industry, suffering from loss of sales due to competition from imitation jet manufacturers in France and America. Jet, and its imitations, became the perfect jewelry accompaniment to the heavy mourning fabrics and crape industry, which exploded in popularity in 1861, due to the deaths of the Queen's mother in March, and the Prince Consort in December. The widowhood of the Queen set an example for American mourning customs, occurring as it did coincident with the casualties of the American Civil War. Americans had always followed English mourning practices, and the increasing prosperity from industrialization and commerce occurring between the two countries enabled large quantities of English Whitby jet to be exported to America during the height of its popularity in the American Civil War years.

In addition to jet and its imitations, other materials such as bog oak, tortoiseshell, horn, ivory, and iron-work were fashioned into mourning jewelry. Even though some mourning jewelry was being produced in 18th century America, the perception was that the best memorial pieces were those created and imported from England and Europe. Thus, Whitby jet from England, mosaics from Rome and Florence, lava items from Italy, and shell cameos from Greece were imported and worn by middle and upper class Victorian Americans in all the stages of mourning.

Many years later, when the Queen was forced to emerge from her self-imposed seclusion and re-open Parliament, she modified her mourning jewelry (but not her mourning dress), by wearing brooches, bracelets, pendants and earrings with turquoise, coral, amethyst, and other gemstones. These in turn became popular in England and elsewhere as mourning jewelry for third-stage or "light mourning" attire.

Hair-work devices in Victorian mourning jewelry changed from the delicate mourning scenes of the Georgian era to hair plumes, plaited hair, and cutwork hair designs. Mourning scenes of hair-work disappear in Victorian mourning jewelry altogether as the larger and heavier frames were not conducive to the delicate hues and designs of the 18th century. Earrings became much longer to accommodate the higher necklines, heavier fabrics, and hairstyles during the mid-century, and the materials of jet, vulcanite, bog oak, and gutta percha lent themselves much better to these longer styles than the tiny drops of 18th century fashions. Necklaces too became bolder for the same reason, and many vulcanite and gutta percha pieces with large heavy-appearing (although surprisingly lightweight) "links" were popular in the mid-Victorian period, especially in Civil War America.

By the 1860s, photographs of the deceased became available in small enough formats to be used in jewelry, and these supplanted the painted portrait miniature for many less wealthy bereaved. These miniature photographs were usually daguerreotypes, but later photographic jewelry included ambrotypes, tintypes, and paper images. Photographic portraits could be mounted in brooches, lockets, and bracelets, with crystal bezels, with or without separate compartments on the reverse containing plaited hair. Many brooches were made to swivel, allowing the wearer to show the portrait on one side and the woven hair on the reverse, depending on dress and mood. Some photographic pendants were worn with a narrow black velvet ribbon, especially during the American Civil War era. Also by mid-century, large brooches with black enamel and the words "In Memory Of"

were ubiquitous, and good examples are available today for moderate prices, depending on condition.

Victorian bracelets were usually cuff in style, clasping close to the wrist, and here again, jet, gutta percha, vulcanite, and gold cuffs replaced the delicate pearl bracelets of the 18th century in popularity, as they were more fitting to the heavy fabrics and sleeve styling. In the following pieces we can see the changes in mourning jewelry of the Victorian era.

A palette-worked "tree" on milk glass ground commemorates the death of "Francis S. Crichton," whose birth and death dates, inscribed as "Born 18th May, 1840; Died 7th March, 1861," appear underneath the beautifully executed hair-work tree. The workmanship on the inscription is similar to the fine engraving of a watchmaker, and it is possible that this piece was inscribed or worn by someone in this profession. The gold-filled brooch swivels, and the reverse shows a tintype or ambrotype of Francis in his well-dressed suit. *Courtesy of Judy Jay's Time Dances By.* $1,100.

Reverse of English swivel brooch showing photograph of the deceased Francis S. Crichton. *Courtesy of Judy Jay's Time Dances By.*

A beautiful English "IMO," or "In Memory Of" brooch, c. 1830-50, with black enamel surrounding black onyx set in 15K gold; reverses to display Prince of Wales curls tied with gold thread and seed pearls, set under a crystal bezel. *Courtesy of Things Gone By.* $895.

Reverse of English "IMO" brooch showing Prince of Wales curls. *Courtesy of Things Gone By.*

An outstanding mid-19th century Masonic memorial pendant is shown on the next page, and the detail of symbolism and workmanship is truly exceptional. The "All-seeing Eye" represents God; the globe represents the world and the universe; and the instruments of Masonry are seen in the trowel, ruler, plumb line, compass, gavel, and square. Deeper symbolism is seen in the archways, symbolic of the canopy of heaven in which reside the seven stars and crescent moon. The archways of mother-of-pearl are made up of two columns, the first denoted as the "Boaz column," meaning strength, and the second column denoted as the "Joachim column," meaning "to establish." The meaning here is taken from God's promise to King David: "In strength will I establish you." The numbers 3 and 7 have significant meaning in Masonry as seen in the three steps before the archway, the three candlesticks, etc., and refer to the "three lesser lights" of Masonry: the Bible, the square, and the compass. The number 3 also refers to the three architects of the Great Temple in Jerusalem, and the number 7 symbolizes the arts and sciences. The coffin with skull has memorial symbolism, as well as deeper significance in some Scottish Rites and other branches of Masonry.

The art of cameo-carving can be traced back to ancient times, with the earliest Egyptian examples showing carved beetles or scarabs. During the Renaissance period, with the renewal of interest in classical themes, cameo carving reflected the designs of Neo-classicism in the form of the gods and figures of Greek and Roman mythology. During the Georgian period, it was fashionable for a wealthy woman to wear a cameo on the belt fastening her high-waisted dress, along with a necklace, two bracelets, a diadem, and a decorative jeweled band around her forehead, all with matching cameos.

By the Victorian era, with the new love of the "Romantic-Gothic" style in art and literature, famous people such as Napoleon, Lord Byron, and well-known Court and Romantic figures, male and female, combined with allegorized and feminized classical images dominated the themes in cameo carving. Of all the materials employed in creating cameos, hardstones (such as agates and sardonyx) were the most highly prized, reaching their zenith in popularity in the 1850-60s. Given their variously-hued layers, the craftsman's skill lay in carving away the design in relief to reveal the bands of color as they stood out from the dark ground. Hardstone cameos could also be colored through the use of stains. Shell was the most common material used in creating cameos, as it was most successful in imitating hardstones; the layers produced the same effect of coloring in relief as was achieved in carving agates, albeit with less dramatic effect. The best shell cameos were made in France, possibly by Italian craftsmen, during the 1860s, and along with hardstone and shell, other unusual materials for cameos were used, such as tortoiseshell, lava, and jet.[17]

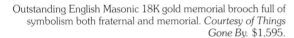

Outstanding English Masonic 18K gold memorial brooch full of symbolism both fraternal and memorial. *Courtesy of Things Gone By.* $1,595.

The outstanding 15K gold mourning cameo shown here commemorates the loss of two children, as an angel carries them heavenward in her arms. This c. 1850-70 brooch is allegorical to a design by Danish sculptor Bertel Thorvald, entitled "Night," whose companion piece, "Day," depicts an angel with an infant on her back carrying a torch, probably symbolizing Resurrection Morn. Note the owl, also symbolic of night. The darkness of "night" has routinely been a poetic metaphor for death and melancholia, particularly among the Romantic poets of the 18th and 19th centuries.

An extraordinary 18K gold cameo with unusual symbolism is seen in the horizontal Victorian cameo shown next. This beautiful brooch shows an angel reading the "Book of Life," or a record of the deeds of the deceased, whose mausoleum is visible on the left. Next to the angel is a lion that dominates the scene as much as or more than the angel. The lion guarding the tomb of the dead against evil, or evil spirits, is an ancient symbol and an unusual one in this context.

Extraordinary 15K gold cameo of angel taking two children to heaven, while an owl, symbolic of "night" (or death) flies in the background. *Courtesy of Judy Jay's Time Dances By.* $1,195.

Outstanding cameo of angel reading "Book of Life" at the tomb of the deceased, with a lion guarding the tomb from evil. 2" x 1.25". *Courtesy of Things Gone By.* $1,195.

A truly exceptional Italian hardstone cameo of a weeping martyr in an 18K gold frame is shown above. "Hard stone" was actually banded agate, by which the various layers in the colored stone were enhanced into the *bas relief* design when the cameo was carved. This banded agate cameo was created by a tremendously skilled Italian carver, who enhanced the overall dramatic effect of the suffering martyr by revealing the vivid purplish hues of the agate as seen around the neck of the woman who appears in agony. Even tears falling down her cheeks are visible – truly the cameo is a sculpture in miniature. The Italian carver signed this piece, "Coreg-Pinx-Beren, Scult.," thereby adding considerably to the value of this piece.

The iconography of the shrouded infant is a common one seen in Victorian cemeteries, having the dual symbolism of the death of a child and the birth of the infant Jesus in swaddling clothes. Shrouds date back to ancient Egypt, and were traditional burial clothing for many ancient cultures. Interest in all things classical fascinated Victorians, who extended these artistic elements into cemetery, monument, and mausoleum design, as well as other death iconography such as urns, which were often depicted with draped shrouds, or palls. The infusion of Neo-classical design elements in mourning jewelry and art reflected the exoticism of the Near East, unveiled from the excavations of the 18th and 19th centuries, and the new interest in all things classical by those recently returning from the Grand Tour.

Outstanding Italian cameo of suffering martyr in 18K gold frame, signed by the carver, early 1800s. Note the tears running down her cheeks and bruising on her throat. 2.5" x 2". *Courtesy of Things Gone By.* $3,500.

Ivory pendant of a shrouded infant, typical of iconography representative of a child's death, familiarly seen in Victorian cemeteries, c. 1860s. *Courtesy of Things Gone By.* $350.

Snakes have had a long and turbulent history as symbols in Western culture. Beginning as the incarnate Devil in the Garden of Eden tempting Eve to eat the forbidden fruit, thus bringing sin into the world, they have been synonymous for evil or sin for centuries. They did, however, experience a respite during the late 18th and 19th centuries, when they became more benign, and were even symbolically associated with marital love. The beautiful hair-work snake bracelet shown here, c. 1850-70, is a fine example of almost mint-condition table-worked hair over elastic, the snake's gold-filled tail and head forming the fittings for the ends. The head of the snake has lovely chase-work engraving as well as garnet cabochons for eyes and head decoration, and his open mouth has individually pointed teeth.

A very rare memorial "snake ring" for a child is shown in the following two photographs. The snake as a design element is most typically seen swallowing its tail, symbolic of eternity. In Victorian times, after Prince Albert gave Queen Victoria a ring with a snake swallowing its tail, snake jewelry became fashionable for sentimental and memorial purposes, with the entwined snakes coming to represent marital love. As snakes also mate in this manner, the symbolism of intimacy in marriage was doubly illustrated. For a memorial ring of a child to have entwined snakes is quite unusual. Perhaps the intention was to represent the child as the gift of their bond or union of marital love. In any event, the combination of entwined snakes with a child's death would have been unusual for its day, but nevertheless quite acceptable, something that might be unsettling for current tastes. In this piece, the bezel holds plaited brown hair, and is surrounded by seed pearls. Behind the bezel, the inscription reads, "Sophia Smith, Ob 3 April 1827, at 5 Years."

In the late Victorian era, a small revival in the macabre skull and crossbones of the medieval *ars moriendi* made its appearance in mourning jewelry and art, particularly as seen in paintings by the Pre-Rafaelites. Mourning jewelry for men in the form of skull watch fobs, cane heads, snuff boxes, stick pins, etc., began using some of the winged death's heads and skull and crossbones motifs and symbols that had not been visible

for two centuries in death art. Somewhat of a contradiction in the Victorian idealization of the *Beautiful Death*, items with these symbols were often favored by those with secular beliefs.

Beautiful woven hair-work snake bracelet with gold-filled head and tail, and cabochon garnet eyes with serrated teeth, c. mid-19th century. *Courtesy of Things Gone By.* $595.

An extraordinary "snake" ring in memory of a five-year-old child, with plaited brown hair surrounded by pearls. Entwined snakes are more commonly seen in rings commemorating marriages than in memorials for children, making this unusual ring not only beautiful but rare. *Courtesy of Things Gone By.* $895.

Underside of bezel on snake ring, showing inscription of "Sophia Smith, Ob 3 April 1827, at 5 Years." *Courtesy of Things Gone By.*

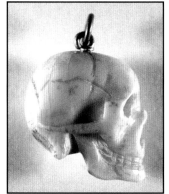

A side view of the skull fob, showing the detailing of the cranial plates. *Courtesy of Things Gone By.*

An anachronistic skull fob for a man's watchchain, c. 1880s. The representation of the skull hearkens back to the skull and crossbones of *memento mori* of the Middle Ages. In this example, the detailing of the skull is quite accurate, even to the cranial plates. *Courtesy of Things Gone By.* $295.

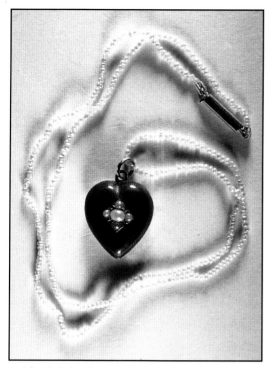

A rare "witch's heart" ring in its original box is distinguished by its curved pointed end. This peculiar shape occurs in Scottish jewelry, and is represented with the heart curving towards the left side. It is found on the crowned "Luckenbooth" brooches and on jewelry associated with Mary Queen of Scots, and probably derives from ancient Celtic designs. This 9K gold English ring contains plaited hair, and is surrounded by pearls, symbolic of tears. *Courtesy of Things Gone By.* $795.

A lovely little red glass heart necklace with tiny seed pearls is an unusually light-hearted digression from the dark, heavy mourning jewelry typical of the mid-century era during which it was made. Perhaps because this piece memorializes the loss of a young person (probably that of a young woman), the red heart symbolic of passion and the white seed pearls symbolic of purity and innocence, the two together seem to represent the loss of youthful promise. The heart encloses a curl of hair on the reverse, and along the edge are inscribed the words, "Ob 21 Nov 1854 at 21." Tiny seed pearls such as these were usually imported from China or Madras and threaded on white horsehair, creating an effect which is quite romantic for a memorial piece. Seed pearl jewelry of this quality, craftsmanship, and condition is very difficult to find. *Courtesy of Things Gone By.* $1,495.

A lovely example of a mid-19th century gold-filled "IMO" ("In Memory Of") pendant locket in black enameling, which could be purchased by mourners and incorporated with the hair or photograph of the deceased. Lockets such as this and others shown here have the typical death symbolism on the outside (such as the urn and garland shown here), and usually contain hair-work or photographs when opened. *Courtesy of Judy Jay's Time Dances By.* $395.

"In Memory Of" locket open, showing photographs of deceased elderly couple inside. *Courtesy of Judy Jay's Time Dances By.*

Another example of an "IMO" or "In Memory Of" gold-filled locket of the mid-19th century, showing black and white enameled floral cross. *Courtesy of Judy Jay's Time Dances By.* $395.

"In Memory Of" locket shown open, with palette-worked plaited hair and Prince of Wales curls inside. *Courtesy of Judy Jay's Time Dances By.*

A beautifully executed pendant made to resemble a "watch," a death symbol dating back to the Middle Ages in Western culture, denoting the brevity of life. The watch is made of double-sided celluloid, one of the newly patented materials invented in the industrial age of the mid-century, and each side encloses elaborate varieties of palette-work hair with sepia designs. *Courtesy of Judy Jay's Time Dances By.* $1,100.

Reverse of pendant "watch," showing palette-worked hair in plumes and cut-work with sepia initials of deceased. *Courtesy of Judy Jay's Time Dances By.*

Lovely black and white "hard stone" cameo brooch with the urn and the willow surrounded by matched gray pearls set in 18K gold. .50" x .75". *Author's collection.* $475.

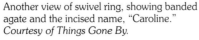

A beautifully engraved 18K gold English swivel ring, possibly commemorating two deaths, with exceptionally fine quality and workmanship. Inside the shank are inscribed the words, "Anna Maria Ob Aug. 20, 1838 at 6 months," yet on one side of the swivel is banded agate, a favorite Scottish stone for mourning and sentimental jewelry, engraved with the name "Caroline." The name is carved into the stone in reverse and can only be read by viewing it in a mirror; possibly the ring was used as a seal. Scottish banded agate was a popular gemstone during the Victorian era, not only because of Queen Victoria's love for Scotland and Scottish gems, but because the castles and crags of the rural rustic countryside as romanticized in literature of this era appealed to Victorian tastes. *Courtesy of Things Gone By.* $1,295.

Another view of swivel ring, showing banded agate and the incised name, "Caroline." *Courtesy of Things Gone By.*

Rare man's watch fob in the shape of an urn. This tiny French 18K gold fob probably contains the plaited blonde hair of the man's wife, and is dated "29 March 1853." 1.25" x .5".*Courtesy of Things Gone By.* $495-595.

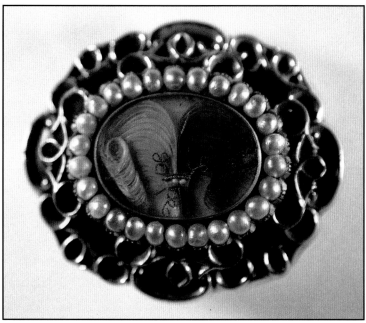

Beautiful gold man's watch fob and lavender glass seal with snake swallowing its tail inscribed "United In Eternity," early 1800s. 1" x .75". *Collection of Laura Bingman Swenson.* $895.

A husband and wife are memorialized in this 14K gold brooch. Two palette-worked hair "plumes" or "Prince of Wales" curls are joined together with seed pearls, and the back of the brooch is inscribed, "Mrs. Mary Acres, Died March 11, 1860, aged 67" and "Mr. Randal Acres, died March 23, 1861 aged 84." Mourning jewelry commemorating more than one death is unusual, particularly in the case of husbands and wives together, and adds to the value of a piece. Hair-work of different colors, as seen here, is also desirable. 2" x 1.5". *Courtesy of Judy Jay's Time Dances By.* $1,100.

Rare 9K gold English memorial studs for man's mourning outfit, c. 1860s. These beautiful studs have two matching gold and black enamel scenes of weeping willow and urn, with one central stud which says "In Memory Of." *Courtesy of Things Gone By.* $595.

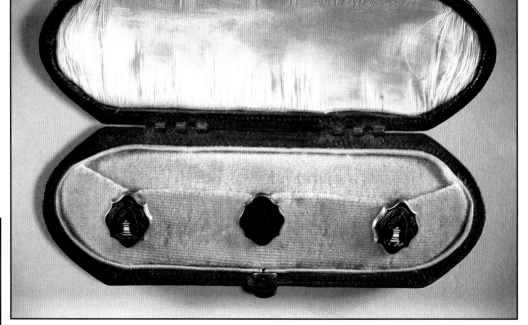

Diminutive 15K gold urn fob with crystal bezel for woven hair, surrounded by garnets, .50" long. *Courtesy of Things Gone By.* $395.

A fine English 15K gold pendant with two Prince of Wales curls tied with gold wire adornment, in memory of a father and daughter. The touching inscription around the edge of the pendant reads, "Mary Hannah Wedge died May 13, 1854 aged 6 years; Earl Wedge died May 1, 1856, aged 32 years." *Courtesy of Things Gone By.* $395-425.

A exceptionally fine English *demi-parure* in 18K gold consisting of mourning brooch and earrings with black enameling and seed pearls, c. 1860-70s. Brooch: 2.75" x 1.5"; earrings, 2" long. *Courtesy of Things Gone By.* $1,295-1,595.

A truly exceptional c. 1870-90 French *demi-parure* in 18K gold, consisting of hair-work bracelet, brooch, and earrings in its original box. The blonde palette-worked hair has been done in the cut-work method, in which the hair is spread over glue-covered paper, then cut out into the shapes of flower petals, leaves, ribbons, etc. and arranged in lovely nosegays of Forget-Me-Nots and other flowers, all in identical motifs. It is very difficult to find matched sets in this outstanding condition and quality, which is near mint. Brooch: 2.75" x 1.5"; earrings, 2" long. *Courtesy of Things Gone By.* $3,700.

Another view of this exceptional French *demi-parure,* showing bracelet with outstanding 18K gold craftsmanship. *Courtesy of Things Gone By.c*

Close-up view of brooch in French *demi-parure* set. *Courtesy of Things Gone By.*

Some of the most popular mourning jewelry today is the type of hair-work piece seen here. This fine quality "rose" brooch, c. 1850-70, is done in two varieties of woven "table-worked" hair and has a small gold center finding. 1.5" in diameter. *Courtesy of Things Gone By.* $225.

Beautiful lady's hair-work watch chain, with rose-gold slide and findings, c. 1860s. *Courtesy of Things Gone By.* $325.

Beautiful, almost mint condition hair-work mourning necklace with cross, gold-filled findings, c. 1810. Hair-work necklaces in this condition are difficult to find, and can easily fetch the $895 value of this exceptional piece. *Author's collection.*

Lovely little c. 1860s hair-work padlock with plaited light brown hair. Padlocks were a favorite sentimental jewelry piece between friends, lovers, and husbands, and easily accommodated a mourning theme when appropriate. *Courtesy of Things Gone By.* $525.

These c. 1850-70 hair-work earrings in the acorn motif, symbolic of power or victory (sometimes in relationship to military funerals), are beautifully executed in the table-worked method over wooden molds (which would be removed after weaving was completed). These lovely earrings were made to have the smaller acorn hang in front of the larger acorn, an unusual arrangement and quite dramatic when worn. 2.5" long. *Courtesy of Things Gone By.* $695.

An 18K gold French pendant commemorating two deaths, which sadly records the inscriptions as "15 Mar 1888" and "29 Jan 1888." A faceted bezel over plaited reddish brown hair is on one side, with woven dark brown hair on the reverse; the pendant opens to reveal the hair on the inside. .75" in diameter. *Courtesy of Things Gone By.* $245-295.

Another view of the pendant at left, showing the locket in the open position with plaited hair of deceased family members on each side. *Courtesy of Things Gone By.*

English 9K gold ring with tiny "book" open to reveal the diminutive photograph of the deceased young woman inside. *Courtesy of Things Gone By.*

An unusual and rare c. 1870s English 9K gold memorial ring with woven hair around the shank. The tiny "book" opens to reveal a diminutive photograph of a young woman inside the crystal bezel (approximately 1/4 inch square). The sadness of the ring is accentuated by the charm of its design, the opening of the little book like the opening a precious reliquary. And, perhaps the intention of the original owner was to convey just such a feeling in the loss of this young woman. *Courtesy of Things Gone By.* $795.

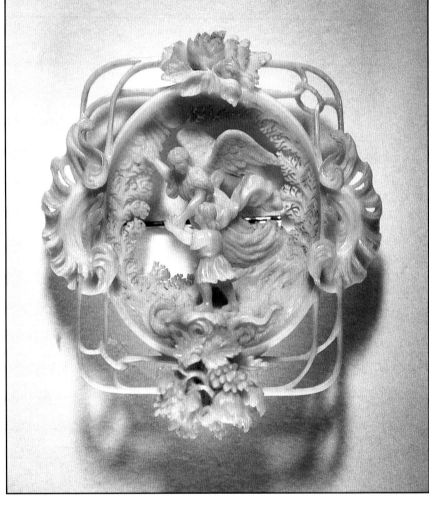

A rare and outstanding ivory brooch commemorating the loss of a child. This ornately carved mourning piece depicts an angel escorting a little boy towards heaven, and no doubt this touching piece brought comfort to his distraught mother. The deeply carved and incised work also includes floral and scroll-work around the perimeter in stylized shell motifs with interior "seaweed" designs, plus a grape cluster and leaves at the bottom. 2" x 1.75". *Collection of Sarah Bolyard.* $1,100.

French onyx and 14K gold brooch, c. 1870s, memorializing three children's deaths. This sad little piece contains the hair and the memories of three little boys, all the mother had left as a token of remembrance. Each of the little hearts encloses tiny blonde plaited hair, and the name of each little boy is inscribed on the reverse: "Henri," "Chas," and "Paul." 1.5" long. *Author's collection.* $595.

Beautiful English memorial ring, c. 1870s, with hair-work under the crystal bezel, overlaid with initials executed in diminutively graduated seed pearls; open sides with gold scrollwork. *Courtesy of Things Gone By.* $895.

Few sentiments are as visually emotional as clasped hands, which convey love and abiding friendship. Also known as "claddagh" or "fede" (from the Italian *mani in fede*, or "hands in trust"), they are often seen in Victorian sentimental and memorial art forms. In this mourning ring in memory of a mother, the clasped hands form the top of the ring, which has open areas along the shank for plaited brown hair. The solid sections in between the open areas spell out the word, "MOTHER" in black enameling. *Courtesy of Things Gone By.* $495.

The American Civil War propelled the popularity of mourning jewelry for American women, much as Queen Victoria's mourning practices set the example for English women. This 14K gold American mourning brooch is in memory of a man lost in the War Between the States; his photograph is on the front, his woven hair under the bezel beneath the pin. *Author's collection.* $350.

Rare "Halley's Comet" brooch, with hair-work under tiny crystal bezel and the words, "In Memory Of" around the black enameling, c. 1870s. 1.5" long. *Courtesy of Things Gone By.* $295.

A mid-19th century 15K gold ring with two black enameled hearts probably memorializes the death of a husband. One heart is inscribed with a cipher, "D" over "A"; the other heart is set with a seed pearl, symbolic of tears, and on each side of the hearts are open areas around the shank of the ring where woven hair is visible. *Courtesy of Things Gone By.* $695.

A poignant mourning swivel pinchbeck brooch in memory of a little boy. This sad memento holds a tintype of the child on one side and a lock of red hair tied with thread on the reverse, overlaying a piece of the mother's mourning crape. The brooch speaks volumes of the mother's grief in losing her son. 1.5" x 1.25". *Author's collection.* $550.

Reverse of mourning brooch in memory of the little boy, showing the curl of his hair laid over his mother's mourning crape. *Author's collection.*

A beautiful 18K gold French mourning lavaliere in its original box, enameled in black and set with pearls and a diamond chip, c. 1800 1840. 3.25" from top of lavaliere to bottom of cross. *Author's collection.* $525.

A crudely made ivory memorial ring in memory of King Edward VII, who died in 1911. This unusual ring, probably one of a kind, was carved out of the tip of a tusk of ivory, and no doubt was made in India during the Colonial period when India was the "Jewel in the Crown" of the British Empire. *Author's collection.* $250.

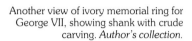

Another view of ivory memorial ring for George VII, showing shank with crude carving. *Author's collection.*

Man's watch fob with a skull and crossbones, 15K gold, English. 1" in diameter. *Author's collection.* $325.

Reverse of man's fob pendant, recording the death of "P. H. Webb 1877," and the initials "F. B. C.," possibly indicating two deaths, or an affiliation or association of Webb. *Author's collection.*

Another view of the man's memorial watch fob, showing lovebirds tying the knot on the two branches of the severed weeping willow executed in sepia and dissolved hair-work. *Courtesy of Things Gone By.*

An extraordinary example of a husband's memorial watch fob in memory of his wife. This fob is actually in the form of a "watch," and is full of memorial symbolism. In the scene we see a severed weeping willow tree trunk with two branches growing from it, symbolizing that although the marital union has been broken in death, it still grows and lives eternally. This is literally true of the willow itself, which will grow from severed branches. Two birds overhead form a lover's knot with a ribbon, also signifying marital union and love. The inscription reads, "The further away the closer together," typifying the romantic belief in love existing after death in the "life to come." The fob swivels by pressing the knob at the top, and reverses to show the plaited hair of the man's wife. 2.5" x 1". *Courtesy of Things Gone By.* $1,595-1,795.

A third view of the man's memorial watch fob, showing plaited hair of his deceased wife. *Courtesy of Things Gone By.*

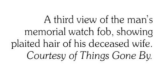

Elaborate 14K gold hair-work brooch with individual Prince of Wales curls of hair from various family members, c. 1870s. 2" x 2.25". *Author's collection.* $595.

Outstanding mourning brooch with enameling in black and white (probably in memory of a child); willow and urn with tiny crystal bezel enclosing plaited hair; approximately 1" square, c. 1860s. *Courtesy of Things Gone By.* $1,295.

Two fine examples of small mourning brooches, one with faceted jet and the other with black enameling and the words, "Sacred to the Memory of a Departed Friend," both enclosing plaited hair-work, c. 1850-60s. .50" x .75". *Courtesy of Things Gone By.* $295-325 each.

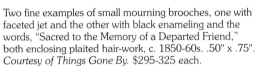

Lovely 15K gold memorial brooch with black enamel and cut-work flowers, Prince of Wales curl set against opaline glass, c. 1860s. *Author's collection.* $695.

An extremely rare and one-of-a-kind hair-work brooch on ivory of a man wearing a top hat, possibly Abraham Lincoln on a sidewheeler during the Civil War. The piece was undoubtedly made by a Union sympathizer, possibly a woman whose husband, brother, or father's hair was employed in creating this scene of patriotic zeal for the Union cause. The man holds a rifle at the ready, and the figures inside the sidewheeler are possibly Union troops. 2" x 1". *Collection of Charles Swedlund.* $2,500.

Beautiful example of a c. 1860s mourning brooch with black enameling and plaited dark blonde hair-work. 1.5" x 1.25". *Courtesy of Things Gone By.* $695.

Lovely c. 1870s sterling silver mourning brooch with gray and brown plaited hair under silver cipher initials. The combination of the silver with the mottled gray hair is quite striking in this brooch. 1.5" x 1.25". *Courtesy of Things Gone By.* $395.

Lovely 9K gold hair-work brooch for "third stage" mourning wear, surrounded by red coral beads. Coral as a mourning gemstone was popularized by Queen Victoria, c. 1860s. .75" x .50". *Courtesy of Things Gone By.* $395.

Hair-work bracelet, executed in table-worked brown hair, with gold-filled clasp containing tightly woven hair; inscribed on reverse, "T. W. Dyer," c. 1860-70s. *Author's collection.* $325.

Three examples of "IMO" (In Memory Of) heart lockets with black enameling and enclosed hair under crystal bezels, c. 1870-80s .50". *Courtesy of Things Gone By.* $295-325 each.

"In Memory Of " heart lockets shown open, with locks and woven hair. *Courtesy of Things Gone By.*

A poignant "strap and buckle" ring inscribed, "Anne Craddock Died Christmas Eve 1875." Strap and buckle rings became popular in the mid-19th century due to Queen Victoria's role as head of the Order of the Garter, and are also commonly seen in Scottish jewelry, where the emblem of a clan would be surrounded by the buckle and strap design. The Order of the Garter was founded in 1348 by King Edward III (1327-77), dedicatory to the King's favorite patron saint, St. George. This exceptionally fine 10K English "buckle ring" has woven hair-work around the shank on each side of the black enameled "buckle." *Courtesy of Things Gone By.* $295.

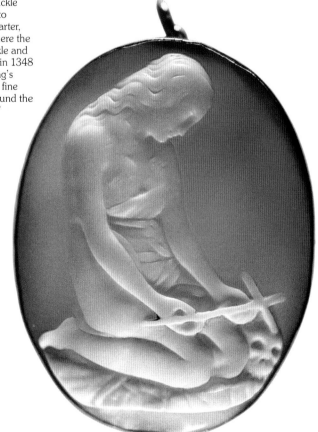

Mourners holding crosses and gazing upon them were popular themes in coffin plates, lithographs, and jewelry designs, including cameos of the mid-19th century. The design hearkens back to the old hymn, "Simply to Thy Cross I Cling," popular during that era. 2" x 1.5". *Courtesy of Things Gone By.* $350.

Lovely "IMO" (In Memory Of) English 18K gold ring, c. 1870s. *Courtesy of Things Gone By.* $595.

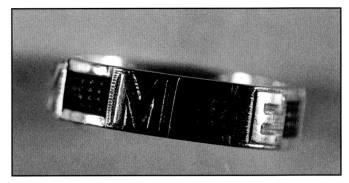

"Leaves have their time to fall,
And flowers to wither at the north-wind's breath,
And stars to set – but all,
Thou hast all seasons for thine own, O' Death!"
[Felicia Hemans, 1793-1835]

Beautiful hair-work 18K gold mourning ring, with open areas of woven hair between letters spelling "M-E-M-O-R-Y," c. 1870s. *Courtesy of Things Gone By.* $795.

Jet as a material with memorial symbolism, and one having the power to ward off evil, dates back to the 7th century where it was first mentioned by the English historian and theologian Venerable Bede. However, even prior to Bede's comments, jet had been valued as a talisman for over four thousand years. Some of the earliest jet jewelry in the form of amulets shaped as animals have been found in Germany, and date to about 10,000 B.C. The ancient Greeks and Romans called the stone *gagates*, and in the first century of the Christian era, the Roman scholar, Gaius Pliny, described the stone even then as having magical properties. In his work, *Natural History*, Pliny wrote:

> *"Gagates is a stone, so called from Gages, the name of a town and river in Lycia. The fumes of it, burnt, keep serpents at a distance and dispel hysterical affections: they detect a tendency also to epilepsy and act as a test of virginity. A decoction of this stone in wine is curative of toothache; and in combination with wax it is good for scrofula."*

Jet is a variety of coal, fossilized from the wood of ancient trees similar to the present-day Monkey Puzzle tree. As these ancient trees died and became waterlogged, they sank and broke apart, and the pressure of accumulating debris over eons altered the wood composition into stone.

Jet is found all over the world, but not all jet is suitable for jewelry, much of

it being too soft to hold carved designs without crumbling. Pure hardened jet, is intensely black, and the expression "as black as jet" has been part of our vocabulary since the 12th century.

The best jet yet discovered is from seams of stone in the cliffs around Whitby, England. The invading Romans in the first century A.D. were very impressed by the quality of the jet stone found there, and by the third century A.D., Roman artisans were creating rings, necklaces, bracelets, pendants, and other pieces of adornment. By the 7th century, Christianity had permeated the ancient British Isles, and jet was predominantly used for ecclesiastical jewelry, such as rosaries, rings, and crosses. As religious pilgrims visited various shrines of saints around Europe, including those in Britain, local jet workers in the 9th century began creating souvenirs to be sold at the sites to those on pilgrimage. In the following centuries, jet mining and jewelry-making continued to rise in popularity, reaching its zenith in the Victorian era. The intensity of the black color made jet jewelry the perfect stone to reflect the deepest grief. An old treatise on jewels proclaimed,

> *'Jeat stone almost a gemme the Libyans find;*
> *But fruitful Britain sends a wondrous kind;*
> *'Tis black and shining, smooth and even light,*
> *'Twill draw up straws if rubbed till hot and bright."*[18]

As noted by Helen Muller in her book, *Jet Jewellry and Ornaments*, the introduction of the lathe took jet mining and jewelry making out of the realm of the primitive and into the industrialization that was occurring contemporaneously in the 18th and 19th centuries. Jet manufacture rapidly formed into a cottage industry through sales of souvenir items to visitors coming to Whitby, and with the growth of the railroad, jet items could be sold and placed into the hands of consumers miles away in London. Americans too favored jet jewelry, as evidenced from a letter written by a South Carolina mother mourning her deceased son in 1833:

> *"[A] jet pin in the form of a heart containing a lock of his precious hair, which I have so often delighted to comb and brush, is all that remains to me of my darling child. I keep it in my trunk, but it is too sacred ever to be exhibited to public gaze."*

Generally speaking, Whitby jet designs reflected the styles currently popular, so that natural, rounded fruit motifs and foliage were popular in the 1850s, geometrical and Greek key motifs in the 1860s, and the largest and heaviest design elements were pieces made during the years between 1870 and 1890. Highly prized by Victorians were the heavy chains carved of single pieces of Whitby jet with no joining seams; such pieces are expensive and difficult to find today. It was not unusual for several artisans to work on a single piece of jet jewelry, as each craftsman developed his own particular skill in carving various designs, such as cameos, floral designs, medallions, bracelets, etc. Hands holding floral wreaths and bouquets were especially desirable as mourning brooches, along with cameos set into wide bracelets formed as a strap, or separate segments threaded on elastic.[19]

Not to be outdone by the English production of jet in the mourning market, France introduced substitute materials, such as the imitation "French Jet." Although never fully able to compete equally with the Whitby jet industry, French glassmakers were nevertheless able to produce a virtually unbreakable material, whose sheen and depth of opacity allowed it to be used in thinner creations, such as glass beading for later, or second-stage mourning clothing. French jet was somewhat stigmatized by the English jet industry as being inferior in quality and a "cheap substitute." In fact, mourning jewelry made of French jet is often as equally beautiful and ornate as Whitby jet, albeit different in design elements and characteristics.

In response to French glass "jet," English manufacturers also produced a glass imitation jet, known as "Vauxhall glass," and identifying this material is fairly easy due to its slightly reddish tint when held at certain angles to the light. In America, Libbey Glass Company in Ohio also produced an imitation jet in 1893, used mainly for glass beads and small items, and Fowler Brothers of Providence, Rhode Island, made a type of abraded cut glass imitation jet advertised as "English crape." American companies also produced a material referred to as "English Crape Stone," which was essentially formed from onyx that had been abraded with acids and colored to produce a dull black surface similar to crape. Onyx mourning jewelry of "crape stone" was exported from America to England, France, and other European countries.

Vulcanite and gutta percha were produced in large quantities and aimed at a less wealthy market consumer. In the case of vulcanite, rubber was "vulcanized," or heated with sulphur to the point of hardness similar to our present-day plastics, the process being invented by Goodyear in 1846. Gutta percha is

another man-made product, manufactured by heating resins from a tree in Malaysia with petroleum by-products. Both vulcanite and gutta percha were mass-produced, and available to virtually every middle class mourning family. While originally quite black like jet, both materials tend to fade over time, especially in sunlight, into a brown or khaki color, which often helps the collector identify a piece's true material.

Some identification is in order for the collector to tell true jet from its imitators. Virtually all Whitby jet brooches have base metal clasps, hooks, and fasteners, which were produced in Birmingham, with gold and silver seldom being used. The pins on jet brooches often extend past the edge of the brooch, another point in identifying jet pieces.

In the case of vulcanite and jet, distinction between the two can be difficult, as both jet and vulcanite leave brown streaks when lightly scraped against porcelain. The only conclusive test is to heat a needle and touch it to the piece; if it is jet, it will produce a smell of burnt coal, and if it is vulcanite, a smell of burning rubber. Since this is not a recommended test for collectors or dealers, other methods need to be employed. Jet is hand-carved, and vulcanite and gutta percha are molded, therefore, a close examination of the piece with a loupe will help in making the determination. Vulcanite and gutta percha will both show mold seams, and in the case of compartments for hair in brooches, the insides of jet will be rough and unpolished; in vulcanite they will appear molded. Furthermore, because molded pieces show a greater intricacy than hand-tooling, de-

Beautiful Whitby jet pendant showing outstanding floral carving for which the Whitby jet industry was famous. 2" x 1.25". *Collection of Laura Bingman Swenson.* $325.

signs will be far more detailed in vulcanite and gutta percha than handwork was able to achieve in carving true jet. Also, vulcanite and gutta percha pieces were mass-produced in the thousands, whereas designs of jet pieces were not as frequently duplicated, and no two pieces are ever exactly alike. Whitby jet is highly polished, and the beauty of handwork is such that pieces stand out from other jet and jet substitutes in quality. French jet, being glass, is fairly easy to identify through its glass-like properties of shine, heavier weight, and coldness to the touch.

The sad loss of a son in the Civil War is seen in this Whitby jet brooch, which is carved, "In Memory of My Dear Son." As Whitby jet was exported in large quantities to American markets, families were able to purchase it either already inscribed or have inscriptions engraved by a local jeweler. In this example, it appears it came from the Whitby jet manufacturer already inscribed with this sentiment. 1.5" x .75". *Author's collection.* $275.

An exceptionally beautiful Whitby jet brooch set with an elaborate
mourning scene in both blonde and light brown hair-work on ivory, c.
1810-30. The three-dimensional arrangement incorporates an urn
and tombstone with an overhanging weeping willow. Cypress trees in
the background along with Forget-Me-Not flowers in the foreground
complete the scene in an intricacy rarely executed in jewelry settings
of this small an area. 2.5" x 2". *Courtesy of Things Gone By.* $1,495-
1,795.

Another beautiful Whitby jet brooch, c. 1850-70, is on its original
card and described as suitable for "half mourning." The brooch has
the lovely deep polished sheen and base metal clasp typical of
Whitby jet. *Courtesy of Things Gone By.* $395.

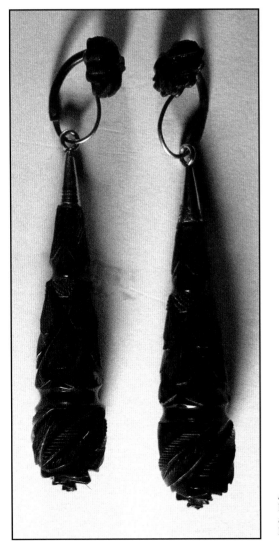

A c. 1840-80 Whitby jet and blonde hair brooch is shown here, with the hair done in
a lovely basketweave pattern, set inside beveled glass. The jet frame has an ornately
carved border of leaves and flowers. *Courtesy of Judy Jay's Time Dances By.* $1,295.

A lovely pair of Whitby jet mourning "day/night" earrings is shown
here. This style of earrings accommodates both daytime and evening
adornment by wearing the smaller "drops" for day and attaching the
longer pieces for evening. 3" long. *Courtesy of Things Gone By.* $495.

A spectacular gold and jet brooch in which large plaits of blonde hair are set into a heavy 18K gold frame surrounded by faceted jet, inscribed "The Right Honorable Lady Ann Hudson, Died 2 April 1818, Aged 43 Years." 3" x 2.5". *Courtesy of Judy Jay's Time Dances By.* $3,500.

A pair of beautiful mid-19th century French jet cameo earrings with male/female in profile, probably the mythological figures of Cupid and Psyche. They were intended to be worn facing each other, and are approximately 2" in length. *Courtesy of Things Gone By.* $295.

An unusual French jet and brass "IMO" brooch, c. 1840-60, shows a tombstone and willow incised into the jet, with the words "My Dear Father" on the tombstone itself. 1.25" x 1". *Courtesy of Things Gone By.* $125-175.

A rare c. 1860s sulphide and French jet mourning brooch is seen in this fine example. Sulphide was a ceramic paste made of potash feldspar, kaolin, flint, talc, and various minerals, with the addition of gum arabic for malleability. The combination of the materials was then pressed into a mold and, when dry, removed, finely shaped by a craftsman, and fired in a kiln. After firing, the form was dropped into a blob of molten glass. Sulphide figures were most often created for children's marbles, and it is rare to see the fine detailing in miniature of a mourning scene as executed here. 1.75" in diameter. *Author's collection.* $550.

Lovely 14K gold onyx and pearl heart locket in mint condition, c. 1860s. 1.25" x 1.25". *Collection of Laura Bingman Swenson.* $395.

Civil War era gutta percha necklace with floral pendant. This type of linked necklace was commonly worn in both England and America in the mid-1860s, and the heavy links were surprisingly lightweight in the gutta percha material. *Author's collection.* $325.

Man's vulcanite lyre mourning watchchain, c. 1860-70s. *Author's collection.* $175.

Example of a Victorian "hand" mourning brooch in gutta percha. Hands holding flowers and wreaths were common motifs both in jewelry, lithography, and cemetery iconography, and represented the popular sentiments associated with affection and love. Mourning "hand" jewelry such as this example can be found in jet, gutta percha, bone, vulcanite, and other materials, c. 1860-70s. Dimensions range from 1" to 3". *Courtesy of Things Gone By.* $225-275.

One last material, which is not a true imitation of jet but is similar in color and often used in jewelry, is "bog oak." Found primarily in Ireland, bog oak is another fossilized wood, but one which does not take a polish well. It is almost invariably rough in design and texture rather than smooth, and its dark brown color as opposed to the deep black of other materials made it generally unsuitable for mourning jewelry, although memorial pieces can be found.

Whitby jet pieces still command the highest prices in the market for jet today. They are generally the most beautiful, and desirable to collectors. However, it should be noted that imitation jet mourning jewelry is increasingly desirable and can often command prices competitive to jet, depending as always on quality, condition, and design elements.

Beautiful pair of articulated bog oak mourning earrings. 3" long. *Courtesy of Things Gone By.* $325.

Jewelry Design

In making the best decision about collecting mourning jewelry, start by examining the finest pieces possible through books, museum collections, and by talking to reputable dealers. By training the eye to visually discern the best qualities and aspects of mourning jewelry, one can better determine how a piece measures up against the finest examples. When considering a piece of mourning jewelry and assessing its condition (and therefore its value), examine the piece under a loupe if possible. Hairwork pieces should be examined for frayed ends or loose pieces, as well as how securely gemstones and materials are fastened under the bezel or within the framework and fittings. Fittings (or "findings") are metal finishing pieces such as end caps, pins, hinges, etc. The condition of the bezel should also be noted, avoiding those with chipping or clouding.

Most mourning jewelry is not hallmarked, and it was not until 1906 that the first law was passed requiring hallmarks specifying gold content to be stamped on jewelry. Because of this, it is important to purchase mourning jewelry from reputable dealers, as they can test pieces for gold content so that a correct determination of value can be made. The most common mixtures of karat gold were 10K, 14K, and 18K, with English jewelry being almost exclusively 18K before 1854; after that date, 9K, 12K, and 15K gold was manufactured. European gold standards have always been 18K but further investigation would be needed in determining whether a piece is French, English, or American in origin, if not readily obvious.

Jewelry findings could also be made of inexpensive pinchbeck, which was an alloy of copper and zinc invented by 18th century watchmaker Christopher Pinchbeck, created to simulate gold and aimed at those of more modest income. The electroplating process was developed by the English firm of Elkinton & Wright around 1840, and allowed for the production of gold-filled jewelry, in which the gold was bonded to the surface of various metals. In America, "rolled gold plate," in which layers of gold were bonded to base metal and then "rolled" into designs, was also produced as a substitute for higher grades of gold. In examining metal content, look for variations in color through magnification, to see if the gold fittings are truly pure, or whether they indicate plating or gilding of gold over base metal. Fittings and mountings of karat gold are more valuable than plated or rolled gold. Colored gold, mixed with copper for a red cast and silver for a green tint, became popular in the 1830s, along with elaborate chasework.

Many mourning brooches have "chased" work frames, which are designs cut into the gold with special tools done by jewelers. Some brooches and pendants, under the influence of Etruscan jewelry design, have tiny globules of gold affixed to the face or edge of a piece, called "granulation," and some mid-Victorian pieces both in Europe and America exhibit granulation of gold beading in mourning jewelry. Other Etruscan design influences are seen in the *intaglio* work of cameos and watch fobs; this is executed by the design being carved into the stone, the opposite of the methods used in cameos.

All early palette-worked and table-worked brooches should have a "C" clasp and tube hinge, and a pin stem that extends past the body of the brooch indicates an early piece. Hair-work bracelets are almost always finished with a box clasp, and sometimes embellished with gemstones or a locket-style compartment for plaited hair, woven mourning fabric, or a photograph. Daguerreotype photographs would date a piece of jewelry to 1840-50, tintype images would place the piece in the 1860s, and paper images would place it in the 1870s.

Pieces with hidden compartments for hair are very desirable, as are jewelry suites of matching bracelet, brooch, and earrings (called a *demi-parure*), or entire matched suites consisting of necklace, brooch, bracelet, and earrings (called a *parure*). If the piece comes in its original box, this too adds considerable value, as do inscriptions.

In addition to the condition of the piece, aesthetic qualities should be considered: these include the overall beauty or design; the colors of hair used; intricacy of weave; embellishments such as gold wire, pearls, or gemstones; rarity; and the gold karat content of the fittings. If the provenance of a piece is available, this also adds to its value.

Keep in mind that here, as with other memorial items, the affective attributes of a particular piece may be so powerful that they outweigh condition or quality problems; the value of the piece then lies either in historical significance or emotive virtues, rather than in its objective clinical merits. It is here that worth truly lies in the "eye of the beholder."

Memorial Portraiture: Mortuary & Posthumous Paintings

Posthumous memorial portraits and mortuary paintings have had a long history in Western culture, having been widely used for centuries in Europe and later in America. Originally appearing in 16th century Europe, posthumous portraiture was once only the privilege of royalty, the aristocracy, or those affiliated with the Church; it became widely available to the English, European, and American middle class after the 18th century, however, in the form of mortuary paintings and posthumous miniatures. As pointed out by photographic historian Dr. Stanley Burns in *Sleeping Beauty II: Grief, Bereavement and The Family in Memorial Photography,* "mortuary paintings depicted the deceased on their deathbeds, but posthumous mourning portraits…portrayed the deceased as if still alive." As mourning is a culturally learned and absorbed form of language, the posthumous portrait and mortuary painting fulfilled significant roles in bereavement both within the average family and in the social hierarchy of the larger community.

With the rise of the middle class in Europe and America, the portrait miniature, both posthumous and mortuary, became universally popular in the 18th century, as large numbers of mourning families were able to afford a personal memorial remembrance. These small tokens offered the owner a private grief memento to be carried in the hand or pocket, or kept in a jewelry box. In contrast to larger portraits hung in the home, halls, and cathedrals visible to all, min-

iatures provided an intimate enclosed "world" to their owners, who could carry the "beloved dead" with them wherever they went. The detail executed in miniatures rivaled in skill portraits done in larger formats, as so eloquently described by Charles Fraser, the Charleston, South Carolina portraitist:

> "[Miniatures are] *striking resemblances, that will never fail to perpetuate the tenderness of friendship, to divert the cares of absence, and to aid affection in dwelling on those features and that image which death has forever wrested from us.*"[20]

The word *miniature* is derived from the word *minium,* the red lead ink used to illuminate medieval manuscripts on vellum, a material of shaved and processed calfskin. These manuscripts often included idealized portraits of saints and religious figures, which later evolved in the 18th century into portrait miniatures of the living and the deceased as tokens of sentiment and mourning. These portraits came to be known as *limnings* after the French word *enluminare,* relating to the illuminated manuscripts of earlier centuries. Primarily French or Dutch in origin and beginning in the 16th century, the practice of painted miniature portraits spread to England, and later America, where they became enormously popular for more than three centuries. Andrew Jackson, the seventh president of the United States, wore just such a locket with a

miniature of his beloved Rachel after her death; it rested on his nightstand along with his Bible.

In addition to vellum, other materials were used, such as ivory, whalebone, and a variety of ivory substitutes. Ivory as a material for memorial art and mourning jewelry was popular in the 18th and 19th centuries. It was particularly suitable because of the purity of its color and the ease with which its surface could be carved or painted to capture intricate detail of mourning scenes in both framed memorials and jewelry. Miniaturists were also quite adept in preparing surfaces to simulate ivory, using base materials such as ivory paper and vegetable ivories. Ivory paper was created by thin sheets of paper glued together with a mixture of limed water and plaster, with sanding between each layer, creating a surface almost indistinguishable from real ivory. Vegetable ivory, which came from two sources (the tagua nut and the seed of the ivory palm), was one of the most frequently used alternatives, as it gave one of the best appearances of being ivory. After the vegetable ivory was heated, the miniaturist would press a piece of real ivory into the still warm resin to make the lines and striations that are found in real ivory. The result was an exceptionally fine ivory-like surface, almost impossible to detect from real ivory. Besides ivory and its substitutes, other media such as painting on copper plate, wood, or enameling on copper were also used for painted miniatures.

Once the base material was chosen, artists ground colored pigments in a solution of gum arabic and water, then painted the portraits on the selected surface. The portraits were then placed in gold frames, often encrusted with gems, paste stones, or gold incised (called "chased") work. Painters generally charged according to the proportion of the sitter (or deceased) represented, e.g., bust, half, three-quarters, or full length. These artists made their living professionally painting portrait miniatures of the living and deceased, but wealthy ladies also practiced painting portrait miniatures privately in their parlors, using both Indian inks, sepia, and watercolors on ivory and ivory substitutes. However, genteel ladies were not encouraged to paint portrait miniatures professionally, as it was considered inappropriately "intimate," according to Dr. Samuel Johnson, who declared:

"[It is] ...improper...for a woman...[as] *public practice of any art and staring in men's faces is very indelicate in a female.*"[21]

In America, in the pre-Revolutionary War era, limned portraits spread from England and Europe to the colonies in North America. Quickly becoming popular, the first watercolor miniatures on ivory appear to have been made in Charleston, South Carolina in the 1740s. Later mediums for American miniatures included graphite on vellum, oil on copper and wood, or enamelwork. The influences of the Enlightenment and Romantic movements changed Western, particularly English and American, philosophies surrounding love, marriage, family, and the afterlife. These newly romantic perspectives were popularized in portrait miniatures at a time when a prosperous middle class, well able to afford these niceties, grew in the post-Industrial Revolution era of the late 18th century. Portrait miniatures were fashionably worn by women as pendants on long chains, or mounted as bracelet clasps. Men carried portraits of loved ones in the pockets of their coats, vests, or breeches. In George Eliot's popular novel, *Middlemarch,* Dorothea Brooke looked upon the "miniatures of ladies and gentlemen with powdered hair hanging in a group" in the home of the dour Edward Casaubon, to whom she was affianced.

Silhouettes, a cheaper form of portraiture, were also set into rings and pendants, sometimes with an enclosure for locks of plaited hair. As described by historian Felice Hodges in her book, *Period Pastimes,* the creation of "shadow portraits" was one of the many forms of parlor crafts taken up by "genteel ladies" of the 18th and 19th centuries. Some silhouettes were done in a cut-work method with scissors; others were drawn in Indian ink and "lamp black" watercolor on paper, vellum, ivory, or glass. The expert workmanship of novices was such that it rivaled the quality of professional silhouette artists. One such amateur silhouettist, who later became professional, was a Mrs. Isabella Beetham, who operated a business on Fleet Street in London in 1782, creating miniature "shadow portraits" in both paint and cut paper for mourning jewelry.[22]

The affluence of the merchant middle class and that of wealthy landowners meant that many early Americans were able to commission portrait miniatures of wives and children for both romantic and memorial purposes. Miniature portraits, along with hair jewelry, became popular as tokens of love and remembrance, and the American Revolution fostered an increasing desire for memorial representations of the deceased among wealthy colonists, due to deaths from the conflict. Abigail Adams had miniatures done of "him I best love," her husband John, as well as two of her children. Martha Washington also commissioned miniatures of her children, Martha and John Parke Custis, along with her husband George, the portrait being painted by the famous miniaturist Charles Willson Peale. These miniatures (usually painted on ivory) were set in gold clasps, with strands of pearls forming the bracelets, hung from gold chains, or sewn to ribbons. Entrepreneurial miniaturist William M. S. Doyle of Boston, Massachusetts, advertised himself in 1803 as a maker of silhouettes and death masks, as well as a being a miniature painter. And, Raphaelle Peale, son of the famous Charles Willson Peale, and a miniaturist like his father and brothers, advertised in the early 1800s that he could create "astonishing likenesses... from the corpse."[23]

A beautiful posthumous portrait miniature on ivory of an early 18th century French woman, her hairstyle and hat clearly visible in the profile view, is shown in the top photograph on the next page. Surrounding the miniature is a ring of palette-worked hair in a chevron design, set into a rose gold frame.

Portrait miniatures where both the sitter and the artist are known are very rare, and the value increases exponentially. In the spectacular 18K gold German posthumous miniature shown also on p. 118, the sitter was a man named "Wilheim Rose" and the expertise of the artist in capturing this man's facial contours and features is truly remarkable. The painter, a German artist by the name of Samuel Gotthelf, was an outstanding miniaturist in an era of exceptionally qualified portraitists. The reverse of this rare piece is as remarkable as the portrait, with a symbolic scene (executed in dissolved hair-work on ivory), of marital love and parting depicted in a weeping willow severed at its base, but still living as the dual branches entwine themselves and grow upward. This is also literally true of weeping willows, which will continue to grow from severed branches. Two columns on the right, once straight and tall as they ascended heavenward, are now interrupted as one life is cut short (that of Wilheim), represented by the broken column. However, ivy entwines itself up the broken column, symbolizing their belief in eternal life. To the left is a rising sun, also symbolic of eternal life and resurrection. The sun and horizon lines are frequently represented in memorial art and mourning jewelry, either as the setting sun representing death, or as the sun rising, symbolizing resurrection.

Rare eighteenth century portrait miniature of French woman with elaborate hairstyle in 18K gold frame with palette-worked hair in chevron design. 3" in diameter. *Courtesy of Things Gone By.* $895.

Outstanding German portrait mourning miniature of "Wilheim Rose"; executed by famous German miniaturist Samuel Gotthelf, c. 1780-1800. 2" in diameter. *Courtesy of Things Gone By.* $4,200.

Reverse of portrait miniature of Wilheim Rose, showing exceptional dissolved hair-work of entwined trees, broken column, and rising sun: symbols of marital love, loss, and eternal life. *Courtesy of Things Gone By.*

A wonderful posthumous portrait pendant, full of pathos, is seen here in the French 18K gold memorial for a deceased infant, surrounded by matched pearls. This tiny portrait miniature, done in sepia, watercolor, and dissolved hair, portrays the baby waving goodbye to his mother at death and is quite heartrending. Yet through the miniature, the feeling is that he is not truly "gone," for he is ever near the heart to be held and embraced in perpetuity; thus he yet "lives." The reverse of this outstanding pendant shows the infant's hair done in palette-work arrangements of entwined hearts out of which "grow" Forget-Me-Nots with ivy (symbolic of immortality) and a branch of a weeping willow.

In the next photograph, we see an extraordinary 18th century painted posthumous portrait on ivory of a French aristocrat, surrounded by dissolved hair embellishments of flowers and overturned torches, symbolic of a life cut short. The provenance of this man is on the reverse, listing his name, that of his wife, and his occupation (attorney). The notation further describes him as a "victim" of the "Terror at Lyons" (during the French Revolution), sometime between December 8 and 22, 1793, the exact date of his execution being unknown to his family. Between October 1793, and the following summer, the city of Lyons endured months of killings and atrocities in which almost two thousand people were killed. The republican revolutionaries overran the city, instituting mass executions by guillotine, and it was during the month of December 1793, that this man was executed. Originally, this memorial was most likely a love token in the form of a pendant containing a painted portrait miniature on ivory of the husband, with his plaited hair-work on the reverse. After the man's execution, his wife then disassembled the pendant, placing the portrait miniature on a larger ivory ground, processing and placing the "dissolved" hair-work artistry around the portrait in the memorial iconography of roses and overturned torches. The effect is a virtual shrine to his memory.

The mortuary painting involved as much or more labor in capturing the likeness as did a portrait executed when the sitter was alive. Miniaturists secured the slack jaws with straps, or as in the case of postmortem photography a few de-

Extraordinary 18th century French mourning portrait miniature of infant waving good-bye to his mother, 18K gold surrounded by pearls. *Courtesy of Things Gone By.* $2,500.

Reverse of rare 18th century mourning portrait miniature of infant, showing hair-work done in cut-work method of ivy and weeping willow branch, with Forget-Me-Nots "growing" out of the two hearts in the center. *Courtesy of Things Gone By.*

cades later, a stick was placed under the jaw inside the clothing to keep it closed. Various methods were employed to keep the eyelids open so as to depict the dead as still "alive," and colors added to remove the pallor and decay of death, as artists continued to work even as decomposition set in.

An extremely rare mortuary painting on ivory of a beatific dead bride is shown in the photograph on the next page. In this spectacular portrait, the bride is painted in all her pre-nuptial loveliness symbolized by her wedding dress and veil decorated with flowers, the traditional emblem of maidenly purity. Never having been "deflowered," she remains forever in a permanent virginal state, a reminder of the Madonna, further represented by the rosary in the

"Who then to frail mortality shall trust, but limns on water or but writes in dust." [Francis Bacon, 1629].

Rare 18th century French memorial to an aristocrat (attorney) executed during the Reign of Terror at Lyon during the French Revolution, sometime in December 1793, at the height of the three-month long "September Massacres." Portrait miniature on ivory set with dissolved hair-work of roses and overturned torches; provenance on reverse. Madame De Stael, a survivor of the French revolution, reflected in her memoirs on the horrors of the event and the loss of most of her friends and family by remarking, "We understand death for the first time when he puts his hand upon one whom we love." 4.5" x 4.5". *Author's collection.* $895-1,000.

bride's hands. The floral bridal wreath worn by this bride was carried by attendants, or in the case of dead brides, left hanging in the church as a "virgin's garland" in the late Middle Ages. When painted "en corpse" as in this case, it became a significant funeral prop symbolic of the chastity of young unmarried women in mortuary paintings and post-mortem photography of the 19th century. The scene here, however, is no doubt somewhat fanciful, as few death-beds were this serenely beauteous. Nevertheless, as families often dressed and posed their loved ones for such portraiture, it is likely that she was dressed post-humously in her wedding clothing to represent her nuptial state. The miniature is cased in an ornate marquetry frame.

An exquisitely painted French mortuary painting in an ebonized frame of a deceased woman floating heavenward in the clouds with the "Evening Star" above her in a twilight sky is shown next. The slight smile painted on her face was intended to evidence her visioning the heavenly realms, which contrasts sharply with medieval *ars moriendi* facial representations, where posthumous paintings of the deceased sometimes depicted them less serenely, even in some instances, horror-stricken as they faced the impending judgment of God.

An extremely rare and one-of-a-kind mourning brooch in memory of two children is seen in the photograph on the following page. This sepia and hair-work brooch on ivory with black enamel-work is an English piece, c. 1810-30. The post-humous portraits were undoubtedly true to life and probably taken from an existing painted portrait of the children and then done in this miniature with sepia and the children's dissolved hair on ivory. It is also quite possible that this portrait miniature is an amateur work, done by the mother or a female relative rather than by a professional artist, thereby adding to the overall poignancy of this piece.

"That Morn which saw me made a Bride,
The Ev'ning witnessed that I died.
Those holy lights, wherewith they guide
Unto the bed the bashful Bride,
Serv'd, but as Tapers, for to burn
And light my Relics to their urn,
This Epitaph, which here you see,
Supplied the Epithalamie."
[Robert Herrick, 1591-1674, *Upon a Maid that Died the Day She Was Married*]

Outstanding late 18th century mortuary painting on ivory of a dead bride dressed in her wedding finery, encased in a beautiful marquetry frame. 5" x 5". *Courtesy of Judy Jay's Time Dances By.* $2,500.

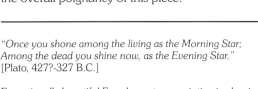

"Once you shone among the living as the Morning Star;
Among the dead you shine now, as the Evening Star."
[Plato, 427?-327 B.C.]

Exceptionally beautiful French mortuary painting in ebonized frame of a deceased woman floating heavenward in the clouds with the "Evening Star" above her in the gloaming sky. The slight smile painted on her face was intended to evidence her vision of the heavenly realms. This portrait miniature was executed on ivory and is in mint condition, with the artist's name and date (1821) just underneath the gold rim at the bottom of the painting. 3.5" in diameter. *Courtesy of Things Gone By.* $2,800+.

Larger-sized posthumous portraiture and mortuary paintings date back to the Middle Ages. The death of Lady Venetia Digby in May of 1653 completely devastated her husband, who commissioned painter Anthony van Dyck to paint a mortuary portrait of her. Van Dyck's painting of Lady Venetia excludes the processes of decay and corruption upon her body so typical of medieval *ars moriendi* representations, and instead portrays her as sleeping the sleep of the "good wife," idealized in her blushed cheek and the broken rosebud fallen on her bedsheet. Another outstanding 17th century mortuary painting, *Sir Thomas Aston at the Deathbed of his Wife,* shows Sir Aston's wife, Magdalene, dead in her bed after childbirth, with various *memento mori* objects placed around the room. Prominent in the room is the dead infant's cradle draped in black cloth, a skull resting on the cradle's hood, and Latin *memento mori* inscriptions surrounding the deathbed scene.

Two centuries later, an English father, contemplating the commission of a mortuary painting of his young dying daughter, asked rhetorically, "In her weak state of health should we not provide against The Spoiler?", a question echoed in numerous households throughout the 19th century. The first known mortuary painting in America was a "corpse portrait" of Elizabeth Royal of Massachusetts, executed by Joseph Badger in 1747.[24] Other widely known portraitists such as Raphaelle Peale, Thomas Cole, William Sidney Mount, and Ralph E. W. Early, also made their livings, albeit often reluctantly, in posthumous paintings and mortuary portraits. Most often the artist came to the house and drew the deceased, then later finished the painted portrait in the studio.

John Callcort Horsley, an English artist, recorded in his diary for 1852 being hired to make a drawing of a deceased child. He notes, "In the afternoon I went to make a drawing of a dead child, thinking it a duty so to do…" John Horsley made his drawings as soon after death as practicable, so that the facial muscles were relaxed and peaceful in appearance, before rigor mortis and discoloration altered the features of the child. Horsley later drew a posthumous portrait of his own father in 1858, and

his mother found that the "likeness is perfect, the peace and beauty of his expression is not to be described."[25] And, in 1868, popular American portrait miniaturist Shepard Alonzo Mount grieved over the death of his two-year-old granddaughter in a letter to family members,

exclaiming, "Alas! How everything fades from us!" He had just finished painting a posthumous portrait of the child, "Camille," showing her face and shoulders rising heavenward in a cloud, a watch denoting her time of birth in the background.

Beautiful sepia and dissolved hair-work mourning portrait miniature of two children painted on ivory and set in a memorial enameled frame. *Courtesy of Things Gone By.* $2,000.

In the mid-19th century mortuary painting on porcelain shown here, a beautiful child is seen almost "floating" in a bed of roses, her garden bonnet laying casually on her lap as though she had fallen asleep while gathering flowers. This watercolor painting is an exceptional example of posthumous paintings of the mid-Victorian era, and was probably originally housed in a black "ebonized" or painted oval frame. Below it is an outstanding framed posthumous photographic portrait of a young child posed seated in a chair, her vacant eyes somewhat unsettling to viewers today. It must be remembered, however, that to parents in grief, these portraits were filtered through psychological lenses into mental images of beauty.

Beautiful mortuary painting on porcelain of a young girl, c. 1870s. She appears "floating" on a bed of roses, her sunbonnet on her lap. 6" x 7". *Collection of Ben Zigler.* $500-700.

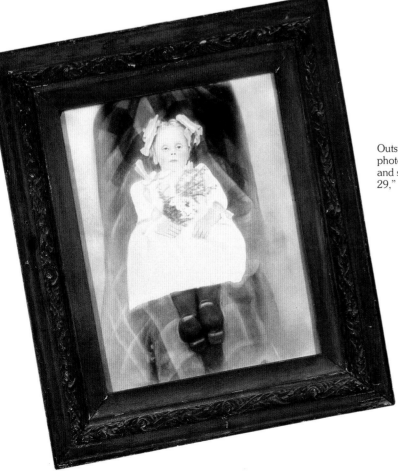

Outstanding large format painted postmortem photograph of young girl posed to appear alive and seated in a chair, large format, c. 1880s. 25" x 29," *Collection of Ben Zigler.* $1,200.

Painted postmortem photographs were also popular later in the Victorian era, after the advent of photography. In this form of posthumous portraiture, a postmortem photograph was over-painted by the photographer or his assistant in the studio to indicate "life." Sometimes a postmortem of just the face of a child was over-painted and an entire "body" incorporated into the portrait as though the deceased had sat for a portrait while alive. The eyes would be painted "open" and scenery and props included in the background tableau, sometimes (but not always) with symbolism included to indicate death. These posthumous mourning photographs frequently have a "painterly" or folk art quality, which is quite appealing and desirable to the collector. Often the disproportion between the photographed "head" and the painted "body" reflect the same disparities seen in folk art portraits of the colonial period in America.

William Gookin, a well known New Hampshire artist, regularly painted posthumous and mortuary portraiture, and in one instance, he was called to the home of a dying child, little Hannah Cushing, where the parents had laid out their daughter in her best dress with her beloved pet dog on the bed. Gookin studied the scene, then returned to his studio to paint a portrait of little Hannah set against a background of trees with the dog at her feet. Determining posthumous paintings can often be difficult unless some indicators are present within the painting to provide evidence that the child was deceased at the time – a broken flower, funeral trees, boats sailing towards the horizon, a setting sun, or other death symbolism. Other painted emblems might be fallen trees, snuffed candles, peeled fruit, broken eggshells, spilt milk, tipped over glasses, etc. Where no indicators are evident, sometimes the only record is that of written references from the artist themselves, or other historical provenance.

When artists were called to the home to take a likeness preparatory for a memorial portrait, they would often draw sketches from death of the deceased (using a measuring caliper for

Painted postmortem photograph in Eastlake frame, in which the eyes of the baby have been over-painted "open" and an entire body and background added to give the impression the child was living at the time and seated for the portrait, c. 1880s. 12" x 14". *Author's collection.* $495.

correct facial alignment) and also draw living family members for similar familial features to incorporate into the posthumous painting. Such a drawing is seen in the example on the next page, in which the artist, Ade Story, drew a pencil drawing of a deceased boy, "Julian," in 1891, preparatory to later painting a posthumous portrait of the boy with his eyes "open" to appear as though he had sat for the painting when alive.

After surviving for centuries, the popularity of posthumous portraits, especially memorial miniatures, waned, eclipsed by the invention of the photograph in 1839. A scholar in 1927 described the demise of the portrait minia-

ture in the wake of photography as being "like a bird before a snake: it was fascinated, even to the fatal point of imitation, and then it was swallowed."[26] Representative of this eclipse of the miniature in the wake of the photograph is the c. 1820s sepia portrait on ivory of a young boy, shown on the next page, which was later enclosed sometime in the 1850s in a photographic case. This miniature is possibly a posthumous memorial portrait and as such represented the only likeness the parents had of this child, lost before the advent of photography would have provided them with the ability to have had a living or postmortem photograph taken.

Nineteenth century artist Ade Story's graphite rendering of little "Julian" after death, preparatory to a posthumous painting of the boy, dated March 20, 1891. In the finished portrait, the boy's eyes would have been painted open to give the appearance of "life." 14" x 18". *Author's collection.* $400.

Rare c. 1820-30 sepia on ivory portrait of young boy encased in c. 1850s photographic case. This anachronistic placement exemplifies the almost overnight substitution of the photograph for the portrait miniature in the decades following photography's invention in 1839. *Courtesy of Things Gone By.* $895.

Memorial Photography

The almost obsessive need to linger over the body, to visually hold onto the face, and to cling to, yet bid farewell to the beloved dead is a universal, and sometimes overwhelming, compulsion. Retaining locks of hair, personal clothing, and favorite keepsakes all provided a substitutionary portion of the deceased too soon consigned to the earth's "cold embrace." However, no personal remembrance provided as satisfying an alternative for the "corruptible body" as the memorial photograph of the face so familiar to family members, and one that they could frequently gaze upon and weep. Like the painted posthumous miniature, the postmortem photograph helped to satisfy the desire to keep the dead within the world of the living. In 1843, the famous British poetess, Elizabeth Barrett, summed up this need when she wrote:

> "I long to have a memorial of every being dear to me in the world. It is not merely the likeness which is precious in such cases – but the association and the sense of nearness involved in the thing...the fact of the very shadow of the person lying there fixed forever! I would rather have such a memorial of one I dearly loved, than the noblest artist's work ever produced."

Throughout the Middle Ages, such memorial portraits were primarily only within the provenance of wealthy and aristocratic families, created in the form of large framed paintings for the home, in miniatures for private viewing in tiny frames, or in mourning jewelry. The invention of photography in 1839 enabled the memorial image to become a democratic remembrance available to virtually everyone. As with posthumous portrait miniatures, the "sun-drawn" (or *helio*-graph) postmortem picture provided the owner with a hand-held object of the "beloved," a shrine to be held, gazed upon, and kissed. In 1850, a daguerreotype with hand-tinting might cost approximately $3 to $6, depending upon the photographer, the amount of added coloring if desired, and the size of the image. However, the average cost of a painted miniature varied between $50 to $250, making a postmortem photograph the obvious choice for most families. The democracy of the daguerreotype was summed up in 1864 in *The Camera and The Pencil,* by M. A. Root, when he stated:

> "In the order of nature, families are dispersed, by death or other causes; friends are severed; and the "old familiar faces" are no longer seen in our daily haunts. By heliography, our loved ones, dead or distant; our friends or acquaintances, however far removed, are retained within daily and hourly vision...The cheapness of these pictures brings them within reach, substantially, of all."

Indeed, nineteenth century photographers earned a great portion of their income, albeit often reluctantly, in taking photographs of the deceased, just as their predecessor portraitists had done with the posthumous painting. In an effort to "secure the shadow ere the substance perish/of those for whom we fond emotions cherish," many photographers went to extraordinary efforts in artistically stylizing the deathbed scene. As noted by historian Philippe Aries, "Death loves to be represented. The image can retain some of the obscure, repressed meanings that the written word filters out. Hence its power to move us so deeply."[27]

The advent of photography began in France with inventor Louis Daguerre in 1839, the resultant "daguerreotype" quickly becoming revolutionary in the 19th century as it gave visual immortality to everyday people for the first time in history. The daguerreotype was a direct-positive process, creating a highly detailed image on a sheet of copper plated with a thin coat of silver without the use of a negative. The silver-plated copper plate first had to be cleaned and polished until the surface looked like a mirror. Next, the plate was sensitized in a closed box over iodine until it took on a yellowish-rose appearance. The plate, held in a light-proof holder, was then transferred to the camera. After exposure to light, the plate was developed over hot mercury until an image appeared, whereupon the plate was then immersed in a solution of sodium thiosulfate or salt to fix the image and then toned with gold chloride.

Although initially having a daguerreotype taken might cost the average family the equivalent of three months' income, photography quickly became so universally available that its cost dropped markedly within months of its inception. The tedium of having a daguerreotype taken, however, was long and uncomfortable for living sitters, as the exposure could take as long as twenty minutes in the early years of photography. Photographing children was even more difficult, as they could not remain motionless for the required time. This difficulty, of course, was removed in postmortem photographs of children, and much posing went into creating a "life-like" appearance, or a countenance of peaceful, angelic sleep. While painters could paint so-called "life-like" portraits of deceased persons, which in reality were simply *illusions* of life, the photographer could, in a sense, mitigate the reality of death within the context of "immortal sleep."

In 1855, a photographer by the name of N. G. Burgess described his occupation as necessarily bringing him "in contact with the most endearing feelings of the human heart, more especially is this true when called upon to copy the human face divine 'after life's fitful fever is o'er.'" Burgess wrote an article for the March 1855 issue of *The Photographic and Fine Art Journal*, detailing the procedures and methods employed in capturing the best postmortem image. He outlined the equipment he took to the house of mourning and the positioning of the body in the most suitable lighting for portraiture. The body of the deceased was placed on tables or in a bed nearest a window to provide sideways lighting – or in the case of infants, photographs were taken of the mother holding her deceased child. While he advised against bodies being photographed inside coffins, this arrangement was routinely done by many photographers, sometimes with the entire coffin visible and other times with cloth coverings disguising the outline of the casket.

Burgess, like other 19th century photographers, realized the significance of the postmortem photograph to family members, stating:

"All likenesses taken after death will of course only resemble the inanimate body, nor will there appear in the portrait anything like life itself, except indeed the sleeping infant, on whose face the playful smile of innocence some-times steals even after death. This may be and is oft-times transferred to the silver plate. How true it is, that it is too late to catch the living form and face of our dear friends, and well illustrates the necessity of procuring those more than life-like resemblances of our friends, ere it is too late – ere the hand of death has snatched away those we prize so dearly on earth. [sic]"

Nineteenth century photographers aimed at displaying the deceased while in the "Last Sleep," a metaphor for death dating back to the Grecian myth of the twin sons of night: Hypnos, god of sleep, and Thanatos, god of death. Biblical references to death as sleep, along with the Huguenot expression of "the sleep of God," appealed to Victorian religious perspectives, and references to the analogy of death to sleep abound in conso-lation literature, letters, diaries, and memoirs of this era. Photographers became expert at conveying the comfort of sleep, and in July 1858, *The Photographic and Fine Art Journal* commented on one daguerreotypist's artistic efforts regarding the postmortem photograph of one young boy:

"We have been shown a daguerreotype likeness of a little boy, taken after his decease. It has not the slightest expression of suffering, and nothing of that ghastliness and rigity [sic] of outline and feature, which usually render likenesses taken in sickness or after death so painfully revolting. How sublime the thought that man, by a simple process, can constrain the light of heaven to catch and fix the fleeting shadow of life, even as it lingers upon the pallid features of death."

"How beautiful those rose-buds are!
The happy brother said,
Whose hopeful heart could have no thought
That sister could be dead;
I'll pluck them for sweet sister now,
And take them where she lies,
I know she'll love to see them there
When open are her eyes."
["The Sacred Flora, Or Flowers from the Grave of a Child," by Henry Bacon, 1847]

A beautiful c. 1850s daguerreotype of a little girl posed to appear serenely napping, the flowers in her hand tinted red. *Collection of Ben Zigler.* $750.

Opposite page:
"We watched her breathing thro' the night,
Her breathing soft and low,
As in her breast the wave of life
Kept heaving to and fro.
For when the morn came dim and sad, —
And chill with early showers,
Her quiet eyelids clos'd – she had
Another morn than ours."
[Thomas Hood, 1799-1845, *The Death-Bed*]

Outstanding full plate daguerreotype, c. 1840s, of elderly woman. Early photographic images focused primarily on the head and shoulders of the deceased except in the case of children, where the entire body could be contained in the various sizes of photographic plates. This exceptional daguerreotype is rare not only for its size, but for the quality of the image. *Collection of Charles Swedlund.* 6.5" x 8.5". $5,000+.

The extent to which photographers were able to create a mourning tableau around the posed body of the deceased was extraordinary. In the 1840s, the well known Boston photographers Southworth & Hawes wrote instructions on how to massage the limbs to enable posing of the body so as to make the deceased appear alive. And 19th century photographers were experienced in other methods to present the deceased to the viewer, such as affixing the mouth closed with a forked stick placed under the chin and against the breastbone, closing the eyes with coins, and preserving the features by placing ice under the body. The extraordinary abilities of 19th century photographers to photograph the deceased is shown in the following images of little children posed to appear "alive," the boy appearing to read a book.

The deceased were photographed inside and outside the family home and in the photographer's studio, and while most photographers tended to shape the facial features into an appearance of sleep, occasionally postmortems show the eyes open, or other undisguised signs of death. While unsettling to viewers today, these images were emotionally and psychologically filtered into beautiful remembrances by family members overwhelmed with grief. Letters and diaries often describe the facial features of the dead with such adjectives as "beautiful," "peaceful," or "serene," in what could only be imaginative perceptions considerably removed from the obvious signs of decomposition.

Occasionally family members desired an arranged "scene" to disguise the fact of a loved one's death. Propping up the deceased in a chair and placing an open book in the crossed arms was a popular arrangement for both adults and children, as in the rare c. 1900 postmortem image shown here. Young "Earl Andrew Pearl" was dressed in his best suit and posed reading a book, but in reality, the fact of his death is evident in the unnatural position of his arms, as well as in his sunken eyes and cracked lips, both common features of the postmortem condition. *Collection of Ben Zigler.* $495.

"Grief fills the room up of my absent child,
Lies in his bed, walks up and down with me,
Puts on his pretty looks, repeats his words,
Remembers me of all his gracious parts,
Stuffs out his vacant garments with his form."
[William Shakespeare, *King John*]

Touching 1/6 plate postmortem daguerreotype of little girl posed seated in a chair. Great effort was expended into creating this poignant scene of a little girl holding flowers, dressed in beautiful clothing, her hair curled over her face. Again, when one remembers that this might have been the only representation the parents had of their child, the significance of this remembrance cannot be underestimated. The conflict between acceptance and denial is often evident in postmortem images of children, such as this one in which the child is posed seated in a chair as though she were still alive; dead children do not sit up in chairs. *Collection of Charles Swedlund.* $495+.

Early in photographic history, there was initially little attempt to beautify the pose, and bodies are sometimes shown tied up preparatory for placement in the coffin. Occasionally, even body fluids at the mouth and nose are seen in early daguerreotypes, attesting to the influences of prevailing Puritan views of death as a consequence of sin and the reluctance to exercise any attempt to "soften" this religious interpretation of death through cleansing of the body. Calvinist views of "predestination" also influenced the harsh visual realities of death in early 19th century postmortem images. An exception to this practice, however, was in the case of postmortem images of children, who are usually depicted as sleeping, often holding flowers or toys in their hands.

Other photographic processes followed the development of the daguerreotype. The ambrotype, an image developed onto glass plate in the wet collodion process, was backed with black fabric, paper, or a piece of tin painted black and placed behind the glass negative to create a positive image. Ambrotypes were only popular from 1855 to 1865, when they were supplanted by other, less fragile mediums.

The tintype, an image processed on tin or iron plate, was popular from its inception in 1865 up to the 1940s. Tintypes, like their predecessor ambrotypes and daguerreotypes, were once-only positive photographs, in which no negative was produced; each image, therefore, is unique and one-of-a-kind.

Outstanding c. 1860s example of a postmortem ambrotype of a young girl. She has been lovingly arranged on two printed Victorian linens, one a jacquard print, the other a printed cloth typical of Oriental-style fabrics popular in this era. The child is dressed in the mid-19th century off-the-shoulder clothing favored by Victorians for both girls and boys under the age of five, and she has the long ringlets styled for little girls of the Civil War era as well. Her cheeks have been tinted, and she holds a single pink rose, hand-painted at the studio. Photographers charged customers extra for tinting and painting images (work usually done by an employee at the studio), with additional embellishment of facial features, flowers, clothing, jewelry, background scenery or props costing proportionately more, depending on the desire of the customer. *Collection of Ben Zigler.* $550.

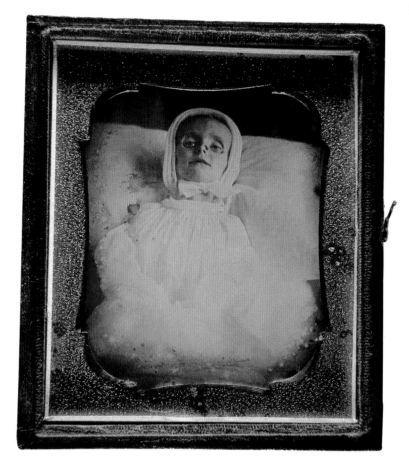

Also shown earlier, this 1/6 plate daguerreotype of a deceased child shows evidence of the child's poor condition prior to death. As was sometimes the case with early postmortem photographs, the fact that the child's jaw and hands were tied up in anticipation of burial can also be seen in the photograph. *Author's collection.* $450-500.

"When we came where lies the child
We lost in other years,
There above the little grave,

O there above the little grave,
We kissed again with tears.
[Alfred, Lord Tennyson]

The earlier postmortem images of adults tended to be rather stark, with the focus of the camera on the face and upper body of the deceased, and little or no background visible. Adult women were usually dressed in their best dress, or sometimes, in the case of young, unmarried women, in white burial clothing to symbolize the purity of a white wedding dress or confirmation raiment.

Following these so-called "hard" images were paper photographs, such as the *carte de visite* developed in 1865, so called because its size resembled the French calling card, and the 1880s 4" x 6" cabinet card in larger mounts suitable for photograph albums kept on the Victorian parlor table. Stereograph photographs, consisting of paired images placed on 3-1/2" x 7" cardboard mounts, were intended for three-dimensional viewing in stereoscopes, a popular Victorian parlor pastime, from the 1850s up to the 1940s. And, by the end of the 19th century, large format photographs were available for postmortem photography. The advantage of these new forms of photography was significant: multiple images could be developed from one photographic negative. Thus, postmortem images could be sent in the mail to family and friends far away and the grief shared. *Cartes de visite* and other paper photographs are most often found unframed, but occasionally images were placed in frames to be hung on the wall or displayed on the parlor table.

"Clasp the hands meekly over the still breast, they've no more work to do; close the weary eyes, they've no more tears to shed; part the damp locks, there's no more pain to bear."

A c. 1860s 1/9 plate tintype of a woman laid out in what was probably her best dress, but in actuality a simple calico. *Author's collection.* $325.

poignancy of empty shoes for bereaved parents:

> *"Two little shoes with knotted strings,*
> *With tears aside we laid;*
> *And for the form they used to wear,*
> *A little grave was made."*

Empty shoes figured prominently in Victorian poet James Russell Lowell's poem, "After The Burial," wherein Lowell argued that faith does not always adequately assuage grief, but is only a "goodly anchor when skies are sweet as a psalm." Lowell compared the death of a child to the shipwreck of a life, and although he acknowledged the consolations of friends as "well-meant alms of breath," he added that "not all the preaching since Adam has made Death other than Death." He summed up his despair in the last stanza:

> *"That little shoe in the corner,*
> *So worn and wrinkled and brown,*
> *With its emptiness confutes you,*
> *And argues your wisdom down."*

Nineteenth century newspaper columnist and writer, Fannie Fern, wrote of "tiny half-worn" shoes as "sad and fitting" monuments for the grave of the "poor man's" child in Mount Auburn Cemetery. In her 1857 book, *Fresh Leaves*, she noted that life was full of "toil and strife," that "wrecks strew the life-coast," and the "plaint of the weary-hearted is unheard in life's fierce clamor." Consequently, she observed that she could not weep for the "infant army who slumber there," but thanked God that the little shoes were "laid aside and the dreary path untrod."

In her 1856 book for children, *The Play-Day Book: New Stories for Little Folks*, Ms. Fern invites her childish readers to "Come – let us go to Greenwood [Cemetery]," whereupon she points out to her young readers the little glass cases

All forms of *ars moriendi* represent a surrogate of the living person, and dating back to the Middle Ages, memorial icons substituted as symbols for veneration, religious instruction, and alternative forms of the *body* of the beloved. The desire to place objects with the deceased that represented them in life (such as wedding rings, family photographs and mementos, or other personal tokens of remembrance), whether in the coffin, the grave, or within the context of the posthumous portrait, is basic to human grief and memorialization. The power of symbols as a substitutive equivalent of the *original* is perhaps nowhere more vividly expressed than in the area of postmortem images, which in the case of children's deaths, assume a kind of sacred veneration. Something of the transcendent force behind the evocative symbols employed by parents and photographers in their memorial photographs still affixes itself in our minds when we hold the postmortem image. Children posed with their favorite toys are especially affecting. Few memories can be as heartbreaking to a parent as seeing the forlorn toys cast aside in the empty bedroom, never to be played with again.

Just as flowers and favorite toys were popular photographic props for children, so too were their empty shoes, which held considerable significance for parents as symbols of childhood. Poems of the 19th century speak of the sadness and emptiness of the tiny pair of shoes cast aside, never to be filled again, and certainly children's shoes have an affecting poignancy about them far more powerfully symbolic than other items of clothing. Representative of a baby's first steps, shoes were associated with a child's growing independence, the "vehicles" which carried the child through countless hours of playtime to the amusement of parents. Like the plaster casts and marble sculptures of children's hands, empty shoes became a prop in postmortem photographs full of the pathos of a childhood gone forever. A poem composed on the death of six-year-old Chester Olson in 1891 summed up the

upon the children's graves containing toys and dolls, locks of hair, tea sets, and, on one little boy's grave,

"only a pair of half-worn little shoes, with the strings tied together, very coarse homely little shoes, with the little toes turned up, just as the child's foot had shaped them. I think the little boy was too poor to have playthings, and this was all his sorrowing mother had to tell us that her little boy lay dead beneath."

The efforts by parents in posing their children, or in instructing the photographer to arrange the last remembrance, can be heartbreaking. As with other previous forms of photography, toys figured prominently as poignant props in relinquishing the symbolic ties to earth. Here the doll has not simply been placed haphazardly on the bed; it has been put in the arms of the little girl just as it was carried when she was alive. The c. 1880s cabinet card is housed in a purple velvet frame with coffin-shaped "doors," which open to reveal the postmortem in a symbolic representation of death and resurrection. The photograph is "vignetted," or fading out at the edges, also symbolically blurring the lines between life and death. *Author's collection.* $300.

In this beautiful cabinet card postmortem, a young girl is posed clutching her doll, the fingers of her right hand wrapped around the doll's body as a mother would with a child. *Collection of Ben Zigler.* $275.

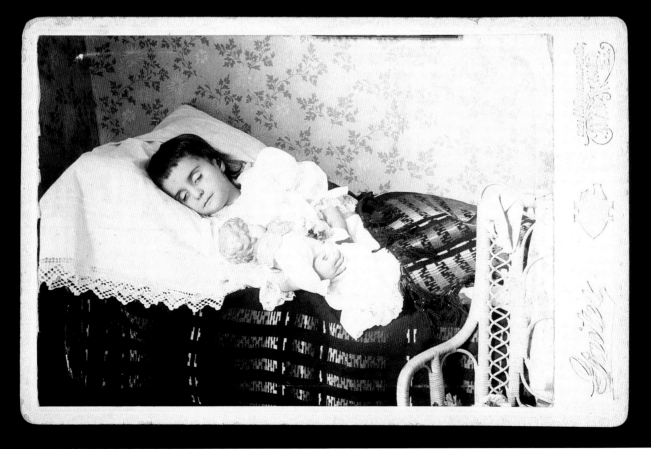

Perhaps it was with these religious views and literary comforts in mind, that the parents of the deceased children shown next chose to place their children's empty shoes in the sad tableaux. In the first c. 1870s *carte de visite* photograph, a little girl's empty high-button shoes are prominently placed beside her on the Victorian sofa. In the second image, another beautiful little girl has one shoe on and the other placed in her hand, as though she had simply fallen asleep while in the process of taking off her shoes for a nap.

Sad *carte de visite* of a young girl with her now "empty" shoes placed beside her on the settee, c. 1870s. *Collection of Ben Zigler.* $250.

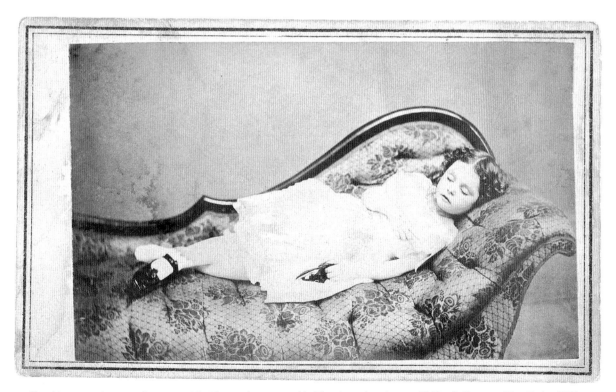

Touching *carte de visite* of a young girl with one shoe on, and holding her other shoe, c. 1860s. *Collection of Ben Zigler.* $250.

A rare pair of c. 1880s cabinet cards commemorating the death of an African-American infant are shown below. In the first photograph, we see the child in its beautiful dress and cap seated at the photographer's studio for its portrait when still alive. However, shortly thereafter, the baby died, and the tragedy of its passing is entirely summed up in its little empty shoes and funeral bouquet, probably placed in the child's hands during viewing in the home.

Empty shoes are props again in a memorial tableau arranged on a front porch, as shown in the c. 1900s postcard at right in which a deceased child's earlier living photograph is surrounded by items such as her chair and clothing intended to indicate her loss. The homely quality of the floral funeral arrangements placed around the portraits and the empty shoes add a particular poignancy to the scene, which is made even more heartbreaking by the mother's written notation on the reverse:

"Dear Cousin, I will send you another postal of Dear Little Mary they hant very good these are the flowers and her shoes [and] it Seams like the hole world has turned against me Since She has gone [sic]."

Touching memorial postcard, c. 1900s, with tableau showing photograph of "Little Mary" prior to her death, plus funeral flowers, her empty shoes, and her mother's mourning bonnet, all placed on front porch of the home. The reverse of this poignant scene has a heartbreaking note from the mother: "it seams like the hole world has turned against me since she has gone [sic]." *Author's collection.* $50.

Unusual pair of cabinet-sized memorial cards for a black infant, c. 1890s, one showing the child while still alive, the accompanying photo showing the "empty shoes" along with funeral flowers symbolizing the baby's death. *Collection of Jim Mathews.* $325.

As noted by photographic historian Dr. Stanley Burns, even such tragic events as murder would be memorialized by postmortem photographs of the victims to be given to family members. If the case was notorious enough, postmortems of murder victims were publicized by newspapers for public interest, or to raise money for surviving family members. Such was the case with the 1872 Columbiana, Ohio, postmortem *carte de visite* photograph of Adaline and Minnie Porter, described on the reverse as "The Murdered Children." The Porter girls lived in a home of domestic violence, in which the father, an alcoholic ne'er-do-well unable to hold down a job or support his family, dispassionately murdered his daughters with an ax one morning in front of their mother. In a previous marriage, Mr. Porter had put his first child outside to die of exposure, and while under the influence of alcohol he murdered Minnie and Adaline, the children of his second marriage. The case was so opprobrious, that these *cartes de visite* photographs were reproduced, possibly to raise money for the grief-stricken mother. Porter was apprehended shortly after the murder and committed to an insane asylum, where he died a year later; what happened to the tragic Mrs. Porter is unknown.

Particularly poignant are images of mothers holding their deceased infants and young children. Called "Madonna" images for their similarity to the iconography of Mary holding the infant Jesus, the facial expressions on the faces of the mothers exhibit a range of emotions from resignation and acceptance to shock and despair, as seen in the following 19th century images.

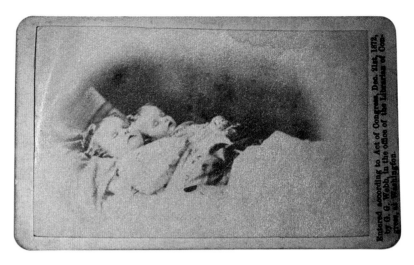

Rare *carte de visite* photograph of murdered children, "Adeline and Minnie Porter," killed by their father in 1872, in Ohio. *Author's collection.* $325.

Sad 1/6 plate ambrotype of a young mother holding her deceased infant, a representative example of the "Madonna" images, so called for their similarity to the iconography of Mary and the Christ Child. These images frequently capture a variety of emotions on the faces of the mothers, ranging from shock to resignation to overwhelming grief. *Author's collection.* $325.

Another example of a "Madonna" image, with mother holding deceased infant; 1/6 plate ambrotype, c. 1850s. *Author's collection.* $325.

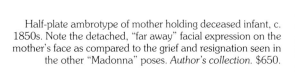

Half-plate ambrotype of mother holding deceased infant, c. 1850s. Note the detached, "far away" facial expression on the mother's face as compared to the grief and resignation seen in the other "Madonna" poses. *Author's collection.* $650.

*"In the corpse we love, it is the **likeness** we see; it is the likeness, which makes itself felt the more keenly because something else **was** and **is not.**"*
[George Eliot, 1819-1880, from *Adam Bede*]

A haunting 1/6 plate ambrotype of woman holding her dead child, c. 1850s. An ambrotype was a photographic image on glass, but this particular ambrotype is unusual in that it was placed behind another layer of glass upon which the background of drapery and vase was painted. Sometimes referred to as *relievos*, ambrotypes such as these are scarce, especially with the skill and use of color as well executed as in this image. The mother's posture and facial expression speak volumes. *Collection of Charles Swedlund.* $750.

Postmortem images of African-Americans are difficult to find. In spite of the fact that postmortem photography continued in popularity in black communities well into the 20th century (far longer than in white communities), early posthumous photographs are rare. Prior to the Civil War, this was simply due to the fact that few African-Americans could afford such images, even those living free in the North; and after the Civil War, most blacks were occupied with the rigors of life after emancipation.

Rare in the postmortem portrait genre are those photographs taken of the dying before they had passed to the "other world." These images, called "pre-mortems," were often chosen by family members who preferred a living photograph to a postmortem, regardless of the dreadful message inherent in the facial expressions of the dying. In calling a photographer to the home, they were essentially admitting that nothing further could be done to save the life of their loved one, and this acceptance of the inevitable was often extremely difficult, as the psychological need to "deny" death could be overpowering.

I know moon-rise, I know star-rise,
Lay dis body down.
I walk in de moonlight, I walk in de starlight,
To lay dis body down.
I'll walk in de graveyard, I'll walk through de graveyard,
To lay dis body down.
I'll lie in de grave and stretch out my arms,
Lay dis body down.
I go to de judgement in de evenin' of the de day
When I lay dis body down,
And my soul and your soul will meet in de day,
When I lay dis body down.[28]

Rare c. 1894 photograph of an elderly black woman, dressed in a black burial garment and laid out for her last photograph. *Collection of Ben Zigler.* $300.

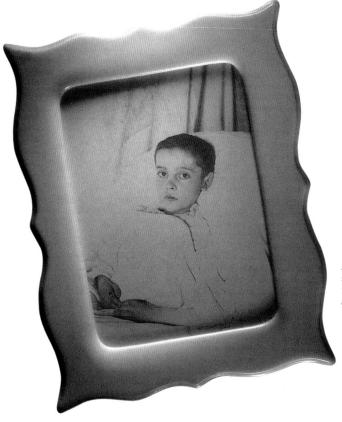

A c. 1880s cabinet card of a terminally ill child taken while he was still alive, but with the expectation of imminent death seen on his face, possibly from consumption, a known fatal illness. *Author's collection.* $75-125.

A c. 1860s rare "pre-mortem" *carte de visite* image of a young boy in his final hours, lovingly wrapped in a blanket. *Author's collection.* $175-225.

In determining values, the daguerreotype, being the earliest process and the most difficult in which to create an artistic result, is the most highly prized by collectors of historic photographica and, therefore, can command high prices for unusual themes or beauty. Ambrotypes and tintypes are generally less costly, although outstanding postmortem images done in these formats can be sometimes competitive with daguerreotypes. Images that include locks of hair, obituary notices, poems, or other tokens also add to the value, as do the quality and rarity of the case in which the postmortem is housed. Tinted or painted embellishments on the image, as well as photographer's stamps on the brass mat or a velvet pad interior, also add desirable value. Condition is critical here, as with other memorial artifacts, in assessing values.

Most postmortem photographs found today are of children, and while these images may seem morbid to our current tastes, it must be remembered that often these photographs were the only visible remembrance parents had of their children, who frequently succumbed to fatal illness within twenty-four hours. James Abram Garfield, later our twentieth president, left the Civil War battlefield to hurry home and be photographed holding his dead infant in his arms.

Even after living photographs became available to middle class Victorians, the acceptability of postmortem photographs was such that these images continued in popularity throughout the 19th and early 20th centuries. Today, family members are still taking postmortem images and many hospitals routinely photograph stillborn infants as a comfort to grieving parents. However, they will probably never reach the zenith in popularity or the artistic beauty seen in 19th century images.

A powerful c. 1840s daguerreotype of a mother holding her deceased infant with her living children surrounding her. The absence of a husband possibly indicates that he too has passed, or is away from home for an extended period of time. The mother wears a mourning brooch containing hair of a deceased loved one, possibly that of her child, on a black ribbon around her neck; her facial expression is a mixture of bewilderment and serenity. This daguerreotype was taken by the well known photographer "M. A. Root" of Philadelphia; images with photographer's names or galleries add more value to an image than those without such identification. *Collection of Charles Swedlund.* $1,500.

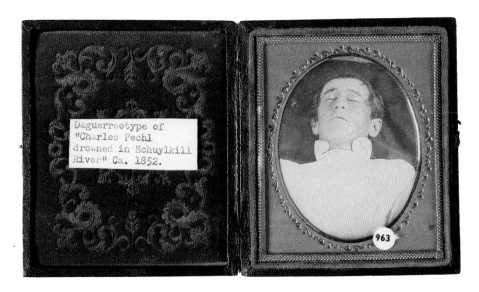

"Mine eyes are robbed of what they loved to see; my longing arms of the embrace they covet."

Exceptional 1/6 plate daguerreotype of man and woman holding a postmortem image of their deceased child. Being photographed holding an image of an absent loved one was a popular method of representing loss in the 19th century, although holding a postmortem image was more rarely done as seen here. In this haunting image, the grief of the parents is quite evident. *Collection of Charles Swedlund.* $595.

A rare postmortem daguerreotype in which an older child holds her dead sibling. This c. 1840s image is unusual in the fact that a parent is not holding the dead infant with the living child standing alongside. Perhaps the parents wanted an image of both children for economic reasons, or it is possible that they feared losing their older child and wanted a living image of her in case of her premature death. The time necessary for this living child to sit motionless holding her dead sister makes this image all the more poignant. *Author's collection.* $750+.

Opposite page:
"Thou art gone to thy rest, brother!
Thy toils and cares are o'er;
And sorrow, pain, and suff'ring now,
Shall ne'er distress thee more."

Rare c. 1850s daguerreotype of "Charles Pechl," with provenance noting that he drowned in the Schuylkill River in 1852. Images with names or information of the deceased add considerably to the value. *Collection of Charles Swedlund.* $750.

A c. 1860s tintype of the head and shoulders of a young boy. A curl of his hair is sewn to the interior pad, along with a poem extolling his loss. Such elegiac poetry was ubiquitous and neutral enough to be applicable to everyone's loss in the Victorian era, and many diaries, memoirs, and images included such poetic lamentations. However, it is difficult to find postmortem images with hair and poems still intact, thus, this image is all the more valuable for the inclusion of these elements. The boy's knotted bow tie and dress shirt show the loving extent to which family members dressed him for his final portrait. *Collection of Ben Zigler.* $595+.

"The death-wind swept him to his soft repose."
[Willis Gaylord Clark, c. 1840s]

Sixth plate tintype of elderly man in early hexagonal coffin, c. 1860s. *Collection of Ben Zigler.* $450.

September 19, 1869: Warm & dry. My dear wife is dying. Oh, my Father, help me to be reconciled to this painful disposition of Thy providence. Let me not sink in despair. September 21, 1869: Cloudy, signs of rain. A sad day, the saddest of my life. My wife, this day is buried."
January 24, 1873: "My dear departed, most beloved – if departed spirits have knowledge of what happens here, you know how lonesome I am. My life, since your departure, has been one of sorrow that no earthly power can charm away. Are poor mortals left here to suffer, forgotten by departed friends in the heavenly world? Have you no memory of your bereaved and broken-hearted husband?
[Nineteenth century diary of pioneer settler Zadoc Long]

Very rare c. 1860s tintype of a man grieving for his dead wife. Postmortem images almost always depict the deceased as the sole focus of the photograph, thus memorial images of a husband or wife with a dead spouse are quite rare. As seen here, they reflect the marital bond of "til death do us part" in a visually literal manner. *Collection of Ben Zigler.* $750+.

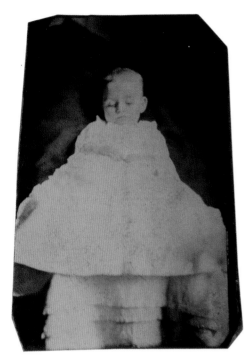

"He has passed away like a delightful vision."
[John Quincy Adams on the loss of his grandson
Arthur in February, 1846]

Sad uncased postmortem tintype of an infant
with large bump on its head; period notation on
reverse states that the death occurred on
Christmas Eve, 1863. *Author's collection.* $275.

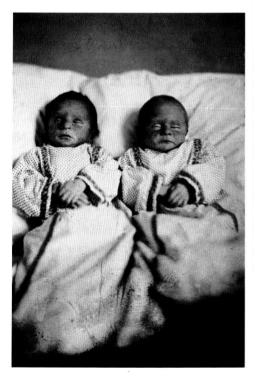

In this c. 1860s postmortem tintype of twins, the
axiom of the Middle Ages, that the "first cry of
the newborn is its first step towards the grave," is
visually represented. These newborn twins are
laid out in matching outfits. *Collection of Ben
Zigler.* $425.

A *carte de visite* postmortem of an infant propped up in its coffin is shown in a bronze frame made of
knots, symbolic of a bond without beginning or ending – an obvious allusion to the Victorian belief in
eternal familial relationships. A close examination of the baby's face shows spots, possibly indicating
that he or she died of measles or small pox. *Author's collection.* $350.

An unusual *carte de visite* postmortem image of a deceased cat, c. 1860-70s. By this time, photography was inexpensive enough for posthumous images of beloved pets to be taken. *Collection of Ben Zigler.* $150.

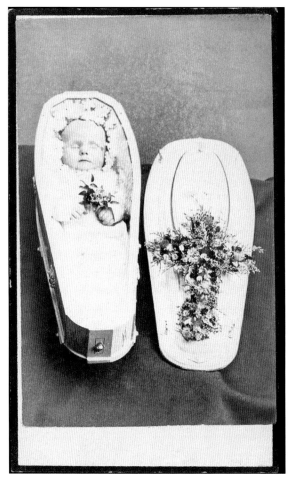

Carte de visite of infant, c. 1860s, encased in its beautifully shaped coffin with viewing window. Flowers are placed in the baby's hands, and a floral cross lies atop the coffin lid. *Collection of Ben Zigler.* $225.

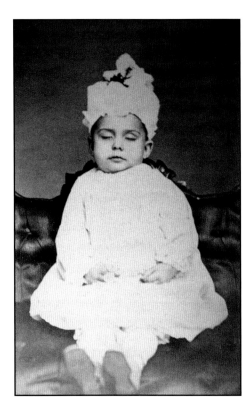

In this c. 1860-70s *carte de visite*, a little girl in her best Victorian dress and hat has been propped up on an elaborate Victorian sofa. Posed to appear alive, her closed eyes and limp body posture evidence of her deceased state. *Author's collection.* $225.

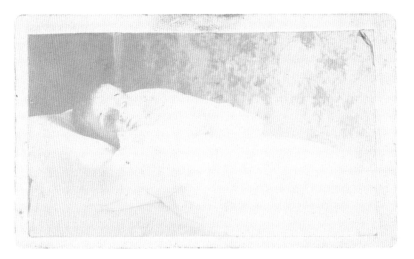

A c. 1893 *carte de visite* of a young girl carries all the pathos of a child's vacant place in the family home, and the despair in the parents' hearts is summed up in the handwritten poem on the reverse of this sad image:

"Baby your chair is vacant,
Baby your toys is idle;
Your mother is lonely;
But she will meet you in heaven."

Little Vivian Caroline Kincaid died August 5, 1893, and is shown in her christening gown, with her hands tied preparatory to placement in the coffin. *Collection of Ben Zigler.* $395+.

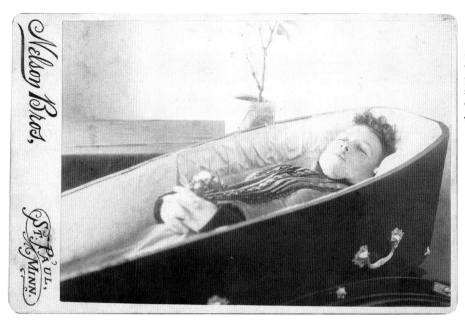

Circa 1880s cabinet card of a young married woman in her coffin. Note the pathetic-looking plant placed nearby, which speaks volumes of the solemnity of the moment, its few leaves indicative of its own death-like condition. *Collection of Ben Zigler.* $275.

A lovingly decorated c. 1910 postmortem cabinet photograph of a beautiful infant laid out in its coffin and covered with flowers. The photograph was placed in a handmade but lavishly embellished frame. This touching memorial goes beyond the simple posthumous photograph, in that the mother created a "framed" memorial of her child, suitable for placement on a parlor table or hung on a wall.

Much effort and design went into this sad memorial, which has an iconographic quality about it as though it were memorializing a saint. Perhaps that was this mother's intention. 7" x 9". *Collection of Ben Zigler.* $300+.

A fabulous mourning tribute to a lost child was created in this c. 1915 memorial tableau, filled with numerous artifacts, religious icons, and symbols representing the child's death and the religious affiliation of his or her family. Prominent in the scene is the canopy over the jewel box casket, in which a white dove is suspended over the baby. Stuffed doves were popular as photographer's props in this decade to represent the soul, or the Holy Spirit. Around the infant's body are numerous religious cards, commonly placed in caskets during viewings at Catholic funerals. Below the casket on the floor are two plaster saints, also popular religious icons among Roman Catholics, and on the table beside the casket are lit candles and floral arrangements. *Collection of Ben Zigler.* $275.

Memorial celluloid "button" photograph, c. 1900s, approximately 6" in diameter. These large memorials had attached wire stands so they could be propped on mantels and parlor tables. *Collection of Lyn Iversen and Chris Lamoreaux.* $125.

An unusual postmortem photograph celluloid pin, c. 1915. Like the pocket mirror of twins, this is another unusual format for posthumous photography; living photographs are more common in these pinbacks. 1.5" in diameter. *Collection of Ben Zigler.* $150-200.

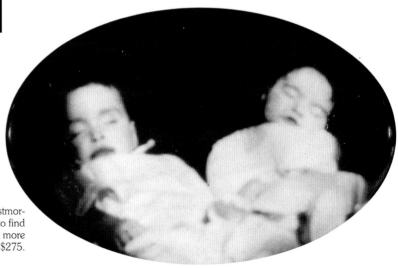

Rare postmortem celluloid pocket mirror of twins, c. 1915. Postmortem photographs in formats such as pocket mirrors are difficult to find today, and twins make this posthumous remembrance even more valuable. *Collection of Ben Zigler.* $275.

Other Memorial Images

Spirit photographs developed in the 1860s as a response to the growing interest in spiritualism among middle and upperclass Victorians, which at times even existed side by side with conventional Christianity. In parlors in America, England, and Europe, spiritualists, mediums, and their followers, as well as skeptics and the curious alike, gathered to contact the world of the "pseudoliving, disembodied spirits." Notorious were the séances conducted by mediums with their "Indian guides," complete with knocking tables, rattlings and shakings, cold blasts of air, and other "manifestations" of the spirit world. And, with the serendipitous discovery in 1861 of so-called "spirit" photography by William Mumler, a Boston engraver and part-time photographer, the possibility of visually revealing the "dead" joined the other activities of spiritualism. Mumler accidentally happened upon the potential for the commercialization of spirit photographs when he developed a plate that had already been twice exposed, showing a weak impression of a head in the background. He established a photographic atelier in New York, taking advantage of the new interest in spiritualism popularized by Mary Lincoln's obsession with contacting her husband's spirit after the assassination.

Grieving family members, desperate for confirmation of their loved ones' future state, fed the growing industry in "spirit photographs" of the deceased. Ghostly apparitions of husbands or wives looking over the shoulder of their living spouses and watching over them, along with the "shades" of children returning to reassure heartbroken parents that they were in bliss represented this new obsession with "scientific evidence" of the After Life. Because photography was viewed as incontrovertibly "true" since it was a "scientific" invention, spirit photographs validated contemporary views of the "domesticated heaven" by offering Victorians "proof" of the spirit world where their loved ones dwelt and where they would soon join them "beyond the grave." So acceptable were spirit photographs in some quarters, than even a new edition of the Bible was published in 1874 with "authentic photographs of Abraham, Moses, David, etc., taken by Spirit Photography."

In fact, spirit photography was a hoax. As one late 19th century account described the practice, "it originated in the land of Barnum, where so many Humbugs have been born." In 1856, Sir David Brewster, an important figure in the development of the medium, described in *The Stereoscope, Its History, Theory, and Construction*, how ghosts could be made to appear in photographs for amusement or "spiritual edification":

"For the purpose of amusement, the photographer might carry us even into the regions of the supernatural. His art, as I have elsewhere shewn [sic], enables him to give a spiritual appearance to one or more of his figures, and to exhibit them as thin air amid the solid realities of the stereoscopic picture. While a party is engaged with their whist or their gossip, a female figure appears in the midst of them with all the attributes of the supernatural. Her form is transparent, every object or person beyond her being seen in shadowy but distinct outline. She may occupy more than one place in the scene, and different portions of the group might be made to gaze upon one or other of the visions before them. In order to produce such a scene, the parties which are to compose the group must have their portraits nearly finished in the binocular camera, in the attitude which they may be supposed to take, and with the expression which they may be supposed to assume, if the vision were real. When the party have nearly sat the proper length of time, the female figure, suitably attired, walks quickly into the place assigned her, and after standing a few seconds in the proper attitude, retires quickly, or takes as quickly, a second or even a third place in the picture if it is required, in each of which she remains a few seconds, so that her picture in these different positions may be taken with sufficient distinctness in the negative photograph. If this operation has been well performed, all the objects immediately behind the female figure, having been, previous to her introduction, impressed upon the negative surface, will be seen through her, and she will have the appearance of an aerial personage, unlike the other figures in the picture."

Even this charade became unnecessary with some fraudulent photographers, who simply asked the purchaser to send money and a photograph of the departed. The scam was eventually exposed in France when a grieving father desired a spirit photograph of his four-year-old son, and received instead one of a fifty-year-old man. The police were summoned, whereupon the photographer was arrested in his shop with a mannequin dressed in blue tulle, and four hundred various heads! In America, William Mumler himself was arrested and prosecuted, but never found guilty of fraud as no proof could be found. Other spirit photographers were not so lucky; many were exposed and arrested or fined, and by the end of the 19th century, spirit photography fell out of favor, becoming part of the carnival sideshow venue. Today spirit photographs are very desirable, especially those by William Mumler and other spirit photographers of the 1860s era. Prices for *cartes de visite* with no backmarks are valued at approximately $175 each; those with photographers' backmarks are $250 and up; images of William Mumler are over $275.

The spirit of a dead child hovering about its father's shoulders is shown in this wonderful c. 1860s spirit photograph. The reverse of this *carte de visite* image advertises the photographer's ability to capture the spiritual occupants of the "unseen" world, revealing the "power" of the spirits "to return and show themselves" as "individualized existences" offering "proof of immortality." *Collection of Ben Zigler.* $325.

Another rare "spirit" *carte de visite* by well known "spirit" photographer William Mumler, c. 1860s. The "spirit" of Ada Isaacs Menkin hovers about the shoulders of Charles Foster, according to a pencil notation on verso. Mumler spirit photographs are rare and highly sought after, and this exceptional image is a fine example of his work. *Collection of Ben Zigler.* $300+.

Top right: Grief has prematurely aged a Civil War era mother, who wears the hairstyle of ringlet curls of a much younger woman, as well as mourning clothing and jewelry probably in memory of this child. This *carte de visite* photograph superimposed with the "spirit" of her little girl standing beside her no doubt brought the mother a great deal of comfort. The photographer of this emotional image was also a woman (unusual for the time), a "Mrs. Stuart" of Boston, who also advertised herself as being able to make "hair jewelry to order." *Collection of Ben Zigler.* $300+.

Cabinet card, c. 1890s, of a women surrounded by the "spirits" of family members. By the 1890s, spiritualism and the "tricks" of photography were no longer widely accepted as "proofs of immortality," and spirit photographs were relegated to the carnival novelty. *Collection of Ben Zigler.* $150.

Aside from the postmortem image, other types of memorial photographs were available to 19th century mourning families as well, and so many of these have survived that collectors have a wide variety to choose from at reasonable prices. Living photographs of the deceased were framed within a "scroll" representative of their passing, and these memorial cards are quite reasonable for collectors to acquire today, usually costing only a few dollars. In some cases, stereoviews of floral or hair wreaths substituted for the living or postmortem image. With these types of memorial photographs, the family could place the stereograph into the stereoscope and once again remember the loved one no longer with them.

From the 1880s, photographs of coffins, by then referred to as "caskets," became popular as memorial representations, and the coffin eventually supplanted the body as the central focus of the image. The popularity of the casket as a symbol for death continued well into the 20th century, and was often virtually invisible amongst the large overwhelming floral funeral arrangements then in vogue. In fact, even photographs of funeral flowers and arrangements, some with inscribed coffin plates, others with banners and the word "Mother," "Father," etc., eventually replaced the postmortem image of decades earlier.

Typical example of a memorial photograph of funeral flowers in cabinet card format of the late 1800s. *Author's collection.* $50.

Unusual c. 1900s photograph of coffin completely covered with Lily-of-the-Valley, symbolic of "purity and humility" or possibly the hope of a future "return of happiness" to the deceased. Towards the end of the 19th century, the coffin substituted for the postmortem image. *Author's collection.* $25-50.

*"Life's blessings all enjoyed, life's labors done,
Serenely to his final rest has passed;
While the soft memory of his virtues, yet
Lingers like twilight hues when the bright sun is set."*
[*The Cypress Wreath* or *A Book of Consolation for Those Who Mourn*, 1844]

Large format photograph, called an "Imperial" photograph, substituting for the postmortem image in the late 19th and early 20th centuries. In this c. 1900s example, a photograph of the deceased ("FATHER"), which was probably standing in the funeral parlor at the time of this gentleman's service, was overpainted, then later framed as a memorial. 14" x 20". *Author's collection.* $275-300.

Finally, symbols began to substitute for the body or coffin of the deceased in many memorial photographs. In the example here, we see a c. 1870s stereograph card depicting symbols immediately recognizable to Victorians as representing the death of a child. On the left we have a marble or parian statue of a child; in the center, an ivy floral arrangement of "Cross and Crown"; and on the right, a white calla lily in a vase, symbolic of purity.

These symbolic and substitutionary photographs, however, represent a double loss to us today, in that because we do not see the deceased as he or she was once known to the family, we are deprived of the face that once gave immortality to the postmortem image.

Stereograph (c. 1890s) of memorial symbols substituting for the postmortem body of the deceased. In this example, the parian statue represents a child, the ivy "Cross and Crown" a funeral arrangement, and a white calla lily in a vase symbolizes purity and innocence. *Author's collection.* $75.

Framed Memorials

Hair-Work Memorials

In the Georgian and Victorian eras, "ladies of taste" were encouraged to participate in sedentary occupations of creativity as part of their societal roles in the "domesticated sphere" of home life. Wealthy young women were raised by their mothers and instructed by tutors in the so-called "pretty arts" of music, dancing, draughtsmanship (pen and ink drawing and pastels), painting, and other parlor crafts. These were part of every well-bred young lady's refinements to be deemed suitably "genteel as an ornament to society." Ladies "repositories" or magazines of the 18th and 19th centuries encouraged the efforts of amateur parlor crafts not only as a means to decorate the home and memorialize the dead, but to "please one's husband." And, *The Habits of Good Society* noted in 1859 that:

> *"All accomplishments have the one great merit of giving a lady something to do; something to preserve her from ennui; to console her in seclusion; to arouse her in grief; to compose her to occupation in joy."*[29]

Thus, all the creativity that genteel ladies pursued in their decorative arts was used as well in producing memorial compositions in both the 18th and 19th centuries. The Victorian penchant for covering every surface with "pretty fancies [and] felicities" also allowed for women's creative handiwork to give expression to grief and loss. In this chapter, we will examine *ars moriendi* of these

centuries using some of the methods of "fancy work" popularly employed.

Most desirable (and generally the most expensive), among collectors today are the hair-work memorials, with examples encompassing variously colored hair, intricate designs, and three-dimensional palette-work methods. All of the methods of working hair as described in the Mourning Jewelry section were utilized in creating framed memorials as well. One sees the same palette methods of cut-work, "dissolved," or chopped hair (along with the use of sepia for fine detailing) used to create the iconography and inscriptions employed in the larger formats of framed pieces. Scenes of weeping willows, grieving mourners, tombstones and urns, etc., are as ubiquitous in hair-work memorials as they are in mourning jewelry.

An antebellum visitor to the mansion of a wealthy Charleston, South Carolina family noted a framed hair-work memorial scene in the home, composed of,

> *"the hairs of [his] late parents, brothers, wife, twelve children, and his own. The ground work is constituted of shrubbery of his father's and mother. An urn on a monument is shrouded with trees of erect figure and horizontal limbs and thick foliage of his brothers' and sister's hair. Ten lambs, and two female figures occupy a field of his children's hair of various colors, mostly of infantile flaxen. A cot represents his lamented wife, constituted of her hair, shaded by weeping*

> *willows and embraced by fence of his own hair. The hairs chopped fine and mixed, I presume, with oil and perhaps colorless paint. I hope my dear daughters will find in these hints materials for a family piece of our own."*[30]

The photographs in this chapter illustrate hair-work memorials created in England, Europe (primarily France, but also Germany and Switzerland), and America. American creators generally favored the method of winding individual strands of hair around thin wire, then shaping the hair-covered wire into floral shapes or design elements such as crosses, lyres, anchors, crowns, wreaths, etc. European hair-work artists tended to prefer palette-worked methods in their memorial works. Additionally, European examples usually included sepia work in the form of obituary information on tombstone plinths and/or grief sentiments (either personal or the standard parlance) within the memorial scene, something not generally seen in American examples. American hair-work pieces also tended to be large (often wreaths set into shadowboxes), whereas French and English hair-work scenes were usually quite small – generally under ten inches, although there were some exceptions as will be seen in this chapter. An additional distinction is that American hair wreaths often included coffin plates, something not seen in European hair-work memorials.

The first example of hair-work memorials we will look at is an extraordinary mourning scene set into a photographic case. This exceptionally fine French remembrance includes the hair of various family members and employs a variety of palette-work methods of cutwork, dissolved hair-work, etc., to create an intricate cemetery scene unbelievably full of memorial symbolism. The rays of sunshine shining down upon the scene convey a happiness not normally seen in memorial art, and the entire tableau exudes a joyful aura in spite of its subject matter. A central tombstone with two adjoining hearts is garlanded and trimmed, while two lovebirds build a nest in its top, the male bringing the nesting female a flower in his beak, symbolic of domestic life, not death. Butterflies float in the warming rays of sunshine, symbolic of two souls joyfully flying heavenward, while birds, also representative of the immortal soul, are visible in the background by the church. Next to the monument, two torches point upward, one burning, one with an olive sprig, with a shield in front bearing the initials "I.H.P." in sepia. A faithful dog, symbolic of loyalty, reclines at the base of the tombstone but looks towards the large oak tree representing victory and strength – no doubt the attributes of his deceased master. Other floral funereal symbols such as cypress trees and Forget-Me-Nots complete this fabulous scene.

An outstanding French memorial on water-colored ivory is shown in the next photograph, in which chopped and dissolved hair create the scene of a large oak tree with three smaller oaks alongside. This memorial is mysterious, and its meaning difficult to interpret. In the background is a large river with a Roman aqueduct, foliage, and hills. Each of the smaller trees has a corresponding initial, obviously intended to represent an individual, and the large oak symbolically signifies strength, endurance, and vigor, qualities typically viewed as predominantly "male." In painted sepia is the following inscription: "Si nous sommes egaux por vous Soyez toujours un abri pour nous," which loosely translates to "If we are your equal, then be a shelter for us." The meaning here is religious in intent, alluding to the Heavenly Father, or God, although it could also possibly refer to an earthly father. The protective haven provided by the large oak for the three smaller ones depicted in the scene is also typical of the growth habit of young oaks under the large overhanging limbs of older trees. The scene of the Roman aqueduct could be a real location, somewhere in France, or possibly Italy.

Beautiful memorial executed in macerated hair-work on ivory, with detailed painted background of hills, cypress trees, and Roman aqueduct. In the foreground, a large oak and three smaller oaks – each with a dissolved hair initial – symbolically represent the inscription, "Si nous sommes egaux por vous soyez toujours un abri pour nous," which loosely translates to, "If we are your equal, then be a shelter for us," a mysterious inscription whose true meaning is now unknown. 4" x 5". *Courtesy of Things Gone By.* $595.

Opposite page: Outstanding hair-work scene set into a six-plate size photographic case. The design and workmanship of this rare memorial are technically incomparable, involving various colors of hair and numerous symbols of familial relationships and meaning. Memorial elements of tombstone monument with garland, cypress and oak trees, lovebirds and torches, the faithful dog, butterflies and sunshine all add to the remarkable composition, making this memorial one of the finest and most unique examples ever seen. *Courtesy of Things Gone By.* Approximately 3" x 4". $2,800.

A pair of extraordinary three-dimensional hair-work memorials in gutta percha frames is shown on these two pages, and the workmanship is almost beyond description. Not only are the scenes executed on water-colored ivory, but the monuments and urns are carved pieces of ivory placed three-dimensionally against the background. The initials on the monuments, along with the rare iconography of skull and crossbones, scythes, and hourglasses, are all done in sepia, and the hair-work weeping willow branches fall around and between the elements of the scenes. In one of the memorials, a cherub executed in sepia with palette-worked hair "wings" places a wreath on the tomb. Background cypress trees, foliage, butterflies (symbolic of immortality), and stream done in dissolved hair and sepia complete the scenes in both pieces, which are placed under embossed paper mats inside the frames.

One of a pair of outstanding hair-work and ivory memorials in gutta percha frames. Hair-work is executed in both cut-work and macerated methods of palette-work, and the scene of ivory tomb and weeping willow are three-dimensional with branches of the willow hanging behind and over the tomb. Note the skull and crossbones, hourglass, and scythe in the foreground, symbols from the Middle Ages *memento mori* iconography. 6.5" x 8". *Courtesy of Things Gone By.* $4,200 pair.

Close-up of hair-work scene, showing detail of workmanship. *Courtesy of Things Gone By.*

Second of extraordinary pair of ivory and hair-work memorials in gutta percha frames, showing ivory cherub placing wreath on tomb, with two butterflies in the sky overhead, and hourglass, skull, and scythe in front of the monument. Note that the cherub is memorializing two deaths and the date on the tomb is 1872, a period when *memento mori* iconography enjoyed a brief resurrection in popularity in Victorian design. *Courtesy of Things Gone By.*

Close-up of memorial cherub placing wreath on the tomb, with details of initials on the tomb and plaque in the cherub's hand. *Courtesy of Things Gone By.*

An unusual method of hair-work was employed in this memorial; the scene was actually embroidered using individual strands of hair as "thread" to create the memorial tableau. Examples of this form of memorial art are rare and constitute the earliest form of hair-work done in memorials, dating to the early 1800s. In this French memorial, the entire scene is embroidered using single strands of hair in shades of blonde to light-brown hues, probably the hair of a wife and child[ren]. The strands of hair are embroidered over single threads of silk, with the shading under the trees along the riverbanks lightened and darkened by the increase and decrease of tiny stitches. Victorians were readily familiar with mourning symbolism, and would thus have been able to "read" the message intended here: that of the death of a spouse. The two equal-sized weeping willows, one living in "this world" as symbolized by the tree on one riverbank, and the other having gone to "the other world," as represented by the tree on the opposite embankment, are separated by the "River of Life" flowing through the two "worlds." Symbolic flowers of lilies and Forget-Me-Nots grow on each of the riverbanks, and the bridge symbolizes the connection from "this world to the next," yet brings the dead spouse near to the "land of the living," while they await their future reunion. The expression "Separated But Forever United" in French is embroidered over the scene.

The next three examples are c. 1870s French memorials, all approximately 12" high by 10" wide, done in various methods of palette-work and surrounding *carte de viste* photographs of the deceased. The touching French child's memorial, with an image of the little girl taken when alive and riding her elaborate Victorian hobby horse, is surrounded by her blonde palette-worked hair done in the cut-work method and set on a milk glass background.

The other child's memorial, showing a *carte de visite* of a three-year-old child, incorporates her brown hair executed in another form of hair-work design set against white satin, symbolic of

Rare French hair embroidery on silk, c. 1860s. In this extraordinary memorial, individual strands of hair of a wife and child[ren] were used to create the scene by embroidering over single strands of silk. The technical expertise by this needlewoman is evident in the use of greater or fewer stitches to achieve the desired effect of gradations in shading. Symbolism of the weeping willows over the River of Life and the bridge "from this world to the next," as well as the Forget-Me-Nots and lilies on the riverbanks, add to the melancholy theme of widowhood, along with the inscription, "Separated but forever united" in French above the scene. 5" x 7". *Author's collection.* $895.

the child's purity and innocence and made to appear like the interior of a casket. In this piece, the child's hair was wound around thin wire and fashioned into both floral designs and the letters, "M C," with a large central "Forget-Me-Not" flower in the foreground.

In the third memorial, we see a piece dedicated to a mother. In this fine example, the mother's hair was done in the cut-work method of palette-worked hair, which was then further embellished with gold leaf. In sepia are the words, "In memory of my good friend, Mother," and the mother's photograph has been cut out of its original *carte de visite* format and placed inside the palette-worked hair designs.

A beautiful c. 1870s French hair-work memorial to little girl whose *carte de visite* photograph in the center shows her riding on a fancy Victorian hobbyhorse. Her blonde hair was created in the palette-worked method, by laying her hair on glue-covered paper, then cutting it into shapes when dry and placing it in flourishes on milk glass surrounding the central image. 10" x 12". *Author's collection.* $695.

A poignant, c. 1870s French memorial to a little girl created by wrapping strands of her hair around thin wire, then fashioning the hair-covered wire into floral shapes and initials to form this sad tribute. The large "Forget-Me-Not" flower also created in her hair was formed by another method of looping the hair and was placed below a *carte de visite* photograph of the child. 10" x 12". *Author's collection.* $695.

A beautifully executed, c. 1870s French memorial to a mother is shown here, with elaborate palette-worked hair on watercolored milk glass. The mother's photograph has been cut out from a *carte de visite* image and placed in the center, surrounded by hair-work executed in superb workmanship. Three-dimensional flowers with tiny leaves, gold-painted stamen and pistils, and sepia detailing add considerably to the beauty and value of this memorial. "Souvenir de notre bien aimee Mere," or "In Remembrance of my good friend Mother" in sepia, gold paint, and dissolved hair form the inscription. 10" x 12". *Author's collection.* $695.

An extremely rare and possibly singular example of its kind, the hairwork memorial on ivory set into a larger ivory frame shown here is an early 19th century piece employing dyed palette-worked hair. In this exceptional memorial, the hairwork is extremely fine, even to the thorns on the rose, and the entire arrangement has been executed after having bleached the hair white, then dying it the pale tints shown in the flowers and leaves. The large full rose represents the deceased having reached adulthood, and the inclusion of a pale pink bud alongside possibly represents an only daughter – perhaps the artist who created this masterpiece. Pale blue Forget-Me-Nots are included in the arrangement as memorial flowers as well. The simplicity of the design belies the complexity in creating this memorial, and few dyed hairwork arrangements of this quality are extant.

The following three 18th and 19th century French memorials are rare and truly exceptional. Various methods of palette-worked hair design, primarily comprising styles of cut-work and dissolved hair, have been employed to create scenes of historical and memorial interest now lost to time. In the first mourning scene, we see an 18th century town or military outpost somewhere in France, with a weir and cannon in the foreground. At the time this memorial was created, France had already endured the horrors of the Revolution, to be followed by other conflicts suffered during the reigns of Napoleon I and III. It is possible that this memorial commemorates an official from the military post during this time of tumult.

A rare and outstanding memorial of dyed hair-work on ivory, c. 1840s, probably French. *Collection of Sandra Johnson.* $1,100.

Wonderful scene executed in dark brown macerated hair on ivory of military barracks with cannon emplacements alongside a large river weir, no doubt a real fortification somewhere in Europe, probably France, during the Napoleonic Wars. *Collection of Sandra Johnson.* $895.

Another military scene with ramparts in the foreground is commemorated in the next hair-work memorial. This time, a harbor view in Louverne, Italy is shown with cannonade in place, and it was here on "14 October 1806," as noted in the banner overhead (written in sepia), that a battle took place during one of Napoleon's many invasions when he was attempting to expand the French empire into Italy. An eagle triumphantly displays the banner, the eagle being the symbol for Napoleon who was often referred to as *"L'aiglon"* by his countrymen. The initials "RB" no doubt refer to a soldier in Napoleon's army who fought and died in this battle.

Hair-work scene of a harbor area in Italy with breastworks, probably the site of a battle during the Napoleonic Wars where the soldier being memorialized was killed on October 14, 1806. *Collection of Sandra Johnson.* $895.

A spectacular depiction of a rare historic chateaux in France dating back to the 11th century is shown in the third outstanding French hair-work memorial. Housed in a beautiful rococo frame, this 18th century French memorial is done entirely in various methods of palette-worked hair and sepia. The history of this castle is as fascinating as this memorial is spectacular, and the scene is rich with visual impact and detail. The Castle of Moulineaux, also known as "le Chateaux de Robert le Diable," was built by the father of William the Conqueror, who was also the Duke of Normandy. It was here at the chateaux that possession of the province of Normandy changed hands multiple times from English to French occupation throughout

the many wars of the Hundred Years' conflict. When it was in English hands, Richard the Lion Heart stayed there in the 12th century, and attempted to make the castle impregnable to French recapture. His successor however, returned to England, and the chateaux, along with the province of Normandy, returned to the French within a few decades. King Philippe of France built up the small town of Rouen in 1430 (some of which is pictured in this memorial) to fortify and protect the entry to Rouen against subsequent English invasion. And it was here in this castle, that Joan of Arc was imprisoned before she was burned at the stake. Continuing wars between the French and English laid the castle low, and for centuries after it fell into ruins, the local inhabitants avoided them until they became only the refuge of owls and phantoms. If forced to walk by the mysterious castle, the Rouennais would make the Sign of the Cross on their chests for fear of the ghosts and spirits said to haunt the ruins, made all the more frightening by the dense fog and darkness which settled over them at night. It was said that in the evening, the low clouds transported the spirits of all

who had perished there throughout the walls of the ruined castle.

The modern history of the castle is still one of conflict and devastation, as only one of the tower keeps now remains. Attempts to excavate and restore the castle have been attempted since 1903, but thwarted by both world wars. However, some of the ramparts still remain, and the view of Normandy from its heights is said to be incomparable.

The exact date of the creation of this memorial is unknown, but it probably dates to the 18th century, as the castle is in much better condition in this scene than it presently appears. All of the elements in the chateaux, the foliage and trees surrounding it plus the pathway leading to it, have been executed in the palette-worked methods of cut-work and dissolved-hair. The small town of Rouen is in the distance executed in sepia, as are the distant hills and the small boat with boaters; detailing of sepia is also seen throughout the scene in the touches of brown-black on the foliage and trees. The sky and river have been water-colored in pale blue, the only areas in the scene to be so embellished.

Rare, one-of-a-kind hair-work scene of the castle at Roeun where Joan of Arc was imprisoned before being burned at the stake, 18th century, French. *Collection of Sandra Johnson.* $2,895.

An extraordinary dissolved hair-work and sepia watercolor on ivory memorial, rich with symbolism, contains many motifs representing marital love and loss. This c. 1840-50s French memorial shows the idyllic pastoral cottage, scene of wedded happiness in the earthly life, while lovebirds build a nest in a tree overhead on the right. Underneath the lovebirds, the clasped hands of a husband and wife symbolize the affection and friendship of marriage. The one who has died first is the one who clasps the other's hand; thus, in this case, it is the husband who has died and is being mourned. Central to the scene is an interesting bit of symbolic theatre: a tombstone inscribed with the words, "L'Amitie Les Unis A Jamais," or "Our love is forever united," is crowned by the twin burning hearts above it, the figurative motif of marital passion and love. A sheep hiding behind the monument (representative of an adult child of their union), is seen timidly peeking around the tombstone at the little dog (emblematic of fidelity and loyalty), who bravely barks at the three-headed serpent who appears to threaten the monument. This three-headed snake is somewhat mysterious. Throughout the 18th and 19th centuries, snakes represented benign, even sentimental qualities such as eternal love, as seen in the familiar design of a snake swallowing its tail, and the number three has always represented the Trinity in *ars moriendi* from the Middle Ages through the Enlightenment. Here, however, the three-headed serpent appears more malevolent than charitable, perhaps representing those sinister causations which forecast marital discord – such as infidelity, dishonor, and maltreatment, to name just three possibilities. Another possible interpretation is that the three-headed snake represents Cerberus, the guard dog of Hades (the underworld in Greek mythology), who had three heads, a row of snakes sprouting from his neck, and who greeted the newly dead with relish.

German and Swiss hair-work memorials are more difficult to find, and the techniques employed are somewhat different from French examples. Where French memorials tended to contain a great deal of palette-work in the form of cut-work and sepia, and were generally more vivid because of the darker hues of hair, German and Swiss examples are paler in hue (with more blonde rather than brown hair), and employ more watercolor in background designs. Another typically German technique is the use of two panes of glass in the scene, one upon which a background of sky and hills are painted, and another upon which the hair-work is applied. When placed together, they give added depth and dimension to the overall mourning scenery and iconography. Here we will look at three beautiful German and Swiss hair-work memorials to see similarities and differences in workmanship and design.

The first lovely German memorial, c. 1839, shows a man (probably the father) kneeling at a monument in memory of "Ann Brunner, born 18 Jan. [18]39; died 14 Feb. [18]43. Rest in Peace, Not Forgotten." The background was executed in Ann's blonde hair, in the dissolved hair method, against a pale water-colored sky. The technique is simple, yet very well-executed with a minimum of strokes needed to convey the melancholy scene. The small size of this memorial adds to its overall charm.

A beautiful little German memorial, c. 1840, is shown next. This piece is an example of the German use of the double panes of glass to create the memorial scene. In this case, the background of a gloaming sky at sunset with a lake and distant hills gives a horizon to the eye. The symbolism of a body of water with a far-off horizon line invariably represents the journey of the soul to heaven, and in this case, the message

Extraordinary 18th century French memorial to a husband, full of symbolism, c. 1840-50s. A scene of domestic bliss interrupted by the death of the husband is seen in the clasped hands, the marital "cottage," and the loyal and faithful dog, all executed in macerated hairwork on ivory. *Collection of Charles Swedlund.* $895.

is further emphasized by the boat seen to the right of the weeping willow. The little ship is not painted on the background glass, however, but rather on the foreground piece to give depth to the scene. The hair of the deceased ("In Remembrance V. B." and "M. B.") has been used to create the cut-work and dissolved hair scene on the foreground pane of glass, in which a tomb, a cross, a weeping willow, an anchor, and Forget-Me-Nots convey the message of loss.

A beautiful small German memorial of a man grieving at the tomb of his child, c. 1839; dissolved hair-work and sepia on ivory. 4" x 4". *Courtesy of Things Gone By.* $695.

A lovely c. 1840 German memorial with dual panes of glass, one of which was painted to form the background, and another upon which the cut-work and dissolved hair-work of the deceased was executed in the foreground. 4" x 4". *Courtesy of Things Gone By.* $695.

A rare one-of-a-kind hair-work memorial, full of mourning symbolism, is representative of some of the finest workmanship seen in German and Swiss commemorative art. This outstanding c. 1840 German or Swiss memorial is almost entirely executed in dissolved hair, with cut-work elements, sepia, and watercolor also incorporated into the scene. Several remarkable techniques and symbols have been used here: the use of the double panes of glass, the background glass being painted with the lovely sunset sky, distant hills and lake, and the foreground glass containing all the hairwork motifs and design. Prominent in the foreground is an island in the middle of the lake, in which a large columnar temple encloses a monument upon which sits a burning heart, symbol of passionate love. Note that the temple is garlanded by tiny slivers of cut-work hair, and the contours of the temple and its columns has been achieved by the use

of slightly darker hues of hair, an extraordinarily skillful accomplishment. Funereal trees, a weeping willow, and a "broken" tombstone in front of the temple with the initials "KR" are also depicted. Grazing underneath the willow is a sheep, exquisitely detailed, and probably symbolic of the death of an adult child. A swan swims along the lake in the foreground, reminding the viewer of the love of swans, grottoes, and the lakes of Germany so frequently extolled in Wagnerian operas. A bird, symbolic of the soul, flies heavenward in the sky, and the idyllic scene is framed in its original gold-painted wood frame.

Hair wreaths were a popular parlor pastime like many other crafts for Victorian women, particularly those living in America. Incorporating both familial sentiments as well as memorial remembrances, hair wreaths personalize a family as succinctly as the family photograph album, as relatives could often easily

point to and identify the hair of various contributors, living and deceased. Some hair wreaths were strictly sentimental in nature; others were exclusively memorial. Thus, without additional evidence, it can be difficult to identify the true nature of the wreath arrangement, whether memorial or sentimental. Some historians believe that if the hair wreath is "closed," that is, in a circular rather than an open "horseshoe" shape, it is memorial. However, clearly identified memorials wreaths are seen in both open and closed arrangements, so this cannot be a true determination. As described earlier, most hair wreaths were created by winding individual strands of hair around thin wire, then the hair-covered wire was fashioned into the floral and leaf shapes. Among the following memorials are exceptional examples of hair wreaths showing outstanding workmanship in beautiful frames, making them fine examples of their genre.

A spectacular German or Swiss memorial, c. 1840s, of an island in a lake executed in dissolved hair, sepia, and watercolor against a painted background on glass of hills and a lake. This scene was also arranged employing the dual panes of glass for foreground and background scenery typically used in German and Swiss memorials. 9" x 10.5". *Courtesy of Things Gone By.* $995.

A c. 1830-40 French hair-work memorial executed in blonde hair and sepia paint on ivory, with tombstone and initials "ATW," cypress and willow trees, and stream flowing in the foreground. Note the skull and crossbones over the tomb, a rarely seen symbol in memorial art after the 18th century. The plaque is placed under a convex glass inside an "ebonized" wood frame, which is base wood painted with black enamel. 4.25" x 3.5". *Courtesy of Things Gone By.* $595.

French hair-work memorial depicting a man placing a wreath on a tomb with an urn. The palette-worked hair scene is executed on water-colored ivory, and the tomb is inscribed with a farewell to the family. On the reverse is a period written provenance for the Thevenin family deaths in 1834. 4.5" x 4.5". *Courtesy of Things Gone By.* $595.

A lovely and delicate urn done in blonde dissolved hair-work on ivory. This quality of workmanship in this c. 1830-50 memorial is so finely executed, one must look closely to see the tiny Forget-Me-Nots almost gaily floating overhead and the tiny lines in the garland which trim the pale-blue water-colored urn. The macerated hair of the deceased also composes the mosses, grasses, and leaves below the urn. 4.5" x 4.5". *Courtesy of Things Gone By.* $495.

A rare English hair-work on ivory inside a gutta percha standing frame. The oval scene depicts the weeping mourner placing a wreath on the shrouded urn at the top of the monument. The epitaph of "Regrets" on the monument speaks volumes in itself, unusual in obituary idiom, and one wonders at the story behind this sad piece. Willow and twining ivy complete the scene. 5" x 3". *Courtesy of Things Gone By.* $2,895.

A very poignant memorial to the deaths of four children is shown in this c. 1840 French memorial depicting the mother grieving over the tomb of her four children, whose names are inscribed on the plinth. The entire scene is full of pathos and executed in dissolved and finely chopped hair on ivory. 4" x 4". *Courtesy of Things Gone By.* $1,395.

A close-up view of the craftsmanship of dissolved hair-work in the scene of the mother grieving at the tomb of her children. *Courtesy of Things Gone By.*

A c. 1840 French memorial to a husband and father, executed in cut-work hair on watercolored ivory, conveys the loss of marital love with the flaming hearts over the tomb. Overhead in sepia is the inscription, "Nos cheveux te couvrent epoux et pere!!," or "Our hair covers you O husband and father" in French, indicating that both the brown and blonde hair of mother and child[ren] were used to create the intimate remembrance. *Author's collection.* 4.5" x 4". $550.

A c. 1840 memorial to a mother, with a lovely basket of flowers (Forget-Me-Not and thistles) executed in both cut-work and dissolved hair methods. The inscription reads, "Restes precieux de ma mere," which means, "Precious remembrance of my mother". 5.5" x 5.5". *Courtesy of Things Gone By.* $525.

A sad French memorial to a six-year-old boy named "Paul," with his blonde hair worked into the symbols of a weeping willow and monument with plinth. The epitaph in French reads, "Paul mort le 15 november 1821 age de 6 ans ½," which translates to "Paul died November 15, 1821, at 6-1/2 years of age." Another plaque alongside the monument reads, "C'est tout ce qu'il ni'en Reste," which loosely translates to "This is all that remains," a heartbreaking statement of despair that the tomb and the memorial of hair is all that is left of the precious "Paul." 6" x 6". *Courtesy of Things Gone By.* $696.

A c. 1850s memorial to a beloved mother indicates the possibility of two contributors in the hair-work: the brown and blonde hair being either that of a husband and daughter, or possibly two children. In any event, the monument and urn garlanded with a funeral wreath and overhanging willow executed on ivory, is inscribed, "In memory of the best and most beloved of Mothers." 4" in diameter. *Courtesy of Things Gone By.* $695.

As childhood death was such a common experience, memorials to children abound. In this French memorial, three children are remembered in the curls of their blonde hair; their names and the dates of their deaths written in sepia around or inside each curl. The largest curl at the top is of little Marie Agatha, who died March 31, 1871; the others are of her twin brothers, Rene and Andre, who died together April 10, 1876. A poignant inscription in sepia over the palette-worked hair is loosely translated as, "Your three children now dwell in the Temple of the Sky and are beautiful blooming lilies." 5" x 7". *Author's collection.* $895.

In this touching c. 1870s French memorial to a young boy, an entire pastoral scene incorporating cemetery and memorial symbolism surrounds a c. 1870s photograph of him holding his toy gun. The background scenery employs many of the elements seen in other hair-work memorials and mourning jewelry of the 18th and 19th centuries, such as the cypress and yew trees and the distant mountains done in the dissolved hair method, along with a three-dimensional weeping willow executed in palette-worked hair. The River of Life promised in the biblical "New Heaven and New Earth" is shown meandering through the scene, and typical Forget-Me-Not flowers grow at the boy's feet, certainly an unnecessary reminder to grieving parents. 5" x 7". *Author's collection.* $795.

Anchors were popular as a mourning motif for *ars moriendi*, sometimes representing a loved one lost at sea, as in this example, or referring to the three symbols of Christianity: Faith, Hope, and Love, with the anchor being the representative motif for Hope (Hebrews 6:19). Four sailor knots in each corner are the probable indicators that this memorial does in fact commemorate someone lost at sea, and the beautiful palette-worked hair is exceptionally well done. A wreath of tiny cut-work slivers of leaves and flowers entwines an anchor, the cord of which has been done in the table-worked method of hair-weaving. A large Forget-Me-Not flower is on the right side of the wreath near the anchor and two white twisted cotton "ties" appear to "fasten" the wreath to the anchor. The small size (4" x 6") of this c. 1860s memorial in its black frame makes it all the more charming. *Courtesy of Things Gone By.* $515.

An exceptional hairwork memorial and one of the finest examples of curled *loupe* or "Prince of Wales" methods of palette-worked hair. Deceptively simple in appearance, yet quite dramatic in its arrangement, the initials "E M" have been elaborately designed as a cipher with individual strands of hair laid out against the ivory ground. This c. 1870s French memorial was created by an expert in palette-worked hair devices. *Collection of Sandra Johnson.* $895.

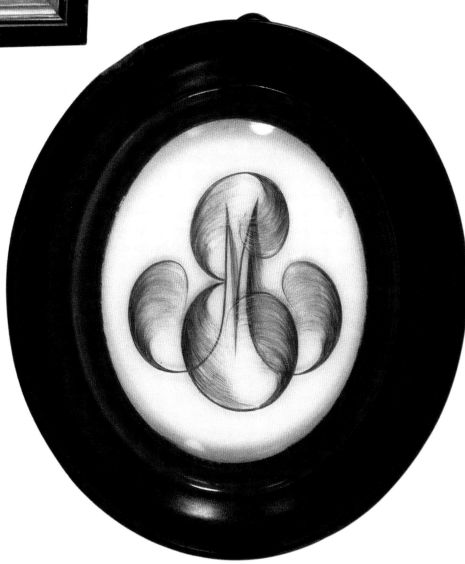

A spectacular round walnut "porthole" shadowbox frame crammed full of variously-hued hair "flowers," c. 1860s. 9" in diameter. *Collection of Jerry Lesandro and Larry Martin.* $795.

A lovely c. 1880s memorial with intricately executed hair-work in the unusual color of pale blonde hair. This remarkable memorial in a lovely oak frame has tightly woven hair flowers in virtually mint condition surrounding a cabinet card photograph of a husband and wife. The length of hair required for the flowers in this memorial indicates that the wife is undoubtedly the deceased being remembered here. 13" x 14". *Collection of Charles Swedlund.* $500.

A beautiful vase or urn of "flowers" all made from the hair of family members is shown in this c. 1880s shadowbox memorial. The outstanding hair-work on this piece was executed using different methods of wrapping the hair around wire, then fashioning the hair-covered wire into the floral shapes. Note that the urn itself was created by densely packing the hair-covered wire in such a way that by incorporating lighter-hued brown hair, the contours of the vase were highlighted. 12" x 14". *Courtesy of Lyn Iversen and Chris Lamoreaux.* $550.

A beautiful hair-work cross laid against white satin in a walnut frame is shown in this lovely c. 1870s memorial. The method of hair-work "buttons" was executed over wooden molds, with tatted hair as additional decoration, and the inclusion of white satin background possibly indicates that the deceased was a young unmarried woman. *Collection of Charles Swedlund.* 17" x 13" including frame. $400.

This interesting c. 1860s hair-work cross with floral arrangement was composed of wire-worked light-brown hair, wherein the hair-covered wire was layered back and forth to form the three-dimensional cross "bars," the tips of which were formed by the hair-covered wire wound in a trefoil pattern. At the base of the cross, floral motifs in various methods were arranged with one individual blonde hair "bow" added, possibly the hair of the maker, executed in a table-worked pattern similar to the techniques employed in creating bobbin lace. 7" x 8". *Author's collection.* $325.

A wonderful Civil War-era memorial with a hair wreath and linen leaves surrounding a *carte de visite* photograph of a deceased woman set inside a walnut shadowbox frame. Here the wreath is completely closed, symbolizing a death, the life having come "full circle" and now "closed forever." 17" x 18", including frame. *Collection of Charles Swedlund.* $400.

A c. 1880s cabinet card of a deceased young woman is framed by beautiful hair-work flowers executed in her lovely dark brown hair, both enclosed in a carved walnut Victorian frame. The hair-work here is executed in the method of covering wire, then fashioning the hair-covered wire into flowers and stems in the wreath surrounding her photograph. *Collection of Charles Swedlund.* 13" x 15", including frame. $350.

A touching "homemade" floral "bouquet" of flowers with blue beaded centers set inside a lovely frame, c. 1860s. The limited amount of hair, and the white ribbon indicate this was probably the hair of a child who died. 12" x 14". *Collection of Jerry Lesandro and Larry Martin.* $325.

A poignant memorial to the loss of a little girl is shown in this c. 1880s shadowbox. In contrast to the elaborate mourning scenes executed in technically sophisticated palette-work of French and German pieces, this touching piece simply shows the ringlets of hair as though we were looking at the back of the little girl's head as she walks into eternity. 10" x 12". *Author's collection.* $300.

An expertly crafted c. 1880s hair-work memorial to a mother, in which a tiny "bouquet" of flowers in brown hair is held together with a paper "shield" inscribed, "Remembrance of Mother." The hair-work here was created by wrapping strands of hair around thin wire, then assembling the hair-covered wire into the tiny individual flowers and leaves. 9.5" x 11". *Author's collection.* $395.

A rare mid-19th century nun's memorial enclosing a small rosary crucifix, hair "flowers" with blue glass beads, and lead calla lily coffin screw. This memorial is unusual in the inclusion of a lead coffin screw as a memorial piece, as opposed to the inscribed casket plate more commonly seen. As the heads of nuns were closely shorn in the 19th century, the lengths of hair used in this memorial were extended by being wrapped with black thread on wire in order to make up enough quantity to create the flowers. 4.5" square. *Courtesy of OBJX.* $395.

A beautiful c. 1860s hair wreath with hair-work cross in a walnut octagon shadowbox. This large memorial displays an intricately executed hair wreath composed of the hair of various family members, living and deceased, surrounding a hair-work cross of the one being memorialized. 2.25 feet in diameter. *Collection of Lyn Iversen and Chris Lamoreaux.* $895-1,000.

A touching memorial to a young boy, whose cabinet card photo shows him dressed in an elaborate velvet skirt and blouse, with his hair in long ringlets. Clothing and hairstyles such as was worn by this child were favored among some Victorian upperclass parents, most notably the only son of Robert and Elizabeth Barrett Browning, who wore such outfits and long ringlets until well past young childhood. This memorial shadowbox includes the little boy's white leather gloves and two of his ringlet curls fastened to the hand-painted interior on black velvet. 10" x 18". *Author's collection.* $275.

An outstanding hair memorial set into an oval frame (possibly walnut), incorporating the family members' variously-hued blonde and gray hair, elaborately woven into hair flowers. Note the blonde ringlets attached with a white ribbon in the center which memorialize a child. 20" by 12". *Collection of Jerry Lesandro and Larry Martin.* $895-1,000.

Framed Memorials of Other Materials

In addition to the hair-work examples shown previously, other types of memorials were created in 18th and 19th century European and American households. Mourning paintings were often composed on ivory, milk glass, and wood. Home crafts employing elements such as flowers made of wax, feathers, linen, paper, dried petals, and "skeletonized" leaves are seen ubiquitously in 19th century memorials, particularly American pieces. These and other materials, such as collected seashells, ferns, and sea-weeds, were sometimes combined with coffin plates and photographs of the remembered loved one, either while living or deceased. In this section, we will look at other types of memorials, such as pieces utilizing various craft materials or unusual arrangements.

In the first example, an elaborately grand cemetery scene created by an Italian-American family member to memorialize the loss of a mother and child (probably in childbirth), incorporates several elements into the memorial tableau. In the lower left, we have a mica-covered paper "mausoleum" with its door standing open and an attached white paper cross "monument," possibly denoting an earlier death of someone other than the mother and child being memorialized here. Little wooden "coffins" of mother and child, painted black with silver stars and glass glitter, seen on the lower right, are ready to be carried along the rock "pathway" through the sphagnum moss leading to the mausoleum for burial in the vault. Above the mausoleum is a hair-work weeping willow made of the mother's hair with tiny glass beads at the ends of the "branches." Above the willow is a coffin plate of a woman kneeling at the cross. In the center of the scene is a large wooden cross entwined with hair-work "grapes" and grape "leaves," and to the right of them is a wooden altar with parian ceramic Madonna and Child and the name "Rosa," with flowers all executed in hairwork, entwined around the statuary. This extraordinary memorial lacks some of the intricacy in detail and workmanship of fine 18th century French hair-work pieces, but has all the wonderful qualities of 19th century American folk art.

During the 18th century, decorating with shells was a favorite occupation of aristocratic ladies, and the pleasures of creating "shell grottoes" and other forms of shell art were extolled by Mary Delaney in England, an accomplished 18th century artist in paper "mosaicks" and shell displays for drawing rooms. She described her "new madness,…running wild after shells" in a 1734 letter, while she accumulated an enormous collection which she kept in a specially-constructed cabinet. The Duchess of Portland, a friend of Mary's, was also enamored of shell collecting and art, so much so that she killed over a thousand snails to acquire their shells. Louis XVI had a Shell Cottage built at Rambouillet for Marie Antoinette, and a grotto of "marine art" was a favorite pastime of the Duchess of Richmond and her two daughters at Goodwood House in Sussex.[31]

Shell work creations were also easily modified into the venue of memorial arts, similar to the other decorative skills of wax work, feather work, and embroidered pieces. Women living near coastal regions collected seashells on beach walks, as the love of nature collecting became a popular pastime in the 18th and 19th centuries. Shells and "sea ferns" (sea weeds), were gathered, just as souvenirs from woodland nature walks such as leaves, acorns, nuts, twigs, etc., were collected and used in parlor crafts. For women living inland, shells could be purchased through *Godey's Ladies Book* or other repositories, and many sailors brought shell souvenirs home to wives and sweethearts from trips taken to the Mediterranean and Far East.

The shells were first sorted as to size, shape, and color, and elaborate floral arrangements fabricated into designs on pasteboard. The shells were glued down with a mixture of wax and mucilage, which was warmed and softened to allow placement of petals and stems. Roses and Forget-Me-Nots were relatively simple to execute, but other memorial blossoms were tedious and complex. Frequently the shell designs were augmented with watercolor tints, and when completed, the entire work varnished with a light coat of copal varnish. Often they were placed in shadowbox frames, and backed with black cloth to symbolize a memorial piece.

A spectacular "cemetery" scene memorializing an Italian-American mother and child who died in childbirth, c. 1890s. A cardboard "mausoleum" covered with mica, at the lower left, has an open door with white monument indicating an earlier death in the family. A "rock trail" leads from the open door of the mausoleum to the two coffins at the lower right representing the mother and child memorialized here. Overhanging the mausoleum is a hair-work weeping willow, and above that is the mother's coffin plate. A wooden cross in the center is entwined with hair-work grape leaves, and the name "Rosa" and flowers also done in hair-work surround the Madonna and Child in the upper right. 24" x 24.5". *Author's collection.* $850.

Many of these shell work creations were fashioned into frames around memorial images or lithographs such as the one shown here. In this piece, shells probably collected on a beach excursion, along with paste stones, jewelry findings, and mother of pearl buttons, were arranged on a board frame in a decorative arrangement around a lithograph of a woman and her child in a cemetery. The mother is weeping, holding a handkerchief to her eyes, and both mother and child are in mourning dress. A braid of hair in a heart shape, tied with blue silk thread, and the name "Hattie" is in the upper left, and curls of hair over a pencil notation, "June 1, 1861, Pleasant St, Auburn Village" is on the right. The absence of a husband in the lithograph possibly indicates that the lock of hair over the pencil notation is that of a dead husband, and "Hattie," that of a deceased child.

Wax was another craft material suitable for memorial art. Initially wax creations were decorative, much like feather and shell work pieces, but they were easily modified to convey a mourning theme. A home encyclopedia entitled *Inquire Within, or Over 5,700 Facts for the People*, published in 1856, introduced readers to the art of wax creations, thusly:

> *"There is no art more easily acquired nor more encouraging in its immediate results than that of modeling flowers in wax."*

Wax flowers were created primarily in three different ways. Sometimes the wax petals were cut out of sheets of wax and assembled on stems, then curled by means of rolling and twisting the wax around curling sticks. Another method employed scraping thin "petals" from a block of wax, and the third technique involved melting the wax and pouring it into molds of petals and leaves. This last method was the most expensive, as the molds were individually priced at 50 cents each, and thus wax creations, like most memorial arts, were primarily the hobby of upperclass Victorian women. Bell-shaped flowers made of warmed and softened wax were shaped over wooden molds so that they "drooped" in sadness, then removed and mounted. Like feather and shell work, wax could be purchased tinted, or dyed at home. Once the wax flowers were formed,

camel's hair brushes were employed to paint thin lines and highlights of various hues onto the flowers. Leaves were formed from green-tinted wax, or sometimes pressed on top of embossed cloth leaves, with "hairy" surfaces created by dusting the wax leaf with hair powder.

Wax memorials are difficult to find in the excellent condition seen in the fine examples here. Over time, heat and atmospheric conditions usually take their toll on the fragile wax flowers and leaves, rendering them a pale and damaged shadow of their former beauty.

Shellwork memorial, probably in memory of a husband, with a lithograph of a young widow and her child, is shown here. The shellwork frame includes bits of jewelry and buttons as well as collected shells, and is varnished on wood. On top of the lithograph is a braid of hair formed into a heart, with the name "Hattie" inside on the left, and on the right, a curl of hair with the pencil notation, "June 1, 1861, Auburn Village." 8" x 9". *Author's collection.* $350.

The following three mid-19th century small memorials were created in memory of a child, and are full of the pathos inherent in such a loss. In the first lovely little oval shadowbox, a nosegay of wax flowers fastened with a white ribbon and the sentiment "Our Darling Babe" beautifully expresses sadness in the loss of an infant. The memorial of a

tiny white wax floral nosegay set into a hand-carved "tramp art" style frame set against black velvet also bespeaks a painful poignancy in its simplicity. And the oval shadowbox with wax roses, dried fern leaves, and fine hairwork flowers is unusual for the fact that the funeral flowers themselves were dipped in wax and used in this child's remembrance.

Poignant wax floral tribute to "Our Darling Babe" in beautiful walnut oval frame, c. 1860s. *Collection of Jerry Lesandro and Larry Martin.* $400.

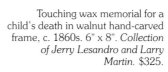

Touching wax memorial for a child's death in walnut hand-carved frame, c. 1860s. 6" x 8". *Collection of Jerry Lesandro and Larry Martin.* $325.

Child's wax memorial in beautiful oval walnut frame, with funeral flowers dipped in wax, dried fern leaves, white ribbon, and fine hairwork flowers. 9" x 7". *Author's collection.* $400.

An outstanding and rare shadowbox memorial for a child, c. 1870s, is shown next. A lovely wax floral wreath of calla lilies and orange blossoms surrounds a postmortem *carte de visite* of a little girl laid out on a Victorian fainting couch, with her lunch pail and toys beside her. Lilies, of course, are a traditional funeral flower; however, orange blossoms decorate the bridal veil, one this little girl will never wear. It also appears that shortly after her death, the couch where the postmortem image was taken was placed in her bedroom, as her rumpled bed is visible in the background, possibly where she died. The coffin plate above the postmortem image, originally removed from the little girl's casket, is engraved, "Suffer the Little Children to Come Unto Me" (Matthew 19:14).

In 1853, visitors to New York City's Crystal Palace marveled at the beautiful feather floral creations, and shortly thereafter, in 1857, a popular home encyclopedia published directions to create a copy of the Crystal Palace arrangements. Materials were relatively inexpensive for middle class Victorian women, and most of the flowers were made from goose or swan feathers, which were easily obtainable.

The feathers were first soaked in hot soapy water to remove the down, and after rinsing, draining, and separating, they were dipped into colored dyes, which were developed from a variety of ingredients. Yellow dye was made with tumeric and boiling water; added soda turned the dye orange. Blue dye contained oil of vitriol and indigo, and green was obtained by mixing indigo with tumeric. Lilac was created using cudbear, a color obtained from processing lichens, and adding cream of tartar turned the lilac into amethyst. Red was achieved by preparing cochineal (processed from a species of crushed beetle), muriate of tin, and cream of tartar. Afterwards they were laid before a fire to dry, being shaped by fingers into curls and shapes.

Once the feathers were dyed and shaped, they were glued down with a dyed starch paste, made of ground rice and gum water, onto the prepared pasteboard or wood. Foliage was made from dyed green feathers, cut into leaf shapes, serrated at the edges with fine scissor cuts, and attached with thin wire. The feather bouquet could then be fashioned into a wreath form similar to what was done with shell and hair work, sometimes surrounding a coffin plate or memorial photograph, sometimes placed alone against a black fabric background.

A c. 1890s shadowbox memorial for a mother, composed of a dyed feather wreath set into a padded interior and surrounding a funeral photograph of the deceased, is shown in the next photograph. The "flowers" are made of dyed, cut, and arranged bird feathers, which have been fashioned into lilies and other fanciful flowers and leaves, along with wax-dipped stamen. Of interest is the word "MOTHER" in the center; it is made of pussy-willow material and was obviously removed earlier from the funeral floral arrangement that is seen in the central photograph.

*"Can we believe that the dear dead are gone?
Love in sad weeds forgets the funeral-day,
Opens the chamber door and almost smiles, —
Then sees the sunbeams pierce athwart the bed
Where the pale face is not."*
[George Eliot, 1819-1880, from *The Spanish Gypsy*]

A rare and extraordinary memorial shadowbox with a wax floral wreath, postmortem image of a child laid out with her toys, and her coffin plate inscribed, "Suffer Little Children to Come Unto Me," c. 1880-90s. 12.5" x 12.5". *Collection of Ben Zigler.* $695+.

Ornate memorial to "MOTHER," made of dyed and painted bird feathers fashioned into floral wreath around a funeral photograph. Central letters are formed of pussy-willow material, c. 1890s. 24.5" x 24.5". *Author's collection.* $495-525.

Other natural materials such as dried flowers were commonly used in memorial art, as seen in the c. 1890s remembrance for a mother and child who died in childbirth shown here. The central wreath of dried straw-flowers is further embellished with wax calla lilies, linen Lily of the Valley, and wax-dipped linen ivy leaves, and surrounds the mother's coffin plate engraved "MOTHER." A ribbon banner with purple chenille letters reading, "Sweet Rest" drapes over the straw-flower wreath. In the lower right hand corner, the child's coffin plate, engraved "Our Darling," and handmade tissue paper flowers probably once held in the hands of the infant during viewing, are tacked to the black cloth interior.

Memorial for a mother and child who died in childbirth, c. 1900. Straw flower wreath with wax calla lilies, with central coffin plate engraved "MOTHER"; child's coffin plate inscribed "Our Darling" in lower right, paper roses in lower left. 24.5" x 24.5". *Author's collection.* $495.

Two children's memorials typical of many seen in the 1880s are shown in the following examples. Children's memorials from this decade are usually seen in these painted white enamel and gesso frames, the white being symbolic of the innocence and purity of children. In the first, a cabinet card photograph of the infant taken when still alive is centered inside a wreath of wax-dipped linen flowers, and placed over a lace background. Underneath the photo is the child's coffin plate, inscribed "Our Darling," often kept by parents as a mourning keepsake.

The second memorial is a touching remembrance of a child of German immigrants who settled and farmed in Eastern Iowa. The central coffin plate is inscribed "Our Darling" in German, and is surrounded with the white linen flowers and ribbons also typical of the 1880s decade, and placed in an interior designed to resemble that of a casket. The mother clipped a small snippet of her baby's christening dress (typically used as burial clothing as well) and placed it in the floral wreath in the lower right at about the 4:00 position, a touching addition to this piece.

Child's memorial of wax-dipped linen floral wreath surrounding cabinet photo with coffin plate, c. 1880s. 12" x 18". *Author's collection.* $295-325.

Child's memorial from German-American immigrant family, with interior designed to appear like that of a casket; linen flowers around coffin plate inscribed "Our Darling" in German; snippet of lace from christening dress at lower right. 16" square. *Author's collection.* $295-325.

A Canadian memorial to a ship's captain who drowned while attempting to save his crew and passengers is shown at right. Captain William Carr of the side-wheeler *John Fraser*, which took loggers to and from camps along the shores of Lake Nippising (one of the Canadian Great Lakes), caught fire on November 7, 1893. Neither Capt. Carr, nor his first mate, was able to quench the flaming engine, which caused the side-wheeler to circle wildly out of control, throwing many of the men into the frigid waters. As the ship quickly sank, Capt. Carr rescued as many of the men as he could push into the few lifeboats, and was last seen clinging to the bow as the ship went down within sight of land and onlookers. Only half of the twenty-four men on board were saved.

Paper as a material for memorials was popular and readily available to any housewife. Some memorials were executed on paper in pin-pricking methods, using variously sized steel needles in which the paper was stippled to form the pattern or design, then mounted against contrasting paper for highlighting. Pen and ink drawings or calligraphy, sometimes alone, sometimes in combination with pin-pricking and other techniques such as watercolors or cut paper, were also executed. Memorials were sometimes created by cutting out floral petal shapes of paper and then assembling the flowers together in wreath form. A simple paperwork memorial of folded paper "stars" is a poignant testimonial to the practice of "making do" when elaborate materials were unavailable or too expensive for mourning families. In contrast to the more ornate memorials seen in this chapter, this touching piece was probably made by a poor family in memory of a child. Folding strips of white paper into star-like shapes in an origami-like craft was usually done by German and Swiss families for traditional Christmas ornaments. In this example, the stars were formed into a cross, painted with white milk paint, set against a black velvet-lined interior, and placed inside a crude shadowbox frame made of house shingles.

Memorial to William Carr, Captain of the *John Fraser*, which caught fire and sank on Lake Nippissing in Canada in 1893, killing half of the men on board. Captain Carr sacrificed his life to save the crew and passengers, and was last seen by those on shore clinging to the bow of the ship as it went down. 12" x 15". *Author's collection.* $295.

Primitive memorial made of folded paper "stars" painted with milk paint and enclosed in handmade shadowbox of house shingles, c. 1860s. 7" x 9.5". *Author's collection.* $225.

The following two exceptional children's memorials are Danish in origin, remembering children of an early pioneer family in the town of Ferndale, California. Each memorial has a written eulogy in Danish surrounded by linen flowers, reading as follows:

In Memory Of Peter Jacobsen born June 17, 1875, died May 1, 1883:

In my beautiful childhood days,
Death's cold hand tore me away;
From father, mother, beloved siblings,
And led me off to heaven's land;
Where you will find me once again,
When the Lord calls you home.

In Memory Of Emma Bertha Jacobsen, born February 15, 1877, died October 28, 1882:

Little Emma, your joy is great.
In heaven you are with our Lord God.
Now you enjoy eternity's happiness and peace,
Since here we have no abiding place.
A loving farewell from sister and brother,
A loving farewell from father and mother.
We all hope to see you again,
In joy and happiness in heaven.

Extraordinary pair of memorials to two children who died in the 1880s, in Ferndale, California. The children were Danish immigrants and the two memorials are comprised of linen floral wreaths around obituaries written by the parents of little Emma and Peter Jacobsen. 12" x 18". *Collection of Jerry Lesandro and Larry Martin.* $950+ pair.

"I lingered round them, under that benign sky: watched the moths fluttering among the heath and harebells; listened to the soft wind breathing through the grass and wondered how anyone could ever imagine unquiet slumbers for the sleepers in that quiet earth."
[Emily Bronte, in *Wuthering Heights*]

It is very rare to have provenance surrounding a memorial piece. However, the owners of the two poignant memorials for Emma and Peter Jacobsen, themselves local historians in Ferndale, California, researched and found the graves of the children in the local cemetery, one of the most beautiful historic rural cemeteries in California.

A beautiful oval shadowbox of yellow wax calla lilies and roses, along with dried preserved foliage in the form of a cross. This c. 1880s memorial in a beautiful walnut case probably memorializes a young unmarried woman – the light-hued lilies and white ground being indicative of the purity and innocence of young womanhood. 11" x 9". *Collection of Lyn Iversen and Chris Lamoreaux.* $595-625.

Wax memorial in oval walnut frame with very unusual floral symbolism of drooping stephanotis blossoms. The genus *stephanotis* means "Fit for a Crown" in Greek, and the flower has been the traditional bloom for bridal bouquets and veils for centuries; thus, it appears this memorial commemorates the death of a bride, the stephanotis now "crowning" her death, rather than her bridal headdress. 10" x 12". *Collection of Lyn Iversen and Chris Lamoreaux.* $495.

The interior of this c. 1880s shadowbox has been lined with silk in imitation of a casket interior, exhibiting the elaborate fabrics typical of the emerging funeral and casket industries. Around the perimeter are wax calla lilies and roses, with glitter trimming the cut-out areas which frame portions of a memorial cabinet card used for obituary information in the open areas. 14" x 18". *Collection of Lyn Iversen and Chris Lamoreaux.* $495-525.

The sad loss of an infant is memorialized in this wax floral wreath of yellow roses and white Lily-of-the-Valley in the corners. The small sterling silver coffin plate in the center shaped like a shield is exceptionally beautiful in quality and engraving, and not the usual pot metal or spelter coffin plaques of the 19th and early 20th centuries. 14" x 18". *Collection of Lyn Iversen and Chris Lamoreaux.* $495.

Lovely featherwork memorial wreath in beautiful shadowbox frame, probably created in the mid-1800s. The predominant use of white feathers suggest that it memorialized the death of a young unmarried woman. 12" x 16". *Collection of Lyn Iversen and Chris Lamoreaux.* $395+.

An interesting memorial wreath of yellow wax roses and white calla lilies. Normally wreaths were displayed in shadowboxes in the "horse-shoe" shape, but in this c. 1870s example, an inverse wreath is shown above the name "Josie," the letters of which were created with chenille yarn. 20" x 24". *Collection of Lyn Iversen and Chris Lamoreaux.* $450.

*"Oh, it is hard to take the little corpse and lay it low,
And say, 'None misses it but me.'"*
[George Eliot, 1819-1880, from *Armgart*]

A poignant memorial to a little boy is shown in this c. 1870s shadow-box memorial. The flowers were created in feather-work, then papier mâché holly leaves and berries were added into the wreath, a quite unusual floral ornamentation in memorial arrangements, possibly indicative of the December birth of the child, or his death. Holly was also symbolic of domestic happiness, no doubt tragically altered by the death of this little boy. The tintype photograph of the child is in the center of the wreath above his coffin plate, which is inscribed, "Our Darling." Both are encased in a black-painted wooden shadowbox frame. 14" x 18". *Collection of Lyn Iversen and Chris Lamoreaux.* $395.

A lovely floral wreath composed of stiffened paper flowers and gauze leaves surrounding a pewter coffin plate is housed in a beautiful pressed wood walnut frame. Great effort was made to commemorate the short life of "Lizzie Jane Fisher," who lived only twenty-two days, dying May 23, 1899. 12" x 14". *Collection of Lyn Iversen and Chris Lamoreaux.* $325.

During the post-Civil War era, it was very popular to include a *carte de visite* or cabinet card photograph of the deceased, usually taken when alive, into the memorial context. In this c. 1860s example, a *carte de visite* of a relative of the current owner is shown surrounded by a straw flower wreath, a popular parlor craft of this era, set into a beautiful Eastlake frame. 10" x 6.5". *Collection of Jerry Lesandro and Larry Martin.* $325.

A beautiful c. 1880s memorial of yarn-flowers with dried floral materials surrounding a coffin plate in the center. The inclusion of dried "sea ferns" and wheat with yarn-worked flowers is an unusual combination; most often memorials were worked in one medium only. In this example, the "frame" of neutral tan wheat stalks and sea "ferns" in the bottom corners sets off the colorful floral wreath around the central plate. 12" x 18". *Collection of Lyn Iversen and Chris Lamoreaux.* $425.

An unusual framed memorial enclosing a c. 1880s cabinet card of a young man set inside a wreath of linen flowers against [originally] white crepe paper. The use of crepe paper appears about this time as a background material in shadowboxes probably because of its similarity to crape fabric, from which the name is derived. 10" x 6.5". *Collection of Jerry Lesandro and Larry Martin.* $325.

A simple, dyed green feather-work wreath in a black oval frame. This c. 1900 memorial was created in memory of "Mary Hannah," whose name appears on the reverse of this memorial, and is comprised of simple goose feathers – probably the only material available to the creator of this memorial. 12" x 18". *Collection of Lyn Iversen and Chris Lamoreaux.* $295-325.

Crepe paper as a material to represent mourning crape fabric is seen in this c. 1890-1900s child's memorial shadowbox. This touching piece was designed to appear like the interior of a coffin, with the white crepe paper gathered like the folds of fabric. The coffin handle from the casket made of silver plate and mother-of-pearl is enclosed with a photograph of the infant taken when still alive. Linen flowers also decorate the interior. 12" x 18". *Collection of Lyn Iversen and Chris Lamoreaux.* $450.

A particularly sad 1904 shadowbox memorial incorporating a child's coffin plate, inscribed "Our Darling," surrounded with a white linen floral wreath fastened into a deeply recessed black interior. Underneath the floral wreath is the little girl's braid of blonde hair attached to the back with white ribbons, and on each side of the coffin plate are the two coins used to weigh her eyelids down during viewing, a common practice among immigrants, particularly the Irish. 14" square. *Author's collection.* $425.

A large and spectacular c. 1890s shadowbox memorial enclosing two funeral wreaths, a coffin plate, and two coffin screws is shown here. It is rare to find memorials incorporating the coffin screws, as there was an abhorrence to the concept of the "remorseless screws" which fastened down the coffin lid, forever encapsulating the beloved out of sight. This fine example encases two linen funeral floral arrangements against a black velvet interior set into a walnut and faux-painted frame. 16" x 30". *Collection of Jerry Lesandro and Larry Martin.* $795.

A white-fringed silk casket pall forms the backdrop in this shadowbox (an unusual inclusion for a memorial material), which also includes a crucifix and coffin plate. This lovely c. 1900s German or Scandinavian memorial is beautifully housed in a black and gold frame, making its white, black, silver and gold color combination quite striking. 16" x 24". *Collection of Lyn Iversen and Chris Lamoreaux.* $495.

A rare "funeral pillow" arrangement of linen flowers and chenille-work for "Anna S. Koch," probably taken from floral tributes at the funeral. Most likely, this piece was originally all white, possibly for a young unmarried woman, and the "pillow" form symbolic of her taking her "last sleep." 18" x 24". *Collection of Jerry Lesandro and Larry Martin.* $695.

A lovely yarn wreath in a black octagon frame showing skillful workmanship in the yarn flowers. 12" x 18". *Collection of Lyn Iversen and Chris Lamoreaux.* $325.

Poignant infant's memorial in Eastlake shadowbox frame, with chenille and hairwork "flowers" surrounding coffin plate, for little "Adah Fradenburgh, who died June 11, 1870," at the age of twenty-one months. 13" x 15". *Author's collection.* $300.

Painted Memorials

The earliest form of mourning picture in America, was the hand-painted scene with the troika of mourners, monuments, and willows executed on silk, velvet or paper. These 18th century memorials were quite similar to the mourning embroideries of the same period, employing almost identical grieving figures of women dressed in flowing white, high-waisted garments, dabbing their eyes with handkerchiefs while standing alongside an urn or obelisk monument inscribed with epitaphs. Sometimes, small-waisted men in black with top hats stood alongside their wives, grieving for children, siblings, or parents.

In the spectacular early 19th century mourning painting on silk shown here, we see the high-waisted clothing typical of the 18th century, but the transition now is from the gauzy white to the heavier black of the Victorian era, as seen in the woman's dress. The central mourners grieve over monuments dedicated to three deaths, the epitaphs inscribed as follows: "Sacred to the Memory of Mrs. Betsy Greenwood who died 27th August 1811, aged 29 years and 6 months" in the central plinth; "In Memory of Harriet Morse, who died March 1798, aged 6 weeks" on the left plinth; and "In Memory of Mary Morse, who died August 1819 aged 9 weeks" on the right plinth. The background depicts the usual pastoral landscape typical of folk art paintings of this era, with a small colonial town which may or may not be allegorical. This beautiful painted silk oval memorial is housed in a black ebonized mat with gold gilt "stars" and frame.

Another outstanding New England painted memorial on canvas is seen in the next example, where George Washington's manservant sits at the family tomb at Arlington to grieve. This c. 1825 painting is unusual in depicting an African-American mourning the dead first President of the new country.

Wonderful early painted memorial on silk in memory of "Betsy Greenwood" who died in 1811 at the age of twenty-nine, and her two children. *Courtesy of The Museum of Mourning Art.* Value unknown.

Rare painted memorial on canvas to the memory of George Washington, with his African-American manservant mourning at the tomb. *Courtesy of The Museum of Mourning Art.* Value unknown.

In the photograph below we see an outstanding French memorial set into an ebony frame. The entire scene is painted on ivory and is vividly colorful, showing a cloudy overcast day, indicative of the depth of grief where no sunshine is visible. A weeping willow and infant are the very personification of grief, and the inscription on the monument reads, "D.O.M. A un bon Pere Ses traits son Grave Dans Nos Coeurs; A.E. 6 Septembre 1822," which translated means, "a good father whose memory is etched on our hearts."

Beautiful French painted memorial in ebony frame with weeping cherub at the grave of the father being mourned, c. 1822. Note the dark roiling clouds and melancholy color scheme of despair. 6.5" x 6.5". *Courtesy of Things Gone By.* $1,295.

Embroidered Memorials

Learning to "manage the needle" was regarded as basic and fundamental to every young woman's education and preparation for marriage. The root of the word "sampler," is *exemplum,* and as noted by Dr. Samuel Johnson in his 18th century dictionary, the definition was "a piece worked by young girls for improvement."[32] Various stitches and patterns were learned and practiced, along with designs of birds, animals, flowers, and sometimes genealogical information, pious reproofs, and scripture verses. The exercises were to be more than simple training in the needle arts, however, the admonitions to piety were to shape appropriate female behavior and future roles as virtuous housewives. The earliest samplers tended to be simple exercises in decorative embroidery, signed, dated and framed for proud parents as proof of their daughter's skills learned at the exclusive "dame schools" or academies of the 18th century. American samplers tended to be shorter and squatter than their English counterparts with compositions of decorative borders enclosing the patterns inside, which consisted of the ubiquitous alphabet along with pastoral scenes, gardens, and figures. American samplers were generally worked with silk threads on natural or unbleached linen, while English embroiderers favored "tammy," a fine wool tannery cloth, available in England after 1750. And, working in wool threads on canvas was popular among Scottish needleworkers.

Many early colonial era samplers began as genealogical records, and these easily lent themselves to memorial aspects by the record of deaths listed. As with all other forms of art done in Western culture, embroidery accommodated itself easily to the memorialization of loved ones, and many memorial samplers were done in both England and America in the 18th and 19th centuries. Death symbolism such as crosses, urns, obelisks, mourners, funereal flowers and trees, as well as biblical verses or pious poetry, were added into what was basically obituary information. Embroidered mourning samplers were so ubiquitous and typical in design throughout the 18th and 19th centuries that, in 1889, Harriet Beecher Stowe remarked in *Oldtown Folks:*

"Female accomplishments consisted largely of embroidering mourning pieces, with a family monument in the centre, a green ground worked in chenille and floss silk, an exuberant willow tree, and a number of weeping mourners..."

Needlework skills could be quite extraordinary, with girls as young as eight or nine creating masterful embroidered works. The simple cross-stitch, most commonly employed in a young girl's first sampler, was later to include satin stitch, French knot, running and outline stitches, seed and bullion, couching, and crewel.

Contemporaneous to needlework mourning samplers were memorials incorporating watercolor painting into the composition in addition to areas embroidered using colored silk, wool, or chenille thread on silk or satin ground. Faces of figures, scenic or pastoral backgrounds, and, most frequently, the sky overhead were watercolored for ease in completing the mourning composition, which was prepared by sketching the design onto the silk ground prior to stitching. Portrait miniaturists, such as T. C. Bell, Jr. of Baltimore, Maryland, advertised their services for drawing or painting "Faces, etc., of Needlework" mourners, and other miniaturists and artists could be commissioned for sketching patterns as well.[33] These painted and embroidered memorials enjoyed considerable popularity in England and America between 1790 and 1820, with weeping figures overcome with grief surrounding a central monument for the bereaved, with an overhanging willow draping its branches over the tomb.

In 18th century America, these early painted memorial samplers were created as part of the education and refinement of the young daughters of wealthy American parents, just as in the case of embroideries. Furthermore, memorial paintings and embroideries were popular with impressionable and emotional young girls, who saw in the melancholy subject matter all the maudlin romance of love and death. In addition to personal familial remembrances, many early colonial era painted embroideries

Spectacular embroidered memorial on silk to the memory of George Washington, with a patriot, farmer, minister, winged Victory, and notable Indian chief Cincinnatus paying homage. *Courtesy of The Museum of Mourning Art.* Value unknown.

were dedicatory pieces commemorating patriotic figures, just as was done with mourning paintings.

The detailed memorial to George Washington seen on the previous page incorporates several interesting figures, as well as the use of paint as embroidery on silk ground. The design elements in this memorial were taken from a transfer print design used on a Glasgow, Scotland textile print as well as on an English Liverpool pottery jug. This outstanding 1803 Philadelphia memorial shows an obelisk with profile portrait of Washington encircled with laurel wreath of victory, and his honorary titles of "First in War, First in Peace, First in Fame, First in Virtue" as his epitaph. An eagle grasping a rose in his beak symbolizes the new nation, as does the red flag with blue field and stars in front of the monument. Instead of the typical male and female mourners seen ubiquitously in 18th and 19th century mourning art, we see a Revolutionary War hero with a Puritan minister approach the tomb from the left, while a farmer patriot grieves on the ground in front of the tomb. To the right of the obelisk, Winged Victory dabs her eye with a handkerchief, and Cincinnatus pays homage. The figures represent the first participants caught up together as the new nation emerges out from the wilderness, out from the French and Indian Wars, and out of the War of Independence – with one notable exception: the African slave.

Another patriotic piece is seen in the painted and embroidered silk memorial in memory of Alexander Hamilton, member of the Continental Congress and Federalist architect of the Constitution, who was killed in a duel with long time rival, Aaron Burr on July 11, 1804. Burr had challenged Hamilton to a duel in the belief that Hamilton had spread scurrilous rumors against Burr in the campaign for Governor of New York in which the two were opponents. Ironically, Hamilton accepted the challenge, in spite of having lost his own twenty-one-year-old son in a duel three years earlier and against his own lifelong aversion to the practice of dueling. (The loss of his son had also cast his oldest daughter into a permanent state of melancholia from which she never recovered.) Nevertheless, when Hamilton and Burr met to duel on July 11, 1804, at

Weehawken, New Jersey, Hamilton determined not to injure or kill his old nemesis. Believing there was no way to honorably withdraw from the duel, Hamilton instead "threw away his fire," a dueling practice in which one dualist deliberately aims high and away so as to miss his opponent entirely. Burr, however, did not, and his shot struck Hamilton in his side, mortally wounding him. Hamilton died twelve hours later, and was buried in Trinity Church Yard in New York City.

Although dueling was considered a despicable practice in most areas, and was illegal in New York, this c.1805 memorial gives Hamilton all the honor and prestige due him as a founder of the new nation. Hamilton's portrait and gar-

landed urn decorate the obelisk, and his epitaph (written in ink) reads, "Sacred to the Memory of Gen. Hamilton who Departed this life July 29, 1805." (The date is incorrect; Hamilton in fact died July 12, 1804.) The woman on the left holds a letter as a banner, which reads, "Five years has not elapsed since we buried the Father of our Country. We now with grief attend his eldest Son Hamilton! Fare thee well." The monument to Washington is in the background to the right. A thirteen star flag flies behind the mourner to the right of the tomb, and angels fly overhead in the clouds looking down on the scene below, symbolizing a virtual apotheosis of Hamilton's status to that of Washington.

Extraordinary embroidered memorial on silk to George Washington and Alexander Hamilton. *Courtesy of The Museum of Mourning Art.* Value unknown.

The next three embroideries were executed by schoolgirls in academies for the refinement and education of young women, the daughters of wealthy American colonists. The first, a memorial to the "illustrious Washington" depicts a Revolutionary War era couple mourning at the tomb of Washington, and was executed by a young girl at the Elizabeth Folwell School in Philadelphia, Pennsylvania, one of the earliest schoolgirl academies.

The second schoolgirl embroidery and painting on silk is attributed to the Abby Wright School in South Hadley, Connecticut (possibly executed by daughter Harriet Wright). One of the distinguishing characteristics of embroideries from the Abby Wright School is the use of metallic threads outlining the urns atop monuments, as seen in this example. Here again, the design and layout of the work reminds one of the symbolism seen in hair-work art of French memorials and mourning jewelry of the 18th century, the same approximate period of this piece. In this scene we have the paradigmatic troika of the mourner dressed in the gauzy white muslin typical of French mourning art of the 18th century salon period, grieving over a tomb with garlanded urn, the branches of the weeping willow draping heavily over the monument. The plinth lists in ink the death of a C. Chapin, who died January 12, 1799, and more obituary information is seen on the side of the plinth. Other elements, typically portrayed in mourning jewelry and hair-work art of this era, are also in evidence, such as the broken tree in the right front of the scene, the drooping flowers in the left front, and the sheep in the far left, possibly symbolizing the loss of children. The house in the background is almost completely shuttered except for the two windows in the lower parlor area of the first floor, possibly indicating the "death room."

Another exceptionally fine c.1805 Abby Wright School memorial embroidery, employing metallic and silk thread on paper along with painted areas, commemorates the death of Heziah Moody who "died July 6th, 1803 in the fifteenth year of her age." In the background other plinths record the deaths of two other children, "Mary, aged 2 months" and an unnamed "son who died December 22, 1779, aged 2 days." Heziah's

monument with garlanded urn embroidered in silver metallic thread occupies the central focal point where her parents grieve over her grave, and the monuments of the other children are less prominently placed in the background of the memorial scene. This graphically represents the common feeling among parents that the deaths of their older children were more difficult to endure than those of their infants because early childhood death was not unexpected, and the deaths of older children represented the loss of considerably longer and more deeply invested hopes.

Berlin work embroidery occupied a prominent place in Victorian parlor crafts for over eighty years in the 19th century. First introduced in the early 1800s, the popularity of Berlin embroidery, the ease with which it could be learned, the numerous patterns, and the vividly colorful wool threads insured its success as a parlor decoration. The Victorian love for dazzling, almost garish color and heavy florid designs blended well with the desirably cluttered gew gaws and draperies of the Victorian parlor. Worked in a

simple "tent" or half cross-stitch on heavy perforated canvas according to a colored chart, a seemingly complicated work could be produced with no more effort than counting the holes in the canvas. Patterns were created by sellers in Berlin, Germany, whence the creation of Berlin-work derived its name. Later, thousands of patterns were developed in England and France for export to American women. Threads, originally of silk, were later replaced by vegetable-dyed, and ultimately aniline-dyed wools from Germany and France, and thousands of color variations and shades were available.[34] Because of their use of vivid color schemes, Berlin-work wool samplers on canvas were generally not used for memorial compositions in the same way linen and silk embroideries were dedicated. Furthermore, wool Berlin-work on canvas utilized the entire surface, which was embroidered in the tent stitch. Most memorial samplers referred to as "Berlin-work" today were executed in the perforated paper "motto" sampler technique, rather than the heavy wool canvas embroideries.

Charming schoolgirl embroidery and painting on silk in memory of the "illustrious Washington" made by a female student from the Elizabeth Folwell School in Philadelphia. *Courtesy of The Museum of Mourning Art.* Value unknown.

Wonderful embroidery and painted memorial on silk of "C. Chapin" who died in 1799, created by a female student at the Abby Wright School in Connecticut. *Courtesy of The Museum of Mourning Art.* Value unknown.

Another outstanding schoolgirl embroidery from the Abby Wright School in Connecticut, employing metallic threads on paper, made in memory of Heziah Moody and two children. *Courtesy of The Museum of Mourning Art.* Value unknown.

Berlin and Punched Paper Memorials

Perforated "card work," or "punched paper" embroidery was a form of so-called "Berlin-work" favored by 19th century women which easily accommodated mourning themes. The art of embroidery on perforated paper card stock began in France and Germany in the mid-1800s, at the height of popularity of wool Berlin-work. Most often the card stock was embroidered using cotton, silk, and chenille yarns, and do-it-yourself patterns were available in ladies' periodicals and by mail order. *Household Elegancies,* a book published in 1875, devoted an entire chapter to the creation of punched paper embroidery for "the ladies of America, lovers of home decorations and ardent imitators of every hint and tasteful suggestion."

Most often the patterns employed "mottoes" using biblical themes and symbols, scriptures, and poetry – frequently in English, but occasionally in Latin or other European language. "Gone But Not Forgotten" was a popular motto in memorial embroidery, often seen surrounding a photograph of the deceased. Other mottoes include the familiar phrases of "In Memory Of," "Gone to Bliss," etc., seen everywhere in memorials and cemetery epitaphs of this era. Other forms of Berlin work embroidery were original designs by their creator, and were thus unique works of memorial art. They usually did not employ the standard "motto" seen in most patterns available by mail order from ladies' periodicals.

Each of the following two examples of English Berlin work, or punched paper embroidery, contains beautiful memorial designs executed quite differently from one another. In the first, a large tombstone plinth notes the passing of "Maggie" "eldest and beloved daughter of J & M Wilson who died at Sunlaw's Home Farm [on] 3rd Aug 1885 Aged 20 years." Atop the plinth is an urn, and from behind a large weeping willow frames the monument. Below the obituary information is a poem, which reads:

Asleep in Jesus,
Blessed Sleep
From which none
Ever wakes to weep!

Original design punched paper embroidery in memory of a young woman who died at "Sunlaws Farm" at the age of twenty in 1885. Wool yarns on perforated paper. 18" x 24". *Author's collection.* $495.

We shall meet to part no more,
On the Resurrection Morn!

A Berlin work embroidery, executed similarly to traditional linen sampler designs with the border motif of floral leaves and crosses running around the perimeter, surrounds a funeral card memorializing Thomas Ashford, who died December 26th, 1896 and was interred at Swansea Cemetery. The central design is an elegiac poem taken from a 19th century hymn, the stanzas of which la-ment the transitoriness of human existence:

A thousand ages in Thy sight,
Are like a evening gone
Short as the watch that ends the night,
Before the rising sun.

Time like an ever-rolling stream,
Bears all its sons away.
They fly forgotten as a dream,
Dies at the opening day.

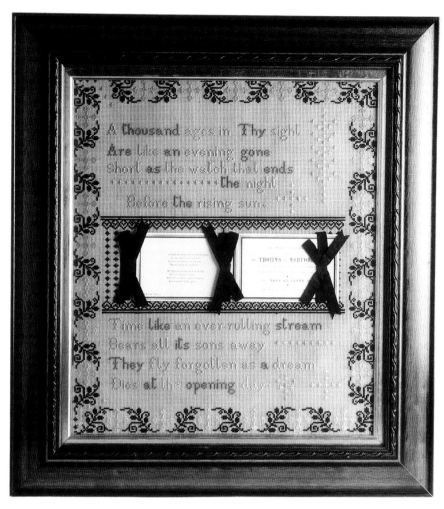

The two punched paper memorials shown below, for a husband and wife who died in 1862 and 1855 respectively, were embroidered in black thread then placed in pressed diecut paper frames. They were then assembled in the black "ebonized" frames by a Philadelphia framer of memorials, whose advertisement on the reverse reads:

"Charles Ogden, Memorial or Funeral Card Manufacturer and Framer, ...the Only Store in America where you can get Memory or Funeral Cards printed and much more beautiful than either a Flower or Wreath Memorial...Having had 24 years experience in Framing and Printing Memory or Funeral Cards, Europeans and Others will have no difficulty now in getting this kind of work done."

Original design punched paper embroidery with silk thread surrounding a memorial card for "Thomas Ashford" who died December 20, 1896. 20" x 22". *Author's collection.* $595.

Original design punched paper embroidery with black silk thread in memory of "Betty, the wife of John Shaw," who died December 7, 1855. 12" x 14". *Author's collection.* $350 pair.

Original design punched paper embroidery with black silk thread in memory of John Shaw who died August 5, 1862. 12" x 14". *Author's collection.* $350 pair.

A lovely punched paper memorial to 65-year-old Sarah Niblett who "fell asleep" on December 16, 1886, shows a weeping willow overhanging a monument with urn. Below, an embroidered inscription speaks of the emptiness left by a missing loved one, the resignation to "God's will," and the call to "preparation."

A light is from our household gone,
A voice we loved is stilled.
A place is vacant from our home,
Which never can be filled.
We cannot tell who may be first
The Lord will call away,
One must be first so let us all
Prepare for that Great Day.
"Blessed are the pure in heart, for they
shall see God."
"Thy will be Done"

Punched paper also lent itself to other forms of memorial art. Victorian women could create raised elements such as tombstones, crosses, monuments, etc. by cutting out a single pattern in ever smaller dimensions on multiple pieces of card stock, then stacking and gluing the pieces one atop the other to achieve a three-dimensional appearance. By using white card stock, these monuments gave a "marble-like" appearance similar to *bas relief*, when done in this 3-D effect. Frames of card stock were also created in "fret-work" designs by intricate scissor-cutting around a central motif or design.

Lovely original design memorial to Sarah Niblett, who died December 16, 1886, with poignant poem of resignation. 10" x 12". *Collection of Jerry Lesandro and Larry Martin.* $300.

A wonderful "Berlin work" memorial sampler, with the popular expression of "Sweet Rest in Heaven" embroidered on punched paper with variegated wool threads surrounding a postmortem tintype photograph of an infant in its christening dress, probably the only photographic remembrance the parents had of their child. 10" x 24". *Collection of Ann McIntyre.* $350.

Another style of c. 1870s Berlin work motto sampler, reading "Absent But Not Forgotten" with a *carte de visite* photograph of an elderly woman; includes embroidered roses as well as the entwined ivy. 8.5" x 20". *Collection of Lyn Iversen and Chris Lamoreaux.* $250.

196

Lithographs

By the mid-1800s, mourning scenes were being mass-produced by enterprising businessmen such as the well-known Boston lithographers Currier & Ives, which replaced the individual hand-done memorial scenes of earlier decades. The first lithographic process was invented in the late 18th century by Alvin Senefelder, a Bavarian, and within a few decades, producers of lithographs of every genre were appearing in American and European markets. The commerce in mourning clothing, fabrics, pottery, and other artifacts prompted brother entrepreneurs William and John Pendleton of Boston to print memorial lithographs on a large scale for marketing. Soon their young apprentice, Nathaniel Currier, was to go on and achieve fame for his extensive lithographic production and variety of designs, ultimately joining with another lithographer, James Ives.

In the following photographs we see typical examples of the many varieties of mourning lithographs available through Nathaniel Currier, James Ives, Kellogg, Pendleton, and other early lithographers. Memorial lithographs had a tremendous advantage over individual homemade works of art. They were readily available and inexpensive to 19th century mourning families, costing only a few cents each. Whereas the time necessary to create the elaborate memorials such as hair wreaths and other floral arrangements was only possible in upper-class families who had such opportunity, mourning lithographs appealed to poorer families hard-pressed and over-worked.

Initially printed in black and white, hand-colored scenes employing green watercolors in weeping willows and foliage with perhaps some touches of red paint on roses in the background could be purchased by consumers for a few cents more. The elements are generally the same in all formats, whether horizontally or vertically rectangular in form. Mourning scenes depicted the general iconography of other memorial art, such as tombstone plinths for handwritten epitaphs and/or poetry, mourners, weeping willows, churches, and foliage symbolic of immortality such as roses and ivy. Most importantly, anyone could purchase the lithograph which most repre-

sented their personal story. Thus, some show a single mourning man or woman in grief for a parents or siblings. Others depict children kneeling or praying at their parents' tomb, and still others show widows and widowers with (and without) children mourning a dead spouse.

These last were most popular during the 1860s when thousands were sold for women widowed by the American Civil War. Many are available to collectors today at prices ranging from $150 to $350, depending on rarity, condition, and value and interest of frame.

A lovely tinted N. Currier lithograph, c. 1830-40s, showing typical elements of mourners, weeping willow, plinth, church, etc., available for purchase and personalization. 16" x 20". *Collection of David and Judith Peebles.* $275.

N. Currier lithograph, c. 1863, showing virtually identical memorial iconography but more vivid, less detailed designs. Inscription on plinth denoting death of original owner's parents in 1863 and 1865. 12" x 16". *Author's collection.* $250.

An early lithograph by N. Currier in a lovely faux-painted walnut frame (shown on the previous page) shows mourners in the clothing typical of the 1830-40s, the coloring in the willows and the techniques of the lithography delicately hued and finely tinted, the monument three-dimensional. The second lithograph, later in the Civil War era, shows mourners in the heavier mourning clothing typical of the mid-1860s, the tinting more vivid and less artistically skilled, the monument one-dimensional and larger for personalized obituary information.

By the 1880s many lithographers were mass producing large numbers of designs for memorials which could be personalized by consumers. A few representative examples are shown here, which are exceptionally nice for their genre.

A memorial lithograph to little "Ernest Ripley," who died in 1897, having lived only six weeks, sums up parental resignation with the words, "It is God's Will," the same sentiments uttered by President William McKinley as he lay dying in 1901. The typical symbols of "Cross and Crown," seen in embroidered samplers of this era (No Cross, No Crown), as well as the anchor, funeral drape, dove, palm branches and lilies are seen throughout memorials of the 18th and 19th centuries. This lithograph was published by The Gray Litho Company, House Life Publishing Co., of Chicago, Illinois, another 19th century producer of lithographs for the consumer. 16.75" x 21.5" including frame. *Collection of Charles Swedlund.* $325.

Beautifully colored lithograph of woman clinging to the cross with the storm waves crashing around her. This familiar scene was taken from the old hymn "Rock of Ages," and the concept of *"Simply to Thy Cross I Cling"* was a ubiquitous concept of religious comfort in the Victorian era. This lithograph was produced by L. C. Brown, Publisher, in Warren, Ohio, who like other lithographers, mass produced such images for mourning families. The deceased, who is "Gone But Not Forgotten," is noted as "Louisa Meleke," born March 11, 1821 and died February 16, 1906. The lithograph is housed in a beautiful walnut and gold rococo frame in almost mint condition, making its value well worth $400. 24" x 28" including frame. *Collection of Charles Swedlund.*

A commercially-produced lithograph, modified by the family of the deceased with wonderful "folky" embellishments. In this memorial, various areas of the lithograph were incised and removed, then backed with sheets of foil and mother-of-pearl, to give the memorial a "fancy work" adornment. The effect is quite charming. *Collection of Ann McIntyre.* $325.

Large format printed lithographs were also mass-produced and available through catalogs, and included poetry verses, funeral iconography, and the appropriate obituary information in the finished ready-to-frame print. This is an example of one style of these memorial lithographs, which were distributed in large numbers by the T. W. Campbell Company of Elgin, Illinois. *Collection of Del & Linda McCuen.* $200-300.

A rare framed lithographed sketch of Abraham Lincoln, "Liberty's Great Martyr," lying in state in his catafalque in City Hall, Chicago. Lincoln funeralia and memorabilia is quite desirable, and not only is this unusual lithograph valuable for its content, it is remarkable for the beautiful original frame. 12" x 16". *Collection of Lyn Iversen and Chris Lamoreaux.* $475.

Tokens of Remembrance

The marvelous thing about memorials is their intimacy; few other fields of collecting provide such a connection to another life in another time. In this section we will look at personal souvenirs in the form of coffin plates and the cherished lock of hair, both kept as sacred treasures.

"Coffin" or "casket" plates were frequently kept as keepsakes by Victorians, as a cherished emblem of the connection between the mourner and the mourned. At burial, the plates were removed just before the coffin was lowered into the ground, an emotionally intense moment for family members. In contrast to today, where funeral practices tend to "sanitize" earth burial in vaults, and where family members may not even be present, in former centuries the committal of a loved one's body to the ground was literally fulfilled in the biblical phrase, "ashes to ashes, dust to dust."

Coincident with the increasing romanticism in Britain and America surrounding death and mourning·in the 19th century, the word "coffin" fell out of favor and was replaced with the word "casket." For Victorians, this word was more suitable with the sentimentalities surrounding the body now seen as a precious reliquary, and epitomized the worth of the remains of the departed. In *Agnes and the Key to Her Little Coffin*, published in 1857, the anonymous author and father of little Agnes framed his consolation book around the "sacred key" that held his daughter's remains within the "receptacle." The author's reference was to the lock and key which had recently supplanted the "remorseless screws and screw driver" of previous years. Memoirs and letters of the 18th and early 19th centuries often described the horror of the sounds of the "remorseless screws" as the lid of the coffin was fastened down by the undertaker, making a "sound like no other" in the deafening silence at the grave.

Coffin plates came in a variety of metals and patterns, from the homemade tin or pewter plaque, to manufactured varieties which were inscribed with the name and dates of birth and death. Coffin plates were engraved by local jewelers, who frequently advertised their expertise in this aspect of the funeral business. Eldridge & Company of Taunton, Massachusetts, manufactured silver-plated plaques, along with those made of so-called "Britannia," a base metal alloy of lead, tin, and zinc. George Gray, a silversmith and jeweler of West Dover, New Hampshire, advertised in 1846 that he could "mark trunk and coffin plates," and other suppliers provided handles and trimmings in addition to coffin plates, along with grave clothes, to fulfill burial needs.

Engraving was done by coating basic "pot metal" plates with a white substance like shoe polish, and then drawing the design onto the surface. Once completed, the jeweler could engrave the final lines and obituary information. For those living in rural areas away from funeral suppliers and jewelers, often the local undertaker or blacksmith could fashion a reasonably attractive coffin plate to fill the need for this keepsake. Designs were generally linear around the rectangular frame so as to appear "embossed," and sometimes death iconography was stamped into the plate, such as weeping willows, urns, crosses, roses, and Forget-Me-Nots. Lambs figured prominently in those plates and trimmings for children's caskets. Rarer (and thus more expensive) coffin plates were molded into a form, rather than simply being rectangular, and examples such as a cross, weeping mourner, lamb, rosebud, etc., were available to wealthier Victorians. These are very desirable today to collectors, along with the molded metal "clocks" with the words "The Sad Hour," which had movable hands so that the time of death could be noted on the plate during and after the funeral. The concept of time standing still or ceasing for both the dead loved one and the mourner was a significant concept in grief expression from the Middle Ages through the Victorian era. The symbol of a stopped watch or clock also hearkened back in the Victorian romantic psyche to one of Emily Dickinson's best known death poems, entitled "A Clock Stopped":

> *"A clock stopped – not the mantel's;*
> *Geneva's farthest skill,*
> *Can't put the puppet bowing,*
> *That just now dangled still."*

Sometimes the coffin plate was simply placed against black fabric (or white in the case of a child's death), and framed "as-is," or hung on the wall by a black cord through holes in the back. Other plates and trimmings were placed inside shadowbox memorials, and surrounded with photographs of the deceased (most often taken when alive, but occasionally postmortem), floral wreath arrangements made in a variety of methods and materials, or hair-work mementos. Coffin plates alone range in price from $50-100, and when placed in shadowboxes with wreaths, photographs, or other mementos of the deceased, they are highly desirable and can often command prices of $300+, depending as always on condition.

Another significant keepsake token to Victorians was the lock of hair of the missing loved one. The author of the 1852 book of consolation entitled *The Mourner's Friend, or Sighs of Sympathy For Those Who Sorrow* described the treasured lock of hair of a deceased friend as follows:

> *"Few things in this weary world are so delightful as keepsakes. Nor do they ever, to my heart at least, nor to my eye, lose their tender, their powerful charm! How slight, how small, how tiny a memorial saves a beloved one from oblivion! Of all keepsakes, memorials, relics, - most dearly, most devotedly, do I love a little lock of hair; and oh, when the head it beautified has long mouldered in the dust, how spiritual seems the undying glossiness of the sad memento! All else gone to nothing, save and except that soft, smooth, burnished, and glorious fragment of the apparelling that once hung in clouds and sunshine over an angel's brow. Ay, a lock of hair is far better than any picture, - it is a part of the beloved object herself. [sic]"*[35]

The exchange of locks of hair was a significant expression of love and friendship in the 19th century and was routinely done between schoolgirls as a symbol of childhood loyalty and affection. Later, as teenage friendships grew into mature, often lifelong relationships, women frequently kept (and gave away) locks of hair throughout their lives from friends, lovers (and later husbands), family members, etc., as symbolic sentiments (or memorial remembrances) of affectionate bonds. Many were saved in handmade hair "albums," placed in small boxes, or framed. Primarily intended to be sentimental keepsakes much like scrapbooks or autograph albums of later eras, hair albums often included memorial tokens as death was so much a part of 19th century life.

Touching coffin plate for little John M. Kearn, who died Sept. 10, 1863, aged 3 years, 1 month, 13 days; silver plate, draped sepulchre, overturned torch, symbolic of a life cut short. 3.5" x 5". *Collection of Jerry Lesandro and Larry Martin.* $75.

Lovely poignant coffin plate for "Our Babe," bordered in white chenille velvet, probably preparatory to placement in a shadowbox memorial, c. 1860s. 3" x 4.5". *Collection of Jerry Lesandro and Larry Martin.* $125.

Wonderful silver coffin plate of sheaf of wheat, with half-ripened grain and sickle implanted in the sheaf, severing the life. In Christian belief, it represents the separation of the grain from the chaff, or the just from the unjust at the Judgment or "winnowing" of God. 2" x 4.5". *Collection of Jerry Lesandro and Larry Martin.* $125.

Molded and silver-plated over spelter coffin plate of flower of the *Liliaceae,* of the genus *Lilium,* whose flowers at funerals represent the restored innocence of the soul at death. Lilies continue to be popular today as funeral and cemetery flora. 2" x 3.5". *Collection of Jerry Lesandro and Larry Martin.* $125-150.

Rare molded coffin plate of a woman's hand holding a broken flower bud, usually representative of a child's death, as the bud has not "fully opened." Molded plates such as this one and the one of the lily are difficult to find today and more expensive to acquire than flat plaques. 3.5" long. *Collection of Jerry Lesandro and Larry Martin.* $150.

Handmade pewter coffin plate for "Rufus Fuller, Aged 56, Died Feb 12, 1864." The primitive quality of this plate indicates that the family did not have access or financial resources available to them to purchase commercially made plaques. It is also possible that Rufus Fuller died in the Civil War, as this plate does not appear to have ever been attached to the coffin, perhaps indicating that Fuller's body was not brought home for burial. 3.5" x 4". *Author's collection.* $100-125.

Rare boxed set of coffin screw plates and casket plaque for 8-month-old "Michael J. Farrell," who died July 20, 1892. The molded screw plates have floral Forget-Me-Nots and drooping buds symbolic of a life cut short, the symbol seen throughout memorial iconography in cemeteries and art of the Victorian era. Plate: 2" x 3"; screws: 1.75" in diameter. *Collection of Jerry Lesandro and Larry Martin.* $150.

Coffin plate, c. 1880s, "The Sad Hour." This plate was used to indicate the hour of death, a sentiment dating back to the Middle Ages in western culture. Examples of this style of plate are rare and desirable to collectors of funeralia. 3" x 4.5". *Collection of Ben Zigler.* $175+.

In the following photographic example, we see an outstanding handmade hair album, assembled by Mary H. Eby in 1856, Lancaster County, Pennsylvania. The album was recovered in 1882 by "MH," also in Lancaster County, and embroidered with rosebuds and leaves in Berlin wool-work on punched paper. Inside the hair album are various locks and braids of hair fastened to the paper pages with pieces of fabric, probably from a favorite dress, or ribbons. In the album, two of the women are in "first stage" mourning, their locks of hair fastened to the page with mourning crape, one of which is shown in the photograph here.

Cover of "Mary Eby" hair album showing wool embroidery on punched paper and date of "Hair Book" as 1882, although it was actually begun much earlier in 1856. 6.5" square. *Collection of Ann McIntyre.* $595.

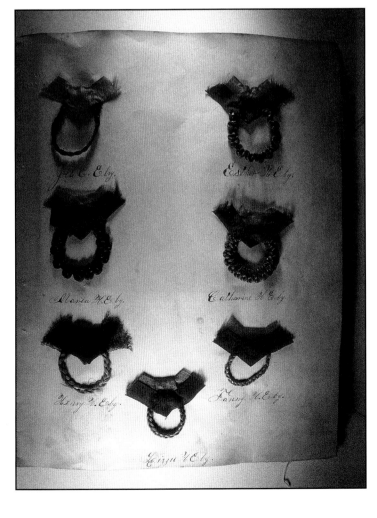

One of the interior pages of the "Mary Eby" hair album, in which one of the family members is in mourning or being mourned. The braid of hair is fastened to the page with mourning crape. *Collection of Ann McIntyre.*

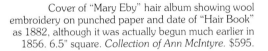

Another touching hair collection, shown below, is a combination of sentimental locks of hair combined with memorial hair tokens. The dominant punched paper piece in the center has steel bead-work, "When This You See, Remember Me," with braided brown hair set inside a steel bead-work sepulchre surrounded with embroidered roses. Below the punched paper piece are separate tokens of sentiment, including interwoven paper hearts and hair braids with ribbons. Note the hair braid attached with black mourning fabric, probably indicating the wearer was in mourning, perhaps for the person whose hair is enclosed in the sepulchre.

In the outstanding mid-19th century example of a unique hair memorial, the hair of a young deceased woman was crocheted into an intimate piece of clothing: the head covering. This extremely rare, and perhaps one-of-a-kind, hairwork "loving cap" was placed on the head of the deceased woman during viewing, then removed prior to interment and saved as a remembrance. The act of cutting, sorting, and crocheting the quantity of hair needed to create this beautiful memorial must have entailed a great deal of love and intimacy between the maker and the deceased.

A poignant memorial to a mother and her son, with their photos and locks of hair, is shown to the right. The intimate inclusion of the curls of hair next to this mother and child make the memorial particularly touching.

Extremely rare hair "loving cap," made from the hair of a deceased woman and worn while in her coffin, 1850s. *Collection of Ann McIntyre.* $2,500+.

Unusual c. 1850-60s collection of memorial and sentimental ephemera and hair tokens of remembrance. Beadwork sepulchre and roses surrounding hair braid, with woven paper hearts and hair braids, one with mourning crape. 5" x 12". *Author's collection.* $395.

Poignant memorial to a mother and her son, c. 1880s. The bond of their love and their lives is exemplified in the adjoining photos and curls of hair, housed in a beautiful, mint condition frame. 12.5" x 14.5"; American. *Collection of Charles Swedlund.* $350.

Nineteenth century essayist Arthur Schopenhauer noted that in every parting was a foretaste of death, an awareness keenly felt by those living in prior centuries. His words are echoed in the tiny poem with two braids of hair shown in the next photograph. This small, c. 1850s rose-colored velvet case (which probably originally held an ambrotype), contains two light brown braids of hair along with a faded poem, written on a piece of paper that has been folded and refolded many times and is barely held together. The poem reads,

> *"Keepsake from M.L.*
> *When forced to parte from those we love*
> *[If] sure we meet tomorrow*
> *We still a pang of anguish prove*
> *And feel a tuch of sorrow. [sic]*
> — *E. Bras"*

A small, c. 1859 handmade box with padded velvet top (probably intended as a pincushion), and painted "Forget Me Not" decoration, contains four hair tokens of remembrance, at least two of which are memorial. Three of the locks of hair are wrapped in different pieces of paper or fabric, one is fastened with sealing wax, two are named, and one is tucked in muslin. The tiny hair curl has the pencil notation "Emily Eliza 7 months" (probably a death), and the large blue paper encloses a gray-brown curl of hair with pencil notation, "My Mother's Hair Mrs. Nancy Gilbert 1859." On the reverse of the blue sheet is a "shopping list" for a milliners, noting a half-yard of black silk, a half-yard of crape, and black ribbon to be purchased, no doubt for mourning.

Lovely little c. 1840-50s velvet keepsake case enclosing two braids of hair with sentimental poem on parting and sorrow. 2.5" in diameter. *Author's collection.* $175.

One-of-a-kind handmade keepsake box with pincushion top, enclosing mourning hair tokens and the Victorian remembrance "Forget Me Not," c. 1850s. 2.5" x 4". *Author's collection.* $275.

In the next photograph, the deaths in a family are recorded by their locks of hair looped in a "chain link" arrangement symbolic of the "links" of human relationships. Underneath most of them are the names of the owners, and two of them are fastened with black mourning fabric indicating their deaths, or that they were in mourning for a loved one. Two others shown have poems underneath their hair as follows:

"This little lock of hair
The baby once did ware [sic]
Although her face you never see
Just look at it and think of me."
Mary Ann Miller

"This is a lock of hair
That jesse once did ware [sic]
It may some memorial be
So I send it there for thee."
Jesse Dewitt Miller"

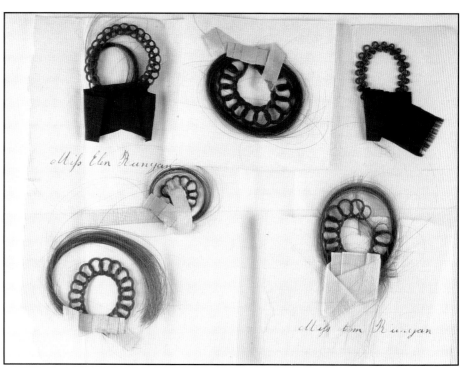

Hair of various family members looped in a "chain link" form, two of whom are in mourning, or deceased. *Author's collection.* $50.

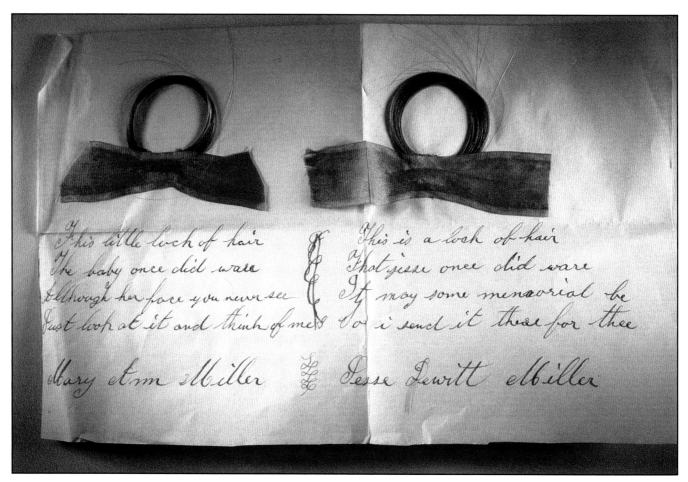

Curls of hair from children who died, along with crudely written poems extolling their loss. *Author's collection.* $50.

Five hair braids sewn onto the back of a letter document the deaths in one family to scarlet fever in a matter of weeks. Each of the braids of hair has the name of a family member written inside as follows: Wesley, Georgeann, Mary C, Mary Eva, and Grandmother. The letter describes the deaths as follows:

"Thare has been a great deal of sickness here this winter, sore throts and scarlet fever and ware it got into a family to or three of them generaly dies. It is mostly children that takes those deseaeds and thare has bin a great many sudent deaths about here among the old and middle-aged." [sic]

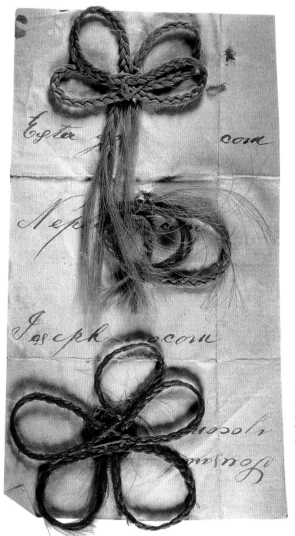

Five braids of hair of family members who died of scarlet fever, including four children and their grandmother, c. 1840-60s. *Author's collection.* $150.

Hair braids arranged into flowers and sewn onto paper record the names of family members who died sometime in the 1840s. The names, Ester Yocom, Nephi Yocom, Joseph Yocom, and Sousanah Yocom are each written in ink beside their braids of hair. *Author's collection.* $50.

208

Yet another family is memorialized through locks of hair shaped into flowers surrounding a *carte de visite* photograph of an elderly woman, no doubt the matriarch of her family. This rare c. 1860s Franco-American memorial for the Marchant family has tiny numbers glued to various hair flowers, and the hand-painted banner at the top lists the corresponding name of each family member from whom the individual lock of hair was taken. A tiny porcelain dove is fastened to one hair flower in the center, possibly denoting the hair of a deceased child.

Close-up view of interior of Marchant hairwork memorial showing flowers and numbers of individuals incorporated into the family wreath.

Rare hairwork memorial of Franco-American family with each hair "flower" numbered and their corresponding names listed at the top in the banner above the *carte de visite* photograph of the matriarch of the "Marchant" family. Small porcelain dove on one hair flower possibly indicates the death of a child. 10" x 12". *Author's collection.* $400.

Beautiful pair of matching hairwork tokens of remembrance, c. 1860-70s. The small amount of fine blonde hair woven into the tiny floral "nosegays" and set into the 4" x 5" frames may indicate the hair of children, possibly twins. *Collection of Jerry Lesandro and Larry Martin.* $400.

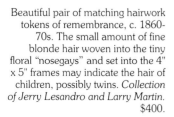

Pottery and Glass

As memorials were created in just about every conceivable material, pieces can be found in pottery, ceramics, and glassware as well. English pottery manufacturers such as Leeds, Staffordshire, Wedgwood, etc., manufactured numerous varieties of memorial pieces with the typical mourning iconography seen in other varieties of art shown and described in this book. Memorial pitchers for George Washington were manufactured by Josiah Wedgwood, and other potteries followed suit, not only for the "Father of His Country," but for other patriots as well. Mourners draped over urns, funeral wreaths, crosses, torches, and commemorative pieces in memory of famous figures were also commercially manufactured in transferware, black basalt stoneware, creamware, polychromed statuary, and Chinese export porcelain.

The jug shown in the photograph here is a creamware transfer-printed mourning pitcher, c. 1800. This commemorative jug memorializes not only George Washington, but Samuel Adams, John Hancock, and the "Proscribed Patriots of America." The plinth reads, "SACRED to the memory of George Washington who emancipated America from Slavery and founded a REPUBLIC upon such just and equitable principles that will serve as a model after ages." In the polychrome decoration, Washington's Memorial is behind the portraits of Adams and Hancock, and below the portraits is inscribed, "Columbia's Sons inspir'd by Freedom's Flame, Live in the annals of Immortal Fame." Around the perimeter of the oval transfer-printed decoration, the surround reads, "Liberty, Virtue, Peace, Justice, and Equity to ALL Mankind."

Rare colonial-era creamware pitcher memorializing the patriot "fathers" of American history, including George Washington, John Hancock and Samuel Adams. *Courtesy of The Museum of Mourning Art.* Value unknown.

For wealthy Victorians, more subtle forms of memorial art for the parlor could be used to convey the message of loss. As the typical Victorian home was chock-a-block with gewgaws of all kinds, crammed to a tasteful extravagance, memorial pieces could be adapted to fit in well to the Victorian love for crowded decorative arts. In the next example, we see the artful use of softened, almost allegorical death symbolism to substitute for the more harsh representations of death, thus making it as suitable for parlor décor as any marble bust or porcelain figure. In a design reminiscent of Thomas Gainsborough's Blue Boy, here the message of death is seen in the act of the child leaning against the cross praying, with a funeral wreath and ivy figuring prominently on the cross as death symbols. Family members could purchase these pre-cast figures of any age and either sex to represent a child's death, and the pieces usually sat on the parlor table under a glass dome to fill the need for a memorial object without the stark realities of the postmortem image.

Funeral china, particularly tea sets, was very popular in England, and a number of pottery manufacturers produced memorial pieces for both private purposes and for commemorating royal deaths. Some funeral china is apparent in the design and color; other china sets were purchased solely for a funeral (wake) purpose and are not recognizable as memorial pieces without corresponding provenance. Among the most popular memorial china was the pink lustre transferware produced to commemorate losses universal to everyone – the loss of children and husbands, for example. Bowls, cups and saucers, plates, and serving dishes were depicted with scenes of children visiting the grave of their mother, parents mourning children, or widows grieving for husbands, rather like the lithographs of Currier & Ives. The pink lustreware bowl stamped "The Mother's Grave," showing three orphaned children grieving at their mother's tombstone in the cemetery, was a popular representational theme in Victorian literature, sheet music, and art. The literary plots of Charles Dickens and other Victorian authors sometimes romanticized orphans as the unknown foundlings of grand estates or inherit-

ances, but the truth was far from such idealized portrayals. In his landmark 1890 book, appropriately named *How The Other Half Lives*, Jacob Riis shocked Victorian American sensibilities by his published photographic exposé of the appalling conditions in the tenements of New York.

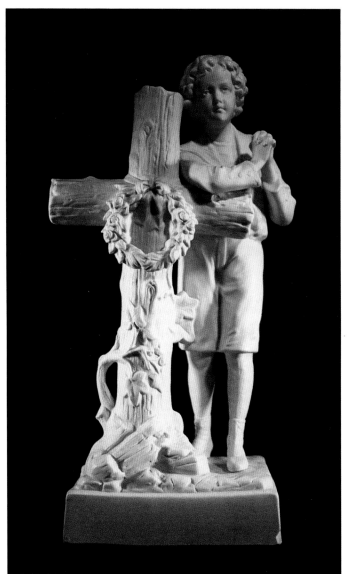

Rare parian ceramic memorial statue of young boy, c. 1880s. This form of statuary could be purchased by mourning families to represent a particular age and sex of the deceased, standing next to the cross with the ubiquitous symbols of death and resurrection common to the Victorian era (seen in the funeral wreath and ivy). They were usually placed on parlor tables under glass domes to indicate a family loss to visitors in the home. 15" x 5". *Author's collection.* $595.

Pink lustreware bowl stamped with transferware pattern of "The Mother's Grave," showing orphans standing by the monument. Pink lustreware memorial china is fairly easy to find today, ranging in price from about $40-50 for a cup and saucer on up for larger or rarer pieces. *Author's collection.* $75.

Also produced were memorial sets for royalty, such as the sauce boat for Princess Charlotte shown in the next two photographs; royal pieces such as this can be expensive and difficult to find. This unusual pink lustreware sauce boat commemorates the November 1817 death in childbirth of Princess Charlotte, daughter of George IV and wife of Leopold of Saxe-Coburg. After being pronounced as "doing extremely well" by her personal physician shortly after giving birth, the Princess was dead in four hours, and the entire nation was plunged into mourning on a scale similar to that which accompanied the death of Princess Diana in 1997. On November 17, 1817, the *London Times* wrote that "chilling regrets and unavailing laments seem the mournful inmates of every mansion, house, and cottage."

The sauce boat depicts Britannia covering her face and weeping with a handkerchief. The grief and loss is such that even an angel in the clouds overhead is grief-stricken, although the soul effigy of Charlotte, seen rising in the clouds nearby, points confidently heavenward. The figures surround Charlotte's monument and obelisk, which is inscribed with the words "To the Memory of Princess Charlotte" on the plinth. A globe symbolic of England's global sovereignty is in the foreground, and another cherub, holding a cross and in rather more "homely" dress, pays homage at the tomb.

The reverse of the gravy boat is equally intriguing and depicts heavenly angels with trumpets in the clouds adoring the Lamb of God seen as a sacrificial lamb on a altar. Overhead, a symbol of three circles within a triangle representative of the Triune Godhead shines rays of light down upon the Lamb.

Pink lustre sauce boat in memory of Princess Charlotte, daughter of George IV of England, who died in childbirth in 1817. *Author's collection.* $275+.

Reverse side of pink lustre sauce boat, showing interesting symbolism of angels in heaven worshiping the Lamb of God, with Princess Charlotte presumably one of them. *Author's collection.*

A rare English temperance plate made by J & G Meakin in the mid-19th century is shown next. This unusual plate is white ironstone with a thin blue rim, decorated around the edge with a poppy, English wood hyacinth, and wheat-ear in *bas relief.* James Meakin began his pottery company in 1851, and was soon joined by his son, also named James. The company produced inexpensive earthenware pottery for many years in the towns of Longton, Shelton, and Hanley, primarily exporting its wares to America and the English colonies.

This unusual plate represents an anomaly in the standard manufactured Meakin pottery. In the tenements of London and New York, temperance societies attempted to educate those living in poverty of the direct connection between alcohol abuse and starvation. As slum dwellers were frequently illiterate, leaving written pamphlets was often futile, thus pictorial material in the form of useful utensils was given away as a means of educating women living in situations of alcohol abuse in the home. In this example, death is portrayed not in a *memorial* context, but as an educational tool in a *socio-economic* message. The father stands in the foreground with a bottle, obviously drunk, guiltily looking askance at his anguishing wife, who is overcome with grief at the loss of her infant, who lies in the coffin in the background being watched over by a weeping older sister. A despondent older brother sits helplessly by the fireplace. The reason for the scene is clearly stated: *Intemperance Produces Starvation.* Thus it was hoped that in using the plate, tenement wives and mothers would be reminded to prevent the starvation of their children by encouraging temperance in their homes, often problematic in such situations at best.

Memorial items were mass-produced commemorating the assassination of President James Garfield, who was shot on July 2, 1881 and died over three months later on September 19, 1881, after enduring a long, lingering, and painful death. The President had sought to escape the heat and malarial conditions of Washington, DC, by taking a trip to Ohio by train on July 2, but was instead shot by an unbalanced assassin named Charles Julius Giuteau. Disgruntled over being denied a job by

President Garfield, and believing that the President was part of a vast conspiracy to remove his political enemies from Washington (including himself), Giuteau emerged from the crowds at the train station to shoot the President in the back. The President endured weeks of painful probing surgeries and inept medical treatments by the two factions of medical thought prevailing during the 19th century: the *allopaths,* who believed that only heroic, invasive, and infection-inducing surgeries would save the

President's life; and the *homeopaths,* who attempted to treat the catastrophic infection and wounds with concoctions of herbs. Ultimately, the massive infections took the President's life.

Numerous memorials were created, including a lovely line of glassware called the "Garfield Drape," a plate and cup of this style of which are pictured here. The "drape," of course, refers to the yards of crape bunting draped from buildings during the funeral processions carrying the President's body to his final

Rare English J & G Meakin temperance plate given away to encourage abstinence from alcohol in the slums of London and New York, c. 1850s. *Author's collection.* $100-150.

Garfield "drape" plate and cup, c. 1880s. *Collection of Lyn Iversen and Chris Lamoreaux.* Plate: $75; Cup: $50.

Remarkable souvenir memorial plate for President William McKinley, originally fired to commemorate his attendance at the Pan American Exposition, then later cold-painted with the words, "Last Picture of Pres. McKinley" after his assassination at the Exposition, c. 1901. *Collection of Lyn Iversen and Chris Lamoreaux.* $125.

resting place, as was also done during the progresses of President Lincoln's and President Grant's funeral trains. Vases, cake stands, plates, cups, relish dishes, etc. are available to the collector, at modest prices of $50-100 each. "Garfield Drape" pieces come in yellow, pale green, light and dark blue, as well as clear glass, but the clear glassware is the most easily acquired. Embossed on this plate are the words "We Mourn Our Nation's Loss." Other types of glassware for Presidents Abraham Lincoln, Ulysses S. Grant, and William McKinley are also available to collectors, some embossed with their "last words," to wit: "It is God's Will" (President William McKinley), and "Let Us Have Peace" (President Ulysses S. Grant).

Two unusual memorial plates for President William McKinley are shown in the following photographs. On September 6, 1901, President McKinley was shot by an assassin, dying of his wounds eight days later and making him the third American president assassinated in thirty-six years by 1901. President and Mrs. McKinley were attending the Pan American Exposition in Niagara Falls, New York, when an avowed anarchist, Leon Czolgosz, approached the President under the pretext of shaking his hand, shooting him instead with a .32 caliber pistol. The bullet entered the President's stomach, and in spite of the efforts of a gynecologist on hand to operate and save his life, gangrene later set in and McKinley succumbed to the fatal infection. Ida McKinley, overcome with grief, only survived her husband by six years.

These plates were originally produced to commemorate the event of President McKinley's visit to the Exposition, and after his assassination were immediately cold-painted with black memorial crape bunting over the already-fired porcelain to commemorate the tragic event in a memorial context rather than a celebratory one. Eager to capitalize on the market in mourning artifacts, this pottery manufacturer probably produced the first pieces memorializing the fallen President.

Matching souvenir plate for President McKinley, with funeral drape over the Canton [Ohio] Courthouse cold-painted onto the plate after the assassination, thus turning the plate from commemorative to memorial. *Collection of Lyn Iversen and Chris Lamoreaux.* $125.

A wonderful English memorial pitcher with inscriptions is shown at right. In painted gold on one side, the inscription reads:

"A Present to James Nilson in Remembrance of Alford Robinson – FORGET ME NOT – 1874."

On the reverse, the inscription reads:

"Although the past is dead,
Its memory still is here;
The happy tones of other days,
Still echo in our ear."

Not only were beautiful porcelains and funeral china created to memorialize loved ones, but even everyday objects commemorated the deaths of patriotic heroes – such as the Duke of Wellington potted meat container seen below. This c. 1850s meat pot would have held ordinary processed beef, and yet its lid memorializes the English military hero of Waterloo who defeated the notorious Emperor Napoleon Bonaparte of France. Son of the Irish Earl of Mornington, the Duke of Wellington entered the army in 1787, commanded troops in India, and served in the Irish Parliament. He went on to serve in the British House of Commons and as Chief Secretary of Ireland in 1807. At the command of British troops, Wellington won victories over the French in Portugal and Spain (as well as in France itself), later defeating Napoleon at the Battle of Waterloo in 1815. He was richly rewarded by English and foreign sovereigns, becoming one of the most honored men in Europe. The "Iron Duke" served as British Prime Minister from 1828-30, and at his death in 1852, was given a monumentally lavish funeral and burial in St. Paul's cathedral, alongside another famous British Naval hero, Lord Horatio Nelson.

The ceramic potted meat container shown here has the Duke's image on the lid, along with his birth date of "May 1, 1769," his date of death as "Sept. 14, 1852," and his age of "83 Years," an extraordinarily long and successfully lived life.

Wonderful English memorial pitcher with inscriptions, 1874. 12" high. *Author's collection.* $300.

Reverse side of English memorial pitcher, showing poem. *Author's collection.*

Ceramic potted meat container in memory of the Duke of Wellington, c. 1850s. 4" in diameter. *Author's collection.* $225.

A rare cremation urn is shown last in this section. This extraordinary piece is not only quite unusual as a memorial keepsake, it also represented a new phenomenon in societal perspectives about the resurrection of the physical body, at the time it was originally created and kept as a remembrance. Both before and after the Protestant Reformation, religious prohibitions regarding cremation as a practice of disposal of remains had existed in Western culture for centuries. It was not until 1876 that the first crematorium was built, and it was done so privately in the home of F. Julius Le Moyne, a Pennsylvania physician. The following year marked the first recorded cremation in the United States, that of Dr. Charles Wilson of Salt Lake City in 1877. Cremation as a popular practice still remained stigmatized until well into the 20th century, however, because of the almost total destruction of the body, causing many to worry about the possibility of future resurrection. However, softened religious perspectives in the early years of the 20th century, emphasizing a loving God promising immortality, helped assuage the fear of death – and by extension, the dissolution of the physical body. This in turn removed some of the reticence surrounding cremation, which has gained steadily in social acceptance ever since. This extraordinary c.1880s glass cremation urn has a portrait of the deceased as well as a receptacle for flowers in the stopper.

Beautiful cremation urn with portrait of the deceased painted onto the glass, 14" x 7" in diameter; c.1870s; American. This rare funerary urn has a stoppered plug with an opening for the insertion of flowers. *Collection of Charles Swedlund.* $700.

Unique Memorial Objects and Artifacts

Mourning keepsakes are as unique as the people who made and kept them; sometimes their significance is obvious, sometimes obscure. If an object is not obviously memorial in appearance, we are dependent upon provenance, and where a story can be known, a mourning artifact has meaning and history. In this section we will look at those pieces which, for one reason or another, are most likely unique, one-of-a-kind remembrances, distinct from other memorials which are typical of their eras and similar to others of their type.

A touching collection of memorial keepsakes for a child is shown first. The items contained in this tiny grouping have almost a "reliquary" quality about them, kept together for over 150 years. The tiny hand-sewn "waist," or bodice of cotton, is lined with muslin and in the dropped-shoulder style of children's clothing for both girls and boys in the Civil War era. Attached to the little waist is a period note, which reads:

> "This waist was made for and worn by my little sister Jennie Leonard who died at the age of 5. She had outgrown it and mother made a larger waist which she wore in her coffin. The yellow skirt like this waist she wore at burial. CJG."

Also accompanying the little waist is Jennie's first attempt at embroidering a sampler. Many of the letters are backwards and the words misspelled, but a few of the words indicate that her mother

had died and that possibly Ireland was her family's country of origin. Three crude handkerchiefs, one unfinished with a needle still in place, and a period note saying, "her sewing as she left it – Jennie's," were enclosed with the sampler and waist. Families' attempts to keep

such mementos to remember beloved children in the face of their often bewilderingly swift deaths is a testament to an era in which most people were forced to continually live knowing that, "In the midst of life, we are in death."[36]

Little handmade bodice (or "waist" as it was called in the 19th century), with period note relating that part of the outfit was worn by five-year-old "Jennie Leonard in her coffin." Also kept with the waist was little Jennie's first attempts at embroidering a sampler, her childish stitches spelling out that she is "weeping," presumably because her "mother died." The word "Irelan" can also be deciphered. Another handkerchief with a period note, "Her sewing as she left it – Jennie's," has the needle still in place in the stitches before Jennie died. *Author's collection.* $500.

The next three photographs show rare memorial vinaigrettes. The first is in the form of a pendant watch, the front cover containing a curl of hair (probably that of a child) inside a crystal bezel, surrounded by pearls. The watch, a common symbol for death from the Middle Ages through the Victorian era, opens in much the same way as that of a pocket watch, with ornate interior layers for the aromatic ointments. Another exceptional memorial vinaigrette is made of carved ivory. The crystal bezel top encloses intricate hair-work and sepia memorial symbolism of urn, angels, and willow branches, executed in a scene of approximately one inch in diameter.

The memorial vinaigrette at left shown open for aromatic ointments. *Courtesy of Things Gone By.*

Wonderful little memorial vinaigrette with curl of hair, probably that of a child, surrounded with matched pearls symbolic of tears. 1" in diameter. *Courtesy of Things Gone By.* $695.

Ivory memorial vinaigrette, shown open with container for aromatic ointment. *Courtesy of Things Gone By.* $595.

A rare memorial lace bobbin, commemorating the hanging of a murderer at Tyburn, England, is shown below. This unusual item is from one of six executions so commemorated at Tyburn – the carved bone bobbins were made and sold as "souvenirs" of these public spectacles. Other forms of memorial lace bobbins do exist, although very rare, and most memorialize the death of a loved one. In this case, however, the souvenir hawkers sold these pieces to spectators at the hangings, in what can only be described as the complete antithesis of the Victorian ideal of *The Beautiful Death* philosophy. The shank on this bobbin was hand-drilled to form holes, which were then filled with red and black melted sealing wax to make the letters, "W. Bull Hung Apr 12, 1871." Records at Tyburn show that a William Bull was in fact hung on this date for the "brutal murder of an old woman."

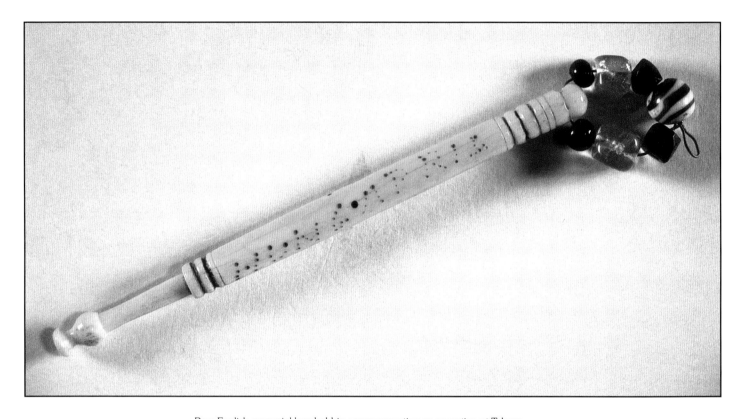

Rare English memorial lace bobbin commemorating an execution at Tyburn, England. Inscribed "W. Bull Hung Apr 12, 1871"; Bull was executed for the murder of an elderly woman. Only six such executions were commemorated in these lace bobbins, which were sold at the hangings by souvenir hawkers. 4" long. *Author's collection.* $400.

A rare scrimshaw whalebone "coffin" with articulated skeleton inside is handmade from carved pieces of whalebone that have been pegged together, the top scene showing a whaling ship and whalers in the process of harpooning a breaching whale. On the reverse is carved the date "3 Sept 1825," indicating that this is probably an English piece. Inside the little coffin, an extremely well-carved and articulated skeleton shows the grinning *memento mori* iconography of centuries earlier but still occasionally seen in 19th century memorial art.

Effigies of the dead date back to medieval times in Western culture, and were made of a variety of materials, such as stoneware, leather, wood, wax, paper, etc. After the death of Lord Horatio Nelson, the English Naval hero in 1805 at the Battle of Trafalgar, a life-size wax effigy was made of him wearing one of his uniforms for display at Westminster Abbey. The likeness was so remarkable that his mistress, Lady Hamilton, overcome with grief at seeing the effigy, almost succumbed to her desire to "kiss his lips" one last time.

During the Victorian era, wax effigies, usually of children, were made in Germany, Belgium, France, and Britain. They were usually encased in wood and glass and customarily left at the gravesite after the burial. Some, however, such as the example shown on the next page, remained in the family as memorial keepsakes. Upon the death of her 21-month-old son Sigismund ("Sigi"), Queen Victoria's daughter, also named Victoria and wife of the Crown Prince of Prussia, sculpted a wax effigy of the little boy and placed it in his crib along with his toys and shoes as memorial objects. The items remained in a small room in the inner recesses of the Neues Palais, locked away from sight for decades after his death. The practice of creating memorial "grave dolls" was brought to America by immigrants, primarily those from Germany, but also from France and Belgium.

Nineteenth century writer Fannie Fern, in her 1856 children's book, *The Play-Day Book: New Stories for Little Folks,* encouraged her young readers,

"Come—let us go to Greenwood [Cemetery]…burial place of the New Yorkers, and a very lovely place it is too. I do not like that children should lie awake nights in shuddering fear of it…I saw some graves of little children; there were no tombstones or monuments over them. [It] is the custom when a little child dies, to place all his toys on the grave with a little glass case over them. I saw [a] little grave and under the glass-case upon it was a little doll,…and three locks of hair, golden, brown, and black, cut from the little heads that lay pillowed there."

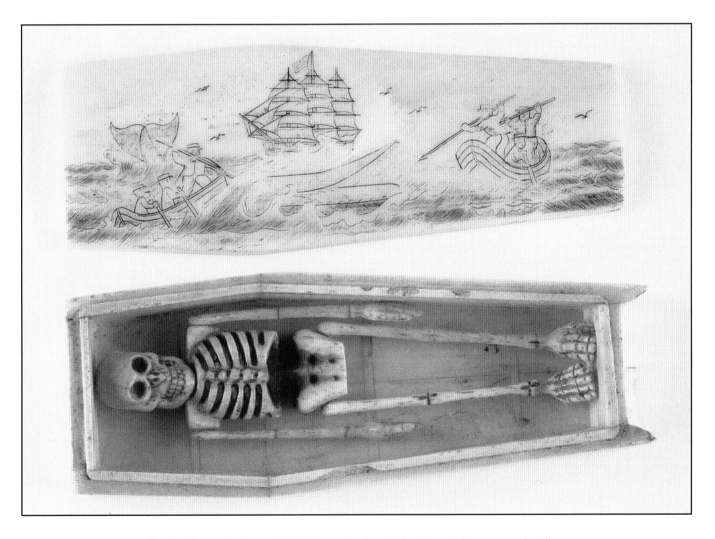

Rare hand-carved and pegged whalebone scrimshaw "coffin," with whaling scene on the lid and articulated skeleton inside; dated 3 Sept 1825. 5" long *Author's collection.* $895.

Because so few survived deterioration from the elements, extant examples of "grave dolls" are rarely found today outside of museums. However, the photograph here shows a rare wax effigy, originally from a German immigrant family who settled in New York State in the mid-19th century. The doll is approximately that of a newborn in size, and laid in a homemade wooden "coffin" painted blue. Locks of the real baby's blond hair were glued to the grave doll, and the christening clothing cut down and fashioned to fit the effigy, which lays upon a small handmade pillow, surrounded by linen flowers decorated with glitter.

A rare c. 1860 ivory memorial plaque depicting the Angel of Death carrying a child heavenward is shown in the next photograph. This figure, primarily evolving from rabbinical Judaism, was the being that extracted the soul from the living at the moment of death. Initially an emissary of God (Exodus 12:23, Isaiah 37:36), this macabre death entity became a figure associated with death (and even evil), in Judeo-Christian iconography, belief, and legend. Sometimes referred to as the "Grim Reaper," this figure stands in stark contrast to the softened Victorian death imagery of cherubs or angels wafting children heavenward. In the depiction seen here, the Angel of Death is cadaverous, carrying a scythe over his shoulder, and walking in the clouds, while holding the baby and staring into its face. The outstretched arms of the infant and its pose hearken back to the story of Abraham offering up Isaac as a sacrifice to God in the Old Testament. Whether or not biblical symbolism is intended here is open to conjecture, but the macabre theme is an unusual anomaly in the Victorian "beautification" of a child's death, and is more representational of *memento mori* images of death and infants as seen in the *ars moriendi* of the Middle Ages.

Rare wax effigy of deceased infant, c. 1860-70s. Popular memorials among German and French immigrants to America for children who died. As these were normally left at the gravesite, few have survived. 24.5" long. *Author's collection.* $2,500.

Unusual ivory plaque of "Angel of Death" carrying infant to heaven in the clouds. Such macabre symbolism of the "Grim Reaper" was rare by the Victorian era, although there was a small revival of interest in this theme in the 1880s (the era of this piece), usually seen in men's mourning jewelry. 5" x 3". *Author's collection.* $795.

Small commemorative boxes for both men and women were popular as memorial keepsakes in England and France in the 18th and 19th centuries. After the death of Louis XV, mourning snuffboxes were produced and sold bearing the portrait of the young Dauphine (now Queen) Marie Antoinette, and the inscription "Consolation in Grief," representing not only the loss of the former King, but the anticipation of the new reign of his son, Louis XVI. Several outstanding French 18th century boxes are shown in the following photographs, bearing all the beauty of this century's fine painting, sepia and hair-work, and craftsmanship. In the first smaller ivory piece, we see a mourning scene done in palette-worked hair of a weeping willow in the foreground with a ship sailing towards the horizon in the background, symbolic of the soul's departure for heaven. The interior of this box is tortoiseshell, and this lovely piece would have sat on a lady's dressing-table, always near at hand to be treasured as a keepsake and to hold additional tokens of remembrance.

One of the larger tortoiseshell boxes shown on the next page is an outstanding c. 1819 French piece with hair-work and sepia on ivory, and 18K gold trim. The scene is extraordinarily detailed and intricate, with palette-worked blonde hair around the perimeter and two-color brown dissolved hair and sepia in acanthus leaves just inside. A mourner sacrificially burning an offering of flowers in memory of the deceased occupies the central scene, and the sepia inscription says, "Souvenir de Vos Amis," or "A Remembrance of Your Friends." This was probably a memorial gift made after death and given to friends named in the will as a bequest, a common practice among wealthy and aristocratic families. Dating back to the Middle Ages, the practice of leaving instructions in one's will to have memorial and jewelry items made after death and given to friends and family members was typically done throughout Western Europe, and this exceptional French piece reflects this continuing form of bequest.

Another beautiful little tortoise-shell box, c. 1780-1800 (also shown on the next page), has a rim of 18K gold and detailed painting on ivory, both in wa-tercolor and sepia with dissolved hair. The scene depicts a grieving woman praying by an urn, which is further embellished with gold wire and seed pearls. A cherub overhead carries a banner with the words, "Not Lost But Gone Before," while background foliage suggests cypress and willows, also done in dissolved hair-work suggestive of melancholia. The bottom of the box has an elaborate entwined cipher.

An extraordinary 18th century French tortoiseshell box with a fabulous painting on ivory set into an 18K gold frame is full of the sentimental and memorial symbolism popular in the centuries influenced by Romanticism and the Enlightenment. An arm reaches down from the heavenly realms to write on a tree trunk the words, "Love and Gratitude," yet the tree appears to "float" upon the sea. A tendril of ivy, symbolic of immortality, entwines the tree trunk, and in the background an iceberg also appears to float in the sea, its meaning unclear.

Lovely ivory box with mourning scene done in macerated hair of weeping willow on an island in the sea, with a boat sailing towards the horizon, symbolic of the soul ascending to heaven. 1.25" in diameter, c. 1840s. *Courtesy of Things Gone By.* $1,595.

Beautiful French memorial 18K gold box, executed in dissolved hair and sepia, of mourner offering floral remembrance to the deceased. Inscription says "In Remembrance of My Friends," probably a memorial commissioned by bequest to friends of the deceased, c. 1820s. 3" in diameter. *Courtesy of Things Gone By.* $1,695-1,895.

Outstanding tortoiseshell and ivory memorial box in 18K gold, with elaborate sepia and watercolor painting of grieving mourner at the urn. A cherub holds a banner overhead declaring, "Not Lost But Gone Before." The urn is spectacular, with tiny graduated seed pearls, black enameling, and gold wire. 3" in diameter. *Courtesy of Things Gone By.* $2,295.

Rare French tortoiseshell box with painted scene on ivory set into 18K gold frame, c. 1760-80. Scene of lady's arm reaching down from heaven to inscribe the words "Love and Gratitude" on a tree trunk floating in the sea. 3" in diameter. *Courtesy of Things Gone By.* $4,800.

Cork work was another form of "fancy work" of the 18th and 19th centuries, and proper upper class ladies would occupy themselves in using *every conceivable material in novel ways* to create beautiful objects for the home as part of their assigned role as "doyennes of good taste." Both straw work and cork work were part of the myriad forms of parlor crafts employed for sentimental, decorative, and memorial purposes, and both materials were done in marquetry designs and "free-standing" arrangements. The fashion for cork work was created by the use of simple tools such as a penknife and sheets of cork, readily available and inexpensive, with directions obtainable through the 1875 ladies publication, *Enquire Within Upon Everything.*

In keeping with the Victorian love for the "rustic picturesque" of crumbling castle fortresses made popular by the novels of Sir Walter Scott and other Romantic writers, Victorian ladies interpreted their love for the gloom of gothic ruins in darkened woodlands into melancholy scenes.[37] Sometimes the cork was cut in a fretwork design around an interior mourning scene; in other forms of memorial art, the cork itself was cut out and arranged into the tableau, as in the following outstanding example. This English, c. 1810-30 box with walnut veneer has a beautiful three-dimensionally carved urn and monument with overhanging willow tree against black velvet interior cloth set into a shallow shadow-box-framed lid. The entire scene has been cut from cork, including the tiny leaves.

Rare cork-work and walnut veneer memorial box, with mourning scene of willow and urn set inside shadowbox lid. Cork-work pieces are very rare, especially in this excellent condition. 5" x 8" x 4". *Courtesy of Things Gone By.* $1,495.

A rare one-of-a-kind shell-work obelisk with in-laid tintypes of the deceased is shown in the next photograph. This exceptional piece is an outstanding example of the many varieties of materials and compositions used by Victorians in creating memorials for the home. This miniature of what was probably the family's cemetery monument undoubtedly sat openly displayed on a parlor table in keeping with the unabashed Victorian desire to keep the dead within the circle of the living. Rare objects such as this are difficult to find and highly desirable.

Tear catchers or "weeping bottles" are other unusual examples of grief expression. Weeping bottles are occasionally seen in the hands of Grecian-dressed mourners on monuments in New England historical cemeteries, particularly that of Green-Wood in New York, where a life-size mourner is depicted holding such a bottle up to her eye to save her tears. The concept is based on a verse from Psalm 56:8, where David returns from losing a battle and cries out to God, "Hast Thou not saved my tears in Thy bottle?" The idea of God saving mourners' tears of grief appealed to Victorian religious beliefs, and thus women would hold these receptacles up to their eyes, saving their tears, and keeping the container on their dressing-table. Some traditional accounts hold that the weeping bottles would then be emptied over the grave on the first anniversary of the death.

An outstanding one-of-a-kind shellwork obelisk with set-in tintypes of four deceased individuals. On each side of this wonderful remembrance are 1/6 plate-sized photographs: one of a young man, one of a young woman, one of a young boy, and one of an elderly man. This unusual memorial shows a unique concept in creating a three-dimensional remembrance, probably a miniature of a familial cemetery monument, to be placed on the parlor table or mantel. 19" x 9" at the base. *Collection of Charles Swedlund.* $900.

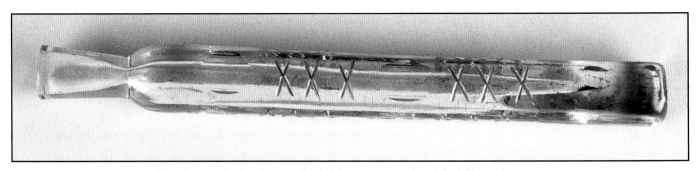

Glass "tear catcher," or "weeping bottle," for saving tears of grief. Such blown glass receptacles were placed on dressing-tables, and on the first anniversary of the death, the tears were poured over the grave. *Author's collection.* 6" long. $325.

A rare, one-of-a-kind "Sacred Casket," a gift from a husband to his wife at their betrothal in April 1855 is shown in the following photographs. This extraordinarily complex "Love Box" contains three "layers" enclosing objects, as well as panels extolling love and sentiment. Each exterior side or panel has a "message" from the husband to his wife: "Virtue Reward is True Bliss"; "Fidelity Is a Casket of Jewels"; "Leaves Taken is Not to Be Mistaken"; and "True Friendship Cannot Fade," with a final sentiment, "Presented to Mary J. Croxal by her Frend R. L. D., Balt. 1855." on the back of the "Sacred Casket."

The lid of the casket has velvet "forms" for pin cushions, and its use as a sewing box is also evident in the small compartments inside intended for thimbles and other small sewing notions. Upon opening the first lid (see photo, next page), one sees a daguerreotype of each of the betrothed couple taken individually in 1866. Over each of the individual tintype portraits is a braid of their woven hair. A calligraphic poem written by husband Robert L. Dickey, full of the terms of endearment and affection typical of the Victorian era, is framed inside the interior lid of the upper section, as follows:

"Accept of me a friendly token,
This box, a pledge of friendship unbroken
That will appear as a Violet by a mossy stone,
Half hidden from the eye.
Or as a fair stone, when only one
Is shining in the sky."

And,

"I have had no other means M.J.C.

Of offering a pledge to thee,
Therefore this except [sic], and if by distance or the tomb,
I should ever be hid from your longing gaze,
Still shalt thou, by viewing this treasure boone,
Find the fond remembrance of the days."
Robert L. Dickey, April, 1855."

A lower section opens to reveal another velvet compartment, full of tintypes of children and family members with their names and dates (from 1853-1860) listed in the lid, which has a satin "curtain" framed to appear like a theatre stage open to reveal each of the participants of a pageant.

This rare betrothal "Sacred Casket," made by a husband for his wife prior to their marriage, is an extraordinary sentimental and memorial family token of remembrance, c. 1850-60s. The casket (made to serve as a sewing box), contains daguerreotypes of the husband and wife on their wedding day, with braids of their hair, along with various images of their children and family members. The sentiments around the perimeter of the box were hand-painted by the husband as an expression of love for his bride. Sentimental and memorial reliquaries such as these are extremely rare and quite desirable to collectors, making this extraordinary "Sacred Casket" almost impossible to value on today's market. 12" x 8" x 8". *Collection of Charles Swedlund.* $3,000+.

"The Sacred Casket" with first lid open showing daguerreotypes of the betrothed couple, their braids of hair, and handwritten calligraphic love poems from the husband to the wife on their wedding day. *Collection of Charles Swedlund.*

Another view of the "Sacred Casket," showing a second layer of the casket revealed with family images. The names and dates of each are framed by the "theatre curtains" in the lid. *Collection of Charles Swedlund.*

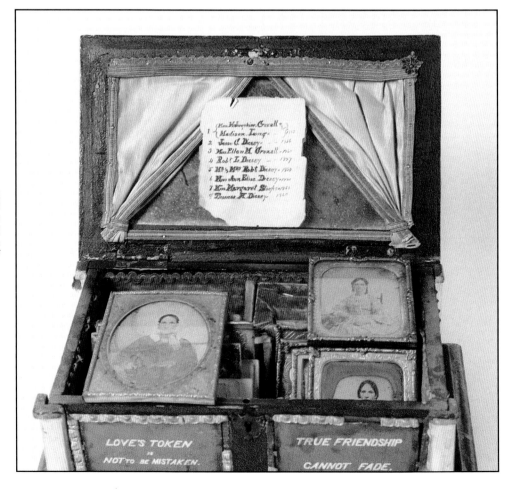

As seen in several poignant post-mortem images of children in the section on Memorial Photography, children's empty shoes held great emotional impact for Victorians, an impact which can still be felt today in viewing those images and the child's memorial shown here. The brightness of the red bows decorating Dorothy's little black shoes with their scuffed toes is an incongruous and emotionally affecting counterpoint, almost belying the fact of her death as noted in the chiseled marble date of Oct. 12, 1905. No doubt red was Dorothy's favorite color, and one can almost see her dancing in these tiny shoes.

Death masks were created by commissioned artists in the Victorian era, usually among the European wealthy or aristocracy, and in the art world of 18th and 19th century European impressionists as well, who used plaster casts to mold the facial features of the dead, later using them as molds for sculptures or busts. The emotional and psychological value placed upon death masks as memorials for Victorian mourners, like their European medieval counterparts, stands out as a visual antipode to current tastes. Fanny Fern, the well known 19th century American writer, wrote to her brother Richard in Germany in February, 1844, of the death of their sister Ellen to pleurisy, noting,

"Ellen, our Ellen, is in Heaven! One week of blessedness has she already passed there; one week of agony and desolation have we mourned her, each long, weary day, as it has passed, but reminding us the more painfully of what we have lost. Was she not too fair to die? A cast was taken of her face, and a drawing made by Alexander, both of which will be invaluable to us all."

Louise Colet, mistress of Gustave Flaubert, the 19th c. French writer of *Madame Bovary,* kept a sculpted likeness of her infant son on her desk, causing another of her lovers to note in a letter, "I've often seen you grow tearful at the sight of the mysterious little plaster bust standing in your study; your heart still bleeds…." And the English artist John Horsley made a cast of the head and shoulders of his three-year-old son, Harry, as a memorial of his death

in 1854 to scarlet fever.

The creation of death masks and the casting of hands in plaster appears to have been a more popular practice in England and Europe, as fewer examples of 19th century American pieces are extant. Rare, individual examples occasionally turn up, however, as in the early 20th century American piece shown below. The story behind this sad memento has been lost, but the desire to look upon, and remember the face of beloved children too soon gone from sight, is a universal need.

"Dorothy's" little shoes with red bow ties. This touching memorial of a little girl's shoes embodies all the heartbreak of childhood death in otherwise ordinary, inanimate objects. The scuffed toes, and the name "Dorothy" with her date of death, are all that remain of this little girl's existence and the memories of her parents. *Collection of Jim Mathews.* $395-475.

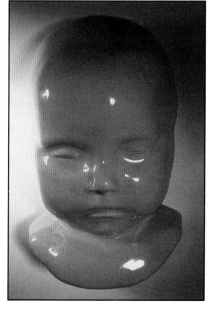

Rare ceramic infant death mask, early 20th century. Death masks date back to the Middle Ages in western culture, and represent the basic human need to visually hold onto a memory of the deceased's face. *Author's collection.* $175.

A beautiful memorial beadwork anchor embroidered on silk ground is shown next. The technique of beadwork, although dating back to ancient times, came into vogue as a needlework art in the 17th century, particularly in England. Originally seen in combination with "stumpwork" (embroidered and appliquéd fabric pictures with raised, stuffed embellishment on elaborate backgrounds), beadwork began to develop as its own form of needlework. Pastoral scenes, allegorical motifs, biblical and court figures, and fanciful animals, birds, and insects cavorting in exotic gardens were among the favorite compositions decorating young girl's slippers, jewelry caskets, pictures, bonnets, etc.

Vividly colorful glass beads of various sizes were exported throughout England and Europe from Italy, France, and Germany, and dozens of shades of glass were incorporated into a single design, sometimes with clear glass beads worked into the background for sparkle. Each was sewn on by hand to the silk ground. The popularity of beadwork continued into the 19th century with the publication of designs and instruction in ladies' publications for such articles as firescreens, table tops, trays, lambrequins, tea cosies, foot stools, etc. Personal accessories too, such as purses, jewelry, spectacle cases, etc., lent themselves to beadwork, and as with other forms of parlor crafts, memorial objects were made. For mourning dress, the writers of *Elegant Arts for Ladies* advised "grisaille" beaded accessories in "black, white, or gray bugle beads [which] make up very prettily." And, jet beaded items were worn during bereavement as well, as seen in the jet mourning reticule in this book's section on Mourning Clothing.

In this beadwork anchor, the designs commemorate the loss of a husband, as seen in the two burning hearts, symbolic of marital love. Above the mausoleum is a torch burning upward; in contrast to the usual display of the torch represented as upside down, this possibly symbolizes the fiery passion of love. A fully opened rose, representing the death of an adult in the prime of life, and a daisy, symbolic of gentleness and purity of thought, are also shown in the beadwork.

A small reliquary, completely handcarved out of solid wood to resemble a "coffin," is shown at right, full of the pathos inherent in handmade memorials

to a lost child. This piece was probably made by the child's father, and has the attached coffin plate inscribed "Our Loved One" on the hand-hewn lid. Inside the little "coffin" is a postmortem tintype of a figure covered with a "shroud," made of a homespun bed-cloth. The figure, presumably the mother, is seated on a chair and is holding her deceased infant, whom she has turned towards the camera to record the face for probably the one and only time. Also enclosed inside the little reliquary is a tiny handmade silk heart made from a piece of the dress the infant is wearing in the tintype, containing something inside (probably a lock of hair), along with black and white silk ribbon. This extraordinary memorial came from eastern Iowa.

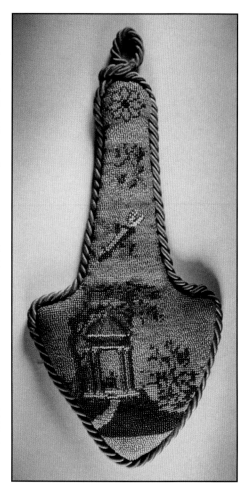

Lovely beadwork "anchor" in memory of a husband, executed in diminutive beads sewn onto silk ground and finished with silk cording, c. 1820. Mourning symbols of burning hearts over a monument inside a mausoleum represent marital love, and a burning torch that of passionate emotion. 8.5" x 3". *Author's collection.* $595.

Rare, one-of-a-kind handcarved "reliquary" coffin with mourning ribbon, postmortem tintype, and silk heart made from the dress worn by the infant in the image. 8" x 4" x 4". *Author's collection.* $1,200.

A "Souvenir of Clara Hurst" encases an entire collection of childhood memories in a little bound book, and what a precious reliquary this must have been to Clara's parents. The beautiful leather binding, obviously done by an expert bookbinder, contains locks of Clara's hair, a scribbled drawing, a piece of blue ribbon, her obituary, a photograph of her tombstone, and letters, all tucked inside her first reader.

Clara was born on December 30, 1861, and died June 20, 1869, the daughter of John and Catherine Hurst, a minister and his wife living in New Jersey. Her parents lovingly collected the little relics of her life, wrapping each one in tissue or newspaper, noting on one enclosure, "Precious Clara's hair cut while she was living in March, 1869" (she died the following June), and on another, a description of her eyes as "gray."

In 1875, Catherine evidently felt it necessary to pass on the reliquary to her son, Carl, and noted in the inside cover of the reader, the following:

> "Carl, I wish you to be very careful of this little book, for it belonged to your dear sister Clara. It was her first book, and from it she learned the alphabet and then to read the "beautiful little stories and prayers" that she used to speak so often. Madison, N.J. 1875."

One wonders if John had already passed, and Catherine was herself terminally ill, and was seeking to preserve the remembrance of Clara by passing it on to her son. Although the reader and some of the papers are in German, the written English is grammatically perfect, so it appears that the Hurst family had earlier immigrated from Germany and settled in America, but retained their German connection through newspapers.

Beautiful leather-bound case with hair tokens, snippet of ribbon, obituary and photograph of tombstone, and other remembrances for "Clara Hurst," who died at the age of seven in 1869. The touching remembrances were tucked inside Clara's first reader, in German, her family being immigrants to America from Germany. 5" x 7.5". *Author's collection.* $595-795.

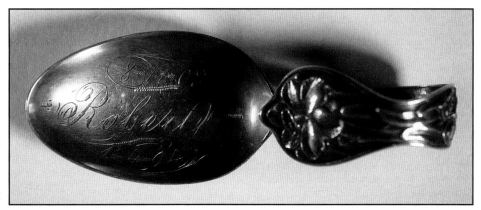

A child's memorial spoon, engraved with his name, "Robert," and dates of his birth and death in 1903 and 1904, has a daffodil flower formed in repousse (in which the pattern is formed in relief from pressure applied to the other side), the daffodil being symbolic of the "death of youth." *Author's collection.* $150.

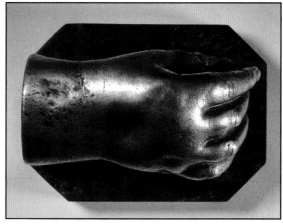

The cast hands of children were especially affecting, and the example shown here is a tiny silver-plated cast hand of an infant, attached to a marble base. This sad little token no doubt sat on a parlor table in the family home in memory of a child. 3.5" long. *Author's collection.* $175.

This little marble Bible or "prayer book" was a gift from a stonecutter to the family of the deceased after the cemetery monument was completed. Such tokens of remembrance were often given to family members, as stonecutters used leftover scrap marble to create these personal tokens. Here the name "Ossie" is inscribed on one side, and the clasped hands of a man and woman are carved in *bas relief* on the reverse. This piece probably commemorated the death of a husband, as the man's hand in a coat sleeve clasps that of his wife in her dress sleeve. 2.75" x 3". *Author's collection.* $150-175.

A small crudely molded chalkware "recumbent child" memorial parlor piece, c. 1860s. The figure of the "shrouded infant" or "recumbent child" is often seen in the tombstone carver's art to represent childhood death, and smaller versions of this iconography were made in marble, parian, pottery, chalkware, and other materials for mourners to keep at home as a remembrance. *Author's collection.* $100.

A small handmade cast iron "tombstone," painted red, with the name "Eugene" and the words, "Mar 29-95," is shown here. This sad relic was no doubt made to remember the loss of a child, the first name only being memorialized. Possibly made by a blacksmith or foundry worker, this piece might have been in the family plot, or kept as a memorial in the home. 6" x 6". *Author's collection.* $75-100.

Brass "Sacred Heart" keepsake container, c. 1880s. This Catholic token of remembrance enabled the mourner to tuck away locks of hair, obituary notices, written notes, a rosary, and other personal tokens inside a religious receptacle similar to a reliquary. *Author's collection.* $125.

Paper Ephemera

A large area of paper goods is available to the collector, whether for historical research or to fill out a collection of memorial art. As memorialization of the deaths of loved ones permeated all aspects of Victorian life, it also influenced personal correspondence, journals and diaries; printed funeral cards; sheet music to be sung in the parlor; handwritten poetry and small paper tokens of remembrance. Letters detailing the deaths of family members during the 19th century abound, and many are available to the collector at prices ranging from $25-$30 each to $100 or more, depending on content, early date, or area of interest. Letters written by soldiers wounded or killed during the Civil War command high prices, often in the hundreds of dollars. Handwritten accounts of deaths which include a lock of hair are also very desirable, and thus more expensive to acquire.

The following extraordinary deathbed account of 21-year-old Lewis Kerr, of Steubenville, Ohio, was handwritten by his brother in 1815 for relatives who were unable to personally witness the long dying process and the young man's religious conversion. The memoir is handsewn on rag paper and includes a short biography of Lewis, noting that he was born in 1794 and contracted the dysentery from which he died after visiting family and friends while away from home. The account includes the futility of the "medical arts to restore him," Lewis' conversations with his family members regarding his spiritual state and struggle to achieve salvation, his final resignation to his imminent death, the disposition of his possessions, and his committal of his family to God. As death approaches, he utters, "Is this death? How comfortable! Do you not see death liteing [sic] upon me?" to which his brother replies, "We think we see the appearance of it." His brother noted his last words as "O Lord I commit my spirit!"

This account is typical of early Calvinist beliefs that salvation involved more than faith alone, but painful suffering and endurance in dying. Memoirs and letters such as these are important historical documents in understanding social and cultural history, as well as – such as in this case – geographical history, as this account was written shortly after Ohio's statehood, but when it was still very much the "wilderness frontier."

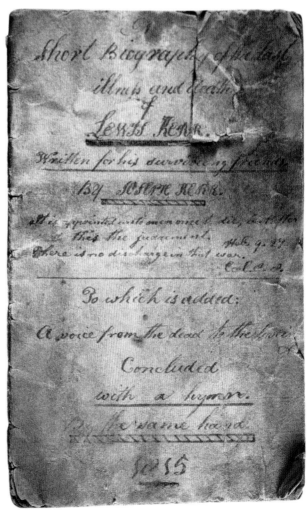

Handwritten and hand-sewn death account on rag paper, of 21-year-old Lewis Kerr from Steubenville, Ohio, who died of dysentery in 1815. Details religious conversion, dying utterances, and futility of the medical arts to save him. 3" x 5". *Author's collection.* $150.

An extraordinary 1883 letter on mourning stationary details the death of a wife in the language of mourning typical of the views surrounding death during the Victorian era. James Brock grieves over the passing of his wife of forty-five years in a letter to his brother, detailing the dying hours and deathbed scene:

"My house is left desolate indeed. She who was the light and ornament of it is no more. She who was the companion of my pilgrimage for upwards of forty five years has passed on before me in the Journey and has left me behind. He who has the right to recall his gifts, "has taken away the desire of my eyes with a stroke" and has left me to weep."

Brock had already endured the deaths of seven children before that of his wife, so the "stroke" was particularly bitter. In a style reminiscent of the Middle Ages, he anthropomorphizes death by ascribing to it human characteristics, e.g.:

"Death has seven times come up to our windows, and entered into our chambers, and has taken away the children, but now he has entered the eighth time and has taken away the Mother of the Children."

The tone of the letter alters however, to the Christian hope of resurrection and reunion, and changes to the scene of the deathbed where he describes his wife's passing from influenza as a mixture of sinking and revival, until she "sank down gradually [and] the weary wheels of life stood still [sic]." Letters of this caliber are very desirable and difficult to find, and thus well worth the $100-150 price range.

While mourning covers (envelopes) are fairly easy to acquire for minimal cost, letters of this rare content are becoming increasingly difficult to find and correspondingly more expensive. Like other deathbed accounts, letters, and memoirs, these personal narratives are desirable to historians as well as collectors of mourning and funereal artifacts.

Civil War era letters are another genre of collecting popular with both ephemera collectors as well as Civil War historians. The value placed on such items is determined by the content and whether the identity of the soldier is known or can be determined; higher values being placed on known soldiers, those who fought in specific battles, or those were prisoners of war. Prices range from $100 to $450 and up depending on content and identity and importance of soldier and/or writer.

After attending Sunday services, Victorians frequently gathered around the piano or organ to listen to mournful tunes extolling the sad experiences of widows and orphans, the deaths of Civil War soldiers, or the early passing of children. Note the two piano pieces commemorating the loss of a child. The first, entitled "Mother Put Me in My Little Bed," shows the child kneeling in prayer beside her bed, but its accompanying sequel shows the child placed instead in her *grave bed*, with her soul being wafted heavenward by angels. Examples of mourning sheet music with elaborate lithography are the most desirable to collectors today, and prices range from $20 up to $50 each, depending on condition and appeal of lithography.

An extraordinary volume of sheet music contained in one volume is partially shown in the following photographs of Flora Lynn's songbook, and is a window into a young woman's life during the Civil War years. Music books in the 19th century could be purchased with the owner's name inscribed on the cover, and the one here belonging to "Flora Lynn" is a rare example because Flora personalized her music book as though it were her diary. Thus, this volume is more than simply a collection of 19th century sheet music: it contains news-

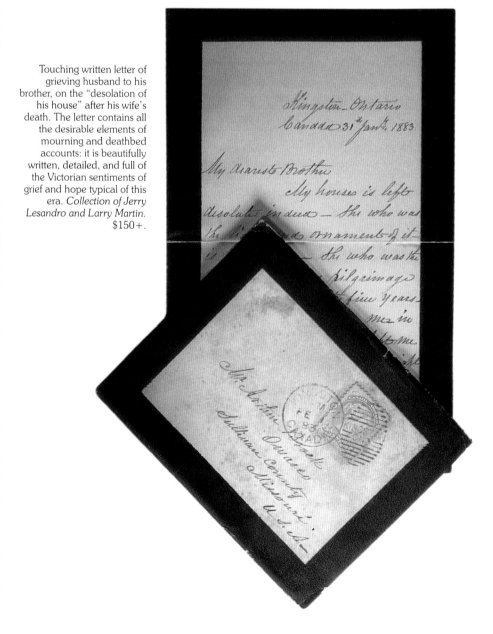

Touching written letter of grieving husband to his brother, on the "desolation of his house" after his wife's death. The letter contains all the desirable elements of mourning and deathbed accounts: it is beautifully written, detailed, and full of the Victorian sentiments of grief and hope typical of this era. *Collection of Jerry Lesandro and Larry Martin.* $150+.

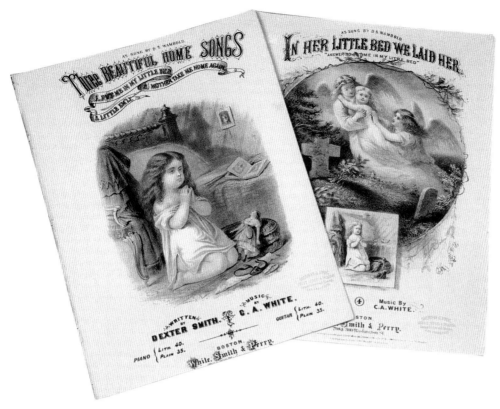

Sheet music extolling the sadness of childhood death. The first song sheet entitled, "Mother, Put Me in My Little Bed," shows the child praying beside her bed; the lithograph on the sequel piece depicts the child's grave bed while angels carry her soul effigy heavenward. *Author's collection.* $50 each.

written poem, inserted between the pages of sheet music, now empty of scribbled insertions or happy doodlings:

Faded Flowers

Oh! The flowers that I saw in the wild wood,
Have since drooped their beautiful leaves.
And the many dear friends of my childhood,
Have slumbered for years in their graves!

Oh! The bloom of the flowers I remember,
And the smiles I shall nevermore see.
For the cold, chilly mists of December,
Stole the flowers my companions from me!

Other roses may bloom on the morrow,
And many a friend have I won.
Yet my heart it can beat but with sorrow,
When I think of the ones that have gone.

T'is no wonder that I am broken-hearted,
And stricken with sorrow should be;
We have met; we have loved; we have parted,
My flowers, my companions, and me!

Oh! How dark looks this world and how dreary,
When we part from the ones that we loved:
But there is rest for the faint and the weary,
And friends meet with loved-ones above!

And, in heaven I can but remember
When from earth my proud soul shall be free,
That no cold, chilly winds of December,
Can part my companions from me.

It is evident from the transition of the music book, that George must have been lost in the Civil War. A lithographed song sheet entitled, "Let Me Kiss Him for His Mother" is the final clue. Flora scratched out the word "Mother" penciling in the word "Girl" instead, and the lithograph shows a young woman's tender ministrations over her dying lover. The words of the song speak of the death of a young man whose "cold, pallid lips" could not feel the final kiss. The songbook ends, and one is left wondering what happened to Flora and her youthful joys and idealism.

paper articles, poems, little drawings, and pencil notations that are a picture into Flora Lynn's life other than at the piano. Flora Lynn was part of a small coterie of young women, one of whom, Jennie Dugan, burned to death when an oil lamp caught her dress on fire. The opening piano piece, "Good Night, Good Night to All," was written in memory of Jennie, and its title are the last words spoken by Jennie as she died. Several newspaper memorial obituaries written on the anniversary of Jennie's death are pinned together and placed inside the volume, testifying to the closeness that Flora and her friends felt for Jennie.

As one leafs through the music book, beginning in 1860, the tone is light-hearted as Flora reveals her idle doodling at the piano and her love for a young man named "Marc," who himself also draws flowers and the ubiquitous "Remember Me" sentiments back to Flora on several song sheets. As the handwriting is different in places, it appears the two sat at the piano and probably flirted and doodled idle hours away.

As the music book progresses however, along with the early months of the Civil War, we find Flora experiencing the loss of male friends from her circle of acquaintances. She altered a song entitled, "Where Are the Friends of My Youth?" by penciling in the words, "gone to war" behind the title. And, after an-

other song entitled, "T'is Hard to Leave Our Childhood's Home" Flora added the words "to go to war," no doubt thinking of the young men she knows who have "gone for soldiers."

Soon a change appears as Marc's doodling tributes to Flora disappear, and her new love, "George" comes on the scene in the song, "In Dreams I See My Mother." Here Flora has scratched out the word "Mother" and substituted the name "George Henry," the new object of her affections. Unfortunately however, George too "has gone for a soldier" in the Civil War, and Flora misses him immensely. She continues her love for him by altering another song, "O Give Me a Home By the Sea," adding the words, "with my fellow George." She even dreams of him and substitutes his name for the word, "Her" in the Stephen Foster song, "I See Her Still In My Dreams." Virtually every song throughout the volume was converted by Flora to express her love for George: After the song "Star of the Evening," she penciled in "George, Thou Art My Star"; to the Civil War song, "Willie We Have Missed You," she substituted George's name for "Willie," and added the words, "Indeed we have" after the title.

However, as the songbook progresses, a cloud appears over Flora's life. George too disappears altogether, to be substituted with the following hand-

Song sheet from Flora Lynn's songbook, with sheet music taken from Jennie Dugan's dying words, "Good Night, Good Night to All." *Collection of David and Judith Peebles.*

Sheet music altered by Flora Lynn expressing her grief at the loss of George in the Civil War. She fancies that she kisses him good-bye as he dies. *Collection of David and Judith Peebles.*

Sheet music altered by Flora Lynn to express her longing for her beau, "George," soldiering in the Civil War. c. 1860s. *Collection of David and Judith Peebles.*

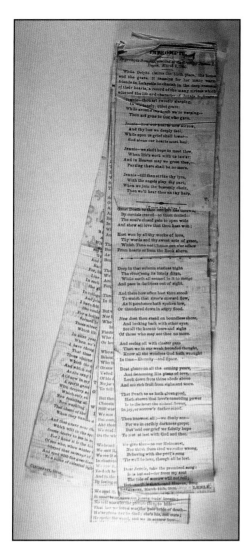

Poetic linen paper obituaries to Jennie Dugan found in Flora Lynn's songbook, c. 1860s. *Collection of David and Judith Peebles.*

A poignant c. 1850s poem written by an older sister in memory of her younger sister, with an attached "chain link" braid of the child's hair, tied with a pink bow and fastened with red sealing wax, is shown below. The emotionally affecting poem reads as follows:

> *"Sister, thy lov'd form is lying*
> *Peaceful in the grave's still gloom;*
> *And the mourning winds are sighing*
> *Sadly o'er thy lonely tomb.*
>
> *Life was opening gay before thee,*
> *Wooing to its wearying roam;*
> *Bright the skies were beaming o'er thee,*
> *When thy maker called thee home.*
>
> *By no terror was thou shaken,*
> *When thy spirit might not stay;*
> *Like some flower by spring forsaken,*
> *Thou didst fade in death away."*

Memorial cards, with and without photographs of the deceased, were also widely popular and available to all income levels. These memorial cards were usually done in the cabinet card format (approximately 4" x 6" in size) and sometimes contained a photograph of the deceased while alive, in combination with obituary information and sometimes poetry. These memorial cards were mass produced by manufacturers such as H. F. Wendell, who, in addition to English formats, offered to the consumer cards in German, French, Danish, Swedish and Norwegian languages. Wendell employed women around the United States to gather obituary notices and submit them to the company for a penny apiece. The company then printed a sample card, and sent it along with literature to the family of the deceased for placing orders.

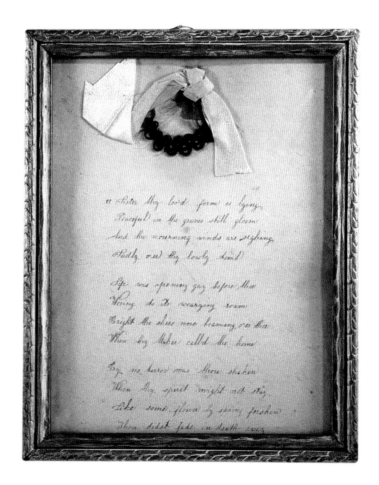

Simple framed poem to a "baby sister" with lock of infantile hair in "chain links." The grief of the older sister is palpable in the last line of the final stanza, "Like some flower by spring forsaken, thou didst fade in death away." 5" x 6.5". *Author's collection.* $150.

In the following two examples, memorial cards have been framed and become in themselves decorative parlor art. In the first one, the card has been placed in a hand-carved wooden frame embellished with gold paint, and in the second example, an elaborate Eastlake easel holds the memorial card, which is embellished with black mourning ribbons at each corner.

The memorial cards on the following page are examples of mourning cards given away at funerals in remembrance of loved ones in the 19th century. Mourning families could purchase sample cards and have them printed with stock Biblical verses and/or obituary information, much in the same way as is done today. These printed style cards are the least expensive and most easily acquired. The elaborate "fretwork" memorial cards, given away at upper-class American and European funerals, typically show the same iconography seen in other varieties of commercially printed mourning accessories, such as grieving mourners, angels pointing heavenward, weeping willows, draped monuments, urns, roses, etc., These diecut cards, however, are fragile due to the considerable amount of open "fretwork," and examples in good condition are sometimes hard to find. Thus, prices range from $15 for poor pieces to $30 and up for nice examples in good condition.

An outstanding Eastlake easel frame with black mourning ribbon holds a memorial card for Sarah Parker. The quality and beauty of this frame make this otherwise commonplace memorial card desirable to the Victorian home and antique memorial collector. 12" high. *Collection of Jerry Lesandro and Larry Martin.* $350.

Framed memorial card for Sophia Pfeiffer, who died in 1892. The beautiful hand-carving and gold painting of this frame considerably enhance the attractiveness and value of this memorial card. 5.5" x 8". *Collection of Jerry Lesandro and Larry Martin.* $275.

Various examples of 19th century memorial cards given away at funerals and wakes. *Author's collection.* $15-25 each.

Graphite and pen and ink drawings used for design patterns and layouts in hair-work memorials and mourning jewelry. *Courtesy of Things Gone By.* $50-75 each.

Cards and stationery, bordered in black, were commonplace throughout the Victorian era, along with memorial calling cards; all are readily available to the collector at reasonable prices. The width of black borders on stationery, as with calling cards, signified the depth of mourning, from wide indicating deep mourning to thin for half-mourning. Once the required period of seclusion was over, pale gray, silver, and lavender borders signaled the return to social visitation. *Collection of Jerry Lesandro and Larry Martin.* $25-50 each.

Examples of beautiful mid-19th century die-cut and embossed memorial cards. Designs of female figures grieving at the tomb while angels point confidently heavenward remind the mourners that the deceased are "not dead, but liveth." Another card depicts a mother and child grieving at the tomb, and a third shows the typical iconography of angels draping the tomb with funeral shrouds. 2.5" x 4". *Author's collection.* $35-50 each.

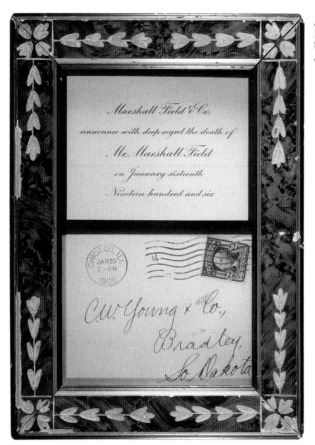

A rare framed memorial card announcing the death of the founder of Marshall Field's Department Store. Although early 20th century, the card is bordered in black just as in Victorian precedents, and set into a lovely Eastlake frame. *Collection of Jerry Lesandro and Larry Martin.* $125.

A burial permit for an 82-year-old immigrant from the Alsace region of France and Germany, who tragically committed suicide on July 5, 1897, in Ferndale, California, ironically includes the stamped notation that his death was "non-contagious." *Collection of Jerry Lesandro and Larry Martin.* $50-75.

A handwritten calligraphic memorial card made by the under-taker, W. W. Westphall, for the funeral of eleven-year-old Charles Edgar Burkhart, is especially touching in its simplicity and notation that Charles is in "God's Care." It is possible that no pre-printed memorial cards were available for the family and the undertaker created this beautifully executed remembrance. *Collection of Jerry Lesandro and Larry Martin.* $50-75.

Here, an unusual juxtaposition of a memorial die-cut placed inside a photographic case is similar to that which was done with the c. 1820 sepia portrait on ivory of the small boy shown earlier, the meaning of which is now lost. The die-cut is that of a young boy standing on a tomb, his faithful dog by his side, symbolic of fidelity and loyalty. Symbolism such is this is more commonly seen in hair-work memorials, but occasionally scissor-cut silhouettes are seen in this style of funereal art, and thus, this die-cut could well have been a similar form placed in the brass mat of a photographic case for preservation. *Author's collection.* $75.

English graphite drawing and watercolor painting of sepulchre design and burial landscape for Charles Augustine Gell, son of Rev. Phillip and Elizabeth Gell, of St. John's in Derby, who was born May 8, 1808 and died April 11, 1829, at the age of twenty-one. The drawing was executed by Elizabeth Gell, mother of Charles. 3" x 4". *Author's collection.* $175.

Large size diecut memorial cards were also available to mourning families, in which various standardized mourning iconography could be chosen, framed, and smaller individualized mourning cards added to personalize the piece. Here we see an elaborate English silver-embossed memorial diecut commemorating the death of a fifteen-year-old girl, "Elizabeth Ann Fox," daughter of "William and Charlotte Fox of Wymeswold," on August 12, 1875. The card has the typical symbols of the weeping mourner, the angel pointing heavenward, cross with wreathes, shroud and urn, weeping willows, gothic designs, urns and ivy, etc., surrounding the memorial card. *Author's collection.* $125-150.

An outstanding English diecut memorial scene set into a frame which has been further embellished with weeping willows painted onto the glass. The paper diecut is particularly "fancy"; it not only incorporates the customary Victorian mourning figures and symbols in gothic cathedral design, but silk "veils" have been added to represent the entrance into the heavenly realm on each side of the memorial card. Akin to the veil in the Temple "Holy of Holies," separating the Hebrew people from the rites performed by the High Priest on the Day of Atonement, the veil in Christian iconography came to represent the entrance of believers into heaven. A die-cut angel set against the black interior heralds the entrance of the deceased by blowing his trumpet overhead. 14" x 24". *Collection of Jerry Lesandro and Larry Martin.* $350.

Mourning Art Among Minorities

Memorial art in Western culture was created within a predominantly Christian framework (Catholic and Protestant) throughout the Middle Ages, albeit later influenced by the secular humanism of the Enlightenment of the 18th century. Perspectives on dying and death remained within this Christian structure relatively unchanged in Britain and Europe until the 20th century, due to their relatively homogenous societies. Similarly, in America, Christian death philosophy and ritual were dominant during these same centuries in spite of a non-homogenous society, racially and culturally mixed from its inception. Early in American history, Puritanism shared its religious influence among colonists, with a somewhat secularized deism favored by the founding fathers. And, under the fires of religious fervor of the Great Awakenings of the late 18th and early 19th centuries, America, like England, was heavily saturated by evangelical doctrines concerning the After Life.

The 18th and 19th centuries brought an influx of hundreds of thousands of immigrants swarming American shores – arriving in desperation, servitude, or seeking a better life. Most were European Catholics or of Protestant sects, and thus nominally considered "Christian" in their views surrounding death and mourning, views which were similar to the prevailing beliefs of so-called "native born" Americans, only recently arrived themselves. Other large immigrant (and slave) population groups, particularly Jewish, African, and Asian (mostly Chinese), held quite different mourning practices, and where possible, hid their customs within their homes, neighborhoods, or family gatherings, for fear of ostracism, punishment, or persecution.

Catalysts occurring simultaneously in America in these centuries created an environment that swallowed up as many immigrants as stepped ashore. When gold was discovered in California in 1849, "the world rushed in" to the California gold fields, as noted by 19th century diarist William Swain, himself a "Forty-Niner." As the famous 19th century French statesman, traveler, and writer Alexis de Toqueville observed:

"Millions are marching at once towards the same horizon – their language, their religion, their manners differ, but their object is the same. Fortune has been promised them somewhere in the West, and to the West they go to find it."

Immigrants sold everything they had, borrowed whatever money they could, and sailed, rode, and walked to California from all over the world. Most did not find their fortune and returned to their native countries, but many stayed and built new lives. They brought their religious views, along with their burial and mourning practices with them, establishing cemeteries for their dead within Christian burial grounds. This was especially true of Chinese immigrants, one of the largest immigrant populations in the West.

Later, during the building of the Transcontinental Railroad in the 1860s, Asians, particularly the Chinese, came in the thousands to California and engaged in back-breaking labor as dynamite blasters tunneling through the Sierra Nevada. America was desperate to employ as much of a labor force as possible to fulfill the demands of increasing expansion and population growth all across the country, and the swarms of immigrants provided the manpower necessary to keep up with the industrialization of post-Civil War era America.

Within all these so-called "non-Christian" populations, memorial art remained culturally distinct to their religious views and practices – in some cultures more than others. In the case of Jewish immigrants (most of who fled to America from pogroms in Europe), memorial art tended to be similar to that of the prevailing religious art in their native Catholic European countries, with the exclusion of conventional or standard Christian iconography. For Asian populations, memorial art remained culturally true to religious practices in their homelands, with little or no Western influence. Attempts by African slaves to maintain funeral and burial practices, mourning customs, or art of their native lands was virtually impossible under slavery, and little is known of their early colonial-era customs. As time went by, slavery altered beliefs and customs into a marriage of the "old ways" with the new Christianity introduced by their masters.

Memorial art within all these groups *was* created, however, but is much more difficult to find than pieces from Christian-influenced sources simply because the culture of mourning fostered the creation of memorial art through religious and domestic literature containing *only* Christian themes. In the following photographs we will look at some examples of memorial art and mourning pieces from minority cultures and non-Christian religious sources.

Photograph of a Chinese funeral in Deadwood, South Dakota in 1901, showing the strong tradition of cultural practices being maintained on American soil, even in the "Wild West." $10.

This rare photograph of a Japanese-American family in mourning typifies the Asian religious focus of ancestor worship and familial ties, within a Western context. Note the older traditional dress of the living sitters, combined with the photographs in the background of young dead family members, including one first generation *issei* son in Western dress.

White (along with yellow) is a mourning color in China as well as other Asian countries. A rare pair of 19th century Northern Chinese lady's mourning shoes are shown in the next photograph, their size evidence of the practice of foot binding as a feature of beauty modification among Chinese upperclass women. The shoes measure 6" inches long by 2" inches wide, and are entirely handsewn of linen with leather soles.

Hispanics hold a long tradition of honoring the dead, with many Mexican homes containing small altars that are usually present year-round, but particularly decorated during the *Los Dios de Los Muertos* or Day of the Dead ceremonies held October 31 through November 1 of each year. Hispanic-American customs were generally shaped within a Catholic framework just as in other traditional European Catholic countries, and thus memorials retained artistic elements of various saints, the Virgin, and other Catholic elements in memorial art.

A c. 1860s tintype of a Hispanic woman on the next page shows her with black lace *mantilla*; although considered proper dress for a married woman, it is typical of mourning dress for Mexican-American women as well, and in this case, its mourning focus is evidenced by the hair-work necklace with cross that she is wearing.

Photograph of Japanese-American family in traditional dress with dead family members incorporated into the image, both in ancestral and western clothing, c. early 1900s. $25.

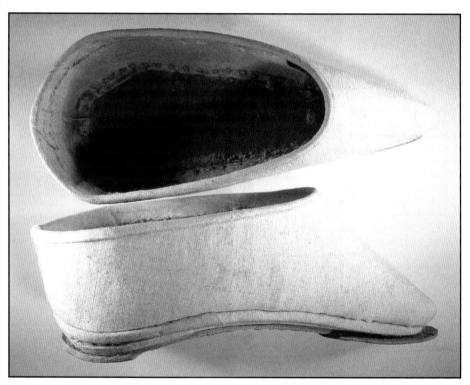

Rare nineteenth century handmade linen Chinese woman's mourning shoes, 2" x 6". *Courtesy of OBJX.* $275.

Tintype of young Hispanic woman in mourning clothing with hair-work necklace and cross similar to one shown in the Mourning Jewelry section of this book, c. 1870s. *Author's collection.* $75.

Handcarved wooden memorials of deceased loved ones were created by Hispanic family members as remembrances to be placed on altars in the home. Called *foto-escultura,* these c. 1915-45 framed "shrines" to the deceased were made from black and white photographic prints which had been enlarged and sepia-toned. The face was then cut out and glued to a relief-carved wooden "bust," which was itself cut out around the head and shoulders, and then set into an ornate wooden "frame" of red cedar or mahogany. While the photograph was still damp during gluing, lines were scribed into the hair and clothing for added depth and detail, and facial features enhanced with French pastels or watercolor tints imported from England or Germany. Women's clothing was sometimes accessorized with bits of jewelry, and "buttons" and "medals" of modeling paste were added to men's military uniforms. The early frames were carved in styles of arched "colonial," gothic "chapel," or "continental" motifs with rosettes, fleurs de lis, or acanthus leaves. Later Art Deco influences are seen in the horizontal lines of 1930s frames similar to radio consoles.

Mexican wood *foto-escultura* of deceased man, photograph on wood, with carved embellishments, c. 1920s-30s. *Courtesy of OBJX.* $75.

Postmortem photography also occupied a prominent part of memorial ritual among Hispanic families, especially in the case of the uniquely Mexican death of the *angelito*. For most Hispanics, postmortem photographs generally followed the pattern of American posthumous portraiture in style and layout, but for those immigrants from the Mexican countryside, the art of "Child Death" was closely linked to the "Cult of the Virgin." According to author Margaret Hooks, an Irish writer living in Mexico, postmortem photographs of *angelitos* were modeled on 17th century paintings depicting the death of the Virgin. Thus, symbols of purity such as lilies and spikenard, along with emblems of Virgin worship such as palm fronds and the crown, are seen dressing the postmortem image of the *angelito*. Ms. Hooks adds that the dead girl child is almost always dressed as the Immaculate Conception and the dead boy child as Saint Joseph. The apparel and adornments symbolize the child's state of innocence as that of the Virgin, and his or her transformation into a heavenly being, victorious over death through resurrection. These death images are venerated among Hispanics, passing from generation to generation, and are difficult to find on the market in good condition.

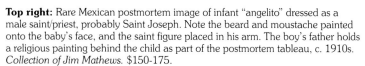

Top right: Rare Mexican postmortem image of infant "angelito" dressed as a male saint/priest, probably Saint Joseph. Note the beard and moustache painted onto the baby's face, and the saint figure placed in his arm. The boy's father holds a religious painting behind the child as part of the postmortem tableau, c. 1910s. *Collection of Jim Mathews.* $150-175.

Center left: Poignant c. 1910 postmortem image with Hispanic mother and family members around the infant, who is lavishly laid out for its final (and probably only) portrait. The efforts that impoverished Mexicans expended to provide beautiful funerals and memorial photographs was considerable, and the heartbreak of a child's death just as evident on the faces of this family as with Anglo-American families. *Collection of Jim Mathews.* $150-175.

Bottom right: A grief-stricken Mexican father mourning his infant is almost overwhelmed in the floral displays in this postmortem photograph, c. 1920s. Note that the child is again dressed as a saint ("angelito") with a crown on its head and priest's clothing, typical of funeral clothing for children in Hispanic funerals. *Collection of Jim Mathews.* $150-175.

Jewish immigrants, frequently fleeing persecution, confiscation of land and property, and pogroms in Eastern Europe, were the fourth largest population group to come to America, behind English, German, and Irish immigrants. Like Asian minorities, Jewish immigrants maintained religious integrity, along with their burial and mourning practices, with little to no melding into predominantly Christian societal customs. Nevertheless, both in America and in Europe, Jewish memorial art employed some of the same symbolism as that seen in Christian cemeteries and mourning art, with the obvious exceptions of the Cross, the Bible, Madonna and Child, etc. Typical motifs such as the standard funeral flora of weeping willows, cypress trees, and cedars; urns and shrouds; overturned torches; etc., are seen in Jewish memorials just as in Christian examples. Such is the case in the following memorial for a young Jewish man, Bension Moshe Arie, who was born in 1873 and died in 1905, at the age of thirty-two. In this Hebrew and Latin lithographic calendar, many of the elements and symbols seen in conventional Christian lithography are present: the mausoleum, weeping mourners, cypress trees, stylized torches, urns, and palm fronds, as well as the typical Grecian shell, funereal acanthus, and wreath motifs. The calendar notes all the Hebrew memorial days in which Mr. Arie was to be remembered, his photograph placed prominently in the memorial as a reminder. The lithographer left his mark at the bottom: "From me, the young Haim Reuven Peretz, Writer/Painter."

Africans, brought as slaves to America, came with cultural practices and beliefs unique to their various tribal backgrounds. African-American burial and mourning practices provide a singular window into the perspectives of African customs married to 19th century American beliefs. From colonial times, African-Americans buried their dead in ways typical of their native countries, when and where those practices could be remembered. Burial grounds excavated under Wall Street in the 1990s showed early slave labor in building colonial "New Amsterdam," as New York was originally called by its Dutch settlers. Hundreds of Africans were buried in these sites, many with bracelets and waist belts around their bodies. Such items were made from glass bead amulets and treasures spirited over the Middle Passage from African homes and secreted from discovery.

As generations grew up under slavery, many of these mourning and burial customs were either forgotten or modified by American (Christian) beliefs. By the 1800s, burial customs became an amalgam of traditions done in Africa combined with those practices adopted under slavery. Funerals were held after the evening meal; pennies or coins were placed on the deceased's eyes to keep them closed; shrouds were draped the body; and hands were placed across the chest with glass beads around the wrists.

African folklore continued even within the framework of Christian beliefs and burial customs. In African belief, the dead returned to visit the living, sometimes returning in their burial clothing to see their children or relatives. The "visitations" were usually not malevolent or ill-intentioned in nature, and were achieved via the direction of a conjurer, who would walk back and forth at daybreak rubbing tokens of spiritualism.

Jewish memorial lithograph calendar for Bension Moshe Arie, who died in 1905 at the age of thirty-two. 12" x 15" *Author's collection.* $125.

Also employed before and after slavery, was the practice of decorating the burial mound with "grave goods" consisting of the belongings of the deceased. Plates, bowls, pitchers, glass items, and utensils, were broken up and placed atop the grave, in the belief that doing this would "break the chain of death." In the late 19th and early 20th centuries, these broken shards were gathered from the grave after a period of time had elapsed, and then glued into pottery "memory jars" using putty or cement, as seen in the photograph here.

Memory jars as hollow vessels were believed to contain the spirit of the deceased, and the seashells and bits of glass hinted at the watery underworld or nebulous realms of death. While this form of memorial art eventually became popular in both white and black communities and is now collectively referred to as "tramp" or "folk" art, often without the association with death, the custom of preserving grave goods by African-Americans both before and after emancipation is one of the few visible links to original African customs. By the end of the 19th century, middle class blacks were employing the same memorial customs as whites, such as wearing mourning clothing and jewelry and decorating the home in mourning bunting. Black Americans also turned portraits and mirrors to the wall in the belief that this would "fool" the spirit of the deceased and prevent it from re-entering to haunt the family home. Middle class black women of the 19th century also adhered to the requirements of mourning etiquette, as seen in the tintype photograph of a c. 1870s African-American woman (probably a widow), in "first stage" or "deep" mourning attire. Interestingly enough, the taking of postmortem photographs remained a significantly more meaningful memorial tribute in black families than in white, continuing in popularity well into the 1960s, decades after white families had ceased to find posthumous photography openly acceptable. James Van Der Zee, the famous Harlem photographer of the 1920s, was well-known for his postmortem photographs superimposing "spirit" images of the deceased taken when alive, or images of Christ and other religious iconography, into the posthumous scene.

African-American "memory jar," with shells, beads, jewelry findings, buttons, etc., embedded in putty, c. 1900-1920. 5" x 3.5". *Author's collection.* $125.

"So I say to my heart, "Be silent,
The mystery of time is here;
Death's way will be plain
When we fathom the main,
And the secret of life be clear."
["The Mystic Sea," by Paul Lawrence Dunbar, 19th century black poet and son of slave parents]

Tintype of African-American woman in first-stage or "deep" mourning attire, probably a widow, c. 1870s. *Author's collection.* $125.

The Death of Mourning

I am often asked why the extensive mourning practices and memorial art have "disappeared" in European and American social customs and funeral practices. And, truly, universal artistic memorialization of death has essentially vanished within one or two generations in Western culture. What had taken centuries to evolve, has died out virtually overnight in western consciousness. Several factors contributed to the "death" of mourning customs and its visual panoply.

Throughout the Middle Ages, death was viewed as God's judgment for sin, and few attempts were made to interfere with what was considered as sin's inevitable consequences. Even after the Protestant Reformation, religious views surrounding dying and death carried much of the *memento mori* philosophy that existed in the medieval past. The 18th century American theologian, Jonathan Edwards, continued to promulgate this *memento mori* view in his classic sermon, "Sinners in the Hands of An Angry God." The dying were encouraged to approach death "heroically," enduring pain and suffering with fortitude and courage. Calvinist views of the pre-determination of "sinners" to heaven or hell, along with the doctrine of "infant damnation" predominated death philosophy after the Reformation, in spite of the softened perspectives of the Enlightenment and Romantic Movements of the 18th century.

Nevertheless, these harsh doctrines ultimately fell out of favor, and a new aestheticism began influencing religious views on death and dying, permeating visible memorial symbolism and design. Evangelicalism provided promises of future family reunion and the love of God replaced the God of judgment and damnation. Rural cemeteries, once abodes of horror, became the first community parks in England and America, their bucolic heavenly scenes of natural beauty altering burial places of the dead into desirable venues of visitation rather than abhorrent areas of putrefaction and disease.

But, by the end of the 19th century, the comforts of evangelical beliefs began to wane with the publication of Charles Darwin's *On the Origin of Species*. Individual death was now seen as part of the "natural law" of species survival and the new philosophy of "scientific naturalism" promoted the idea that death can be brought under control through an understanding of the laws of nature, thereby prolonging human life. Now science, with its advances in understanding life, disease, and death, modified the perspective that God directly orchestrated every death and that one could do nothing to change His will. Where once Christian views governed the national perspectives about life, death, and immortality in Western culture, now science, humanism, and secularism supplanted these religious views. With new inventions increasing industrial productivity, commerce, and science in the late 19th century, machines, not mankind, became the focus of Victorian interest.

Simultaneously, great strides were made in medicine during and after the American Civil War, as well as in Victorian England. The discovery of the "germ theory" of disease as a cause of illness (as opposed to the belief in "noxious miasma," or foul air pollution) continued the progress in understanding, and thereby avoiding, death. Scientists worldwide began to look for germs as the source of disease, resulting in the introduction of revolutionary medical treatments and "miraculous" cures by the end of the century. New medicines were being developed and patented for public consumption with the introduction of Bayer Pharmaceutical Company's landmark drug called "heroin," so named for the "heroic" praise its newly produced aspirin received when first released to the public. Development of the pasteurization process for milk prevented the deaths of thousands of children, and new understandings on the prevention and treatment of childhood illnesses considerably reduced childhood mortality. Furthermore, the fear of imminent death could be "put off" as life spans increased by the end of the 19th century due to medical advances and new emphasis on personal hygiene and disease prevention for health. People were now living the "three score and ten" years promised in the Bible, so that death was no longer seen as an expected "intrusion" into daily Victorian life. For the first time in centuries, death no longer preoccupied daily conscious thought.

With the development of anesthesia, the idea of death as "sleep" emerged as a cultural consolation, supplanting the heroic deathbed struggle as a requirement for salvation. As pointed out by historian Dr. Stanley Burns, in anesthesia "was the meeting of the concepts of sleep and death; this became a powerful consoler in addition to the respite from pain."[38] Delivered from the idea of the heroic and painful death struggle, late Victorians embraced the concepts of sleep as a metaphor for death, with preparation for death as elementary as going to sleep. No longer the "King of Terrors," an 1899 essay on death describes it simply as, "a kindly nurse who puts us to bed when our day's work is done. The fear of death is replaced by the joy of life."[39]

Coincident to the changing perceptions surrounding death, embalming, first performed during the Civil War, became an acceptable practice when President Lincoln's young son, Willie, was embalmed, to be followed by the President himself in 1865. Shortly after the Civil War, in 1876, the first cremation was performed in Philadelphia, and while initially rejected by church prohibitions, cremation slowly expanded in acceptance and popularity.

Once only the last abode of the destitute and the alcoholic, hospitals gained new respectability towards the end of the 19th century, becoming acceptable places where the dying could be cared for by strangers instead of by family members. As Victorians began to distance the dying from their physical midst, they also further distanced the philosophies surrounding imminent death from their minds.

By the end of the 19th century, the rigidity of mourning etiquette was beginning to relax. In response to pressure from Parliament, Queen Victoria resumed her duties after decades of seclusion by opening her Jubilee in 1887. In America, the post Civil War prosperity and westward expansion gave rise to renewed optimism about the future, and a desire to put aside the depressing mourning customs of recent decades. The frontier was officially closed in 1890, signaling both the end of the wild, untamed wilderness, and the beginning of the fulfillment of the promised prosperity ahead.

In 1890, *Ladies Home Journal* published an editorial proclaiming that the family parlor would no longer be called by the word *parlor*, because of its asso-

ciation with the dead body – this room of the house being formerly the place where viewing of the deceased was held. From now on, declared the *Journal,* it would be referred to as the *living room*, a place for the living, and not the dead. Thus, the word *parlor* faded from our vernacular to be adopted by the emerging funeral industry, and we now refer to that room of the house as the *living room*. In earlier decades, this proclamation would have been unthinkable, but by the end of the 19th century, these editorial views simply expressed what was already taking place in America and England, that of putting death permanently out of the Victorian conscious. With the new changes in death perspectives, the heavy mourning attire and rigid rules of etiquette began to alter and disappear. Queen Victoria's death in 1901 ushered in an end to the era of the Victorian "*Beautiful Death.*"

The catastrophic loss of life of the First World War ultimately sounded the final death knell for mourning customs. More than 8,538,315 men died or were killed in action (Allied and Central Powers combined), and casualties totaled 37,508,686 men for all armed forces between 1914 and 1918. British casualties were listed at 3,190,235 men (908,371 killed), those of France were 6,160,800 (1,357,800 killed), and American losses were 364,800 (126,000 killed). Of these horrors, Rudyard Kipling, the famed British poet, wrote, "There has never been anything like this in all history: the embalming of a race." The Kiplings lost their own eighteen-year-old son, John, on some unknown spot of ground near Loos, France, fought over three times between British and German forces; his body was never found.

As was typical throughout the war, virtually all were buried in mass graves, and the enormous loss of life on battlefields meant there were few bodies brought home to their communities. Thus, adherence to mourning customs was almost impossible, and consequently, families were deprived of their ability to perform obsequies and funeral services. There was no longer any framework of mourning with which to provide comfort, and families could not ritualize their loss by keeping locks of hair or taking postmortem images. English family

members were discouraged from wearing mourning clothes, because the mere sight of thousands of men and women in black would be demoralizing to English troops home on leave. Furthermore, so many women were involved in war work, or taking over the responsibilities as breadwinners, that there was little time and even less ability to adhere to mourning etiquette.

The Spanish flu pandemic of 1918, which took the lives of an estimated 20-30 million people worldwide (500,000 in America alone), followed closely behind the "winds of war," and was one of the catalysts to the termination of World War I. Men were simply too ill to fight, and deaths from influenza began to rob the already-weakened armies of manpower and strength.

The enormous loss of life in World War I brought Americans and Europeans out of their insular world. Robert Graves, the famous English poet and writer, and himself a memoirist of the First World War, knew when he departed England for the war front as part of the Royal Welch Fusiliers that England would never again be the same. It was *Good-bye to All That,* the title of his memoirs, that expressed so fully and poignantly that sad finality of the Victorian age.

Within a few short years of Queen Victoria's death, Europeans and Americans were brought quickly into a world of international complexities and conflicts for which they were emotionally, and to a certain extent psychologically, ill prepared. They did not have what we would call today, a "global mentality," and the shock of the horrid deaths of the First World War shattered 19th century fading illusions about the *"Beautiful Death."* The perspective of the "domesticated heaven," along with the "cult of memory" in the Victorian home disintegrated completely in the catastrophic losses of the European conflict. And, in the War's aftermath, the ravaged cities of Europe required progressive determination to look forward and rebuild, rather than stagnation in sorrow.

Courtauld's in England, which had previously enjoyed an annual profit in sales of black crape at about 200,000 pounds per year, found their sales dropping off precipitously in 1919, never to be recovered. Although wearing black crape continued to be popular during and after World War I in France, a new generation rose up in the early years of the 20th century, and this generation did not want to remember the old mourning customs and the memorial arts. The waning of Christian belief in Western culture, advances in the social equality of women, and changing attitudes towards marriage and remarriage also altered perceptions about the visible display of grief. Although wearing black mourning clothing is still seen in rural areas of Italy, Greece, and Eastern Europe, it has all but disappeared in Britain and France. In America, probably the last vestige of mourning clothing seen publicly was that worn by Mrs. Jacqueline Kennedy at the funeral of her husband, the assassinated President John Kennedy, in 1963.

Social changes occurring during and after the World War I years were irreversible. Millions of pieces of hair-work jewelry and memorials were thrown out or burned in the mistaken belief that they spread disease, and few of the living remembered, much less mourned, the dead of past centuries. The topic of death went into the closet and stayed there, becoming the last *taboo* in the Western psyche, considered an "inappropriate" subject matter for "polite conversation."

Although public memorials for diseases such as cancer and AIDS, or for the terrorist attacks of September 11, 2001, are well-known today, they are *corporate* memorials, and while sometimes composed of individual names, they still retain a unified memorial content. Roadside or on-site floral arrangements for vehicular and catastrophic deaths are placed at the scene of tragedies, but soon fade away. Private *individual* tokens of remembrance and postmortem photographs are still being taken and cherished, but they are rarely shared with others outside a circle of accepting friends and family members. There is often shame associated with postmortem photographs in spite of the fact that hospitals routinely offer them for stillborn infants and children's deaths as a comfort for grieving parents. And, rarely are individual memorials today presented for public viewing in an artistic venue. Death is a private, not a public matter. Internet website memorials provide a *public ex-*posure, yet retain a sense of "barrier" between the mourner and others, an artificial, or pseudo-anonymity. Closeness is provided only through email correspondence should the mourner choose to do so, and creativity in the website is not material in form to be held, worn, and perhaps kissed, but exists only in a nebulous cyberspace. And, of course, no tangible and personal essence of the "beloved" remains as a "token of remembrance."

(Author) "Have you news of my boy Jack?
(Boatman) – Not this tide.
(A) When d'you think that he'll come back?
(B) – Not with this wind blowing, and this tide.

(A) Has anyone else had word of him?
(B) – Not this tide.
(B) For what is sunk will hardly swim
(B) Not with this wind blowing, and this tide.

(A) O Dear, what comfort can I find?
(B) – None this tide, nor any tide.
(B) Except he did not shame his kind,
(B) Not even with that wind blowing, and that tide.

(B) Then hold your head up all the more,
(B)   This tide, and every tide.
(B) Because he was the son you bore,
(B)   And gave to that wind blowing, and that tide!"
["My Boy Jack," by Rudyard Kipling (1865-1936), written in memory of his son's death in World War I]

Beautiful French World War I cameo of the "Angel of the Battlefield" tiptoeing over soldiers standing beside cannon and expended shells at any one of a number of battle scenes in France, Belgium, or Germany during this conflict. Note that the angel carries laurel wreaths (representative of victory) in each hand, symbolically encouraging a hoped-for French victory, and it is probable that this one-of-a-kind commissioned piece memorialized a French soldier who gave his life in this War. *Collection of Julia Logan.* $895+.

In summary, it can truly be said that Victorians knew how to "mourn well." The many consolation books, along with a strong faith, an accepting social community, and a structured mourning culture that supported the grieving enabled them to cope with frequent deaths in ways completely unfamiliar to most of us. Nonetheless, however we may be forced to privately endure our grief today, it is still important *that* we mourn our loved ones, regardless of *how we* give expression to grief, and notwithstanding our current societal lack of understanding or acceptance. This was summed up so well by one anonymous widow in 1887, when she wrote to a friend:

"Mourning is a form of memory. When we mourn, we keep our loved ones alive in memory. Without memory, the living lose connection with the dead. When the dead have no place in our lives, we have a different view of life itself."

The End of An Era.

Glossary of Symbols[40]

Flora

Acacia tree. Immortality of the soul. Held to be sacred because it was believed to be the construction material used for the Ark, and for Christ's crown of thorns.

Acanthus. Believed to be a flora of the "Heavenly Garden." One of the oldest (and most common) cemetery motifs, associated with the rocky ground where ancient Greek cemeteries were located. Usually seen at the tops of Corinthian columns in architecture, and is symbolic of the triumph of the soul over life's sorrows and sufferings.

Acorns. Power or victory; see "Oak tree" below.

Almond. Sweetness; hope of heaven.

Anemone. Anticipation. If the flower is red in color, it represents the transience of life.

Apple. A means to immortality; fruitfulness.

Arbor-vitae. Unchanging friendship.

Ash. The mountain ash deters evil spirits from bothering the dead.

Asphodel. "Flower of death"; said to cover the Elysian Fields of poetry; means "field of ashes."

Bay. Love and victory; glory.

Birch. Safeguard against evil; the ancient Celts covered their dead with birch branches, believed to be necessary for entrance into the After-Life.

Boxwood. Traditional material for making coffins.

Buttercup. Cheerfulness.

Calla Lily. Symbolizes marriage, often used as a funeral flower as well.

Cedar. "Think of me"; also refers to the biblical Cedars of Lebanon.

Chestnut. Curative powers.

Corn. Possibly an occupational symbol.

Crocus. Youthful gladness.

Columbine. The Holy Ghost.

Cypress Tree. Death and hope of immortality; also despair. Its dark foliage represents death; their tall shape points towards heaven; also once cut down, they do not regenerate. Used by Romans to adorn the vestibule while the body was lying in state, and branches were carried in funeral processions. In both Rome and China, cypress trees trimmed as hedges were planted around graves, as it was believed they had the ability to ward off black magic and evil.

Daffodil. Death of youth.

Daisy. Innocence of child; Jesus as an infant, purity of thought, gentleness.

Dead leaves, dead branch. Sadness; melancholy; lifelessness.

Dogwood. Christianity; divine sacrifice; triumph of eternal life; resurrection.

Evergreens. Everlasting life and victory over sin.

Fern. Sincerity; sorrow.

Figs, pineapples. Prosperity, eternal life.

Fir. Time, especially as it relates to future resurrection.

Flower. Frailty of life.

Flower, broken. A life terminated; often seen in memorials of children or young adults cut off in their prime.

Forget-Me-Not. Remembrance and love.

Fruits. Abundance, representing accomplishments in life, fruitful life; many children.

Garland. See "Wreath."

Garland, Maiden's. A garland of white paper or linen was embellished with white streamers and roses, carried at the funerals of young, unmarried women, and hung in the church after the funeral and allowed to decay. The pieces would then be buried in the graveyard.

Grapes, leaves, and grapevines. Represents Christ, Christian faith.

Hawthorn. Hope, springtime.

Heliotrope. Faithfulness and devotion.

Holly. Foresight. In ancient times, holly bushes were planted near tombs in the belief they protected them from lightening strikes. Also symbolic of domestic happiness.

Honeysuckle. Bonds of love, generosity, and devoted affection.

Hyacinth, purple. Sorrow.

Ivy. Immortality in marital love, friendship; fidelity; undying affection; eternal life.

Laurel. Love and victory; special achievement, distinction, triumph (ancient athletes and victors in battle were crowned with it); because laurel leaves do not wilt, they also represent eternity.

Lily. Purity, innocence, and resurrection. Also associated with the Virgin Mary; often used on women's graves. Use of lilies at funerals represents the restored innocence of the soul at death.

Lily of the Valley. Return of happiness; purity; humility.

Lupine. Dejection; sorrow.

Mountain Ash. Deters evil spirits from bothering the dead.

Morning Glory. Farewell, brevity of life as symbolized by the flower's opening and closing within one day; departure, mortality. Also represents the flower opening in the morning to sunlight ("goodness") and closing at night to the darkness ("evil").

Myrtle. Love and victory; also love in absence.

Moss. Merit.

Mulberry. Grief unto death; or "I will not survive you."

Narcissus. A popular flower with the Greeks to decorate their graves.

Oak tree. Stability; strength; honor; endurance; liberty. Oaks, their leaves and acorns represent power, or victory; often seen on military tombs.

Palm, and palm branches. Since earliest times, the palm has represented the triumph of peace and victory over death. Egyptians commonly laid palm fronds on coffins and mummies; Romans etched fronds on their tombs; and the Jews of Jerusalem laid palm branches in the pathway of Jesus as He entered the city. The palm became synonymous with resurrection, and thus was used in religious services on Palm Sunday.

Pansy. Love and remembrance; humility.

Passion flower. The passion of Christ as seen in the lacy "crown of thorns" center of the flower; the five stamens being the five wounds, the ten petals representing the ten Apostles.

Pine tree. Fertility, regeneration; fidelity.

Poppy. Peace, rest, sleep, eternal sleep, consolation.

Poplar. Where other trees represent immortality, the poplar symbolizes memories and sorrow.

Rose. A symbol of love and death; a common motif in posthumous mourning paintings.

Rose, bud. Often depicted as "broken," representing the death of a child under twelve years of age.

Rose, partial bloom. Death of a teenager or young adult.

Rose, full bloom. Death of an adult, in the prime of life.

Rose, white. Symbol of purity, often used in memorials to young unmarried women and children.

Rose, wreath. Beauty and virtue rewarded.

Rosebuds, joining. Strong bond between two people, e.g., mother and child who died at the same time.

Rosemary. Remembrance; also used during wakes for powerful aroma.

Shamrock. Ireland as country of deceased.

Tree. The all-covering love of Christ, The Tree of Life.

Tree, severed branch. Mortality.

Tree, sprouting. Life everlasting.

Tree branch, dead. Mortality.

Thistles. Sorrow over sin in earthly existence, or symbolic of Crown of Thorns; also country of origin of deceased (Scotland).

Vine. The sacraments; God's blood, God.

Weeping Willow. A tree that appears to be bowing in grief, its mournful growth habit due to its falling branches; also symbolic of Resurrection through its capacity to re-grow from a cutting.

Wheat, sheaf of. Divine harvest; also represents death of the aged.

Wreath. Ancient symbol which predates Christian era and symbolizes victory of the deceased, and redemption. The laurel wreath is usually associated with someone in the arts, literature, etc., or the military, and the wreath and festoon together symbolize memory.

Wreath, bridal. Represents death of a bride.

Yew Tree. Sadness; immortality. Frequently planted as a cemetery tree in early English graveyards, adding somberness. William Wordsworth, the English poet, referred to Yew trees in his elegiac poem, "Lines Left Upon a Seat in a Yew Tree." As yew was the wood used in the powerful English longbows, the planting of Irish yew trees in English burial grounds was viewed as a deterrent to invading armies.

Fauna

Birds. The human soul; hearkens back to ancient Egypt as a symbol; birds are frequently represented as the carriers of the soul to the underworld. They are sometimes seen as a "death omen," as when a bird flies into a home or flap its wings at a window. Blackbirds and owls who roost near homes are thought to presage a death.

Birds in flight. The "winged" soul.

Butterfly. Symbolizes the soul in resurrection; represents the three stages of life – the caterpillar, the chrysalis, and the butterfly, or life, death, and resurrection. When used in children's memorials, it represents a shortened life.

Dog. Loyalty, that the master was worth loving.

Dolphin. Portrays the idea of resurrection.

Dove. The soul; the descending dove is common on gravestone iconography representing the Holy Spirit; when represented with olive sprig, it symbolizes hope and promise.

Dragon. The defeat of sin and evil by St. George; triumph over sin.

Eagle. Courage and possibly a military death; symbol for St. John.

Frog. Depicts sin and worldly pleasures.

Hart (male deer). Faithfulness, thirsting for God (Psalm 42:1).

Horse. Courage or generosity; attribute of Sts. George, Martin, Maurice, and Victor, all of whom are represented on horseback.

Lamb. Common symbol for a child's death; symbol for Christ (John 1:29); meekness, gentleness, humility, purity, and innocence; sacrificial love as personified in Christ.

Lion. Power of God; guards the tomb against evil spirits; eternal vigilance; courage and determination.

Owl. Wisdom; also represents the night.

Peacock. Incorruptibility of the flesh, beauty of the soul, immortality. Also, the transience of beauty and futility of vanity.

Pelican. Charity.

Rooster. Awakening; the Resurrection.

Serpent, Snakes. Snakes have held a long fascination in religions of many cultures. In Western culture, primarily biblically based, the story of the fall of mankind in the Garden of Eden by the duplicity of the Satan as personified in the serpent is well-known and seen throughout religious *ars moriendi* of the Middle Ages. In that context, the snake was associated with Adam and Eve's consumption of the fruit of the Tree of Knowledge of Good and Evil, thus introducing death into the world, leading to the expulsion from the Garden and the curse upon the Serpent. In Judeo-Christian religious tradition, snakes held very negative connotations, until the Enlightenment when more benign interpretations of serpents came into vogue. One characteristic of snakes which influenced these positive views was their periodic shedding of skin which came to symbolize regeneration, rebirth, and immortality, qualities increasingly popular in Enlightenment and Romantic views. The quality of perceived rejuvenation became a positive enough symbol for the medical profession to adopt the serpent for its caduceus. In the late 18th century and throughout the Victorian era, the design of a snake swallowing its tail became a cherished symbol of eternal love, popularized by Queen Victoria, whose engagement ring given her by Albert, the Prince Consort, was just such a snake ring.

Squirrel with a nut. Religious meditation or spiritual striving.

Swallow. Indicates a child or motherhood.

Objects

Amber. Tears, courage.

Amulet. Protection from death.

Anchor. Symbol of hope and steadfastness; when set amongst rocks, can represent the death of a mariner, or St. Nicholas, the patron saint of seamen; was used by early Christians under persecution as a disguised cross. An anchor with a broken chain stands for the cessation of life.

Angels. From the Greek, *angelos,* intermediary spiritual beings or agents fulfilling their role as messengers of God. They are assigned to watch over or protect human beings, as opposed to evil spirits or demons, sometimes referred to as "fallen angels." Angels in iconography are often depicted pointing heavenward, or taking the soul effigy of the deceased towards heaven, and comforting the mourners left behind.

Angel, blowing horn. Call to judgment or resurrection; also the angel Gabriel.

Angel, carrying sword. Represents the archangel Michael.

Angel, flying. Rebirth.

Angels, in clouds. Represents heaven; often seen escorting soul effigy of deceased towards heavenly home.

Angels, weeping. Grief, or mourning an untimely death.

Angels, kneeling, praying. Called "Adoring Angel," shown in act of benediction.

Arch. Victory in death.

Arms, outstretched. A plea for mercy.

Arrow. Denotes mortality.

Baby's empty chair. Represents the child now gone; sometimes depicted with little empty shoes, also representative of deceased child.

Bell. Protection from evil.

Bible. A religious lay person or a cleric.

Boat, or ship. Especially sailing towards horizon. The passage of a soul to the After Life is often symbolically represented by a ship sailing towards the horizon. This relates to the Greek myth of the souls of the deceased being ferried on a boat across the River Styx to Hades, the underworld, by Charon, the ferryman. The Greek practice of routinely burying their dead with a coin in their mouths with which to pay the "toll" to Charon is well known, and the concept of a boat carrying the souls of the departed is also an ancient one in Western Europe. Drawings of grave boats date back to the neolithic period, especially in seagoing cultures, and ships and boats have been popular forms of artistic death iconography in *ars moriendi* in Western culture for centuries.

Book. Represents an educated person, scholar; or a person of faith. Also symbolic of the Book of Life, and shown as a Bible, usually shown open.

Bow. God's power.

Bridge. The structure by which the dead traverse from the land of the living to the land of the dead, usually over a body of water.

Candle, lit. Individual light or life.

Celtic Cross. Circle around the crosspiece symbolizes eternity; traced back to Celtic culture of Britain.

Chains. The bonds of family relationships; friendships. Broken link in a chain represents severance of that relationship.

Chalice. Represents the sacraments.

Cherubs, cherub's head. Symbolizes the death of, or graves of children.

Cherub, Winged. "Soul effigy" of deceased; replaced Death's Head of Middle Ages and Puritan eras.

Children. The untimely death of the innocent; they may be shown mourning a parent or sibling; but if shown holding a skull, it means they are also deceased.

Children, sleeping. Represents the tie between life and death; artlessness, innocence of children.

Chrisma. A cross-like shape formed by combining two Greek letters, chi (X), and rho (P), a symbol for Christ.

Cinquefoil. Member of the rose family with five-lobed leaves; maternal affection, beloved daughter.

Circle. Symbolizes eternity; predates Christian era; one circle above another connotes earth and sky; three circles intertwined represent the Trinity.

Clover, three-leaved Trefoil. The Trinity.

Coffin, sarcophagus, cemetery monument. Mortality.

Column, unbroken, with urn on top. Represents memory.

Column, broken. An early death; life cut short too soon, sometimes shown when representing the death of the head of the family, a father's death. May be girded with flowers.

Columns, with archway. Heavenly entrance.

Cross. The crucifixion of Christ; circle in combination with Latin cross, means never-ending existence.

Cross, with anchor. Christ as "hope" (Hebrews 6:19).

Cross, Calvary. A cross standing atop three steps or blocks, represents faith, hope and love (or charity).

Cross, Eastern. Used in Russian and Greek Orthodox religions, cross has upper horizontal cross piece or "shoulder," representing the inscription over the head of Christ while on the cross; the lower slanting "shoulder" represents the footrest of Christ when crucified.

Cross, Gothic. Floral cross with open flared out ends; symbolizes the adult Christian.

Cross, Greek. Four equal length arms.

Cross, Ionic. Similar to Celtic Cross; symbolizes everlasting salvation, love and glory. The circle around the cross piece represents eternity.

Crown. Immortality; righteousness, victory and triumph, also symbolic of honor and glory, esp. of life after death. May be shown being offered by angels to those on earth.

Crown. Symbolizes Crown of Life, given to righteous dead by God.

Crown, with a cross. Sovereignty of the Lord.

Curtain. Usually depicted partially open to reveal the heavenly realm; represents the parting of the "veil" between this world and the next.

Doors and gates. Passage into the After-Life; heavenly entrance to After-Life.

Drapery, esp. over urn. Sorrow, mourning.

Eye of God/All-seeing Eye. The all-knowing and ever-present God. Sometimes depicted during medieval art inside a triangle, often with radiating rays of life, symbolic of the Holy Trinity.

Feather. The wind; faith; contemplation.

Finger pointing upwards. Indicates the ascension of the deceased to heaven.

Finger pointing downwards. Indicates the Finger of God taking the deceased home; sudden death or mortality.

Fleur-de-lis. Flame, passion, ardor.

Flame. Eternity.

Garland. A bond.

Gates, ajar. Usually represented as "The Pearly Gates Ajar," a favorite symbol of the Spiritualist movement of the 19th century.

Gates, heavenly. Usually depicted open to welcome home the faithful deceased.

Grim Reaper. Death personified.

Hand of God (plucking link from chain). Symbolizes God taking a soul to Himself.

Hands, clasped. Symbolic of marital love, representing "hands in trust forever," or "hands in friendship." Also unity and affection after death; and symbolic of a farewell or last good-bye. The spouse who dies first clasps the hand of the hand of the other, leading him or her to heaven.

Hands, praying. Devotion.

Harp. Dispels evil spirits; bridge between heaven and earth; associated with David in the Old Testament; also symbol of St. Cecilia, patron saint of musicians; symbolic of worship in heaven.

Heart. Love, mortality; love of God; the center of the soul; the source of love.

Heart, bleeding. Christ's suffering on our behalf.

Heart, encircled with thorns. Christ's suffering.

Heart, flaming. Extreme religious fervor; where two flaming hearts are depicted, symbolic of marital love and passion.

Heart, pierced by a sword. The Virgin Mary (regarding Simeon's prophecy at Christ's birth (Luke 2:35).

Hourglass. The inevitable passage of Time; symbolizes the shortness of life.

Hourglass, on its side. Time has stopped for the deceased.

Hourglass, winged. Time's swift flight.

Keys. Spiritual knowledge; or if held in the hands of an angel, represents entrance into heaven.

Knot. Interlaced Celtic knot represents resurrection and everlasting life.

Labyrinth. The passage of life.

Lamp. Knowledge; love of learning; immortality of the soul.

Lyre. Union, especially marital.

Menorah. Seven-branched candlestick, symbolizes presence of God in Judaism; seven branches represent the seven days of creation.

Mirror. Self-contemplation.

Moon. Cycles of the heavens.

Obelisk. Ancient classical design; symbolizes memory, eternal life.

Phoenix. Rising from the ashes; incorruptibility of the flesh in resurrection.

Pick and Spade. Mortality.

Pitcher. Jewish symbol for the Levites, high priests in the Tabernacle, representing the washing of hands.

Pomegranate. Oneness.

Pyramid. Eternity; also legend held that a pyramid-shaped monument would prevent Satan from reclining on the grave.

Ring. Wholeness; continuity.

Rock. Everlasting strength.

Rod or staff. Comfort.

Rope. Eternity.

Rosette. The Lord, messianic hope, promise, and love.

Scales. God's ultimate weighing of souls; justice.

Scroll. Symbol of life and time. With both ends rolled up, indicates that a life is unfolding like a scroll of uncertain length, with the past and the future hidden. Often held in the hands of an angel, representing life of the deceased

being recorded; can also symbolize honor and commemoration.

Scythe or Sickle. Death, as the "last harvest" of souls at the end of time. When depicted as severing flowers, it symbolizes a life cut short.

Shell. Fertility, resurrection and pilgrimage; predates Christian era.

Shell, scallop. Symbol of the Crusades, pilgrimage, resurrection; one's "life journey"; a traditional symbol of the Puritans.

Ship. The grave of a seafarer; when depicted in memorial art, it represents the death of a mariner, or the soul of the departed sailing towards heaven, represented by the horizon line on the ocean.

Skull, skeleton. Mortality, death.

Star, five-pointed. Symbolizes life of Christ; also possibly the five wounds of Christ. Stars also represent the spirit, as piercing the darkness of life and death through faith, and the triumph over struggle and oblivion.

Star, of David. Symbol of Judaism.

Stump. The cutting down of life, especially prematurely. These are usually seen in cemetery monuments or memorials of the fraternal organization of the Woodsmen of the World.

Sun, setting. Death.

Sun, shining or rising. Renewed life; resurrection.

Sundial. Passage of time.

Sword. A military career; justice, fortitude.

Swords, crossed. Indicates a death in battle.

Torch, Overturned Torch. Symbolic of being cut off too soon, before one's time, in the prime of life. Originally symbolic of a soldier's death in battle, this symbol became universal for any life prematurely cut short.

Trumpet(s). Victory and resurrection.

Urn. Representative of classical Greek grave furniture; also symbolizes the body as a vessel for the soul. By itself, the urn represents sorrow; if draped, it symbolizes mourning; and with a flame on top, it represents sorrow, mourning, and eternal life.

Winged face. Effigy of the soul of the deceased.

Winged globe. God, the creator of the world.

Winged skull. Flight of soul from mortal man.

Winged wheel. The Holy Spirit.

Woman clinging to Cross. Common motif of faith, originated with hymn, "Rock of Ages."

Appendix II

The Language of Gemstones[41]

Agate. Long life; health and constancy.
Amber. Disdain.
Amethyst. Peace of mind.
Aquamarine. Hope.
Beryl. Forget me not.
Bloodstone. Farewell, I mourn your absence.
Carnelian Onyx. Distinction lies before thee.
Cat Sapphire. Affability, power.
Cat's Eye. Platonic love.
Coral. Thy choicest jewel is thy heart.
Cornelian. Friendship in sorrow.

Diamond. Forever Thine, true love.
Emerald. Success in love.
Fire opal. Adversity cannot crush thee.
Garnet. Fidelity in every engagement; virtue.
Jade. Remembrance.
Jasper. Pride of strength.
Jet. Sad remembrance.
Lapis Lazuli. Nobility.
Moonstone. Pensive beauty.
Natrolite. Female friendship.
Obsidian. Mutual amity.

Onyx. Reciprocal love.
Opal. Pure thoughts.
Pearl. Modest loveliness.
Rose Quartz. Remembered in prayer.
Ruby. Courage in dangerous enterprise.
Sapphire. Innocence.
Topaz. Fidelity.
Tourmaline. Generosity.
Turquoise. Fortune favors thee.
Zircon. Respect.

Latin Inscriptions[42]

The following inscriptions are usually seen on monuments in cemeteries, but may appear on memorials or mourning jewelry, and are thus included for help in deciphering inscriptions.

ad patres. "To the fathers," dead or gone away.
anno aetatis suae. In the year of his/her age.
anno Domini (A.D.). In the year of our Lord.

annos vixit (a.v.). He/she lived (so many years).
beatae memoriae (B.M.). Of blessed memory.
Dei gratia. By the grace of God.
hic iacet or hic jacet (H.I.). Here lies.
hic iacet sepultus (H.I.S.). Here lies buried.
in hoc signo spes mea (I.H.S.). In this sign (the cross of Christ) is my hope.
in hoc signos vinces (I.H.S.). By this sign you

will conquer.
laus Deo. Praise be to God.
memento mori . Remember you must die.
Obit (ob.). He/she died.
requiescat in pace (R.I.P.). May he/she rest in peace.

Sources

The following sources are listed here for readers to view museum quality antique pieces, acquire additional information, or purchase outstanding examples of sentimental and mourning jewelry and memorial art.

Antiques & Goodies
Sandra Hall, Proprietor
1128 Third Street
Eureka, CA 95501
(707) 442-0445

Museum of Funeral Customs
1440 Monument Avenue
Springfield, IL 62702
(217) 544-3480

Museum of Mourning Art
Anita Schorsch, Ph.D., Curator
2900 State Road
Drexel, PA 19026
(610) 259-5800

OBJX
Memorial Art and Artifacts
Kellen Perlman, Proprietor
531 2nd Street
Eureka, CA 95501
(707) 476-9058

PEKL
Historical Ephemera
P. O. Box 4150
Portland, ME 04101

Charlotte Sayers
Mourning Jewelry
360 Grays Antique Market
58 Davies Street
London W1K 5LP
England
Telephone: 020 7499 5478
E-mail: charsayers@hotmail.com

Things Gone By
Mourning Jewelry and Memorial Art
Darlene Bolyard, Owner
Website: www.thingsgoneby.com
E-mail: darlene@thingsgoneby.com

Judy Jay's Time Dances By
Mourning Jewelry
Judy Jay, Owner
Website: www.timedancesby.com
E-mail: jjay@timedancesby.com

I am frequently asked for sources of contemporary hairwork artistry, as many people have saved locks of hair of loved ones and desire to memorialize them in jewelry as was done in prior centuries. I became acquainted with Sandra Johnson through the creation of this book, and found that her knowledge and skill in creating beautiful examples of contemporary sentimental and memorial hairwork jewelry are worth noting here. Shown are two examples illustrating the exceptional quality of her work. Sandra's contact information is provided below.

Sandra Johnson, Hair Artist
Heritage Hair Art, Inc.
Website: www.victorianhairjewelry.com
E-mail:
sandra@victorianhairjewelry.com

Endnotes

Section I – Historical Background

[1] Michael Ignatieff, *Lodged in the Heart and Memory*.

[2] Henry Beston, *The Outermost House,* by Henry Beston, 1888-1968.

[3] Michel Vovelle, "On Death," from *Ideologies and Mentalities,* 1990.

[4] Nigel Llewellyn, *The Art of Death* (London, England: Reaktion Books, Ltd., 1991).

[5] Ibid.

[6] Sir Thomas More, English statesman and author, 1478-1535.

[7] Stanley B. Burns, M.D., *Sleeping Beauty: Memorial Photography in America* (Twelvetrees Press, 1990).

[8] Comtesse de Bohm, from her memoirs, 1830.

[9] Laurel Thatcher Ulrich, *A Midwife's Tale: The Life of Martha Ballard Based on Her Diary, 1785-1812* (New York: Vintage Books/Random House, 1991).

[10] Margaret M. Coffin, *Death in Early America* (New York: Elsevier/Nelson Books, 1976).

[11] John Mack Faragher, *Daniel Boone: The Life and Legend of an American Pioneer* (New York: Henry Holt & Co., 1992).

[12] Anita Schorsch, *Mourning Becomes America: Mourning Art in the New Nation* (Clinton, NJ: The Main Street Press, 1976).

[13] Pat Jalland, *Death in The Victorian Family* (New York: Oxford University Press, 1996).

[14] Sally G. McMillan, *Motherhood in The Old South* (Louisiana State University Press, 1990).

[15] Ibid.

[16] Jean H. Baker, *Mary Todd Lincoln: A Biography* (New York: W. W. Norton & Co., 1987).

[17] Margaret M. Coffin, *Death in Early America* (New York: Elsevier/Nelson Books, 1976).

[18] Jean H. Baker, *Mary Todd Lincoln: A Biography* (New York: W. W. Norton & Co., 1987).

[19] Ibid.

[20] Ibid.

[21] Ibid.

[22] Cecil Woodham-Smith, *Queen Victoria: From Her Birth to the Death of the Prince Consort* (New York: Alfred A. Knoph, 1972).

[23] Ibid.

[24] Lou Taylor, *Mourning Dress: A Costume and Social History* (London, England: George Allen and Unwin, 1983).

[25] John Cannon and Ralph Griffiths, *Oxford History of the British Monarchy* (New York: Oxford University Press, 1988).

[26] Lillian Schlissel, *Women's Diaries of the Westward Journey* (New York: Schocken Books, 1982).

[27] Ibid.

[28] Ibid.

[29] Ibid.

[30] Ibid.

[31] Ibid.

[32] Ibid.

[33] Willard Sterne Randall and Nancy Ann Nahra, *Forgotten Americans: Footnote Figures Who Changed American History* (Cambridge, Massachusetts: Perseus Publishing, 1999).

[34] Charles Phillips and Alan Axelrod, *My Brother's Face: Portraits of the Civil War* (San Francisco, California: Chronicle Books, 1993).

[35] Albert Castel, *Touched by Fire: Photographic Portrait of the Civil War; Comrades, A Story of Lasting Friendships* (New York: Black Dog & Levanthal Publishers, 1997).

[36] C. Vann Woodward, Editor, *Mary Chestnut's Civil War* (New Haven, Connecticut: Yale University Press, 1981).

[37] Drew Gilpin Faust, *Mothers of Invention: Women of the Slaveholding South in the American Civil War* (North Carolina: University of North Carolina Press, 1997).

[38] Ibid.

[39] Ibid.

[40] Ibid.

[41] Albert Castel, *Touched By Fire: Photographic Portrait of the Civil War; Comrades, A Story of Lasting Friendships* (New York: Black Dog & Levanthal Publishers, 1997).

[42] Sally G. McMillan, *Motherhood in The Old South* (Louisiana State University Press, 1990).

[43] Ibid.

[44] Stella Tillyard, *The Aristocrats* (London: Chatto & Windus, 1994).

[45] Cathy Luchetti, *Children of The West: Family Life on the Frontier* (New York: W. W. Norton & Company, 2001).

[46] Ibid.

[47] Ibid.

[48] Laurence Lerner, *Angels and Absences: Child Deaths in the Nineteenth Century* (London: Vanderbilt University Press, 1997).

[49] Sally G. McMillan, *Motherhood in The Old South* (Louisiana State University Press, 1990).

Section II – Memorial Art and Artifacts

[1] Lou Taylor, *Mourning Dress: A Costume and Social History* (London, England: George Allen and Unwin, 1983).

[2] Alison Weir, *The Wars of the Roses* (New York: Ballantine Books, 1995).

[3] Lou Taylor, *Mourning Dress: A Costume and Social History* (London: George Allen and Unwin, 1983).

[4] Anthony Trollope, English novelist [1815-1882], from *"Can You Forgive Her?"*

[5] Alison Weir, *The Wars of the Roses* (New York: Ballantine Books, 1995).

[6] Lou Taylor, *Mourning Dress: A Costume and Social History,* (London, England: George Allen and Unwin, 1983).

[7] Joan Severa, *Dressed for the Photographer: Ordinary Americans & Fashion, 1840-1900* (Kent, Ohio: Kent State University Press, 1995).

[8] Vivienne Becker, *Antique and Twentieth Century Jewellery* (Essex, Scotland: N.A.G. Press, Ltd. 1980, reprinted 1992).

[9] Alison Weir, *The Princes in the Tower* (New York: Ballantine Books, 1992).

[10] Pat Jalland, *Death in the Victorian Family* (NY and London: Oxford University Press. 1996).

[11] Tom Pocock, *Horatio Nelson* (London, England, Random House, 1994).

[12] Ibid.

[13] Ibid.

[14] C. Jeaneane Bell, *Collector's Encyclopedia of Hairwork Jewelry* (Paducah, Kentucky: Collector Books, 1998).

[15] John Cannon and Ralph Griffiths, 1988, *Oxford Illustrated History of the English Monarchy* (New York: Oxford University Press, 1988).

[16] Vivienne Becker, *Antique and Twentieth Century Jewellery* (Essex, Scotland: N.A.G. Press, Ltd. 1980, reprinted 1992).

[17] Ibid.

[18] Ibid.

[19] Ibid.

[20] Robin Jaffee Frank, *Love and Loss: American Portrait and Mourning Miniatures* (New Haven, Connecticut: Yale University Press, 2000).

[21] Felice Hodges, *Period Pastimes: A Practical Guide to Four Centuries of Decorative Crafts* (New York: Weidenfeld & Nicolson, 1989).

[22] Ibid.

[23] Robin Jaffee Frank, *Love and Loss: American Portrait and Mourning Miniatures* (New Haven, Connecticut: Yale University Press, 2000).

[24] Ibid.

[25] Ibid.

[26] Ibid.

[27] Philippe Aries, *Images of Man and Death* (Massachusetts: Harvard University Press, 1985).

[28] Roberta Hughes Wright and Wilber B. Hughes, *Lay Down Body: Living History in African American Cemeteries* (Detroit, Michigan: Visible Ink Press, 1996).

[29] Felice Hodges, *Period Pastimes: A Practical Guide to Four Centuries of Decorative Crafts* (New York: Weidenfeld & Nicolson, 1989).

[30] Ibid.

[31] Ibid.

[32] Ibid.

[33] Ibid.

[34] Ibid.

[35] Starr Ockenga, *On Women and Friendship,* (New York: Stewart, Tabori & Chang, 1993).

[36] *Burial of the Dead,* from the English Book of Common Prayer.

[37] Felice Hodges, *Period Pastimes: A Practical Guide to Four Centuries of Decorative Crafts* (New York: Weidenfeld & Nicolson, 1989).

[38] Stanley B. Burns, M.D., *Sleeping Beauty: Memorial Photography in America* (Twelvetrees Press, 1990).

[39] Ibid.

[40] *City of the Silent* website (under construction): *Rochester's Glossary of Victorian Cemetery Symbolism,* http://www.vintageviews.org/vv-tl/pages/Cem_Symbolism.htm.

[41] Starr Ockenga, *On Women and Friendship* (New York: Stewart, Tabori & Chang, 1993).

[42] *City of the Silent* website (under construction): *Rochester's Glossary of Victorian Cemetery Symbolism,* http://www.vintageviews.org/vv-tl/pages/Cem_Symbolism.htm.